The Italian Baker

The Italian Baker

The Classic Tastes of the Italian Countryside—
Its Breads, Pizza, Focaccia, Cakes, Pastries, and Cookies

REVISED

Carol Field

PHOTOGRAPHY BY ED ANDERSON

TEN SPEED PRESS
Berkeley

CONTENTS

When Don Abbacchio came to the reading of the gospel, he turned to us and preached us a little sermon about San Giuseppe da Copertino. We knew the story, but we always liked hearing it again. For this saint was a *cafone* who became a monk but never managed to learn Latin, and whenever the other monks recited the Psalms, he gave praise to Our Lady by turning somersaults wherever he might be, even in church. Our Lady must have been delighted with the innocent spectacle, and to encourage and reward him she gave him the gift of levitation, and after that he had no difficulty in somersaulting all the way up to the ceiling. He died at an advanced age, after a life of severe privations, and it is said that when he appeared before the heavenly throne, God, who knew him by repute and wished him well, because Our Lady had talked about him so often, embraced him and said, "I will give you whatever you want. Don't be afraid to ask for whatever you like."

The poor saint was utterly bewildered by this offer.

"May I ask for *anything*?" he asked timidly.

"You may ask for anything," the Almighty encouraged him. "I give the orders here. I can do whatever I like here. And I am really fond of you. Whatever you ask for will be granted."

But San Giuseppe da Copertino did not dare confess what he really wanted. He feared that his immoderate wish might arouse the Lord to anger. Only after much insistence on the Lord's part, only after He gave His word of honor that He would not be angry, did the saint confess what he most wanted.

"O Lord," he said, "a big piece of white bread." [For the only white bread he had ever seen was in Jesus' hand in a painting on the church altar.]

And the Lord was as good as His word and did not grow angry, but embraced the *cafone* saint, and was moved and wept with him. And then, in His voice of thunder, He summoned twelve angels and gave orders that every day from morning till evening for all eternity, *per omnia saecula saeculorum*, they should give San Giuseppe da Copertino the best white bread that was baked in paradise.

Ignazio Silone, *Fontamara*

ACKNOWLEDGMENTS

This book owes an enormous debt to so many people, both in Italy and in America. It wouldn't even exist without Carlo Veggetti, who so generously shared his formidable knowledge of Italian baking and introduced me to bakers all over Italy. For this edition he persuaded several of them to bake the many specialties that illustrate the book in its new incarnation. And of course it owes everything to the bakers themselves. Special thanks are due to Renato Veggetti, whose generous spirit and helpfulness were endlessly tested by my requests and questions. Renato was patient and kind to an incredible degree.

I couldn't even have written this book without the boundless help of Diane Dexter, who assisted me from beginning to end. Her knowledge of baking and her extraordinary patience as we tested recipes over and over again kept me going. I don't think I could have faced so many go-arounds if Diane hadn't been as curious and as willing to keep searching for solutions as I was.

When I met Joann Carmody, she was a young baker at Il Fornaio in San Francisco who had gone to Italy to bake in Florence and Venice because she wanted to know how things were done there. She was an invaluable help, not only sharing her knowledge but actually traveling to Italy with me for her entire vacation and baking alongside the pastry bakers.

In America, numerous friends have tasted and tested these recipes. Joyce Goldstein, then the chef at the Café at Chez Panisse, came to taste as often as she could, and she was so pleased with what she found that she served several of the rustic breads at Square One, her restaurant in San Francisco. Her encouragement and help meant an enormous amount to me. Carol Sinton, Maxine Bloom, Marjorie Traub, Pat Berkowitz, and Leslie Freudenheim tested for me and gave me wonderful feedback. Paola Bagnatori was spectacularly helpful, tasting much that I made and even seeing bakers for me when she was in Italy, to help get answers that I needed. Francesca Vattani not only brought back special sweets from Venice, but she helped me in Italy as well, and she and Alessandro were fabulously encouraging to this non-Italian admirer of their country's heritage. My father, James Hart, brought me books that I needed and discovered that he loved Italian bread after all. Other special help came from Joanne Hayes, a young baker; from Holly Pugliese, who provided baking help in this current edition; from Barbara Winkelstein, who parted with her wonderful *panforte* recipe; from Bob and Maggie Klein; from Fred Hill; from Amanda Pope and Celeste Gainey; from

Rose Scherini; from numerous Italians living in America who shared memories with me, but especially from Elisabetta Nelsen and Eugenio Pozzolini, who remembered so much of their Tuscan childhoods and the role that bread played in them; and from Loni Kuhn and Carlo Middione, who tasted my breads and discussed them with me.

In Italy, I don't know what I would have done without the friendship of Shirley and François Caracciolo in Todi and Rome, and of Gianna and Riccardo Bertelli in Tuscany. John Meis at Badia a Coltibuono, in Gaiole in Chianti, and Maria Caterina and Franco Crespi in Perugia, were wonderful sources of information and help. Silene Veggetti and the children—Mattia, Stefania, Alfonso, and Giulia—were wonderfully helpful and hospitable during my stays in Italy years ago, and for this edition, Silene and Moira Marelli were invaluable in coordinating the bakers with the photographer's visits. I am very grateful to Claire Hennessy for helping the photographer for this edition. Thank you to Faith Willinger for helping me find her. Thanks to Bonnie Nadell who stepped in when I really needed her. Christian Hansen and Adolfo Veggetti are two others to whom I am very grateful for much help. Nando Tosoni baked in Rome but answered questions for me and baked in San Francisco as well, and Agostino Di Vella was a wonderful guide to the breads and sights of Altamura and Matera. Nella Galetti showed me old-fashioned ways of baking at home.

Barbara Ottenhoff and Helen Huckle were unstinting in their hard work on the first edition of this book. Clancy Drake was a meticulous proofreader who understood the spirit of the book. Most especially I thank Ann Bramson, whose belief in this book from its inception was phenomenal. Her kindness, her caring, her sensitivity, warmth, and real dedication were so remarkable that I marvel at my enormous good fortune in having had the opportunity to work with her. Lisa Regul, who inherited the book for this new printing, has been patient and supportive from the very beginning. Her calm manner and unstinting dedication to getting things right has been remarkable.

I give special thanks to Kathleen Weber for spending two amazing days with me photographing at her house and her bakery, Della Fattoria in Petaluma, along with Aaron, her very talented baker son, and her daughter, Elisa. Thanks to Jan Schat of Il Fornaio and to Marjorie Traub.

Very special thanks go to Matthew and Alison, my children, whose encouragement has meant the world to me. They have been so enthusiastic and helpful over all these years. Now Camilla, Alex, Owen, Eric, and Sofia have joined the family and they too love Italian bread and sweets. There is no way to thank my husband, John, for his support. He believed in me and helped with this book in every possible way. He made special trips to travel with me to Italy when it looked as if I would never survive a crazy schedule and itinerary, he ate endless breads and sweets, and he even became addicted to having his own Italian bread at home. His enthusiasm and belief and willingness to tolerate my obsession with Italian breads and baking made it all possible.

PREFACE

Bread in Italy takes the form of rough country loaves with thick chewy crusts, and flat disks of focaccia seasoned with the wild herbs of the fields. Their tastes and shapes are fragrant reminders of a tradition of baking that is older than the Roman monuments and Romanesque cathedrals that we rush to Europe to see. These breads are expressions of an earthy culture that still talks about its most fundamental experiences in terms of bread. In Italy, a down-to-earth man with a real heart of gold is described as *buono come il pane*—good, like bread. When Americans talk about being direct and straightforward, we say we're calling a spade a spade, but Italians say *"pane al pane e vino al vino,"* calling bread bread and wine wine. Bread gives us real glimpses into the complex and fascinating history of all the regions of the country. Italy wasn't even united until a little over a hundred and fifty years ago, so many of the roots have remained a little more exposed than might be true elsewhere. All the rivalries and bloody battles between neighboring cities and regions bred an intense pride in the most local expressions of place, so that just as each *paese* and city had its own bell tower overlooking its fraction of countryside, ready to call citizens to arms and alert them to danger, in the same way its breads expressed a passionate attachment to local customs and ingredients.

Bread is so fundamental to everyday eating that the Italians are forever using the word *companatico*, an all-purpose term for what one eats with bread. "What's for lunch?" *"Pane e companatico"*—bread and something that goes with it. And bread is such a basic part of life that while there are very few cookbooks devoted to baking bread at home, many recipes begin: "Take 500 grams of bread dough that you've bought from your baker." Pizzas, *focacce*, enriched breads, and holiday breads often begin just that way.

Each day in Italy more than twenty-five thousand artisan bakers rise early to knead their doughs and shape their loaves. Working on a small scale and dedicated to keeping family and regional traditions alive, they are preserving the past by making it a living part of the present, but they are also showing the baker's dazzling imagination, producing modern breads that turn the luscious provender of the vines and fields into tantalizing loaves.

They have taken the olive paste of Liguria, made from the first crushing of salty, aromatic olives grown near the sea, and incorporated it into a bread. They have taken pesto and sweet peppers and tomatoes dried by the sun under a dappled screen of latticework arbors, the humble potato and the most expensive aged cheeses, and the dark grains that once belonged to a peasant culture, and given them new companions and shapes to make an inventive and tantalizing range of breads that appeal to the Italian passion for *fantasia*.

Life without bread is inconceivable in Italy, and yet if I had decided to write this book in the 1950s or 1960s, it would have been an elegy, a bittersweet testament to breads of another time. In those years, massive companies took over the bread baking of Italy, turning out airy white loaves that resemble the spongy, cottony slices Americans know from our own supermarket shelves. These companies threatened to homogenize the breads, pastries, cookies, and pizzas that were once the culinary equivalent of Italy's numerous dialects. Gone were the indigenous specialties. The tastes and flavors of the past were eclipsed by high-speed rollers that milled grain to a bland, highly refined flour without texture or nutrients, by huge machines that mixed and kneaded faster than the human eye could see, by automation that removed the human touch from the most basic of all human food.

Suddenly giant Italian companies were making deals with American consortia to produce biscuits and crackers by the million to be eaten instead of bread. They were replacing *grissini*, the archetypal artisan-made breadsticks, with pale little batons all the same color and width and length, extruded from the dies of a machine. Gone were the thick, knobby breadsticks whose length was determined by the span of the baker's arms. Blandness suddenly ruled, leaving the centuries-old tradition conquered, as one writer put it, "by the imperialism of city bread."

But just as the monks kept culture—and bread—alive during a dark time in the country's history, so there were a few bakers who refused to follow the new ways. To them—those who safeguarded tradition and perpetuated the taste of the countryside—this book owes its inspiration and its recipes.

In the early 1970s Carlo Veggetti, whose family had been in the business of furnishing the interiors of bakeries for three generations, found himself increasingly discouraged by the institutionalization of baking in Italy. The handmade regional specialties that had been baked for hundreds of years were disappearing with alarming speed, so he set about to create a network of bakers and bakeries that would preserve traditional breads from every region of Italy and bring them back to the public. By now, a full-scale revolution has been achieved and more than 2,500 Il Fornaio bakeries exist in Italy, with several other chains visible across the landscape as well. It was Carlo Veggetti, an expansive and energetic man—the Fellini of Italian bread—who opened the doors of his bakeries to me. I baked with his bakers in Como and Milan, in Florence and Rome, in Palermo and Lecce, in Venice and Lugano, in small towns and big cities. His feeling for these breads and the artisans who are masters of their trade is contagious. He talks about eating bread with the eyes as well as the mouth. He speaks of bread as the ultimate art form: "Imagine any work of art with such variety in form, color, aroma, and taste. A work of art that you eat!" There's even music involved in the eating. "Listen: cric-crac, cric-crac."

Through Veggetti I met Giancarlo Grignani, a Milanese baker and a scholar of bread who read anything he could find on his chosen subject. He even had a clipping service that saved everything relevant in the Italian newspapers. He re-created the breads of Pompeii as they were baked in Roman times and made numerous twentieth-century versions of breads of the Lombard countryside from much earlier times—breads made with corn flour, crunchy crusted loaves of Como, and earthy regional breads baked with organically grown flours produced as they were before 1900. He even put together an exhibition of regional Italian breads in the main piazza of Milan.

Other Il Fornaio bakers included Georgio Gobbi in Lugano and Giovanni Pesenti in Florence; Luca Cucumazzo, a baker from Puglia; and Salvatore Sacco, who dreamed up the *picce calabresi* and showed me the secrets of some breads made in southern Italy.

Giovanni Galli in Florence, who bakes both pastry and breads, is giving life again to the Tuscan specialties that were once part of country life and tradition. He has put the tastes of this extraordinary landscape into oil-drizzled *schiacciate* and *pizzette* and into festive specialties like rosemary-scented buns and breads bursting with fat zibibbo raisins. Gianfranco Anelli made one hundred kilos of pizzas a day in his wood-burning ovens in Rome, rendered the rustic loaves of tiny towns like Genzano and larger cities like Terni, and created a *coccodrillo* (crocodile) bread that people in Rome traveled far across the city to get.

Giorgio Puppola began baking in Venice when he was a very young boy. His skill with pastry and his flights of imagination created the *ossi da morto* (page 399), focaccia laced with zabaglione cream (page 208) and the *bolzanese* (page 187) in this book. In Venice, too, Severino Scarpa shared forty years of baking experience and showed me how breads and rolls were made before machines had such a large part in the cutting and shaping of doughs. Also in Venice, Carlo Cavaliere, Ferruccio Bellemo, and Renato Milanese all showed me secrets of bread and pastry baking. Sergio Saturnino in Genoa makes the true focaccia of the region, crammed with the pungent tasty olives of Liguria and the fresh herbs of the hillsides.

I learned the special shaping of the myriad forms in the region of Emilia-Romagna from Margherita Simili, the rare woman baker in a world dominated by men. In Altamura, Vito Forte opened a small artisanal bakery in 1965. In the 1980s his extraordinary bakery was divided into two sections, one where some loaves were produced industrially—no human hand touched the dough from its mixing to its baking—and the other where loaves were made by simpatico and knowing artisans, who shaped them to look like a woman's pompadour, the traditional shape of Altamura bread. Truckloads of his breads continue to fan out across the countryside, to Milan and Turin in the north and to tiny *paesi* and larger cities in central and southern cities deep on the heel of the boot.

I have shaped and dimpled pizza doughs in Naples, watched bakers in Palermo make calzone and *cassata*, and eaten their brioches filled with ice cream for breakfast, as all the Palermitani do. The brothers Spinnato in Palermo took me under their collective wing, taught me about *mafalda* and *sfiuncini*, the bread and pizza specialties of the city, and wouldn't hear of my leaving without tasting everything on the premises.

Pino Micoli taught me about *rustici* in Lecce, where Avvocato Marangio made sure that I felt and smelled all the flours and learned about the variables of baking in the heat of a southern Italian summer, and introduced me to the bakers of *calzone, puccia,* and other Pugliese specialties. Carla Schucani of the famous bakery Sandri in Perugia was very gracious, inviting me in to watch the Easter baking and allowing me to witness everything from the cutting of a wheel of three-year-old Parmigiano-Reggiano to the mixing of Umbrian specialties.

In San Francisco, Luciano Pancalde, who comes from Ferrara, shared secrets and recipes with me, tasted what I baked, and gave me more pointers. He was my first baking link to Italy in this country.

These and many more are the sources of the recipes and folklore of Italian bread, and they are the ones who day after day make the breads and sweets that bring these tastes to the fortunate Italians who eat them at breakfast and dinner, over coffee and aperitifs in the trattorias and restaurants, coffee bars and *piazze*, where the people of Italy live out their lives.

The revival of bread and a new pride it its myriad forms has led real aficionados to wonder why a different bread isn't served with each course, in the same spirit as wine. Giancarlo Grignani was avant-garde in designing a bread menu for the restaurant Malatesta in Milan in the early 1980s, where it was possible to choose one loaf to go with the appetizer, a second for the main course, and a third for the salad. At a quite ordinary restaurant in the Galleria in Milan at that time, I was surprised to find a basket with five very different breads automatically set on the table. Now it is not at all unusual for chefs to make the breads they serve in their restaurants.

Angelo Albini, a baker from Cividale, whose *gubana* (page 219) is one of the great discoveries of my travels, talked about breads much as winemakers talk about wine. "Smell it," he said to me, "taste it, put it on the back of your throat, and taste it again." It was his dream to achieve a D.O.C. classification for such regional breads just as winemakers have their Denominazione di Origine Controllata. D.O.C. on a wine label means that the wine was made under carefully controlled and specified conditions in accordance with traditional procedures; it verifies the authenticity of the character of the wine and indicates quality. If wine is made by transforming grapes, yeast, and water, and bread is made by the alchemical fusion of flour, water, yeast, and salt, why not confirm its regional authenticity with some special, highly respected authority?

In 2005 the European Union granted DOP (Denominazione di Origine Protetta) status to Pane di Altamura and Pagnotta di Dittaino, in Sicily. The award is very specific about the natural processes, precise techniques, and locally produced flours with which the bread is made. A different designation, IGP (Indicazione Geografica Protetta), was conferred upon three breads, Coppia Ferraresi, Pane Casereccio di Genzano, and Pane di Matera, confirming a strong historical bond between the area, its agriculture, and the local culture.

Seeing really good bakers at work can be eye-opening. When they roll out the dough, their touch can be as delicate as a lover's caress, and when they knead, their authority can almost command the dough to respond. They can take an inert and colorless piece of dough and with their fingers give it form, elasticity, and vitality. The pale white dust that sifts over everything, and the sounds—the slapping and banging of the dough, the thud as it hits the table right out of the mixer, the thunk of the canvas carrier being snapped into the oven and then retracted—the smells, and the sights make the bakery a special world of its own.

Knowing the story and tastes of the regional breads that come out of these ovens is like taking a trip through the Italian countryside. Saving and honoring them is like preserving the stone villages on the hillsides or their churches and frescoes, for saving the taste of the past keeps it alive in the present. The bakers who are committed to rediscovering the past and creating new ways of eating in the present do honor to the oldest of man's foods and to authentic Italian tradition, for bread is one of the most persuasive images of man's struggle to survive. No wonder baking is called *l'arte bianco*, the white art, for the mystical life-giving magic of yeast creates nourishment that sustains people and keeps alive memories connecting the collective past to the world of today.

Bread in Italy

Bread is merely flour, water, yeast, and salt as the world is merely earth, water, fire, and air. These four elemental ingredients—grain from the fields, water from the rivers and mountain streams, leavening from the wild yeasts of the air, and salt from the sea—have been combined since Roman days to make the breads of Italy. In a country where the family is the primary source of physical and emotional sustenance, bread celebrates the richest and simplest pleasures of daily living. It is the single inevitable presence at the table during all three meals of the day, for no Italian would contemplate a meal without bread.

Bread is such a basic part of life in Italy that every restaurant automatically sets it on the table and imposes a cover charge (*coperto*) to cover its cost. Almost every street in Italy's large and middle-sized cities seems to have at least one *panificio* (bakery) and *pasticceria* (pastry shop), and even tiny towns without bread ovens have a grocery store where bread is delivered warm in the mornings.

Under the circumstances, it is not surprising that Italians express many of their most intensely felt sentiments through sayings and proverbs that use bread as their common metaphor.

Buono come il pane: As good as bread (said of a big-hearted, down-to-earth person).

Senza il pane tutto diventa orfano: Without bread, everyone is an orphan.

I miei parenti son i soldi in tasca e il pane nella casa: My family is money in my pocket and bread at home.

Issu esta unu cantu de pane: He is a piece of bread (he is a good and reliable man, a man who can be trusted).

Uscire di pane duro: To leave behind hard bread (to have a change for the better).

Dire pane al pane e vino al vino: To call bread bread and wine wine (to call a spade a spade).

La prima parola della guerra è pronunciata dal cannone ma l'ultima è sempre detta dal pane: The announcement of war is given by cannons, but bread always has the last word (when there is no more bread, the war is lost).

Trovar pane per i propri denti: To find bread for one's very teeth (to meet one's match).

Se non è zuppa è pan bagnato: If it isn't soup, it's moistened bread (it's six of one or half a dozen of the other).

Nutrirsi a pan bianco: To eat white bread all the time (to live on easy street).

Avere per un pezzo di pane: To get it for a piece of bread (to get it very cheap).

Essere pan e cacio: To be like bread and cheese with someone (to be thick as thieves).

Distinguere pane dai sassi: To know the difference between bread and rocks (to know what's what).

Render pane per focaccia: To give bread for focaccia (to give tit for tat).

E tanto pane!: It's so much bread! (said upon seeing rain where there's real need of water).

Il pan di casa stufa: Homemade bread makes you fed up (the grass is always greener on the other side).

Meglio nero pane che nera fame: Better dark bread than the dark despair of hunger.

Mangiar pan a tradimento: To eat unearned bread (to be a sponger).

Riuscire meglio a pane che a farina: To succeed more with the bread than with the flour (to have more success than expected).

Per il vecchio e il neonato, il pancotto è prelibato: Bread soup is the food of the old and the newborn (who have no teeth).

Chirurgo come il pane, medico come il vino: Look for a surgeon like bread (young) and a doctor like wine (well aged).

Non è pane per i suoi denti: It is not bread for his teeth (it's not his cup of tea).

Even the academic body that serves to maintain the purity of the Italian language is called Accademia della Crusca—the Academy of Bran—for it sees itself as sifting the wheat from the chaff. Its symbol is an agricultural flour sifter.

Walk past a bakery and you'll often see displays of grain set in the window so people can learn about what they are eating. Go inside and you'll notice that every bread is labeled not only with its name but with every ingredient, as well as the price per kilo. Bread is so basic to a sense of well-being that local governments regulate the prices of the traditional breads of the *commune*, keeping it affordable for anyone with a few hundred lire in a pocket. The saltless bread of Tuscany, which is very cheap in Florence and Siena, can be sold for any price outside regional limits—though most of the people of, say, Milan and Rome have no cravings for or childhood ties to saltless bread. Anyone from the countryside around Chianti, however, or from the little hill towns that have sat on this landscape since the Etruscans first established them, will tell you that saltless bread is part of a heritage that stretches back long before Dante.

Until recently a Tuscan would no more choose to eat a Roman *pagnotta* or a Milanese *michetta* than he would expect to find Wiener schnitzel on his dinner plate. So how could it come as a surprise that each region boasts variations on its breads and ingredients and makes its local tastes into breads that define a small geographical area?

When I was in Altamura, a town in southern Italy famous for its golden durum-flour bread, I went to talk to a baker and watch the bread being made, and to taste it, of course. Later in the day, at a restaurant about fifteen kilometers away, a big basket of golden bread with a chewy crust and a porous interior was brought to our table. I exclaimed to my host with pleasure, "Oh, wonderful—more bread from Altamura." A disgruntled look fleeted across his face and disappointment clouded his eyes. "Well," he said grudgingly, "more or less." I had insulted the tradition. We were a little less than ten miles from Altamura, but no matter, we might as well have been five hundred. The bread of Altamura comes from *its* bakers and *its* grains and *its* tradition. Although the bread on our table was similar, it just wasn't the same.

I should have known better. How could it be otherwise in a country that has a dial-a-message service for regional recipes? Each day the recording gives a new recipe for a dish from each of the regions of Italy. And how could it be otherwise in a country scarred in medieval times by cities that chose to fight ferociously with the closest neighbors to prove their supremacy, their dedication to local alliances finally leading them to stamp their own identity not only on the landscape but on the foods as well? This rich, complex, and combative heritage influences Italian baking and is embellished by the reality that everyone from the Saracens to the Austrians conquered different regions and left their culinary signature behind. The porous and crunchy Pugliese bread of the south is a legacy of the brown country loaf brought by the Turks who long ago walked the streets of Apulia; and the famous *michetta* roll of Milan was born of the *Kaisersemmel* of Vienna, which was brought to Milan by the Austrian cavalry in the late 1800s.

In the country at large, there are more names for the shapes of bread than Eskimos have words for snow. This is a very incomplete list: *azzimo* (unleavened), *casareccio* (homemade), *ciabatta* (slipper), *ciambella* (wreath), *corolla* (crown), *manini* (little hands), *mattone* (brick), *pagnotta* (round loaf), *panino* (roll), *piadina* (flat disk), *quattrocorni* (four horns), *ruota* (wheel), *schiacciata* (flattened), *sfilatino* (long, thin thread), *stella* (star), *tegola* (tile), *treccia* (braid). Italian bakers say there may be somewhere between one thousand and two thousand different breads in the national repertory, although "only" a few hundred are commonly available, and while there are numbers of typical regional breads—*biove* from Piedmont, *ciopa* from Venice, *crocetta* from Ferrara, *michetta* from Milan, and saltless loaves from Tuscany—each type may have slight variations attributable to the individual bakers. The taste of bread is so much a product of local ingredients, the humidity of the air, the quality of the water, and even the fingers and hands of the baker that people know immediately when a local baker has died, because the bread suddenly tastes different.

Secrets and techniques for making bread have been handed down from baker to baker over the years, and they belong to an oral tradition like folk tales and peasant wisdom. Apprentices learn by watching and asking and doing, since this is a tradition that relies not on specific recipes but on formulas that are expressed in proportions. I once asked a baker how he made the chewy, crunchy crusted bread of his region and he told me, "Use 2 percent yeast, 2 percent salt, 60 percent water, to 100 percent flour." Of course the baker understood exactly what he meant, but his answer left a few loose ends for me. How long did he mix the ingredients? Did the dough rise to twice or three times its original size to produce the special texture? Was the water cool or lukewarm? The bakers' formulas are merely guidelines, for knowledgeable baking depends on touch, taste, sight, smell, and experience—knowing when to add a little water or when to work the dough a little longer. Clearly, the flexible formula leaves room for the baker's individuality, his personal touches, and the flashes of imagination that put his stamp on the bread and make it his own. Unlike the French, who make numerous regional breads and sweets according to quantified recipes and a codified tradition, Italian bakers are forever experimenting and dreaming up new interpretations. If forty bakers in Puglia are making *pane Pugliese*, you can be sure there will be forty loaves that taste slightly different.

These breads of Italy have their fragrance, their color, and their flavor, but most also have their raison d'être. Most Italian breads are soft, but the tradition of hard breads is rooted with a people who needed their basic nourishment to keep for a long time. Sardinian shepherds carry wafer-thin *carasau* bread, big, flat, crackly disks that are also called *carta da musica* (sheet music bread) for their parchment color and fine veining of horizontal lines. The *frisedde* of

Puglia, the *gallette* of seagoing sailors, and the *ciambelle valtelline* of the cold north, where snow isolates regions for weeks at a time, are all hard breads made to last for months. When eaten, they are dipped into water or broth, moistened with slices of tomato, or flavored with oil, salt, pepper, and herbs such as oregano, which grow wild in the countryside. They are sometimes then topped with slices of cheese, which might come from the milk of the sheep tended by Sardinian shepherds. The standard Venetian *pani biscotti*, biscuits that are rather like hardtack, were a perfect provision for sailors or even businessmen who went to sea for months at a time. They were made, as their name implies, by being twice cooked (*bis cotto*) to draw off almost all the moisture and produce a very light, long-lasting biscuit that couldn't possibly mold or go bad. It is said that both Marco Polo and Christopher Columbus relied on biscotti on their long voyages.

There are many rituals and elements of etiquette connected with bread. In Tuscany and Puglia, big rounds of crusty rustic loaves are always held in the crook of the elbow and sliced toward the chest. Knowing how to cut bread is as important to an Italian man as learning to carve meat is to an American.

In Italy, bread is an object of respect, a sign of the grace of providence that is treated with almost sacramental reverence. Mothers teach their children that no one is allowed to waste a crumb of bread. Should a bit accidentally fall to the floor, it must be picked up, immediately cleaned off, and eaten. It is said that anyone wasting bread will be condemned to purgatory for as many years as there were crumbs and will be compelled to collect each little bit upon the eyelids, one at a time. Bread placed upside down on a table will bring bad luck. No one should ever leave a knife plunged into the crust of bread because it is like the flesh of the Lord, and the person responsible will never again partake of grace. Bakers always make the sign of the cross over the oven and often make it in the dough itself before baking, as many peasants do before taking a first bite of freshly baked loaves. Bread is so powerful that even the smell is believed to have healing powers.

Some forms of bread have roots in prehistory and are charged to this day with symbolic significance. Round *pan di morte* (bread of the dead) appears in late October, and cookies called *ossa di morte* and *fave di morte* are eaten in honor of the dead on the Day of the Dead and All Souls' Day. On those days families participate in ceremonies meant to prove to the dead that they have not been forgotten and continue to share in the life of the family. The tibia-shaped *ossa di morte* are eaten all over Italy, from Lombardy to Sicily, and are known, regionally, as *ossa da mordere*, *oss de mord*, *ossi da morto*, or *stinchetti*. Outsiders may find these little nougats a bit strange, as Paul Valéry did on a trip to Italy in 1834, when he made it very clear that he didn't care for "this horrible confection," to which he attributed the ancient reputation of the Umbrians for ferocity. He had a point—Umbrian history is nothing short of hair-raising before the seventeenth century—but the bone-shaped cookies seem a bit more abstract than the serpent-shaped cakes of Perugia and Umbria, which are bristling with primitive associations.

In Calabria for the feast day of San Rocco, whose specialty is protecting against contagious diseases, bakers shape *panpepati*, which are like spicy Italian gingerbread cakes, into ex-votos that represent various parts of the body. A parade of local pilgrims winds through the city streets on its way to a statue of the saint, where they offer these baked arms, legs, heads, and various organs decorated with all the imagination of the local baker. They are collected the next day in a huge basket and sold at an auction to support the singers, comics, puppeteers, actors, band players, and makers of fireworks whose art is displayed at the ceremonies for the saint's day.

In three of the most rustic regions of Italy, Puglia, Basilicata, and Calabria, where the poor generally eat only the darker, lesser grains, wheat bread is given only to the dying ("He has arrived at the bread" is a local proverb) and to women about to give birth.

In some remote mountain communities in the Alto Adige, the Val d'Aosta, and the Trentino, far in the north of Italy, superstitions surround the choice of which days are most

propitious for the baking of bread. It is universally agreed that bread must never be made on days when the furrows of the earth are open for the sowing of wheat, for then the bread would mold. Some say that the moon must be rising, others that it should be in its last quarter, but there is no question that the worst time for making bread is at the first sign of the new moon, which would surely bewitch the loaves. Some folk wisdom maintains that bread must be baked in the early morning, for it swells in the oven in harmony with the ascension of the sun. In the same spirit, breads in their round shapes are seen as being like the sun, which appears anew every day to keep away darkness and make the earth grow.

Braided breads, which surfaced in the late Middle Ages, are also richly symbolic. In ancient days, women were expected to join their dead husbands in their tombs, but over time human sacrifice was replaced by the symbolic sacrifice of the woman's hair. When women were finally allowed to keep their hair, the symbol was replaced by a loaf of bread plaited like a braid, which was given to the poor instead of being placed in the grave.

Some breads are literally meant to carry the blessings of home and church. Traditional rolls made only for Calabrians who are leaving their native countryside are stamped with an image of the Madonna and then blessed by a priest before they are entrusted to the departing family.

Breads created to celebrate New Year's Day, Easter, and marriage ceremonies are hard to tell apart because all three deal with beginnings, which must be nourished with the most affirmative symbols. Votive breads in south and central Italy take the form of wheat sheaves, clusters of swollen grapes, and doll-like figures called *pupazze*. All three forms suggest fertility and religion. The *pupazze* made for Easter in Sicily always have a red egg tucked under each arm. Red is the color of fertility, and an egg represents renewal in both pagan and Catholic traditions. These breads celebrate birth and rebirth and new beginnings—whether physical, emotional, or religious—and they celebrate as well the sensuality inherent in the stalks of wheat that are planted and plowed in the warmth of mother earth.

The simple aromatic breads of the countryside are more than the flavors and smells of an ancient culture: they are rife with sexual symbolism, too. The *banana* and *barlino* from the Emilia-Romagna region and various Venetian breads are rolled into unmistakably phallic shapes or curved into a round *ciambella* with a hole in the center. The high swollen shapes of softer *pagnotta pasquale* (Easter bread) are as round as breasts or pregnant bellies. Some breads, such as the *coppiette* of Ferrara, are barely disguised images of coupling that were once made to propitiate the forces of nature and encourage the fertility of the fields. Bakers in some small towns in Lazio still make breads in the form of women with three cone-shaped breasts, recalling Diana of Ephesus, who had one hundred breasts and represented the mythic ferocity of fertility.

The sweets and breads of Sicily are especially rich with sexual imagery. Little almond treats called "breasts of the virgin" (*mammelle di vergine*) are shaped just as you might imagine and, surprisingly, they are prized most by the nuns who created them. Don Fabrizio in Lampedusa's *The Leopard* asks for the "virgin's cakes" at a sumptuous party in Sicily. As he looks at them on his plate, he sees a profane caricature of St. Agatha and exclaims, "Why didn't the Holy Office forbid these cakes when it had the chance? St. Agatha's sliced-off breasts sold by convents, devoured at dances! Well, Well!" To this day, phallic babas and plump round brioche cakes with a squish of cream and the crown of a single fat berry, all succulent images of sexuality, line the glass cases of bakeries all over Palermo.

Italy is a landscape of hundreds of small protected valleys enclosed within mountain chains and dramatic seacoasts. Its valleys and soft open plains are etched with pale ribbons of rivers and stone walls, and they are punctuated with silvery olive trees, rows of grapevines, and ancient stone villas. Even today, much of it still looks as it does in the Renaissance paintings from which we preserve our image of the country. Here the historical roots of bread are no less significant than the geography that produced the regional traditions and the peasant culture that gave it its flavor.

The Romans learned to bake from the Greeks, who followed the victorious Roman armies back to Rome in 170 B.C. and revolutionized the practice of bread baking, which had belonged to housewives for centuries. The Greeks were great bakers who made more than fifty kinds of bread, milling their grain to a very fine flour. They actually worshiped bread, which was intimately tied to religious rituals that centered on Demeter, the goddess of grain and abundance. Demeter originally made the earth dry and infertile while she searched for her daughter Persephone, who had been kidnapped by Hades and taken to the underworld. She pleaded with Zeus for the girl's release, but only after she refused to allow grain to grow was the god forced to restore Persephone to her mother for half the year, the season when the sowing, ripening, and threshing of the fields takes place.

The famous Eleusinian mysteries that revolve around Demeter celebrate the force of feminine fertility, which is profoundly tied to the fertility of the earth. To this day in Sicily an annual holiday in honor of Demeter and Persephone involves offerings of sesame-and-honey *focacce* shaped like women's sexual organs. They are intended to make the goddess laugh and to distract her from the sadness brought on by her daughter's disappearance.

Before they ever tasted or made bread, the Romans ate *puls*, a mush of grains boiled in water, a predecessor of polenta. It was made of millet or, more commonly, spelt, a grain called *farro* in Latin, from which comes *far*, the root for *farina*, which is the Italian word for flour. By 147 B.C. the Greek slaves who tended the ovens in Roman bakeries had taught the Romans their trade, and those Romans had become so important that they were given social status and rank and had formed a professional corporation that had very strict rules about the quality and ingredients used in making bread. Bakery owners were generally freed slaves—the second mayor of Pompeii was one—but once a man became a baker he could never change work, and his sons and sons-in-law after him were obliged to follow the trade as well.

Bread baking reached its apex around 25 B.C., in the time of Emperor Augustus, when there were 329 public bakeries in Rome alone. The bakers leavened bread by using a bit of dough from the baking of the day before or by adding beer yeast, which they had learned about from the Gauls and the Germans. They made saltless sponges, which were called *biga*—as they still are today—by fermenting wheat flour with grape must, sprouted barley, or bran soaked in white wine. They also made enriched breads with milk, eggs, oil, honey, anise, poppy seeds, nuts, cheese, and sesame seeds. They even developed some baking forms, such as the long, thin sandwich bread molds that are still in use today.

The big central bread market in Rome boasted round breads; breads notched into eight sections, which were easy to break off into individual pieces; breads shaped like keys, cubes, or braids; breads that looked like mushrooms; and breads that looked like wreaths. There was a bread for each social class, including senators, knights, citizens, and peasants. White bread was already a status symbol, even though some writers knew that darker, coarser loaves were healthier and gave sustenance to hard-working peasants and farmers. The rich ate *siligo*, the finest wheat flour, which was so white that the women of Rome powdered their faces with it. Pliny noted that "in some places bread is named after the dishes eaten with it, such as oyster bread, in others from its special delicacy, as cake bread, in others from the short time spent making it, as hasty bread, and also from the method of baking, as oven bread, or tin loaf, or baking pan bread."

In those days, breads were made with wheat, millet, and rye. Bran was usually baked into loaves that were tossed to the dogs; oats were fed to cattle. A clever Roman baker dreamed up a labor-saving mechanical kneader that was powered by a horse or donkey trudging in circles, churning the water, flour, and leavening inside its big basin—the KitchenAid mixer of its day. Animals eventually took over from men to provide the power for mills as well. Whereas flour was originally made by crushing grain with a mortar and pestle, then sifting it through a fine cloth, it was now ground between two hourglass-shaped stones that were rotated by mules. The word that defined the grinding action was *pistor*, a term still used today in Venice to define a baker; elsewhere in Italy a baker is called a *fornaio* or *panettiere*, from the words for "oven" and "bread."

Bakers' brick and stone ovens insulated hot air in a hollow space set within an arched opening; wood from tree branches provided the heat, and there was even a container for water to increase the humidity for making crisp crusts. The Romans celebrated June 9 as the festival of Fornax, goddess of the ovens, by decorating oven mouths with flowers and by hanging wreaths from the necks of the mules who turned the mills.

Wheat and bread shaped the destiny of Rome and were intimately tied to its rise and fall. In early Roman days all land belonged to the state except for small parcels given to soldiers returning home from the wars. The state protected the farmers, but as its ambitions grew, its need for more capital led to the decision to lease land to the rich. As a result, wealthy landlords, who forced small farmers to abandon their fields, were able to combine parcels of land into vast estates. Rather than grow wheat, they turned their farmland into pasturage, which was more profitable. Wheat growing was virtually abandoned, and the small farmers were forced to the city, where they melted into the growing mass of the dispossessed and unemployed. Julius Caesar, Augustus Caesar, and Nero provided free grain to keep the restive unemployed from rebelling, hoping that bread and circuses would distract them, but each ruler was forced to import ever greater amounts. The constant search for more grain was partially responsible for the expansion of the empire. While Trajan established the first bakers' school in 100 A.D., and the architect Vitruvius discovered hydraulic milling, which could produce much more flour from the same amount of grain, Rome continued to swallow up territory until the empire stretched from Britain to the deserts of Africa and grew too large to be controlled by a single ruler. When the empire was divided between east and west, Rome lost control of the vast wheat fields of Egypt and Africa, which fed its population. The end of the wheat supply coincided almost precisely with the fall of the empire. Barbarian tribes plunged across the borders and virtually dismembered the state. The once rich arable land, which had been given over to pasturage, reverted to swamp. Bread as the Romans knew it disappeared from Rome and the farther reaches of Italy. For a while, whatever bread was baked at home consisted of roots, beans, acorns, and minor grains.

Surprisingly enough, even the barbarian conquerors knew bread. The brilliant Byzantine general Belisarius built mills at the edge of the Tiber, where he produced enough grain to fill the needs of sixth-century Rome. But it was at the monasteries that the earth was cultivated and bread was first baked again, this time under the watchful eyes of the monks. To get on with their work and studies, these monks needed every labor- and time-saving device they could find. The powerful hydraulic milling machines they put to work again were a major force behind the rebirth of baking. Bread making became more important after 800, when Charlemagne came to power. Mills multiplied and eating became more than keeping body and soul together. In the years that followed, rich lords with great castles and estates took control of much of the countryside. What grain wasn't collected for these great landholders went to the monasteries, whose huge tracts of land gave them substantial clout. Farmers and peasants were compelled to take whatever grains were left to make their daily bread. People collected in cities once again—in self-defense as much as anything else, since they needed security against those nobles who were decimating the landscape with their power struggles. As urbanization proceeded, bakers organized guilds as they had in Roman times.

The breads of the Middle Ages were as stratified as Roman bread. There was a bread for the pope, bread for knights and pages, bread for the cavalry, bread for canons and priests, and bread for soldiers, as well as the little loaves of rye and wheat meant for everyday eating. Bread was so basic to daily nourishment and survival that whenever a battle was fought—and in these crisis-ridden centuries there were many battles—a bread baker always rode off with the soldiers, bringing his iron oven and his grains to bake *gallette* and loaves for the army.

These medieval centuries were the years of a new spirit of independence, when regional identities were being forged. Just as each area had its own currency and customs (imagine having to clear customs several times on a trip between Milan and Florence and you begin to get the picture), each region had its own ingredients, and its own attitudes about bakers and bread. Verona and Padua had baking corporations before 1200, which made them avant-garde for the times. In Venice, where bakers had already been at work in the first years of the eleventh century, there were strict laws about quality control. If bread was discovered to be short-weighted, it was distributed for free to the poor; if the quality was substandard, it was crumbled into pieces and tossed off the Rialto Bridge. By 1280, artisan bakers in Florence had organized themselves in professional guilds and were baking breads and sweets in the city's 146 ovens. Although Florence's sumptuary laws prohibited serving more than three courses per meal, some bakers got around the problem by layering all kinds of meats and vegetables in a single dish, wrapping them in pastry, and cooking the whole thing under the embers. What they pulled out of the fire were meat and vegetable tarts, born as a strategy to have one's cake, so to speak, and eat it too.

Things were entirely different in Rome, where bread making, like everything else, had fallen into a deplorable state when the popes decamped for Avignon. When they returned in 1378, there were only thirty thousand people in the city. The popes knew that they had to do something to revive urban life, so they imported a number of foreigners, including German bakers. We know that bread was the basic food of the city, either by itself or with *companatico* (something to eat with bread), because carefully kept records show that bakers used 85 to 90 percent of the grain that came into the city. Pasta was almost never eaten, and bread baked at home by individuals was extremely rare. Dark loaves accounted for the vast majority of what was baked and eaten, but white breads were made and sold in special luxury shops.

And what of Milan, the city that now symbolizes urban sophistication? Milan didn't have a single independent baker in the Middle Ages because until the end of the sixteenth century the bakers were all under the thumb of the powerful ruling Visconti family. This isn't to say that

bread didn't have a powerful position. On the contrary, the only people in the city who could be elected to the medieval parliament of Milan had to produce their own bread and wine, which says a lot about who the producers were as well as the position of bread. Please understand that we're not talking about white bread here. The Milanese ate a millet bread called *pan de mei*, the ancestor of today's corn loaves, or they ate breads that were either totally dark or made of mixed grains.

Progress was substantially set back by the plagues of the fourteenth century. The Black Death marched across the cities of Italy, decimating as much as 40 percent of their populations and bringing with it famine. For many Italians, bread became a mere memory. The high cost of wheat compelled some bakers to come up with whatever substitutions they could. Many of them found themselves mixing rye and millet or grinding acorns, using hard wheat instead of soft, adding poppy seeds, or even baking with elm or bay leaves and herbs and roots mixed in. Some bakers resorted to mixing in clay from the earth to make their loaves look whiter. To cope with the shortage, the pope effectively municipalized bread by opening numerous bread ovens in Rome. Still, as late as the eighteenth century, the poor were rioting around the famous fountains of the Piazza Navona with placards lettered "Let these cobblestones turn into bread."

Although cooks in Renaissance Italy devised sophisticated techniques of bread baking, the Italians lost their supremacy as bakers to the Viennese, who opened their first coffeehouses in 1782, offering the phenomenal sweets and pastries that made Vienna the capital of elegant baking. New high-speed roller mills turned out the cheap and plentiful white flour that was the basic material not only for these sweets but for bread.

The French shared honors with the Viennese in the field of baking. While white bread had once been reserved for the rich, the soldiers of Napoleon's army introduced it to the masses as they made their way across the continent. French bread became synonymous with bread. When Napoleon sold Venice to the Austrians in 1797, the Hapsburgs brought with them an army of inhabitants whose gastronomic traditions were enthusiastically accepted. They made the *Kipfel*, a croissantlike pastry that is still a great favorite at breakfast, and a century later the Austrian cavalry brought the *michetta*, the quintessential roll of Milan. The contribution of other cultures made an impact in Italy as well. America contributed her ingredients: the tomato, which eventually made a perfect marriage with Neapolitan pizza; the potato; the pimento; vanilla; the chocolate that transformed the pastries of Turin; and the corn that was milled and then baked into delicate pound cakes and heartier breads. Much earlier gifts from the Saracens—citrus fruits, grappa, and distilled spirits—and the Arab contributions of anise, nuts, almond paste, spices, and sugar gave special inflections to the cooking of Sicily and the south. The culinary signatures of invaders, conquerors, and explorers are all part of the heritage that remains today.

It wasn't until the beginning of the twentieth century that Pellegrino Artusi, a Florentine, rekindled Italian culinary pride by writing a cookbook that preserved genuine Italian cooking and gave respect to the regional tradition of middle-class food in the north. The book is chatty and amusing, and a fair number of its recipes are based on bread.

It could be said that an undercurrent common to these centuries was a class struggle between the *bocche da pane*, bread eaters who had white breads on their tables, and *bocche da biada*, literally "fodder eaters," peasants and members of the rural and urban poor who ate only dark breads made of whatever grains and beans the land offered up. In Italy, bread has always been a symbol of quality of life (a meal without it is unthinkable), and the quality of bread has always been a statement of social distinction. The privileged ate white bread even in Roman times. Until the last decade, dark breads have been identified with deprivation and hunger in the collective memory of Italy. The identification was particularly intense during the years when scarcities forced people to rely on *pane selvaggi*, breads made of whatever seeds and grains could be harvested from the countryside. (For centuries, scarcity has been the mother of invention in Italian baking. A baker in Venice told me that as recently as World War II, he mixed sawdust with whatever grain he had, and he used water straight from the sea to compensate for a scarcity of salt.)

Today it is rare to find many people baking at home—with a bakery on every block or in every neighborhood, there's scarcely a need to—but there are still pockets where the old ways prevail, among both the poor and the more privileged. In those places, which are almost always in the countryside, bread is baked in wood-burning ovens every few days by women who keep a nugget of natural yeast from one baking to the next. In the south, women share the yeast, passing it from household to household. Where once there were numerous communal ovens, today there are very few, where women of the community still take turns baking the breads, with hours assigned on the basis of seniority. These women know the temperature of the interior of the brick oven as it changes during the day, know where the hot spots are and where to put the breads so they will bake correctly. In the heyday of communal ovens, when there were numerous loaves being baked together, women would score their doughs with a special identifying mark on top.

The old and honorable bakery tradition, with its roots that reach deep into the Roman past, changed with the advent of high-speed machinery, but things really took a turn for the worse in the 1950s and 1960s, when huge machines were introduced that mixed and kneaded practically at the speed of light and produced cottony breads and bland *grissini*. To many people they were a denial of the art of the Italian baker, which was nourished by an agrarian past and by a passionate attachment to local ingredients and customs. The counterrevolution of the last several decades changed the face of baking. It is not that industrial methods have been banished, but that the conformity and lack of imagination connected with them are being challenged by artisan bakers. These men (and a tiny number of women) have touched a profoundly sensitive nerve in Italians who remember the true tastes of breads, pizzas, *focacce*, and sweets. They are restoring a real taste to bread, and bringing back a tradition that offers the best of the tastes that have given pleasure to Italians for centuries.

A NOTE ON ITALIAN USAGE

Terms and spellings for breads and sweets vary from region to region, and the same term can have different meanings in different regions.

Baking Basics

About the Recipes

In these recipes I have tried to re-create the breads and pastries, the *focacce*, biscotti, and cakes that I have lingered over in Italian cities, towns, and those tiny entities called *fraz*, for *frazione* (fraction), because they contain only a handful of buildings and really are splinters of the larger nearby community. The recipes are meant to bring the tastes of the Italian countryside to the American table and evoke memories of a way of life in which bread and the food it accompanies are shared among friends and family. As many of the recipes come from small towns that are off the beaten track or are baked for special holidays or to commemorate ancient regional practices, only travelers who have strayed from the usual hotel and restaurant route will have found them. No matter: try the breads and pastries this way first, then go to the country and sample them in context.

I have tried to keep these baked goods tasting as they do in Italy. I haven't sweetened the breads or added ingredients that would please the American palate, though I have reduced the amount of sugar in a few of the desserts and cookies—the Italian sweet tooth didn't get its fame undeservedly. Occasionally I have made an ingredient or two optional; the Italian passion for candied fruit is not reciprocated in America, so I have used candied orange peel as a substitute from time to time and required candied fruit only when a recipe truly couldn't do without it. When I have made an ingredient optional, I have often noted how the Italians would use them. I have specified the best-quality ingredients, using butter where some bakeries use vegetable fats or oils (if your preferences run to safflower and/or corn oil, you can certainly use it, especially in the breads). In light of the current national preoccupation with reducing our intake of animal fats, you may prefer to use olive oil in place of lard, although it is lard that gives some of these breads and *focacce* their special taste and texture. I do suggest that Americans try to use whatever Italian ingredients are available here.

The recipes in this book are all Italian. They began in huge quantities—20 kilos of flour is not an uncommon starting point—but they have been scaled down, reworked, and tested so that they can be made in an ordinary American kitchen, using American ingredients that most closely approximately their Italian counterparts. I've given volume as well as weight for measures of most ingredients but using metrics is a much more accurate way of measuring— 4 cups of flour can vary by as much as 100 grams depending on how the flour is scooped and packed into the measuring cup. I much prefer weighing ingredients for just that reason. I have given all measurements for active dry yeast in teaspoons, using $2^{1}/_{4}$ teaspoons per packet as a general rule of thumb, and in weights.

Many of these recipes, especially those calling for a starter, use much less yeast than traditional American recipes, and as a result they bring out the mellow, nutty flavor of the grain. Italian bakers never use sugar to activate yeast, and neither do I. Where sugar is called for, it is part of the recipe's ingredients. Italian bakers have used mixers since a baker designed the first automatic kneading machine in ancient Rome, and their tools have only grown bigger and faster since that time. I have given instructions for making the breads by hand as well as with a stand mixer such as a KitchenAid. (Please don't even think of using a hand-held mixer; it doesn't have the power to knead these doughs, and all you'll get for your trouble is a burned-out motor.) I decided to convert a number of the recipes for the food processor as well, because so many people are delighted by the speed and ease with which this machine can handle bread dough.

On the following pages you will find descriptions of the various ingredients and equipment called for in these recipes, and a review of the basic steps of bread baking and pastry making. Please read these sections carefully and refer to them whenever you need a bit of clarification. The one ingredient and technique not listed in this section is patience. Rome wasn't built in a day, and some of its breads need a little time to let their character mature. Should your plans change after you've begun a bread and your presence is required somewhere other than the kitchen, just leave the dough in a cool spot or in the refrigerator. Please don't let bread baking dictate your day.

Ingredients

The regional breads of Italy are made with only flour, water, yeast, and common salt, because that is the law of the land. "Special bread," another category entirely, may be enriched with milk, oil, or lard and flavored with the dazzling products of the countryside, including myriad types of olives, vegetables, grains, spices, herbs, fruits, raisins, nuts, and various essences and aromas. But it is the basic four ingredients that become the traditional rustic breads of the country, and to trace their flavors from Lugano in the north to Sicily at the toe of the boot is to make an odyssey in history and tastes. It is how the breads are measured and mixed, and in what proportions, and how they are left to rise and be shaped that determine their ultimate texture and taste, for these are the variables that give each bread its individual personality.

The Basic Four

FLOUR *Farina*

Flour in Italy. Bakers in Italy think it's impossible to find flour in America that isn't wonderful. I can't count the number of times during my work with Italian bakers that I heard the word "Manitoba," which becomes *Mahn-ee-TOE-ba*, four liquid syllables, in an Italian accent. It's a code word for fine flour, since the powerful wheats of the American and Canadian prairie absorb considerably more water and produce larger and more expansive doughs than

common Italian grain. Bakers spoke of it with admiration and a tone of distant longing, for the Italian earth, which remains so hospitable to grapes and olives, has been so consistently exploited that today it produces weak grains that lack the strength and flavor of the grains of the past. Some Italian flours may have as much gluten as ours, but they are unable to absorb water and then free it when the baking process requires. Many Italian bakers give a boost to their doughs by mixing in some of the higher-gluten, stronger American flour they admire, to approximate our all-purpose flour.

To capture the true taste of bread as it used to be made, some impassioned professionals, such as Giancarlo Grignani of Milan, have gone in search of grain cultivated as it was in earlier centuries, before chemicals and industrial fertilizers were introduced, and they have found millers who stone-grind it to a coarse texture that retains some of its bran. But, of course, most bakers make do with the common flours of the country and are able to prepare wonderful breads with them.

Flour in Italy commonly comes from the species *Triticum aestivum*, which is divided into two major varieties—soft wheat and hard wheat (*grano tenero*)—and from which all bread is made. Durum hard grain (*grano duro*), or *Triticum durum*, a different species, is the hardest wheat grown and is usually milled into semolina. It is a golden grain that has a higher protein and gluten content and is used almost exclusively for pasta production. The creamy, silky golden durum flour also makes wonderful bread, used alone or in combination with unbleached or all-purpose flour, but it does need to be mixed and kneaded for a longer time. The Italian baker has five grades of *grano tenero* to choose from, although they are classified not by strength and protein content like ours but by how much of the husk and whole grain have been sifted away. The whitest flour has the least fiber. The lower the number, the more refined and whiter the flour, so that of the five categories, "00" is the whitest and silkiest flour; "0" is a bit darker and less fine, since it contains about 70 percent of the grain; and "1" is even darker. Darker and even coarser yet, "2" has almost entirely disappeared from Italy. *Integrale*, or whole wheat, contains the whole wheat berry—husk, wheat germ, and all—and varies only depending on how it is milled. It is now possible to buy "00" flour in the United States. If you want to bake bread or pizza with it, the Source Guide to Ingredients and Equipment (page 401) provides information on purveyors.

The color of the flour is determined by the amount of bran present, but ironically, the white flours, which have the fewest nutrients and vitamins, are very expensive since the refining process is so costly. Unfortunately, it doesn't follow that healthier whole wheat flours are cheap, because most mills have been adapted to produce the refined flours; bran is taken out in an industrial process and used frequently for feeding animals. For all the talk of the prevalence of whole grain in the healthy Mediterranean diet, only a fairly small percentage of Italian breads are made with whole wheat. And in one of the stranger twists in the contemporary story of flour, I have heard of millers who simply take refined white flour, stir in a quantity of bran, and pronounce it whole wheat.

Flour in America. In America, we are used to thinking of flour in terms of its strength, which is measured by the amount of gluten-forming protein, although there is enormous variation in flours from region to region. The hard winter wheat produces strong bread flour with a high 13 to 15 percent gluten-forming content, and it must be kneaded longer and harder than other flours. Soft wheat, grown in the hot months between spring and autumn, when it is harvested, is much lower in gluten—usually 4 to 9 percent—and is generally used for cake and pastry flours.

Most of the recipes in this book can be made with all-purpose flour, which is a blend of hard and soft wheats, although at 11 or 12 grams of protein per cup, which is how we determine the percentage of gluten, it is slightly stronger than its Italian counterpart. If you can find stone-ground flour that hasn't lost its natural qualities from a speeded-up milling process, I'd strongly encourage you to use it for bread baking. I generally use Pillsbury, Gold Medal, or King Arthur unbleached flour, which is confusingly misnamed, as it is in fact bleached by the aging process, a characteristic it shares with Italian flours. No chemicals, however, give it its color. Our flours are enriched with thiamine, riboflavin, niacin, and iron and have a small amount of added malt. (Italians add malt as a grain extract to their dough to encourage their rising and the golden bloom of their crusts; they are also allowed a tiny addition of ascorbic acid, a form of vitamin C, intended to mature the dough.)

Many of the major brands of all-purpose flour note on the package that the flour has been presifted. Actually, once a bag of flour has left the miller and been trucked to a grocery store, put on the shelf, and then brought home with you, it couldn't possibly still be sifted. Just treat it like unsifted flour and, if possible, weigh it on a scale to measure it correctly. Never sift flour for bread; follow instructions in individual recipes for pastries, cakes, and cookies. If you weigh your ingredients, sift the flour after measuring; if you use cup measures, sift before measuring.

Go to any supermarket these days and you can find the basic flours—all-purpose, unbleached, and whole wheat—but you'll also probably find pastry, cake, durum, rye, high-gluten bread flour, or even the "00" white flour used by bakers and pizza makers in Italy. They may appear in small packages or in the big bins of bulk ingredients that hark back to the general stores of the last century. If, however, you have any difficulty finding a particular type of flour, see the Source Guide to Ingredients and Equipment (page 401) to learn where to purchase them.

In addition to the basic flours, other grains include:

Bread Flour. All the bread baking going on in this country has impelled large flour companies like Pillsbury and Gold Medal to market their own high-gluten bread flour with 12.5 to 14 percent protein content. Very few recipes in this book call for its use. Please do not substitute it for all-purpose flour, even if you are tempted by the promise of its more expansive doughs, because it is much too powerful for traditional Italian breads. Those that do call for it or for durum must be mixed and kneaded much longer and at a higher intensity than those made from all-purpose flour.

Corn Flour. Corn first appeared in Europe when Christopher Columbus brought it back from America, but the first boatload didn't reach Italy until the eighteenth century. And then, against all evidence, it was called *grano turco* (Turkish grain), on the theory that such a strange import must come from an exotic eastern locale such as Turkey. Corn became the grain of the poor, for whom polenta to this day replaces bread in some areas, but it was used particularly widely in Lombardy, where it grows in profusion and is made into wheels of fairly dense but delicious corn bread. Corn flour, which is essentially a finely ground version of cornmeal, can be stone ground, so that it retains a bit of its grittiness, or water ground, for a silkier texture. Since it has no gluten, it must be combined with wheat flour unless it is being used for an unleavened bread like *pan meino*.

Cornmeal. Cornmeal is used for baking and for dusting baking stones. When it is used as an ingredient in a bread or cake, I recommend stone-ground golden cornmeal, which retains a bit of its traditional gritty texture. Do not buy the degerminated variety for baking, because you'll get a lot of starch without any food value. Be sure to store the stone-ground variety in the refrigerator, so that the oils in it don't go rancid.

For dusting a baking stone or sheet, degerminated cornmeal is just fine. It costs less and can be stored at room temperature in a cupboard, and all the starch dries out the bottom of the dough and keeps it from sticking.

Durum Flour. Durum flour is a creamy, silky, fine golden flour milled from durum wheat, which is different from the hard wheats that are used for almost all bread making. It grows in very cold climes, such as Montana or Manitoba, as well as the great Tavoliere plain in Puglia, on the heel of the boot in southern Italy. Durum flour is the hardest kind of wheat flour. It is very high in gluten and, contrary to general opinion, it makes wonderful bread, either alone or in combination with all-purpose flour.

Graham Flour. Graham flour is actually a whole wheat flour from which the bran and wheat germ were extracted, finely powdered, and then reincorporated. It is named for Sylvester Graham, a militant nineteenth-century reformer from Boston who crusaded against the lack of nutritional value in white flour and was such an ardent advocate of the entire wheat grain that his name has become synonymous, in some parts of Italy at least, with whole wheat. You wouldn't expect to find such flour in Italy, but it has become rather stylish and it makes a wonderfully rich, nutty-tasting bread that has a decidedly lighter and flakier texture than whole wheat.

Oat Flour. Oats are the grains richest in proteins and minerals, but since they have minimal gluten, they must be combined with wheat flour to make a risen bread. Oat flour is used to add flavor and fat to bread dough and also helps it last longer, since it prevents fats from becoming rancid. If you can't find oat flour, you can grind rolled oats to a fine powder in your blender or food mill.

Pastry Flour. Pastry flour is made from soft wheat and is lower in gluten than all-purpose flour. It is perfect for baking pastries, tarts, and cakes. Although figures vary from brand to brand, pastry flour tends to have 8 or 9 percent protein, or gluten, content, while cake flour has 7 percent. If you are unable to find pastry flour, you can approximate it by mixing one part cake flour with two parts all-purpose flour.

Rice Flour. Rice produces a fine, silky flour that has less gluten but more starch than wheat flour. Regular rice flour is made only of the interior of the rice, while brown rice flour comes from the entire grain, including the bran and the germ, and it lends its nutty, rich taste and smooth, if somewhat dense, texture to multigrain breads. These are having a small boom in some parts of Italy, where there is a strong interest in health and nutrition. *Cinque* and *sette cereali* breads (five and seven grain) are where these special grains are most in evidence.

Rye Flour. The truest indigenous rye tradition in Italy comes from Lombardy's far northern valley of Valtellina, which is wedged right up against the edge of the Alps, and from Alagna Valsesia at the foot of Monte Rosa on the Swiss border. The rye is dark and the flour contains the bran of the grain. Rye breads were common in Italy in the Middle Ages and today are found extensively in the Trentino and Alto Adige, which were part of the South Tirol until the end of World War I, so that they essentially represent an Austrian tradition. A little grappa is still added to the rye bread of Venice in memory of days when slices of rye were flavored with aquavit. Rye has a low percentage of gluten, so it is combined with wheat in various proportions to help it rise effectively. Always make a rye starter to give a boost to the fermentation process and to add a lovely sour taste. Rye makes dough sticky, so it is usually easier to handle if you use a dough scraper as an extension of your hand in the kneading process. When kneading dark rye in a mixer, keep it on low speed so that the delicate gluten strands don't break.

Semolina. Coarse, grainy, cream-colored particles of semolina, milled from the hearts of durum wheat berries, are perfect for dusting your baking stone or sheet. The starch will keep your bread dough from sticking. Don't, however, substitute semolina granules for semolina flour; they simply won't make bread.

Semolina Flour. Semolina flour is made from the amber-colored granular grain that comes from grinding the heart of the durum wheat berry. If you read most imported pasta packages, you'll notice that they list *semolina di grano duro* as the major ingredient; this hard, high-gluten wheat flour is the basis of the best industrially made pastas, as it cooks up firm and absorbs less water than softer flour products.

In Italy, semolina is ground especially for bread making, but here it is hard to find and never quite as silky as its Italian counterpart. Always use pale golden durum flour, which comes closest to the Italian equivalent.

YEAST *Lievito*

Yeast is considered the soul of the bread, the source of its life and its character. A bread made without it ends up as flat as the *piadina* of Emilia, a thin disk that looks very much like a Mexican tortilla. Virtually every bread in this book is made with an infusion of yeast.

Yeast is a living product suspended in a dormant state until it is reactivated. Active dry yeast, fawn-colored granules packed in small $1/4$-ounce (7-gram) envelopes, needs to be brought to life in water that is 105°F to 115°F. When recipes in this book call for "warm water," it should be in this range. Water at room temperature, roughly 70°F to 75°F, allows for a slower rise so the bread can develop its full flavor.

I find that I use active dry yeast almost exclusively. It is easy to store and can be kept at cool room temperature; it stays fresh in the refrigerator for as long as three years. If you are going to buy individual packets, I recommend Fleischmann's or Red Star. If you do much baking, I strongly recommend buying active dry yeast in bulk. Not only does it come without preservatives, but the money you save is absolutely astonishing. A pound can be bought in bulk for between $1.50 and $2.30, while three of the small $1/4$-ounce (7-gram) envelopes can cost as much as $3.75 in their individual packets.

Now that yeast is successfully standardized, I never proof it to verify its freshness. I have baked hundreds and hundreds of loaves of bread for this book and never had the yeast fail me. But, if you are uncertain, simply dissolve the yeast in warm water along with a pinch of sugar and wait about 10 minutes to see that it foams.

Professional bakers are now using instant yeast in their recipes. Contrary to what the name suggests, the instant yeast does not speed up the fermentation of the dough, but it is convenient because it does not need to be dissolved in water and it can be combined directly with the flour and other dry ingredients. If you want to try using instant yeast in any of the recipes in this book, you can convert active dry yeast to instant by multiplying by 0.75. Do not confuse instant yeast with the new high-speed yeasts, such as Red Star's Quick-Rise and Fleischmann's RapidRise, that work in a miraculously short time, because that speed is achieved at the noticeable expense of flavor.

Although baking with fresh yeast was common in the past, fresh yeast is now almost entirely unavailable to home bakers. Anyone searching for fresh yeast can try to buy some from a baker at a local bakery or from the bakery department at a supermarket. There is one website that sells fresh yeast in 1- or 2-pound packets (see the Source Guide to Ingredients and Equipment, page 401). Remember that fresh yeast is perishable and keeps only about a week under refrigeration. If you want to convert a recipe using active dry yeast to fresh yeast, it is important to know that dry yeast is about twice as potent as fresh yeast of the same weight (1 package [0.22 oz / 7 g] active dry yeast equals 1 small cake [0.63 oz / 18 g] fresh yeast). To convert fresh yeast to instant yeast, multiply by 0.33.

Starters. Before yeast was manufactured industrially, bakers' choices of leavening were rather limited. Many used a piece of dough left over from the previous day to ferment a new dough. Many of the best bakers do essentially the same thing today, using *biga* (page 70), a simple saltless mixture of flour, water, and a minute amount of commercial yeast left to ferment at cool room temperature for five to sixteen hours. It is basically the same as a fermented day-old chunk of saltless Tuscan bread dough, left to triple and bubble with vigorous activity (don't worry if it then collapses) before it is added to the ingredients of the new dough, which is then left to rise again before it is shaped. In some of the recipes that follow, yeast is mixed with water and a small amount of flour and allowed to stand for an hour or two to form an unfermented sponge (so called because of the spongy texture of the resulting dough). The remaining flour and all of the flavorings are then kneaded in. Yeast breads made by the sponge method or with the added tang of fermented *biga* have a special dimension of texture and flavor. These forms of leavening that create new life are known as *la madre*, the mother, in northern Italy and as *il babbo*, the father, in Tuscany and farther south.

Natural Yeasts. Few bakers in Italy go to the trouble of making yeast from natural fermentation, as the process is as complicated as it is time-consuming. It begins with a batter of flour and water left to sour at room temperature by collecting the wild yeasts of the air, or by feeding on natural yeasts such as those that cling to the skins of organic grapes or raisins. That's only the beginning: the original mixture has to be refreshed with several additions of flour and water. It is a time-consuming and difficult art that results in what is referred to as a "wild horse," since there's no knowing when it will act up on its own and do whatever it pleases.

I have made so much bread in my kitchen for so long that all I have to do is mix up some flour and water and leave the uncovered bowl at room temperature, and within forty-eight hours all sorts of magical bubbling begins. Imagine what a feast of wild yeast spores are dancing in the air, submicroscopic motes waiting for the chance to fertilize two of the simplest elements on earth and start the whole life process again. And it does happen, time and time again. The Romans used must from the skins of grapes as a natural source of wild yeast, and some bakers use organic raisins or grapes to start their natural yeasts. Bakers who use natural yeasts instead of commercial yeast today typically make a flour-and-water mixture, refresh it daily according to a complicated schedule, and then substitute this mixture for an amount equal to 20 to 25 percent of the flour in their bread.

You can also create a starter that resembles one made with natural yeast by making a *biga* with a small amount of yeast and refreshing it over time until it approximates one made with natural yeast (page 72). It will remain active for a few months, but after that, its strength declines, its texture slackens, and its taste becomes more acidic. If you are making a sweet bread or many of the savory breads, be sure to refresh the *biga* 4 to 8 hours before using it. A few doughs call for a *biga* that has soured for longer to achieve the secondary fermentation that gives the breads their flavor. Fewer still have more particular instructions, such as the ciabatta, which calls for a *biga* made 12 hours previously, or the *ciabatta Polesana* (page 81), with its *biga* that is refrigerated for 12 to 18 hours.

Bakers, who have noses like doctors or pharmacists, insist you can cut into a *biga* and smell if the yeast is right. The really expert say that if you set your ear right next to it, you can hear the little "tic-tac" of its growing.

WATER *Acqua*

Water is the one ingredient in bread baking that we tend to take for granted, since we can simply turn the tap to get what we want. Or so I thought until several Italian bakers looked somewhat dubious when I talked about making their breads in America. It wasn't the flour they were concerned about, but the water. "Too many chemicals," said one. "Too much chlorine," said another. "The water's too hard," volunteered a third. Hard water can be a real problem, even in Italy, where bakers sometimes use a filter, and you can do the same if you get really involved in making these breads. Some breads are said to owe their ineffable taste to the water of their towns, and obviously we can hardly hope to duplicate the flavor of water fresh from cool mountain springs, although I admit that I have made some of these regional breads with bottled spring water. True, it's an expensive way to search out the authentic taste of one of the most basic foods in the world. Still, would I recommend it? If your water is heavily chlorinated or full of chemicals, I'd certainly tell you to give it a try. It is imperative if you are using natural yeasts and preferable when you are starting a natural *biga*.

SALT *Sale*

Salt in Italy comes in two forms, the coarser sea salt that is used in the kitchen and the fine grains that appear only at the table. The fatter grains, which still taste a bit of the sea, are considerably cheaper there and are what Italian bakers always use in their breads.

The best sea salt, which still has all its natural nutrients, comes from Europe. In America, the FDA requires that all the magnesium and trace minerals be washed off table salt; many companies go further and use an additive that allows it to pour freely, for salt is naturally moist and tends to clump. Still, I hesitate to tell you to use finely ground imported sea salt because it is so expensive. After all, this is bread, which has nourished the poor for centuries; it is as basic a food as exists and is made of the most earthy ingredients. But, let's face it: the salt of Italy is pulled right from the sea and hasn't been washed free of its nutrients, so it's a question of how much you value the natural qualities and taste of real sea salt. Please understand that I am talking about fine sea salt crystals, not the coarse ones that I use to sprinkle the top of *panmarino* bread, nor big crystals of kosher salt. I personally use fine sea salt from the Mediterranean, which is now widely available; it tastes saltier than other salt, while kosher salt tastes the mildest. Two teaspoons of kosher salt are equal in weight and taste to 1 teaspoon of sea salt. Morton's has recently produced a sea salt without any additives (see the Source Guide to Ingredients and Equipment, page 401).

Until recently salt was a state monopoly in Italy, a national product of such importance that in the old days you could tell whether a region was doing well simply by the price of its salt, rather as we can judge countries today on the price of their oil. Salt has only recently appeared on supermarket and grocery shelves in Italy, after centuries of being available solely at the *tabacchi* where other state-regulated items, such as stamps and tobacco, are sold.

Salt not only gives flavor to bread and adds to the elasticity of the gluten, but it retards the action of the yeast, so that many bakers add it to the dough only at the very end of the mixing process. If, for some reason, you forget to add the salt, don't worry; you can dissolve it in a little water and mix it in slowly even after the dough as come together. If the amount of salt seems somewhat high, remember that Italians never put butter on their bread, while Americans, who almost always do, predominantly use salted butter.

Additional Ingredients for Bread

Luigi Barzini was once asked to contribute an introduction to an Italian cookbook. In it he wrote that "every recipe should begin by advising readers to buy a small estate in Tuscany so they can produce their own cheese, olives and oil, and raise their own chickens for eggs." The editors ended up deleting the section, "because," they said, "it was not practical and readers would be discouraged."

Barzini was perhaps a bit extreme in his approach, although it is hard to disagree with his sentiments given the Italian reverence for food. It is a rare conversation that doesn't sooner or later turn to the subject of eating, so maybe it is not an exaggeration to conclude that the DNA of Italians must include a special gene predisposing them to care passionately about the quality of their food. Italians won't tolerate indifferent ingredients or dishes. They continue to rely on natural products, and enough people live on the land or maintain a closeness to nature that many products still live up to the high expectations created by centuries of good taste. Colors and flavors are clear and clean: bright green basil, darker glossy rosemary, fat red tomatoes, golden and scarlet peppers, rich green olive oil that comes from the first pressing of the fruit. The yolks of Italian eggs are almost orange-gold because the chickens are fed daily rations of corn. The tastes are as clear and clean as the colors, and they embody an attitude about life that is as Italian as Fra Angelico frescoes and the Renaissance palazzi that we identify as the cultural patrimony of the country.

ANCHOVIES *Acciughe*

These tiny, tasty fish are a wonderful source of flavor. They are preserved in olive oil—filleted and conveniently packed in small tins or jars—or in salt. The anchovies packed in salt come in large 1- or 2-pound tins and have more taste, but since they are not filleted, you should clean them under running water and snip out their backbone, a simple procedure. Anchovy paste comes in a tube, and while a paste freshly made from whole anchovies tastes better, there is a lot to be said for the convenience of having mashed anchovies on hand.

CAPERS *Capperi*

Capers are the small unripe buds of a plant that grows wild, anchoring itself in the fissures and cracks of stone walls and cliffs around the entire Mediterranean. I have seen them climbing ruins in Sicily and on walls of ancient buildings in small Italian towns. Capers come in two sizes: plump, fat ones; and the smaller variety, called nonpareils, which are considered finer. Both sizes are sold in vinegar brines and may need to be rinsed before they are used; if you find capers preserved in salt in an Italian market, be sure to rinse them before proceeding.

I drain capers by putting them in a strainer over a bowl. I save the liquid and return it to the caper jar; after I've measured out the capers that I need, I put the unused ones back in the jar along with the reserved brine.

CHEESES *Formaggi*

Caciocavallo. This hard cooked cheese from southern Italy and Sicily has a smooth and firm pale-yellow interior. It is made by warming the curd so that it can be stretched and kneaded into its idiosyncratic shape, which resembles an elongated flask with a small knob on top. The knob has a purpose: it allows the cheese to be tied in pairs, as if to be slung over the back of a horse (*caciocavallo* means "cheese on horseback"). The more mature caciocavallo, aged for six months to a year, is meant for grating. Piquant and tangy, it adds pungency to the southern pizzas and calzones. If you can't find fresh caciocavallo, mild provolone is an excellent substitute.

Crescenza. A fresh, semisoft, medium-fat rindless cheese that comes from the countryside around Milan, crescenza is made with fresh cow's milk. White or very pale golden cream in color, it is especially delicate. *Crescenza* means "growth," and the cheese is so named because when left in a warm place, it begins to expand, as if it were dough rising.

Fontina. One of the most distinctive cheeses of Italy, Fontina, named for Mont Fontin near Aosta, is an Alpine cheese synonymous with the Val d'Aosta of Piedmont. It should only be made of milk from that region, which produces a rich, aged, firm cheese that is golden in color and very lightly dotted with holes inside, rather like a Gruyère. Its slightly nutty, buttery taste is so delicious that Fontina is considered at least as much a table cheese as a cooking cheese. There are a variety of Italian Fontinas, but the finest has on its brown–gold rind the trademark of the producing Fontina corporation in purple dye.

Gorgonzola. A rich, semisoft blue cheese made from the milk of the cows of Lombardy, Gorgonzola was once aged in caves that were home to the mold that invaded the creamy interior and gave it its distinctive blue veins and wonderful taste and smell. Today, quantities of Gorgonzola are made in factories by injecting the cheese with bacteria to encourage the growth of its blue veins; the aging process is speeded up, but the taste is still glorious. You can choose from two kinds of Gorgonzola: *Gorgonzola dolce,* as sweet and buttery as a blue cheese can be, or *Gorgonzola piccante,* which has a more pungent flavor and aroma. Be sure the cheese you buy is fresh and moist. If you can't find an Italian Gorgonzola, you may substitute a mild Oregon blue cheese, as long as it is still creamy and fresh.

Grana. Grana is a grating cheese made in a number of northern Italian locations. The cow's milk differs from place to place and the aging fluctuates between one and two years.

Groviera. This cheese is similar in all ways to French Gruyère except that it began life in Italy and has an Italian name. Gruyère is a perfect alternative.

Mascarpone. This is a fresh thick cheese made from sweet cream, although it sometimes tastes as if it were whipped cream made of fine cheese. What we get in America has been pasteurized so that it isn't as fluffy or delicate as the fresh Italian product, but it is still a lovely dessert cheese that can be flavored and tucked between layers of cake for tiramisu. In its place you can use the freshest possible cream cheese, made without stabilizers or preservatives, or you could beat a half a pound of ricotta with a cup of whipping cream until the mixture is very, very smooth. Both would be more than adequate replacements for this highly perishable snowy-white cheese. Depending on whose story you believe, mascarpone may be named for the Lombard dialect word for ricotta, *marcherpe,* or for the response of a high Spanish official in the seventeenth century who tasted the cheese and exclaimed, "¡Más que bueno!"— "Delicious!"

Mozzarella. The classic pizza cheese because it melts to such a lovely creamy consistency, Italian mozzarella is ideally made from the milk of the buffalo that still roam the marshy plain of Campania outside Naples (*mozzarella di bufala*). More and more frequently, however, the familiar egg-shaped ovals or spheres are made with some, if not all, cow's milk (*mozzarella fior di latte*). Both varieties are flown to America, so should you decide to buy them, be sure they are fresh, creamy, and still sitting in their own milky brine. Artisan cheesemakers such as Belgioso, Belfiore, and Gioia Cheese Company are also producing fine fresh mozzarella in America. The real product bears almost no relationship to the tasteless rubbery ball that Americans know as mozzarella, which is made of skim milk and must be grated to be used. If you are fortunate enough to live in a city where a cheesemaker produces fresh whole-milk mozzarella, leap at the opportunity to use it, or see the Source Guide to Ingredients and Equipment (page 401) to learn about fresh American and Italian mozzarellas.

Parmigiano-Reggiano. This is undoubtedly the most famous of all Italian cheeses. It belongs to a group of hard grating cheeses (*grana*), of which there are many produced in northern Italy. Like the fine French *appellation d'origine contrôlée* wines and D.O.C. wines in Italy, Parmigiano-Reggiano is produced only in strictly controlled areas under very specific conditions. Production begins with the high-quality milk of summer on April 1 and ends on November 11 and can only take place in the provinces of Parma, Reggio Emilia, and Modena, in Mantua on the right bank of the Po River, and in Bologna on the left bank of the Reno River. The cheese is made entirely by hand in a centuries-old artisan tradition and is left to age for a minimum of two years. What is produced at the end of this long process is a straw-colored cheese with an extremely attractive flavor that is clean and somewhat salty. It is slightly crumbly in texture. You will know that you are buying the real thing if the rind is etched with the words "Parmigiano-Reggiano" around the entire circumference. Lesser Parmesans include *grana padana*, which simply means that the cheese comes from the plain of Lombardy. Domestic American Parmesan is bland; Argentinean Parmesan has some bite to it. Both are infinitely preferable to pregrated American Parmesan, which has no real taste at all. Buy a whole chunk of Parmesan and grate it just before using it, so that the taste and perfume of the Parmesan truly becomes part of the bread or pizza you are making.

Pecorino. What Parmesan cheese is to the north, pecorino is to the south of Italy, where it is the most popular of all the hard grating cheeses. Though there are a variety of aged pecorini, all are made of sheep's milk (*pecora* means sheep), and all are sharp-tasting medium-fat cheeses. They look similar to Parmesan with their compact gold-colored interiors. The difference comes on the tongue; pecorino is saltier, tangier, and sharper-tasting, clearly meant only for grating and not for eating at table. The best pecorino to use for these recipes is pecorino Romano, the most widely imported of all pecorini, although you may try an aged pecorino Sardo as well. Be sure the cheese is still moist and crumbly enough to grate. Buy the cheese in a chunk and grate it only when you are ready to use it. You will notice that recipes sometimes call for a mixture of the piquant pecorino and the milder Parmesan, or for pecorino alone.

Provolone. Even people who know very little about Italian cheese seem to recognize the long bulbous provolone, which is divided into sections by the strings that hold it. It also comes in less picturesque shapes, and can be conical or round, in sizes ranging from as small as 2 pounds to gigantic. When well aged, it is always a hard cow's-milk cheese with a smooth golden-yellow rind. Both the sweet, mild *provolone dolce* and the more mature piquant variety are specialties of the south of Italy and can be used interchangeably with caciocavallo.

Stracchino. A rindless fresh cheese produced in the plain of Lombardy, stracchino is made from two milkings: the fresh milk of the morning is mixed with that from the night before. It gets its name from the dialect word for "tired," because the best cheese is said to have come from the evening milking, after the cows have grazed all day in good alpine pastures and have returned home exhausted. Stracchino is creamy in both color and texture and has a slight tang when it is fully mature.

Taleggio. This is another pale golden whole-cow's-milk cheese from Lombardy, rich and semisoft. It is compact, smooth, and buttery, although it gets a delicate aromatic flavor as the cheese ages and grows stronger. Taleggio, stracchino, and crescenza may be used interchangeably. If you have tasted them in Italy, where they are farmhouse cheeses with a wonderful smooth and creamy texture, you may detect a bit of difference when you sample them in America, because the government requires that all cheeses under sixty days old must be pasteurized to be imported into this country

HERBS *Erbe*

Buy a window box or planter to grow your own herbs or convince your local market to carry them. I don't mind sounding like a fanatic: the taste that fragrant herbs give to doughs and pizzas is so fresh and lovely that it would be a shame to miss their aromatic seasoning. Dried rosemary and oregano are fine in any of these recipes, but dried basil isn't even a distant relation of its fresh self and there's no hope of making pesto with it.

Basil/Basilico. The aroma of fresh basil is so enticing that I think it must imprint itself on our sense memories forever. It is what makes pesto so fragrant and what gives the wonderful taste of summer to tomatoes and mozzarella, as well as zucchini and other vegetables. The green leafy herb doesn't grow all year long, but it can be preserved in any of three ways. Pick the leaves and pat them clean with a damp paper towel; you can then pack them in plastic bags for the freezer, layer them in coarse salt in Mason jars, or cover them with olive oil. The olive oil method is particularly successful in retaining the bright green color of the leaves.

There are a number of prepared pestos on the market, and if you choose to buy one, be sure it is still green from fresh basil and is made with authentic Italian cheese, fine olive oil, and pine nuts.

Oregano/Origano. This hardy herb grows wild in Italy and is a sturdy perennial that grows in America without demanding anything other than a bit of land, sun, and water. It is characteristic of southern Italian cooking and appears frequently dusting the tops of pizzas. It is considerably milder in its fresh state, so you should use it accordingly.

Parsley/Prezzemolo. Italian parsley is dark green and flat-leaved and has a much more tantalizing flavor than the curly-leaved variety many Americans know. Luckily, Italian parsley is now appearing almost universally in the produce section of stores. In its absence, substitute regular parsley.

Rosemary/Rosmarino. Rosemary grows wild in many parts of Italy, in thickets and hedges and dense low ground cover. The glossy dark leaves look rather like pine needles and have a strong taste. They will take root easily in most gardens and pots. Rosemary is so often used with roasts and chickens in Italy that the butcher frequently includes free branches with your order, since it is taken for granted that the herb belongs in your roasting pan. Fresh rosemary is preferable to dried, but should you use the dried, be sure to use substantially smaller quantities, since the taste is concentrated. When adding fresh rosemary to bread, cut the leaves with a sharp knife to release the fragrance and strong flavor.

LARD *Strutto*

Italy is a country full of pigs—hence all the salamis, sausages, prosciutto, and pancetta. Good pork lard, cheap and plentiful, gives a smooth, moist, creamy texture to doughs and is commonly used in any number of breads, pizzas, *focacce*, and *grissini*. In diet-conscious America, where high-cholesterol animal fat is frowned upon, good lard is difficult to find. There is inexpensive lard on some grocery shelves, but I strongly urge you to buy the best pork fat you can and render it at home. Try to get leaf lard, the creamy fat around pork kidneys, or use pork back fat, which can be found in cities with Chinese markets. My butcher, who is usually extremely accommodating, has to sell me leaf lard in 10-pound amounts, so I have one busy afternoon rendering it and then can keep it refrigerated in small lots for months. To render it, just cut the pork fat into smallish pieces, put them in a large heavy-bottomed saucepan, and set it over a very low flame. Let it cook until it has become a transparent liquid. Skim off the little pork cracklings—they taste delicious added to bread—pour the lard into an earthenware container, and leave it at room temperature until it cools completely and hardens to a creamy white substance. Keep it in the refrigerator or freezer. If you need to use a substitute for lard, olive oil makes an excellent alternative in nonsweet bread dough. I think Crisco leaves a cottony taste and coating on the tongue, so I would never use it.

LIQUEURS AND WINES *Liquori e vini*

Grappa. An aquavit, the distillation of the residue of pressed grapes, grappa can have a strong, fiery bite and be a little rough around the edges unless it has been adequately aged. Grappas are now easily found in this country. You can use slivovitz or marc as a substitute.

Maraschino liqueur. This is a favorite of Italian bakers, who use it in remarkable quantities. It is distilled from marasca cherries, but is neither very sweet nor red.

Marsala. This fortified Sicilian wine is essentially the Italian equivalent of Madeira in French cooking. Marsala was first made in 1773 by an Englishman who wanted to improve the staying power of good Sicilian wine. Use Marsala Superior or Fine, not the egg (al'Uovo) or cream variety.

Sambuca. The liqueur of Civitavecchia, the port of the city of Rome, sambuca is made from aniseed and sugar and has a distinct licorice flavor.

MALT EXTRACT *Malto*

Italian bakers use malt, a small amount of which is added to Italian flours, to feed the yeast in their dough and to improve their dough in a variety of ways. Malt encourages the growth of a loaf, retains moisture in the dough, and is definitely responsible for a lovely golden crust.

Diastatic malt extract is a grain product in syrup form—made usually of barley, or of barley and corn, that has been mashed and malted—and it should be used in small amounts. It is hard to find (see the Source Guide to Ingredients and Equipment, page 401), so you can substitute malt powder in equal amounts, adding it with the dry ingredients. Be sure to get the type that is *not* flavored with hops. If you can't find malt extract, you can omit it without changing the results drastically.

DRIED WILD MUSHROOMS *Funghi Secchi*

Porcini Mushrooms. These wild mushrooms, which are the same as French cèpes, are the most highly prized mushrooms in Italy, where they still grow in abundance. During the season, markets are full of the huge-capped fresh mushrooms, but they can be found all year long in a dried version. Their rich, earthy taste flavors dishes with a pungent fragrance of the woods. They are traditionally added to risottos, pastas, and main dishes, but I think that adding them to bread is an imaginative new use of one of Italy's most fragrant ingredients. Dried porcini mushrooms are expensive, although a little goes a long way. They are always soaked in warm water for at least half an hour before using, and the soaking liquid should be strained and saved, since it is so flavorful. Be sure to ask for *Italian* porcini mushrooms. I once had the unfortunate experience of being sold an Argentinean variety that looked and smelled the same but had a taste so pallid as to be imperceptible.

NUTS *Noci*

Almonds, Walnuts, and Hazelnuts. Mandorle, *noci*, and *nocciole* constitute the great triumvirate of nuts frequently used in sweet breads and desserts. They all arrive toasted at Italian bakeries, but you will have to toast your own by spreading them on a baking sheet and setting them in a 350°F oven for 10 to 13 minutes. You can tell nuts are done when their smell wafts through the oven door.

Almonds may be purchased whole or slivered, with skins or blanched. If you need to blanch your own almonds, drop them into boiling water and after about 2 minutes, remove with a slotted spoon or skimmer. Cool briefly and squeeze each one between your fingers until it pops out of its skin.

Hazelnuts have much tighter skins than almonds and it takes a bit more work to remove them. Lay the hazelnuts in a single layer on a baking sheet and bake them at 350°F for about 10 minutes, until the skins crack, shrivel, and flake. Remove them from the oven, wrap them in a tea towel, and let them steam and cool off for about 5 minutes. While they are still in the towel, rub them vigorously en masse in your fingers; while this won't get all the nuts to shed their skins, it will make a good start. Then you'll need to take the nuts individually and rub them between your fingers to encourage them to shed the rest of the still clinging skin. Unless the nuts are being used for decorative purposes and must look perfect, feel free to use nuts with some skin still apparent.

The lazy way to remove hazelnut skins is to put the toasted nuts into a food processor with the plastic blade and pulse. This ingenious solution does work, but the drawback is that you lose a third of the nuts this way.

Pine Nuts. Tiny *pignoli* come from the seeds of pine cones and must be individually shelled and extracted, which explains their great cost. Their rich, creamy flavor is unique and they are folded into any number of sweet breads and fillings as well as desserts. They are as well the traditional nut in pesto, although walnuts may be substituted there. Pine nuts used to be served regularly in Liguria during Lent, when clever people skirted the prohibitions of ecclesiastical authorities by adding them to give taste and substance to otherwise rather thin dishes. Italian bakeries have their pine nuts already toasted; you will need to toast your own, where noted, in a 350°F oven for 10 minutes. They are expensive, no matter how you buy them, although little cellophane bags holding fractions of an ounce of this precious cargo are even more so. There really isn't a good substitute for the unique taste of pine nuts. Be sure to look for Italian pine nuts. A small percentage imported from China are suspected of causing taste disturbances that can last for up to two months.

OLIVES *Olive*

Were there but world enough and time, we could talk of olives almost indefinitely. Olives in Italy are a world unto themselves, and many of the most prized come from central Italy. Olives for eating and cooking are either picked green or are tree ripened until they are mahogany or purple-black in color. They may be cured in salt, oil, or brine. Those most commonly used in these recipes are:

Gaeta Olives. Grown in the Campania region around Naples, these are succulent reddish-purple olives with a wonderfully salty, mildly bitter flavor, somewhat like Kalamata olives from Greece.

Ligurian Olives. These come from the Italian Riviera, the region that wraps around Genoa like a boomerang and extends from the border of southern France to the northernmost edge of Tuscany. Benedictine monks first introduced olives to the area, but now many hillsides are silvery gray with olive trees that are nourished by fertile earth, warm sun, and salt water from the Mediterranean, whose moisture is drawn in by the roots of the trees. Black Ponentine olives are tiny and mild, while fat, flavorful Ardoino are saltier and more pungent; both are purplish-black and are perfect for using in pizza or bread. Pitting them takes a bit of time. Tiny black Niçoise olives from Provence are an excellent substitute, since they are the same type of olive, cured slightly differently.

Sicilian-Style Olives. Crisp, big, fleshy green olives that are cured in brine, Sicilian-style olives are somewhat salty tasting. The easiest to find come from California and are cured in the Sicilian style. They are perfect for use in green olive bread, although I have also used cracked green Greek olives with splendid results. Please don't used canned California green or black ripe olives; they simply haven't enough taste and seem to lack all flavor when baked into a bread. What makes the Sicilian-style olive different from others is that it ferments in a brine cure for up to six months. Its pungent, salty taste and crisp texture give bread the strong personality of a full-flavored, well-aged olive.

OLIVE OIL *Olio d'Oliva*

Bread, focaccia, and pizza doughs flavored with olive oil are richer and longer-lasting than regular rustic breads. Use a well-made cold-pressed olive oil, but that doesn't mean you need a fruity, expensive oil with a double-digit price tag. The flavor should be mild and delicate, not heavy. The oil gives lightness, springiness, and moisture to the dough and makes it supple and easy to work with. Since oil is a preservative, some of the *focacce* and breads made with it tend to last several days. Don't forget to brush pizzas hot out of the oven with a glaze of oil.

OLIVE PASTE *Polpa d'Oliva*

Olive pastes, such as the wonderful Olivada San Remo imported from Liguria, are rich and salty mixtures made of pulverized olives that are preserved in extra-virgin olive oil and flavored with herbs. They make wonderful crostini, especially on Tuscan bread, which is a perfect foil for the salty mixture. The dough for *pane di Chiavari* (page 117), which incorporates olive paste, can very simply be treated like focaccia dough by spreading it in a focaccia pan and baking it according to the instructions typically used for that sort of bread. And Genoese focaccia, in a turnabout, can be topped with a liberal washing of the olive paste. Olive paste is sometimes known in Italy as *caviale nero*, black caviar.

PANCETTA

Pancetta is unsmoked Italian bacon that has been preserved in salt, seasoned with pepper, and rolled up like a fat salami. Good pancetta is a nice balance of creamy fat and lean meat with a salty taste and a peppery crunch. It should be easy to find in many markets. If you can't find any, don't use smoked bacon; instead, substitute salt pork to which you have added some pepper.

PROSCIUTTO

In Italy, *prosciutto* simply means ham. If you want cooked ham, ask for *prosciutto cotto*; to obtain raw, air-dried ham cured with salt and seasonings, specify *prosciutto crudo*. Italian prosciutto from Parma and San Daniele is now routinely imported into this country. High-quality American products, such as La Quercia brand, are also well distributed. Don't buy thinly sliced prosciutto in plastic packages if you have a chance to go to a delicatessen or specialty shop, where you'll simply get better value and better taste.

RAISINS *Uva Passa*

Raisins are dried grapes. The Romans were such connoisseurs that they made distinctions between grapes to be eaten at table, grapes to be made into wine, and grapes that should be dried for raisins, usually the biggest and sweetest white grapes. Several types of raisins are used in Italy, for which counterparts are readily available here.

Malaga. These raisins from Pantelleria, the island off Sicily, are a big seedless variety that taste almost as rich as figs. Muscats can be substituted.

Sultanina. These seedless blond raisins from Turkey and Sicily have a wonderful sugary taste. Substitute either a golden or dark seedless raisin.

Uvette. Very sweet tiny raisins, always used in plum cake, these are very much like our currants.

Zibibbo. These big, fat raisins, which can be either amber or chestnut colored and are sometimes as much as an inch long, and have just enough seeds inside to be slightly crunchy. The best American equivalent is a monukka raisin.

Our golden seedless raisins have achieved their color by being bleached in sulfur dioxide; the trick is never to soak them in hot water, which will bring out their strongly sulfurous flavor. Plump raisins in cool water or something stronger, like rum or Marsala.

SESAME SEEDS *Sesamo*

These pale little seeds that give the slightest hint of a peanut taste are often used in Sicily. Buy them in bulk in ethnic markets or in health-food stores and you will be staggered at how much money you save in contrast to what you spend buying them in little spice jars. Store them in the refrigerator in a tightly closed jar to keep their oils from becoming rancid. To bring out their nutty flavor, you can roast them in a dry iron skillet over medium heat for 5 minutes.

SPICES *Spezie*

Many of the imaginatively spiced breads you can now buy all over Italy sound like wonderful creations of an innovative new breed of baker, but the breads of the Roman Empire were flavored with such unusual combinations. The bakers of ancient Rome made loaves with fennel seeds, anise, raisin juices, and poppy seeds, and even perfumed one variety with maidenhair. By the time of Augustus, when a real bread-baking industry was thriving, there were three hundred bakeries in Rome alone, white bread had taken on a class distinction as a status symbol, and there existed a long and astonishing list of the variety of breads available. Breads had even taken on special functions: there was a bread for keeping a beautiful complexion, a bread for sailors to eat on the high seas, a bread meant to be eaten with oysters, and even a bread for dogs, made mostly of bran. Spices were familiar components in these years of the empire. Then in 410 A.D., Alaric, leader of the Visigoths, seized and plundered Rome. The darkness that fell in his wake shadowed all of Italian life in the Middle Ages, and bread making lost its virtuosity.

Spices fell into disuse until the Venetians went to sea and brought back pepper, cinnamon, cloves, nutmeg, mace, and ginger from the exotic East. Some flavorings sat on the table of the poor to pep up monotonous dishes, and by the twelfth century spices were dressing up a whole range of foods, including the still popular *panforte*, a fruitcake-like confection bursting with dried fruits and nuts and flavored with coriander, cloves, cinnamon, ginger, mace, and even white pepper. Spices were much in demand as symbols of conspicuous consumption because they were so expensive and hard to get ("as dear as pepper" was a common saying); some of them were considered aphrodisiacs; and, of course, they also served to preserve fish and meat. The Ligurians' preference to this day for fresh greens and herbs can be traced to the reaction of Genoese sailors subjected to the powerful odors of spices collected in ships' holds. But the spice merchants profited mightily: spices were so important to Venice that an entire stock market based on their value was set up on the Rialto. Speculation gave pepper and cinnamon a value way beyond what they were worth, and all kinds of secret deals based on fluctuating prices were made until the bubble of this craze for kitchen spices inevitably burst, or at least leaked and then declined dramatically once Vasco da Gama broke the Venetian monopoly. Cinnamon and ginger ceased to be such great rarities. All the historic spices continued to be used in Italian baking. Nowadays they aren't tossed into the doughs and mixtures with quite so free a hand, but they do lend their flavors to any number of breads and desserts.

Anise Seeds/Semi di Anice. Anise seeds, according to mythology, have a magic effect on the digestive system, which probably explains why they turn up at the end of the meal in so many desserts. They taste of licorice and are part of an entire tradition of spicing that ranges from the Udine far to the north to Sardinia, Sicily, and Calabria in the south. They are what gives a special flavor to the *brigidini* of Tuscany and the *biscotti anici* of Sicily and Sardinia.

Cinnamon / Cannella. Cinnamon, in stick form and powder, is utilized in a number of Italian sweets and breads, but it has nothing like the popularity it enjoys in American baking. It is, in fact, usually one of several spices blended together.

Clove / Chiodi di Garofano. Part of the arsenal of spices remaining from the Middle Ages and the Renaissance, cloves are used frequently in desserts.

Mace / Macis. The filament covering the nutmeg is ground and used in only a few Italian desserts.

Nutmeg / Noce Moscata. Ever since the Venetians brought spices back from the East, nutmeg has had a prominent place in the cooking of Italy. It is used in both sweet and savory dishes, often bringing out the flavors of spinach and cheeses. Better flavor is achieved by grating the whole nutmeg each time you use it. Ground nutmeg is hard to find in Italy because good cooks know that most of the flavor and aroma is lost as it sits in the tin or bottle.

Pepper / Pepe. Black peppercorns are called for in these recipes. They should always be ground freshly at the time of cooking. The only exception is when making *panforte*, in which white pepper is traditional. You don't even know that it's there, but it wouldn't be *panforte* without it.

TOMATOES *Pomodori*

Canned Tomatoes / Pomodori in Scatola. Even Italians, who live in the land of the sun-ripened tomato, must use canned tomatoes for their sauces in the deep of winter. Like them, you should look for canned plum tomatoes from San Marzano. Failing this, canned tomatoes from America, although less ripe and less sweet, are a good second choice.

Sun-Dried Tomatoes / Pomodori Secchi. These are tomatoes allowed to ripe on the vine, then dried out of direct sunlight. You may find them covered with extra-virgin olive oil and spiced with Ligurian herbs. A less expensive alternative is loose dried tomatoes, which you should steep in boiling water for a minute to soften, then either use straightaway or cover with oil.

Tomato Paste/Concentrato di Pomodoro. Tomato paste is a concentrate of tomatoes, and you don't need much to get the desired taste. Don't expect twice as much to give you twice as much taste of tomato; it will only tend to drown out other flavors. I am particularly fond of the clean, rich tomato flavor of Amore brand. I recommend the types that come in a tube as toothpaste does, since they can be closed and easily stored in the refrigerator, which eliminates waste, although I also like the rich, extra-concentrated flavor of Maria Grammatico's tomato extract, which comes packed in a clear glass jar.

Additional Ingredients for Pastry and Cookies

These few extra ingredients, found mainly in pastries and cookies, are part of a long tradition of *dolci* in Italy.

ALMONDS *Mandorle*

Almond Paste/Pasta di Mandorle. Without almond paste there would be no amaretti, *brutti ma buoni, torta deliziosa,* or any number of Italian desserts to satisfy the famous Italian sweet tooth. You may either make your own (page 325), which will have lots of flavor but will never be as smooth as the commercial product, or you can buy almond paste, a very fine, flavorful mixture of blanched almonds, sugar, and glucose to which almond extract may be added. Odense is a good brand.

Bitter Almonds/Ermelline. Bitter almonds are used in the making of amaretti because they concentrate the powerful flavor of almonds. They grow freely in the Mediterranean basin, but since they are toxic in their natural state, they are outlawed in the United States. I substitute almond extract in the recipes that called for them.

Marzipan/Pasta di Marzapane. This is essentially almond paste that has been rolled even finer and sweetened more. Its name is said to come from *marci panis*, Latin for St. Mark's bread, and that's what *marzapane* is actually called in Venice, the city of which St. Mark is patron saint. It is said to have been invented in the early fifteenth century during a grain shortage, when a clever baker made "flour" by grinding almonds to a powder, adding sugar, and kneading to make a kind of bread.

WILD CHERRIES *Amarena*

These ripe wild cherries preserved in syrup (preferably) or brandy are moist and fleshy. The Fabbri brand is imported from Italy.

BUTTER *Burro*

Italian butter is sweet, so all the pastry recipes in this book are written for unsalted butter. If you use butter with salt, be sure to use less salt than called for in the list of ingredients.

CANDIED CITRON *Cedro Candito*

Citron, a citrus fruit that grows in the Mediterranean, is as big as a quince and has a thick, bumpy rind. Carried in many specialty shops, it is often candied and used in sweet breads and desserts.

CANDIED ORANGE AND LEMON PEEL *Arancia Candita e Limone Candito*

Among the revelations that come with eating in Italy is the chance to taste all kinds of candied fruits and the candied rinds of Sicilian oranges, lemons, and citrons that are used in numerous sweet breads and desserts. "They are like cinnamon in American cooking," someone told me. "They are in everything." The rinds are fat and full of flavor, and the fruits have a concentrated sweetness and clean, fresh taste that is irresistible. And the colors: the deep red-orange of Sicilian oranges is as seductive to the eye as it is to the tongue.

Because I can't find any preparation close to them in America, I often buy the best fruit I can, candy it myself, and keep it on hand for all my baking. Once candied, the peels will last for months. My other solution is to rely on what June Taylor produces (see the Source Guide to Ingredients and Equipment, page 401). The next best alternative is to search out fine candied fruit and rinds in specialty shops, where they are most likely to appear during the holidays. Sometimes cottage industries pop up, offering wonderful examples of the art. Do try to stay away from the tubs of waxen candied fruit sold in supermarkets, which have lots of preservatives and very little taste.

CANDIED ORANGE PEEL

This recipe can also be made using citron, grapefruit, lemon, or tangerine peels in place of the orange peels.

Makes 54 to 72 pieces

9 thin-skinned navel oranges
4 cups (28 oz / 800 g) sugar, plus more for rolling
¹/₄ cup (3 oz / 85 g) corn syrup

Wash and dry the oranges. Cut off the tops and bottoms of the oranges and then cut them vertically into 6 to 8 pieces. Remove the peels from the flesh and save the flesh for

Continued

Continued

another use. Place the peels in a large, heavy saucepan, cover generously with cold water, and cook slowly over medium-low heat until tender when pierced with the point of a knife, 45 minutes to 1 hour. Drain. Cover with fresh water and let sit for at least 1 hour, or up to overnight. Drain.

Pour 2 cups of water into a large saucepan. Stir in the sugar and corn syrup until blended and bring to a boil. Add the orange peels, cover the pan partially, and reduce the heat to very low. Cook for about 2 hours, using a candy thermometer to make sure that the temperature remains between 212°F and 220°F. You may need to add water periodically to keep the sugar from becoming too concentrated and thick, but it is important to cook the peels slowly so that the syrup can penetrate them. Grapefruit and citron rinds may need longer to eliminate bitterness.

After 2 hours, remove the lid, turn up the heat slightly, and let the temperature of the syrup rise to 230°F to evaporate the water. Turn off the heat and let the peels stand until the liquid stops bubbling. Carefully remove the pieces of orange peel with a slotted spoon and transfer them to a rack set over a baking sheet. Leave them until they are cool, 1 to 2 hours. Roll each piece in granulated sugar and let dry on the rack. You can also put the peels in a paper bag with sugar and shake them around to coat. They keep very well in a covered container.

CHOCOLATE *Cioccolata*

Chocolate isn't used as frequently in Italy as it is in other European countries, but that isn't to say that it isn't delicious when it does turn up. The secret is to use a good-quality chocolate, such as Perugina, Tobler, Lindt, or Callebaut. Most of the chocolate called for in this book is bittersweet and should have a rich, deep flavor and silky texture.

COCOA *Cacao*

Italian bakeries use cocoa fairly frequently to give chocolate flavor to cookies and pastries. Use Dutch-processed cocoa, which is the unsweetened powder of cocoa beans that have been roasted, had their oils extracted, and then been ground very fine. The style is darker and mellower tasting than non-Dutch-processed cocoas. I particularly like the Pernigotti brand. If you want to add cocoa to a recipe to give it a chocolate taste, subtract 7 ounces (200 g) of flour for every 3$^1/_2$ ounces (100 g) of cocoa that you add.

EGGS *Uova*

All the eggs used in these recipes are size large. Large eggs weigh about 2 ounces (60 g) each, although there are variations among eggs. They should be at room temperature when they are used. If you've forgotten to take them out of the refrigerator, soak the eggs in a bowl of warm water for about 10 minutes to warm them up.

ESSENCES AND AROMAS *Essenze e Aromi*

The Italians flavor all sorts of sweets and sweet breads with highly potent, concentrated essences. These include essence of panettone (just take the top off one of the bottles and you are transported directly into the center of the panettone) and aroma of *colomba*, special mixtures of the combinations of spices that give these sweet breads their taste signatures. There are also essences of lemon, sweet orange, orange flower, and bitter orange, as well as an essence of bitter almond, which is wonderfully bracing to smell. No one in Italy really expects to make panettones or *colombe* at home, so their essences aren't easy to find, but all the others are widely available in several brands of small jars. Italian essences and aromas are considerably more concentrated than their American counterparts, and these recipes have been adjusted with that in mind. The important thing with orange and lemon extracts is to look for "pure" liquid flavorings, since that indicates the contents are from a plant substance. Lemon and orange oils are extracted from the peels, and in the best ones the harsh volatile oils are removed to leave true fruit flavors. If you don't have an extract available, you can do what some of the best Italian bakers do: substitute grated lemon and/or orange zest. If you choose to use a lemon extract, I recommend Nielsen-Massey. Almond extract is made of oil of bitter almonds, alcohol, and water in varying proportions. A little goes a long way.

POTATO STARCH *Fecola*

A flour made from grinding potatoes, potato starch is extremely fine and makes a lovely, silky *pasta frolla* for elegant tarts and tortes. Sometimes it can be found in supermarkets; otherwise, potato starch is often carried by health-food stores and ethnic markets. Cornstarch is an excellent substitute.

RICE *Riso*

More than fifty kinds of rice are produced in Italy, but only one is really important for pastries. *Originario*, used for *torte di riso*, is a round-grain rice that cooks in twelve to sixteen minutes and absorbs about three times its weight in liquid. If you don't have *originario*, use long-grain rice instead.

TURBINADO SUGAR *Zucchero*

The Italians use baking sugar on top of any number of their sweet breads and cakes to give them a wonderful crunch and lightly sweetened taste. Alas, the ordinary sugars we buy at the supermarket melt under high temperatures, but turbinado sugar—the raw, unrefined sugar crystals washed with steam—keeps its texture even when put in a roaring-hot oven. It is available at specialty stores, and I notice it turning up more and more frequently at supermarkets.

VANILLA *Vaniglia*

The strong sweet smell in Italian *pasticcerie* comes from vanilla sugar, which flavors cakes and cookies and has its own very special qualities. Italian housewives use little packets of vanilla sugar, and bakers use a superfine granulated sugar made with vanilla flavor. There are now some fine crystallized vanilla sugars, very delicately flavored, available in America—and you can, of course, make your own vanilla sugar by burying a vanilla bean in a canister of sugar— but these recipes have been written with vanilla extract in mind. The trick is to find a really good one that captures the lovely delicate flavor of vanilla. I prefer Nielsen-Massey because it starts with the real pod and ends up with a pure essence suspended in an alcohol solution.

Equipment

On one of my stays in Italy, I was introduced to a wonderful peasant woman named Nella who lived in the tiny town of Cordigliano in the Umbrian countryside, just outside Todi. Nella lived in one of several houses clustered among olive and fruit trees, and every ten days she made an enormous batch of bread to feed her family, her close neighbors, and several families for whom she did housework. When I was invited to watch her make bread, in the same way that her mother and grandmother once had, I was immediately impressed that she had almost no equipment. She used a *madia*, a deep chest on legs with a sizable interior trough, which was made to hold crockery but in which she kept a big mound of flour on one side and her natural yeast on the other. She used the trough to mix and knead the dough, which she then covered with a well-worn blanket to let it rise. When the time came to shape the dough, she placed it on a big board on her dining room table, cut it into twelve pieces, formed huge ovals, and set them on a long piece of well-floured canvas so the loaves wouldn't stick to the cloth or each other. The blanket went back over the top and the bread rose again until it was time to set the loaves in the outdoor wood-burning oven. The total of her equipment: a bucket to measure the water, the *madia* in which to mix and knead, the board on which to cut and shape, the cloth on which to set the loaves, and the dough scraper. Bread baking is one of the most basic and enduring activities in human history, and I do not want to suggest that readers rush out and stock up on unusual equipment for the process. You probably have in your kitchen almost all the basics that you need, and if you choose to make some of the regional specialties, you may need to buy (or borrow or invent) a few of the special traditional forms or molds.

The Basic Three

If it were up to me, I would insist on only three items for baking: a scale, a dough scraper, and a porous baking stone or quarry tiles. And if I could issue one decree, it would be that all recipes be written using metric weights. Weighing ingredients is more precise than measuring their volume, and metric weights are easier and clearer to work with than all those pounds and ounces.

SCALE
I prefer a scale that displays both metric grams and American ounces and pounds.

DOUGH SCRAPER
A dough scraper, also called a bench scraper, is simply a rectangular piece of stainless steel with a rolled steel or wooden handle and a sharp edge. As far as I am concerned, it is one of the great inventions of modern life, since it can be used for everything from lifting and kneading the dough to cutting it to cleaning the surface on which you have been working.

POROUS BAKING STONE
Baking stones effectively replace the brick floor of a baker's oven. Made of natural clay stoneware fired at extremely high temperatures, they distribute high heat evenly and absorb moisture from the dough, thereby producing heavier, crispier crusts. Quarry tiles can also be used, but they don't always fit together perfectly and they tend to jiggle and bounce a bit when you're aiming a round of wet dough onto their surface. Baking stones can be either rectangular or round. I prefer a thick rectangular stone to the round ones, and I like to use the largest one I can find so that I can bake more than one loaf at a time.

Whether I am baking pizzas, cookies, pastries, or bread, and whether the item is in loaf pans or on baking sheets, I leave the stone in place to promote the even distribution of heat. Of course, you don't need to use a baking stone when you are making cookies or many desserts. Puff pastry and croissants, for instance, are best baked without a stone. Be sure to preheat the stone or tiles for at least 30 minutes in a hot (400°F or 425°F) oven, and sprinkle with a dusting of cornmeal or semolina just before you slide your dough onto it.

Excellent sources of baking stones are listed in the Source Guide to Ingredients and Equipment (page 401).

Other Essentials

BOWLS

You will probably want bowls of several different sizes, ranging from a small one in which to dissolve the yeast to large widemouthed bowls that can be used for both mixing and kneading the doughs. They can be earthenware, stoneware, ceramic, glass, plastic, or stainless steel, and you can find them at humble hardware and restaurant supply stores as well as in fancier kitchenware emporia. It is a good idea to have a round or square translucent straight-sided container that allows the dough to rise easily and lets you see clearly when it has doubled or tripled. The most useful sizes range from 2 to 6 quarts, although I have a 21-cup container for large doughs that need to triple. If it fits conveniently in the refrigerator, for slowing down the action of the yeast when necessary, so much the better.

SURFACE ON WHICH TO KNEAD

I love my butcher-block table, which is 24 by 30 inches, big enough to hold a scale and basic tools, but any wooden or Formica surface will do handsomely as long as it is at least 2 feet by 2 feet and is high enough for you to work comfortably with your palms extended and your back straight. Stooping or stretching will make it hard to knead correctly and can give you a backache—hardly desirable, since one of the reasons for baking is pleasure in the process as well as in the wonderful loaves that ultimately result. Be sure that your work surface is easy to scrape down and clean after each batch of dough.

ELECTRIC MIXER

I can't imagine my life without my heavy-duty KitchenAid mixer. It can do everything a human baker could wish—stirring, mixing, kneading, whipping—and demands almost nothing in return except that it is sometimes necessary to stop the machine and scrape down doughs that tend to creep up the collar of the hook. I use the paddle to mix doughs, the dough hook to knead them, and the whisk for making pastries and cakes and for beating egg whites (you can even buy a copper bowl for the task). It is a big, solid, old-fashioned maternal presence in my kitchen that I can always depend upon, although I invariably finish kneading by hand because I am convinced that the dough responds to the warmth of the human touch and comes to life beneath my palms and fingertips.

FOOD PROCESSOR

So much has been written in praise of food processors that I scarcely need to add to the verbiage. Although it is rare to find such machines in Italian bakeries, there is no reason not to use them in American kitchens for mixing and kneading bread, pizza, and pastry doughs in a fraction of the time it takes to perform the same processes by hand. The larger-capacity machines are more useful than the smaller, but you should be aware that many inexpensive food processors are not strong enough to process yeast doughs. Be certain to check whether yours is up to the task before you start work on a recipe. The processor is useful for any number of other operations as well: for making pesto, grating cheeses, grinding soaked whole wheat grains, and turning nuts into pastes. Because the motor is so powerful and heats up the contents as it whirs at almost supersonic speeds, you must be careful to use *cold* water for almost all the liquid called for in bread and pizza recipes.

INSTANT-READ THERMOMETER

Lots of cookbooks tell you to dissolve yeast at specific temperatures—active dry at 105°F to 115°F, fresh cake yeast at 90°F to 95°F—and suggest that you will know lukewarm from hot just by touch, rather as mothers do baby formula. When I started baking, I never guessed right and spent untold nervous minutes waiting for thermometers to steer me to where I belonged. Now no one need worry: instant-read thermometers such as those made by BioTherm, Cuisinart, and Taylor can be put into water or the dough itself and they register the internal temperature immediately. It is important not to get a liquid too hot—active dry yeast is killed above 140°F—or too cool, since that will retard or, in the case of ice-cold water, stop its development, but dormant yeasts are reactivated in a wider range of temperatures than the instructions on the little packets would have you believe. Lower temperatures will cause your dough to take a bit longer to rise, but they work.

BAKING SHEETS

If you're not baking on stones you'll need baking sheets, and the heavier the better, especially since breads bake at such high temperatures that flimsy or tin ones will warp. If you don't have a baking stone, preheat a heavy baking sheet and use it like a stone. Dark carbon steel absorbs and retains heat and produces crisp crusts; heavy aluminum sheets retain heat as well. The traditional half-sheet pan, about 11$\frac{1}{2}$ by 17$\frac{1}{2}$ inches, is a very useful size, but you can use any size as long as there is an inch of clearance on all sides so that hot air can circulate freely around it in your oven. When setting shaped breads to rise before they are baked, use either rimless baking sheets or the backs of baking sheets with raised edges and you'll find it easier to get them on and off.

BREAD MOLDS

Most of the breads in this book are free-form hearth loaves shaped by your hands and baked directly on a stone or baking sheet, but a few need loaf pans or pie tins or traditional molds such as:

Covered Pullman Loaf Pan. There is no way to make the Italian equivalent of sandwich bread without this long, narrow rectangular mold with its sliding lid. It is designed to produce close-textured, almost crustless bread used for such dishes as *mozzarella in carrozza* (page 163) as well as for the *tramezzini* that fill the glass cases of Italian caffès. Don't forget to butter the underside of the lid before letting the bread have its final rise inside; otherwise you'll have a devilish time getting the loaf out in one piece.

Pandoro Mold. To make the authentic sweet Christmas bread of Verona, you must have the tinned-steel five-sided star mold that gives it its traditional shape. Otherwise, you may substitute any high-sided mold with an 8-cup capacity.

Panettone Mold. A tall, thin cylindrical mold allows the panettone to expand into the lightly porous sweet bread that comes from Milan at Christmastime. You can also use a traditional paper mold or substitute a 2- or 3-pound coffee can or a charlotte mold with its sides built up with aluminum foil. I have even used a panettone mold with a narrow central shaft, rather like an angel food cake pan, which may not be traditional but certainly bakes a good panettone.

Banneton. This coiled reed basket, which is either round or oval, turns out a rustic-looking loaf with a beehive pattern of flour etched on the surface of the bread. Flour the form well, then put the dough inside for its second and final rise. When it has doubled and the time has come for baking, simply turn it upside down directly on the baking stone or sheet, being careful to dislodge it gingerly from its heavily floured basket. If you don't have a banneton, you can easily make one by lining any basket you have with a coarse tea towel or some heavy canvas.

Charlotte Molds. These tinned-steel pans with heart-shaped handles, which come in 1- and 2-quart sizes, serve as wonderful molds for various breads as well as for tortes, cakes, and dishes made with leftovers, such as apple charlotte. Soufflé dishes and springform pans of the same capacity can be used the same way.

Ring Mold. A flat-bottomed ring mold or 9-inch tube pan with a hole in the center 3 inches in diameter becomes an excellent form for breads baked in a wreath shape.

LA CLOCHE

A La Cloche clay baker, which is billed as an instant bread oven, is an unglazed stoneware dome that fits over a 2-inch-deep stoneware base, and it truly does bake wonderful crusty loaves. I like to soak the top in water for 15 to 30 minutes while the bread is rising in the base with an inverted bowl over it. The humidity created by the dome at the high oven temperature really crisps the crust. You may also leave the dough to rise under the domed top until it has doubled, then simply set it in a very hot oven. I get my best results when I preheat the stone base at 450°F, allowing the bread to rise elsewhere.

RAZOR BLADE

To slash the characteristic cuts on top of rustic and traditional loaves, you'll need a razor-sharp edge. Italian bakers use a single-edge razor blade, but I have a gadget that is essentially a single-edge razor blade with a handle that greatly reduces the danger of cutting yourself instead of the bread. Check your hardware store or the Internet. If you are very nimble, you can simply score the tops of loaves with a sharp knife or the metal blade of your food processor.

BAKER'S PEEL

In Italy there are two ways that bakers set their breads in the oven. Many use an extremely long stretcher-like apparatus slung with canvas. As many as twenty loaves rise on it, and when they are ready to be baked, the device is thrust all the way into the oven and the canvas is snapped back and retracted—something like the revolving cloth towel in some public restrooms—leaving the loaves to bake on the oven floor or shelves. Clearly there's no such equipment for American home ovens, but we can use the alternative, a peel, or wooden paddle, the long-handled version of which is traditionally used for dropping in and scooping up pizzas and breads. A short-handled peel is easy to find in cookware stores. Just sprinkle it with cornmeal or flour so the dough won't stick, let the loaves rise on it, and with a

couple of expert firm shakes, free the loaf or pizza onto the cornmeal-sprinkled baking stone or baking sheet. Pizza peels come in sizes that vary from small—perfect for a single loaf or a small pizza—to as large as 16 by 18 inches, scaled to a giant pizza. A convenient alternative for transferring dough from its rising surface to the oven could be a rimless baking sheet, a thin wooden cutting board, or even a sturdy piece of cardboard, all of which work very well even if they don't have quite the same authenticity.

COOLING RACK

You will need a rack made of wire, coated metal, wood, or even bamboo on which the loaves of bread can cool with air circulating freely around them. Be sure to remove any breads baked in loaf pans or pie forms immediately and set them on the rack so steam doesn't collect around them. Do the opposite with delicate cakes or highly risen sweet breads, which must be cooled completely in their forms before you set them gingerly on a rack. I have known people who carefully remove some breads from their molds and allow them to cool on pillows; there they recline elegantly as the heat dissipates into the air, the absence of steam preventing the formation of moisture on the bottoms. I have found that the high sweet breads like panettone, *pandoro,* or *Veneziana* are less likely to crack or crumble if laid on their sides.

ROLLING PIN

Only a few breads demand the attentions of a rolling pin—*pane in cassetta* (page 236) and *pasta dura* (page 225) are two—but all croissants and puff pastries and a number of sweets have no hope of coming to life without one. Use the French variety, which is a thin, heavy cylinder of wood, or the thicker American kind, which has handles mounted on ball bearings. Whichever you choose, I recommend that it be at least 15 to 18 inches long and have the kind of heft that gives you authority over the dough. Country women use a wine bottle, and you'd be surprised how well it works in a pinch.

BREAD KNIFE

Please do not go to all the trouble of making a wonderful loaf of bread and then not have a sharp, well-made serrated knife with wide teeth to cut it. A good knife also slices delicate *pan di Spagna* and *maddalena* cakes in half horizontally with grace.

Optional but Definitely Nice to Have

PARCHMENT PAPER

Sometimes I am afraid that I sound like a spokesman for the parchment paper industry, if there is such a thing, because I think parchment paper is one of the great products of the age. Use a piece on baking sheets or peels and sticky doughs suddenly become manageable and cookies no longer stick. When you are baking breads, you can slide the bread and the parchment paper right onto the baking stone, wait about twenty minutes, and then pull out the parchment and leave the loaves or pizzas baking directly on the stone. I even use it to line high-sided molds, allowing me to unmold a lovely single loaf that might otherwise be difficult to achieve.

Additional Equipment for Pizza

BAKING PANS

Black steel bakeware is the best choice for pizza making because it absorbs and retains heat and distributes it evenly to turn out crisp pizza crusts. Brush the pan lightly with vegetable oil to season it each time before using it, and don't be disconcerted by the mottling and discoloration that are inevitable with these pans. They come in 10-inch, 12-inch, and 15-inch rounds, and in 12-inch and 16-inch square and deep-dish pans, as well as a 12 by 16-inch rectangular pan for focaccia. (If you have a baking stone in the oven, you can omit the pan and bake the pizza on the stone.)

MEZZALUNA

If you want to be authentically Italian, you might want to do all your chopping and mincing with a *mezzaluna*, a half-moon-shaped knife with two handles that works by rocking the blade back and forth over the parsley, garlic, herbs, or raisins in question.

CUTTING WHEEL

A heavy-duty, finely honed cutting wheel cuts through a pizza with ease. The Dexter is sturdy and has a replaceable blade, which makes it more than worth its price. I have often used a good pair of kitchen scissors to cut focaccia and some thick pizzas as well.

OILCAN

The Tin Woodman wasn't the only person to depend on an oilcan. Bakers brush their pizza doughs with oil before and after baking, and they lightly coat their rising bowls and baking forms with oil. The fine spout of an oilcan pours just the few drops you need.

Additional Equipment for Pastry Baking

NUT GRINDER

For making a delicate flour out of nuts and pastry and nut pastes, nothing works as well as a real nut grinder—not a food processor, which tends to separate out the oils, not a well-aimed knife, and not a blender. A nut grinder can chop chocolate in lovely even flakes, too.

MICROPLANE AND OTHER GRATERS

For grating the lemon and orange zest I put in pastries and breads, I use a Microplane or other flat fine-tooth grater with holes of a single size. They are much easier to handle than the four-sided box grater and are just right for using directly over the bowl (by grating the zest directly into the dough you don't risk losing some of the essential oils).

TART PANS

Tart pans with removable bottoms significantly reduce the risk of breaking a crust. They come in heavy tinned steel and in black steel, which absorbs heat quickly and retains it. They can be found in a variety of sizes, including 8-inch and $9^1/_2$-inch rounds, individual $4^1/_4$-inch tartlets, 2-inch-deep 9-inch tart pans, and an 11 by 7-inch rectangle. Springform pans function similarly, although they are almost always deeper than tart pans and never have fluted edges.

COOKIE CUTTERS

These can be oval or round, fluted or smooth, and generally range from $1^1/_4$ inches to $3^3/_4$ inches. They should have sharp edges so they cut cleanly through the dough. In a pinch, you can use the top of a spice jar or other lid.

PASTRY BRUSHES

There really isn't a substitute for pastry brushes, which will allow you to dust flour onto or off the surface of a dough; glaze the tops of tarts, cookies, and breads; or moisten the interior edges of filled pastries or calzone so they stick together during baking.

SADDLE OF VENISON CAKE PANS

Also called *Rehrücken*—literally, "saddle of venison"—molds, these are long rectangular loaf pans with raised ridges along the sides that are traditionally used for *amor polenta*, the cornmeal cakes from Italy's Veneto region.

PASTRY BAG WITH TIPS

Treat yourself to a plastic-coated cloth pastry bag with a sizable capacity, which is easy to fill and easy to clean. You will need several basic tips, along with a plastic coupler and a nut for the special long-nosed nozzle used to inject zabaglione cream into *focaccia veneziana* (page 208).

FLOUR SIFTER

You should never sift flour for bread and usually sift it for pastries. If you don't have a sifter, simply use your widemouthed fine-mesh sieve, which works perfectly for the task. It will do the same for sifting powdered sugar over the tops of tarts, cakes, and cookies.

PLASTIC DOUGH SCRAPER

This arcs along the contours of a bowl and gets out every last drop of filling or dough.

Techniques

Techniques for Baking Bread

DISSOLVING THE YEAST

Those little packets of active dry yeast or cubes of fresh yeast give life to bread, but they must be reactivated to do their work. If you read pages 22–24, you will understand how yeast works. Almost every recipe begins by telling you to dissolve the yeast in a small amount of warm water. Cake yeast is best stirred into water that is 90°F to 100°F, while active dry yeast returns to life at 105°F to 115°F. Don't worry too much about getting the temperature precisely right; just make sure that it is warm to the touch—neither hot nor cool. If you are using dry yeast, sprinkle it over the water in a bowl and stir in the granules with a small whisk. Cake yeast should be crumbled directly into the water and stirred to dissolve it. Let the mixture stand for about 10 minutes, after which it should look creamy, then whisk it briefly to mix it all up.

MEASURING THE INGREDIENTS

Italian bakers weigh all their ingredients. They have never heard of measuring cups or spoons, and for the purpose of cooking these breads and pastries, I wish Americans hadn't either. I'd like to persuade everyone to use a scale, at least for the flours, whose volume varies amazingly depending on how much moisture they contain and how they have been handled. Many of these recipes begin with 500 grams of unbleached all-purpose flour, which can measure any-where from 3¹/₄ to 4¹/₂ cups, depending on how they are scooped and whether they were sifted or packed down. If you don't have a scale, this is the most accurate way to measure flour consistently: First pour the flour into a large bowl. Stir the flour to aerate it, then dip your measuring cup deep into the flour and level it off with a knife. Never sift the flour for

> I cannot stress enough how important it is to use a scale with metric weights, because metrics are the most precise and the recipes in this book will work best if you use them.

bread making, and never pack it down into the cup. Measure sugar the same way. A large egg should weigh 2 ounces or about 60 grams, but there will be some variation.

TEMPERATURE OF OTHER INGREDIENTS

Warm water is used to dissolve the yeast, but the other ingredients should be at room temperature, with one exception: in bread and pizza recipes using a food processor, which works at such a high speed that it heats up the contents of the bowl in no time, cold water is used. Italian bakers consider 75°F the ideal temperature for water used in bread and insist that baking is most successful when the average temperature of all the ingredients and the room temperature are at that same 75°F. This means that if you are baking in the cold of winter, you may need to heat up the water and warm the flour in the oven, while in summer you should use cool, or even cold, water to keep the same balance.

MIXING THE DOUGH

Mixing the dough itself is straightforward. Dissolve the yeast in the water as directed, add whatever other wet ingredients are called for—olive oil, milk, lard—and mix them in well with a wooden spoon, a rubber spatula, or the paddle of the mixer. When you mix in the flour, please reserve a bit of it until the end; the dough may come together and you might not need it all. If you are mixing the dough by hand, you may want to use a big widemouthed bowl—I have a set that I bought at a hardware store and I have seen similar ones at restaurant supply shops—so that you can knead in it as well and spare yourself the inevitable crusty counter that has to be cleaned.

By Hand. Stir the flour, which is often first mixed with the salt, into the yeast-liquid mixture, 1 cup at a time. I sometimes use a whisk to mix in the first cup or two because it virtually assures a lump-free mixture, but I wouldn't want you to think that there is anything traditionally Italian about that particular method. There isn't. I never saw anything remotely like it in Italy, but it works well, so I've adopted it. After that, you'll want to use a wooden spoon to mix in the rest of the flour, 1 cup at a time, beating thoroughly after each addition. Should the dough become too dense to continue easily, just plunge in with your hands and continue mixing until you have a consistent dough. It will be shaggy and rough and in some cases quite sticky, but that's to be expected. The process usually takes 4 to 5 minutes.

By Mixer. I have made every one of the breads and pizzas as well as the pastries, cakes, and cookies in this book in my KitchenAid stand mixer. It's easy, quick, and tidy. I use the paddle to mix doughs and the dough hook to knead them, although I invariably finish kneading by hand all but the wettest doughs. Just dissolve the yeast in the bowl of the mixer until it's creamy, add the rest of the water and any other wet ingredients, and mix them all together using the paddle. I set a bit of the flour to the side and add the rest all at once, but I would caution you that this is only a good idea when you've weighed the flour, so that your amounts are sure to be correct. If you're using dry measures, set aside a larger portion just to be safe. It takes 1 to 3 minutes for the ingredients to become combined into a rough dough. It's easy to tell when the flour has been absorbed because there will be no dry patches of it left in the bottom of the bowl.

By Food Processor. Making bread with a food processor is incredibly easy, but it works very differently than a mixer or your hands. Some recipes specify using more liquid, and both the liquid ingredients and the butter must be cold. You should begin by setting the steel blade in the processor bowl with the flour and salt, and process with several pulses to sift and mix. Sometimes you will want to change to the dough blade and other times you may not; the recipes vary, and the method you use will vary in great part on the capacity of the processor bowl. Using the dough blade adds to the capacity of the bowl. A standard machine with a $6^1/_2$-inch-diameter bowl will process $3^3/_4$ cups of flour (about 17.5 ounces or 500 grams) and $1^1/_2$ cups of water. The larger machines with larger work bowls accept from 8 cups of flour and $2^1/_2$ cups of water to the huge quantities professionals need. Please note that not all processors have motors powerful enough to mix and knead bread dough, so read the instructions of your machine. If your processor slows down during the mixing, stop it and take out half the dough. You can always combine the pieces when you finish, kneading them together on a floured surface. Once you have mixed the ingredients in the processor by pouring the wet ingredients and dissolved yeast through the tube, process until the dough gathers into a rough mass.

KNEADING

When I started baking bread, kneading seemed the most mysteriously appealing process because it transformed a shaggy clump into silky, elastic dough. I love my KitchenAid, but I always finish kneading by hand because I am convinced that the warmth of human touch communicates itself and makes a real difference in the responsiveness and final feel of the dough. I hope you'll do the same; machines are wonderful, but it's you, not they, that are really making these breads.

By Hand. If you are kneading by hand, choose a work surface that allows you to knead the dough with a straight back. Sprinkle the surface lightly with flour. Pick up the dough from its mixing bowl, put it on the table, and flatten it gently into a disk. Curl your fingertips around the opposite side, lift it, and fold it toward you. With the heel of your hand, roll and push the dough away under your hand, staying parallel to the counter. Press out, not down. Give the dough a quarter turn and do it again. If it looks shredded, you're working too hard; just repeat the motions, but slowly, gently, and with a lighter touch. Sprinkle flour on the work surface and over the dough so that it moves easily on the table without sticking. If a piece does stick, scrape it off with the dough scraper and toss it away. If you sprinkle flour over the ragged dough on the work surface, it will continue to collect more of your dough, and pretty soon you'll be making one loaf instead of two. With wet, sticky doughs, like ryes or the rustic regional loaves, be sure to have your dough scraper handy. You can use it as an extension of your hand, turning and folding the dough with it and working in a little of the flour on your work surface. Keep kneading for the time called for in the recipe or until the dough is silky and elastic, or whatever consistency is described. One Italian baker told me it should feel as soft as a baby's bottom. Try not to mix in much extra flour as you knead, for it changes the texture of the bread you are making. Please note that when substantial amounts of flour are called for in kneading, amounts are given in the method; if no specific amount is mentioned, you can assume that sprinkles will be sufficient.

Firmer doughs, when they no longer stick to your hands or the work surface, can be lifted up and banged down hard against the surface to develop the gluten. In many cases—although not in the porous regional breads—you are aiming for a supple, silky dough that may show definite air bubbles beneath the surface when fully kneaded and spring back when you flatten it with your palm.

If you are kneading in a bowl, follow the same instructions, adding sprinkles of flour as you knead.

By Mixer. Once your ingredients have come together to from a consistent dough, change from the paddle to the dough hook for the actual kneading. Begin by kneading at a low speed, but be sure to follow the recipe instructions; some call for subsequent kneading at a higher speed. The mixer does all the work, but please keep an eye on it. I once turned my back to finish kneading another dough on my worktable and I didn't notice that the mixer was working so hard on a big batch of dough that it had begun to move from the exertion, literally walking from the back of my counter to the front, and then falling to the floor. Needless to say, the dough was a mess; as for the mixer, it spent the next few days at a repair shop. Otherwise, the only effort you'll exert is when you push down any dough that climbs up the collar of the dough hook (be sure to turn off the motor before you do so). Unless the dough is very wet, you can finish kneading it briefly by hand on a lightly floured surface before letting it rise.

By Food Processor. In a food processor, kneading is simply processing for the additional time called for in the recipe—usually between 25 and 40 seconds. Some recipes suggest that you process the dough briefly, then finish kneading it by hand. Even if it is not specifically called for, I recommend that you finish kneading with your hands briefly on a lightly floured surface. Bread whirled into being in this high-speed machine needs the consolation of human warmth.

Windowpane Test. When you are kneading a very wet dough using a mixer or food processor, you may want to test the dough to see whether it is sufficiently developed. Scoop out a piece of dough the size of a lemon and carefully stretch it into the shape of a windowpane. If it is thinly stretched and translucent and holds its shape, it is ready. If it tears, it needs a few more minutes of kneading.

RISING

Like wine or cheese, bread is a natural product that needs to mature at its own pace in an undisturbed spot where it can rise slowly. When the yeast comes back to life and begins to breathe, it emits carbon dioxide bubbles that become trapped in the elastic gluten network built up in the kneading, and they leaven and lighten the dough, pushing it up so that it rises to double or triple its original size. These breads all have at least two rises, and a few have three. The rises allow the flavor of the wheat to mature so that the full taste of the grain permeates the finished loaves. They also encourage the chewy country loaves with big holes in the interior to develop their character. Be sure to choose a container large enough to permit this astonishing transformation. I strongly recommend a clear or translucent straight-sided container. Lightly oil its interior so the dough won't stick to it. (I use olive oil, but any vegetable oil will do.) Cover tightly with a plastic lid or plastic wrap secured with a rubber band, so the heat and moisture generated by the process are contained in the bowl; you'll be able to watch it all happening as the steamy moisture is trapped. Italian bakers let their doughs rise at room temperature, about 75°F, which is quite a bit cooler than the usual American practice, and I encourage you to do the same. It will take a bit longer in some cases, but the final flavor of the bread is well worth it.

Professional bakers work on an enormous scale, of course, using containers the size of garbage cans with tight-fitting lids. I use any number of things, including large ceramic and earthenware bowls and the domestic equivalent of bakers' equipment, which I have found in hardware and restaurant supply stores in the form of outsize refrigerator containers with tight-fitting lids. If you use a straight-sided translucent or transparent plastic or glass container with a 2-, 3-, or 4-quart capacity, or even a large Pyrex measuring cup, you can monitor the process. Otherwise you should put a mark on the outside of the container,

indicating where the dough started in volume so that you can accurately gauge when it has doubled or tripled, as the recipe requires. That's one sure way to tell if the dough has risen enough. The other is to poke your finger gently into the dough and see if the impression remains; if it does, you can be sure that it has risen sufficiently.

TIMING

If you find that things are simply not moving along at the speed you want, you can set the bowl with your dough in a larger bowl containing warm water and cover it well. If you find the rise is going too fast—maybe you have to go out and don't want to take the chance of the dough overrising—you can always put it in a cool place or, even better, in the refrigerator, and let it rise very slowly there. Cold doesn't kill yeast; it just slows its action. When you are ready, take the dough out; let it warm to room temperature, which will take between 2 and 3 hours; and proceed with the recipe. You can do this for the first rise, the second rise, after the bread has been shaped, or even the third rise, if the dough gets that many.

BREADS WITH STARTERS

Many of these doughs fit wonderfully into a busy contemporary life because they begin with a starter that is essentially a dough made with a bit of yeast and water and a goodly amount of flour. See the *biga* recipe (page 70) for a fuller explanation. A small amount of yeast is dissolved in water, and enough flour is beaten in to make a sticky dough. The bowl is covered and the starter is allowed to ferment. It gives a boost to the true dough, which is made with a new infusion of flour, water, and yeast, and it allows the flavor of the grain to mature and the texture to develop. It's a system that has been used in Italy since Roman times, and it fits perfectly into an American lifestyle because you can make the initial starter anywhere from 6 to 24 hours before you put the dough together. Make it anytime the day before you plan to bake—first thing in the morning or after dinner—and then let it rise overnight. The next day, make the dough and let it rise according to your plans. I keep starters on hand all the time, and you should do the same. Should your plans change after you've embarked on a bread, set the dough in the refrigerator and let it rise more slowly. Just be sure to bring the dough back to room temperature before proceeding. And don't worry about leaving your dough in a very cool spot and letting it rise for a long time. I got the same advice from bakers all over Italy: give the dough long cool rises to develop its fragrance and texture. In the same spirit, use very little yeast and rely instead on a starter or dough from the day before to get the intense taste of the grain and the texture that makes these breads so satisfying.

SHAPING

In $1^1/2$ to 2 hours, in most cases, the dough will have doubled in volume. It will look soft and spongy. Do not punch down the dough unless the recipe says so. Turn it out on a lightly floured surface, divide it into the requisite number of pieces by cutting it with a dough scraper, and flatten the pieces (if directed) a bit more to release the carbon dioxide. Now the yeast can begin to work again, after the loaves have been shaped, and the bread can rise a second time before being baked. Because almost all of these loaves are freestanding—unlike most American breads, which are baked in loaf pans and molds—it is very important to give them enough structure in the shaping so they can keep their form. Start by taking the piece of dough and flattening it, and then, using your thumbs as a guide in the center, roll it up toward you in a fat cylinder. Roll it up once again until you have a thick sausage shape. The real secret in shaping the dough into a firm ball is to roll the dough tightly across the surface of the table with cupped hands, then pull it back firmly against the work surface, always using your cupped hands to help form and maintain its firm round shape. Repeat several times until you have the desired taut ball. What you have really done is to pull the gluten net tight and given the dough the shape it will ultimately take. Professional bakers have a learned ambidexterity and can shape two small round loaves or rolls at the same time, one in each hand, so quickly that you can hardly comprehend what you're watching.

Every loaf of bread has a smooth side and a rough wrinkled side, where the dough being pulled downward in the shaping process is collected. Once you have your shaped dough, you will place it with the smooth or the rough side up. Often the attractive veining of flour on the top of rustic country loaves comes from a bread's having risen smooth side down in a light bed of flour; then, when the dough is inverted onto the baking stone or baking sheet, the smooth surface is up, with a pattern of flour on top and the rough seam side on the bottom.

SECOND RISING

The dough now gets a second rise, during which most will again double in volume, but in considerably less time than it took for the first rise—usually 45 minutes to $1^1/4$ hours. A few doughs even get a third rise, but they are exceptions.

Read the recipe carefully for each particular bread. If it is to have its second rise on a baker's peel, or a piece of cardboard or wood, be sure to have sprinkled the surface with semolina, cornmeal, or flour. If the dough is to bake on a baking sheet, be sure it is oiled before placing the dough on it to rise. If it is to bake on a preheated heavy baking sheet, be sure to sprinkle it with semolina or cornmeal just before baking. Parchment paper is a real friend, especially with many of the moist, delicate doughs. After shaping the loaf, set it on parchment paper that has been floured, put it on a peel or the back of a baking sheet, and cover it with a towel. When the time comes for baking, you can slide the parchment paper right onto the baking stone and slip the paper out 15 to 20 minutes later, when the dough has set.

Some of the breads are set in oiled or buttered molds or baking tins. They will look small and somewhat unpromising—doughs should fill only half the mold or tin—but in no time they will have risen to the top. Be sure to cover the top of the shaped dough to keep it from developing a skin, which would be the end of its expansion. Sometimes I use a moist (not wet) kitchen towel dampened with water that's at room temperature, and sometimes a heavy bath towel; both work fine. For any slow-rising or delicate breads, I prefer a heavy towel. To slow down the rise, a baker in Rome taught me to oil the tops of some sticky moist doughs and gently lay plastic wrap over them. When the circulation of air is cut down dramatically by this method, the dough rises slowly, which helps to develop the flavor. If you want to stop the rise altogether, cover the dough well and refrigerate it.

To speed the rise, you can do what Italian women have done for centuries: place the shaped dough in a bed still warm from a sleeping body. Pull the blanket up over it and wait until it has risen. I have given this a modern-day twist by using an electric blanket at a low setting in the middle of winter, protecting the dough well with a towel. Bakers use proofers—warm, moist chambers—at this stage, and you may want to utilize the low heat of a gas pilot light or a briefly warmed electric oven (turn it on at 150°F or its lowest setting for 3 minutes, then turn it off again) to help your loaves to rise; on a cold day you can even set a pan of steaming water on the bottom shelf of the oven to provide the warm moist atmosphere that will encourage the dough to rise. This works particularly well with rich, sweet breads and doughs bursting with fruits and nuts.

SLASHING

Some breads have a pattern slashed on their tops before they are set in the oven. The secret of slashing is to hold the razor at a diagonal slant to the dough and to slash quickly with a firm motion that slices deep. You can always go back and slash again if you are not happy with your first effort, but a single definite gesture is much more successful.

BAKING

The last transformation takes place in the oven, where the doughs get their final rise. Italian bakers slide the risen loaves directly onto a hot brick floor while jets of steam are shot into the oven for the first few minutes of baking. All that vapor lets the yeast work a little longer, giving the loaves an extra burst of volume while delaying the setting of the crust.

You don't need a brick-lined oven that heats to 750°F to make outstanding bread, as long as you take advantage of several secrets of the Italian baker. It makes no real difference whether your oven is gas or electric; what matters is the brick interior. I like to use baking stones or quarry tiles because they distribute the heat evenly, absorb moisture from the bottom of the loaves, and produce crunchy crusts. If you own a La Cloche, which is a wonderful replica of a baker's oven, you will find it perfect for any regional or rustic bread. I wouldn't use it for a sweet or fruit bread, but it is superior for any bread that needs a good crust. If you prefer a golden crunchy crust, be sure to take the top off for the last 15 minutes of baking or you'll get a softer, paler crust. If you have neither baking stones, quarry tiles, nor La Cloche, you still have good options. The easiest is to let the dough rise and bake directly on a heavy baking sheet. Alternatively, you can set a heavy baking sheet or even a $^3/_8$-inch-thick griddle in the oven, heat it for at least 30 minutes, and sprinkle it with cornmeal or semolina just before sliding the dough onto it. If you have baked the breads in a form or special pan, you might want to unmold them for the last 10 or 15 minutes, to let them bake directly on a stone and take on some color.

GETTING THE DOUGH IN THE OVEN

Italian bakers often use a long-handled peel to set the dough in the oven. They stick it in and, with a single expert motion, jerk it back, leaving the dough on the oven floor. You can slide your own doughs onto a baking stone in the oven with a peel, a piece of cardboard, or a wooden board, depending on what they have risen on, or you may choose to deposit a dough that has risen on the back of one baking sheet onto a second, hot baking sheet. Or you may simply bake on the baking sheet that the bread dough rose on, although I prefer the preheated baking sheet. If your dough has risen on parchment paper, you'll find it especially easy to get it onto a baking stone, because it can be transferred paper and all. I always dust the stone with cornmeal or semolina, whether or not I'm using parchment, partly from sheer habit and partly because I usually remove the paper after about 20 minutes, and if the loaf is a little moist, I know that I don't have to worry that the dough will stick.

ADDING MOISTURE

There are several ways to get steam into the oven, but there are two that I rely on. The easiest solution is to fill a spray bottle with cold water and spray the oven vigorously three times during the first 10 minutes of baking. Be certain not to spray the oven light while you're doing all this humidifying, because it might explode.

The other involves putting both the baking stone and a cast-iron frying pan in the oven and preheating them for 30 to 45 minutes before beginning to bake. I put the pan on the bottom shelf of my oven and the baking stone on the rack above it. When you are ready to bake, sprinkle the baking stone with cornmeal, if you are using it, then slide your dough onto the baking stone. Put $^1/_2$ cup of ice into the cast-iron frying pan just before you close the door, and the steam will mist the interior for 5 to 10 minutes. By the time the crust has set, the water will have evaporated and the rest of the baking will take place in a hot, dry oven.

WHEN ARE THE LOAVES DONE?

The traditional method of determining when loaves are done is to knock on the bottom of the loaf and listen for the resonant hollow ring that indicates they have cooked through. If you are uncertain, you can stick an instant-read thermometer into the center of the loaf; by constant checking I have discovered that breads are done when the interior is between 200°F and 210°F, although the crust reaches a temperature of about 325°F.

COOLING

Cool the bread on a rack so that steam doesn't soften the bottom. Cookbooks always specify wire racks, but I have a wonderful Teflon-coated rack that I like to use, and my butcher-block table, which was designed for pasta making, has natural wood racks that work just fine.

STORING

Breads made with only flour, water, yeast, and salt are best eaten the day they are baked. Age—just a few hours sometimes—causes them to go stale. If you make more than you can consume quickly or give away to friends, you can freeze bread with very good results. The best-keeping breads are those made with starters and those made with a little milk, olive oil, or butter. They seem to stay fresh longer than their plainer, earthier relatives and can be stored in a paper (not plastic) bag in a cool, dark spot. It is true that breads keep a bit longer in a refrigerator, but American frost-free refrigerators draw out the moisture in a loaf, and that doesn't seem like a good trade-off to me.

Many of these breads—the ciabatta (page 79), *pane pugliese* (page 98), *pane di Genzano* (page 93), and *coccodrillo* (page 91), for instance—make spectacular toast, as well as wonderful croutons to be sautéed in butter and oil and set in the bottom of a bowl of Italian soup. Italian folklore is full of warnings about the horrible fate in store for anyone who wastes a single crumb of bread, so it is hardly surprising that there are numerous dishes based on leftover breads (see pages 159–176).

FREEZING AND REFRESHING

To freeze bread, wrap the cooled loaf up tightly, first in aluminum foil, then in plastic wrap, and set it in the freezer. I don't let it thaw at all, but instead I remove the plastic and put it, still wrapped in foil, in a 350°F oven for 15 to 30 minutes, depending on how thick it is. Ciabatta, for instance, is ready in 15 to 20 minutes, while *pane pugliese* and higher-domed breads, such as *panmarino* or sweet breads, take about 30 minutes.

BEGINNER BREADS AND HARDER BREADS

If you are new to baking, start with one of the vegetable or herb breads, like the pesto bread or the sweet pepper or rosemary bread; try any of the *focacce*, the *grissini*, or the whole-grain breads. You can also try the rolls—both savory and sweet—which are a vital part of the social life of this most social of all countries. Try the *maritozzi* (page 238) or the *pane agli spinaci* (page 135) formed into rolls or the *ciambelline* (page 112) with oil or salt. These breads are straightforward and uncomplicated, and the proportion of flour to water makes them easy to mix and knead.

The big regional breads with chewy, porous interiors tend to be more difficult to prepare because they are made with starters and because the doughs are uncommonly moist, which takes some getting used to. Italian bakers toss great blobs of them onto the worktable and shape them with ease, but I have to admit to fantasies of someone plunging in to knead and shape one of these wet doughs, only to find him- or herself trapped in the great sticky mass and having to wait for a friend to come by on a rescue mission. Actually, there is nothing tricky about these doughs as long as you are psychologically and physically prepared, with a mound of flour nearby for your work surface, your hands, and even your tools. You might even want a bowl of water since wet hands do not stick to wet doughs. These wet doughs may sound somewhat formidable, but they make spectacular breads. They are survivors of a rustic tradition that remains alive in pockets of Italy today, and they more than repay in taste what they demand in effort. Often all it takes is an extra tablespoon or two of flour to bring an unmanageable dough under control.

Other doughs demand more time than anything else. The addition of butter, which coats the gluten strands of the sweet doughs, slows down the rises, as do the fruit and nut fillings, handfuls of cheese, and chunks of salami. Make sure you've allowed for the hours that the rises will take and the extra few minutes that rolling in the fillings demand. Follow the instructions carefully, however, and you won't have any problems.

Most of the recipes in this book are traditional or variations on the traditional, but what makes this a spirited romp in the fields of the baker is the fact that tradition is constantly being modified by the creative instincts of the very bakers who dreamed up the variations in the first place. More times than I'd like to count, I've gone back to a bakery, drawn by memories of a wonderful bread, only to discover that they're making it slightly differently. Someone's *fantasia* had added a little durum flour or shaped the loaf into a braid or an extravagant big wheel. These bakers start with flour, water, yeast, and salt, but by the time they've finished they've added color, fragrance, and new flavors and aromas, and dusted a surface with a handful of fresh herbs or tiny crunchy seeds. So while you must follow the recipes and learn from the bakers' techniques, once you've conquered the techniques you may decide to follow their lead and invent your own variations. You might make a long, thin baguette of the *pane pugliese* dough (page 98), put salty olives in one of the salt-free doughs, or add herbs from your garden or a bit of Marsala or rum to a lightly sweetened dough.

A FEW BASIC RULES

- As a rule of thumb, the slower and longer the rise, the greater the flavor. But if the dough is left so long that it overrises and slumps, as the carbon dioxide bubbles begin to burst, don't worry. Dough is very forgiving. Knead it, shape it, and set it to rise once more; you will find that it reaches its desired size rather quickly.

- The more yeast, the quicker the rise.

- The less mixing or kneading used in working the dough, the longer the rise will take.

- Dough with less water is more substantial and compact than softer, moister dough, which will need more mixing and kneading and require longer rising times.

- Lower temperatures encourage the formation of acetic acids, which give breads a more aromatic taste.

- Many of the rustic regional breads should triple in the first rising and can take three risings nicely, in case you need more flexibility than the recipes indicate.

- At the second rise, after the dough has been shaped, you can lightly oil the tops of the sticky wet doughs and gently place plastic wrap over them. The circulation of air is cut down dramatically by this method, so the dough rises slowly and develops more flavor.

- Add fruits and nuts after the first rise by flattening the dough and spooning part of the mixture onto the dough in two or three additions. Fold the dough, flatten again, and repeat until all the filling is in the dough. Knead until the filling is evenly distributed.

Techniques for Baking Tarts, Cakes, and Cookies

Putting ingredients together for Italian sweets is much easier than for breads. First of all, no yeast, starters, and rises are involved. Second, many of these desserts are based on *pasta frolla*, a sweet short pastry dough that is a snap to make. Even the shaping is simple, once you get the hang of it. Most of the recipes depend on the few basic processes that follow.

MAKING DOUGH FOR TART SHELLS

By Hand. First place the flour, salt, and sugar in a mixing bowl and stir them briefly to blend. Cut the butter into small pieces and scatter them over the top. Using a pastry cutter or two knives, cut in the butter until the mixture looks like coarse meal. Beat the eggs, egg yolks, and flavorings until smooth. Drizzle the mixture over the flour and work until the dough comes together.

By Mixer. Cream the butter and sugar until they are light and fluffy, abut 4 minutes on medium speed. Add the egg and the egg yolk, one at a time, mixing in the first before adding the second. Beat in the flavorings last. Sift the flour and salt over the mixture and work them in by hand with a wooden spoon or rubber spatula just until blended.

By Food Processor. The processor has this tart dough together almost before you've started. Set the steel blade in place, put the flour, salt, and sugar in the bowl, and scatter the cold butter in small chunks on top. Process with several pulses until the mixture looks like coarse meal. Combine the eggs, egg yolks, and flavorings and, with the machine running, pour them through the feed tube. Process just until the dough comes together on top of the blade. If you wait for the dough to gather into a ball, it will be too tough. Finish by kneading the dough briefly on a lightly floured surface until it is no longer sticky.

SHAPING THE DOUGH

Bring the dough together with your hands and knead it briefly on a lightly floured surface until it forms a single mass. Transfer it to a piece of plastic wrap, flatten it to a round disk, and refrigerate it until cold, about 30 minutes to 1 hour but no longer than a day.

ROLLING WITH A ROLLING PIN

Place the cold dough on a surface that you have dusted lightly with flour, and sprinkle the top of the dough with just enough flour to keep it from being sticky. The point of the rolling is to make an even, thin circle of dough, so start from the center and roll evenly and smoothly away from you about 3 inches in each direction. Don't push the rolling pin very far—2 to 3 inches is fine—and don't press down hard. Lift up the dough, give it a quarter turn, sprinkle a very little bit of flour underneath it if it shows any tendency to stick, and repeat the process, always rolling away from the center. Don't roll over the edges or you might damage them. If your dough sticks at any point, be sure to scrape the offending particles off your work surface with the dough scraper and flour the surface lightly.

TRANSFERRING THE DOUGH TO THE TART PAN

Simply lay your rolling pin lightly on the top quarter of the dough, pick up the edge of the dough closest to the pin, and drape it over the pin. Gently roll the pin toward you, collecting the remaining dough around it. Lift the rolling pin and set it over the tart pan, rolling the dough away from you and allowing it to drape into the pan. With practice, it gets easier to judge how to center it; if you miss the center the first few times, just pick up the dough gently and set it where you want it. Delicately press the dough into the contours of the pan, then gently push the sides up toward the rim. If you accidentally tear it, patch it by using a little of the leftover dough or by collecting the two edges of torn dough and pinching the edges together.

SHAPING THE EDGES

Once the dough has been fitted into the pan, take the rolling pin and roll it gently over the top edges to cut the pastry dough neatly. Once again I push the dough gently upward toward the rim with my thumb, pressing the overflow with my other thumb to make a slightly thicker edge. The pastry-lined pan is usually refrigerated for 20 to 30 minutes to reduce shrinking while it bakes.

PREBAKING A PASTRY SHELL

Many of the tart shells in this book need to be prebaked, which simply means that before it is filled, the pastry must be baked until it can hold its shape. Line the chilled tart shell with aluminum foil fitted to the bottom contours and spread $2^1/_2$ to 3 cups of dried beans on top of the foil. Fold the edges of the foil in slightly so they are easy to grasp later. Bake as directed, usually 12 to 15 minutes at 350°F. The dough should have cooked enough so that it doesn't feel tacky or sticky. Then, depending on the recipe instructions, either take it out of the oven to cool after removing the beans, or remove the beans, prick the bottom of the pastry all over with a fork, and finish baking.

MAKING DOUGH FOR CAKES AND SOME COOKIES

Creaming Butter and Sugar. Although it is possible to cream butter and sugar by hand with a wooden spoon. I'd certainly recommend that you use an electric mixer. It's much easier and less time-consuming, and it produces a cake as professional as a baker's. Creaming the butter and sugar means beating the two ingredients together (butter at room temperature, please) until they are light and fluffy.

Adding Eggs. Add the eggs one at a time, being sure to incorporate each completely before adding the next. If the mixture looks as if it is curdling, speed up the mixer, beat until the batter is smooth again, and then reduce the speed to that called for in the recipe.

Alternating Liquid and Dry Ingredients. Stir the first portion of the liquid ingredients into your initial mixture, always working from the center out. Alternate liquid and dry ingredients, making sure each addition is smoothly blended before continuing. Always end with the dry.

Grinding Nuts. You can grind nuts in a nut grinder, a spice grinder, or a food processor fitted with the steel blade. With all these methods, you must take care that the nuts are ground just until powdery and fluffy. If you overprocess the nuts they will be oily and will ruin your pastries. If you are using a food processor, add a little of the sugar called for in the recipe to the nuts and process with repeated pulses just to a powder—be sure to keep checking.

Whipping Eggs and Sugar Together. Beat the sugar and eggs at medium speed until pale and about tripled in volume. Usually, about half the sugar is added initially, and the rest is added by bits as the eggs get lighter. If, when you lift the beaters or whisk, the ribbon that falls from the beaters onto the surface remains for 10 seconds or so, the eggs and sugar are sufficiently mixed.

Whipping Egg Whites. To whip egg whites to their full volume, be sure that they are at room temperature and that you have a clean, grease-free bowl and beaters. If you are at all in doubt, just wipe the bowl and beaters with a little vinegar before beginning. A balloon whisk and a copper bowl are wonderful if you are beating by hand, but electric mixers work fabulously and save time and energy. Begin by beating at medium-low speed for about 30 seconds, then increase the speed to medium-high and beat until the whites are stiff but not dry and hold smooth peaks.

Using the Pastry Bag and Piping. I'll try to explain the process, but a little hands-on practice is worth a thousand words. To begin, insert the tip in the bag, fold a third of the top down over your hand, fill the bag about two-thirds full, and twist it closed at the top to push the contents down into the tip. Hold the tip between your thumb and index finger at a 45 to 90 degree angle to the baking sheet and squeeze firmly but gently at the top of the bag with your other hand. Hold the bag gently and apply smooth, steady pressure to pipe a line the size of your tip. Squeeze a bit harder and you'll get a larger flow.

Dusting with Confectioners' Sugar. Use a widemouthed fine-mesh sieve to sprinkle an even layer of confectioners' sugar over the top of tarts or tortes.

A FEW BASIC RULES

- Always have your butter and eggs at room temperature.
- If you're baking on the spur of the moment and don't have any eggs at 70°F, set your refrigerated eggs in a bowl of warm water for about 10 minutes and they'll be ready for you.
- Always weigh your flour (or measure it) before sifting.
- Always sift the flour before incorporating it. If you are using baking powder, sift it along with the other dry ingredients.

PANI

Pani Regionali e Rustici
Regional and Rustic Breads

Do they really exist, those mahogany-colored wheels of country bread with creamy interiors, crackly crusted chewy loaves that still taste intensely of the grains of the fields? The question can only be answered both yes and no. For many people, those fragrant loaves belong to a fleeting moment in the golden past when life was slower and simpler, when breads were made by hand and eaten with a few slices of good local cheese and a glass of wine. Today those breads can still be found, but you must look for them. For all their satisfying flavor, their continued existence was severely endangered during the 1950s and 1960s, when mass production and industrialization centralized baking and threatened to do away with these more complicated breads. Fortunately, they have been revived by artisan bakers all over the country, so that their tastes remain part of another generation's patrimony.

These are the traditional regional breads of Italy, made with only flour, water, yeast, and salt. Most get their taste from a starter that has been allowed to mature and grow slightly sour, so that the loaves will have the deep, mellow taste of the grain itself. You will need to start these breads a half day or day before you plan to bake by making a starter. I often make more starter than the recipe calls for and freeze what's left, for frozen starter can be revived within a few hours. The doughs for these rustic breads will be a new experience for American cooks, who are accustomed to firm bread doughs. The biggest challenge is that they are wet and sticky. When I traveled from bakery to bakery in Italy, watching experts shape, with swift, dexterous moves, doughs that fell off the beaters like butter cream, I knew I would have to explain the procedure carefully. Many of the doughs will seem impossibly wet—a couple even ooze right out of their containers after the first rise—but all it takes is a tablespoon or two of flour to make them easy to shape. *Do not punch them down.* Be ready with a small amount of flour nearby to sprinkle on the sticky doughs, and be sure to keep the work surface floured and your dough scraper handy. Scrape the surface clean so that the little ragged pieces of dough that stick do not tear away at your dough. Parchment paper on baking sheets or peels makes turning these doughs over or sliding them onto the baking stone so much easier than shaking them off a peel.

Classic Tastes of Italy

Biga UNIVERSAL STARTER

MASTER RECIPE

Many of the recipes for the classic regional breads begin with a starter dough made from small amounts of flour, water, and yeast allowed an initial fermentation and then used to infuse the actual bread dough. The starter, known as *biga* in Italy (or *bighino* in small amounts), not only gives strength to what in Italy are weak flours, but it also produces a secondary fermentation from which come the wonderful aroma, natural flavor, and special porosity of the final loaves and wheels of bread.

I keep some *biga* on hand at all times; the contents of my refrigerator and freezer are definitely not the typical American sort: there are more bread starters than food. Still, by having *biga* on hand, I can decide to make *pane pugliese* or ciabatta in the morning and have it for dinner that night.

In Italy, bakers use saltless dough from the previous day's baking to start a new dough. Because the first *biga* must come from somewhere, though, you may make it following the instructions below. This *biga* is remarkable. It freezes very well and needs only about 3 hours at room temperature until it is bubbly and active again. It can be refrigerated for up to 5 days; after that, it gets a bit strong. When using it in recipes, I strongly recommend weighing rather than measuring it, for it expands at room temperature. Use chilled *biga* when measuring by volume; when measuring by weight, the *biga* may be chilled or at room temperature.

The bakers I admire most advise 10 to 11 hours for the first rise and then another 3 hours after adding more flour and water, but others are very happy with the 24 hours it takes for dough to truly become yesterday's dough. If you like sour bread, allow your *biga* to rest for 24 to 48 hours, or you might even stretch it to 72 hours. The important point about a starter dough is that the breads made with it develop a wonderful taste because their risings are long and bring out the flavor of the grain. Another benefit is that the loaves remain fresher and taste sweeter than those made with large amounts of commercial yeast. Use bottled spring water, if you can.

Makes about 2¹/₃ cups (18.4 oz / 525 g)

¹/₄ teaspoon active dry yeast

¹/₄ cup (2 oz / 60 g) warm water

³/₄ cup plus 4 teaspoons (7 oz / 200 g) water,
   at room temperature

2¹/₃ cups (11.6 oz / 330 g) unbleached all-purpose
   flour

Makes about 3³/₄ cups (29 oz / 825 g)

¹/₂ teaspoon (0.05 oz / 1.4 g) active dry yeast

¹/₄ cup (2 oz / 60 g) warm water

1¹/₄ cups plus 2 tablespoons (11.5 oz / 330 g) water,
   at room temperature

3³/₄ cups (17.5 oz / 500 g) unbleached all-purpose
   flour

Stir the yeast into the warm water and let stand until creamy, about 10 minutes. Stir in the remaining water and then the flour, 1 cup at a time.

BY HAND

Mix with a wooden spoon for 3 to 4 minutes.

BY MIXER

Mix with the paddle at the lowest speed for 2 minutes.

BY PROCESSOR

Mix just until a sticky dough is formed.

Rising. Remove to a lightly oiled bowl, cover with plastic wrap, and let rise at a cool room temperature for 6 to 24 hours. The starter will triple in volume and still be wet and sticky when ready. Cover and refrigerate until ready to use. When needed, scoop out the desired amount.

   Both recipes can easily be cut in half.

Biga Naturale BIGA AS AN ALMOST NATURAL YEAST

The usual method of producing a natural culture that takes advantage of the wild yeasts in the air normally requires about 5 to 8 days. The baker begins by mixing flour and water and then repeatedly, over the course of the week, adding flour and water to the mixture before discarding most of the culture and kneading in more flour and water the next day. After several days this process produces the classic bubbles of fermentation. A natural yeast culture is fully active when it triples or quadruples in volume within 6 or 7 hours. At that point the feeding and refreshing of the levain begins, a process that is usually performed twice a day at least three times a week for a few weeks before you can leave the *biga* in the refrigerator and start feeding it only once a week.

Instead of following that long process, which requires adhering to a fairly rigid schedule, I use a simpler method to make a *biga* that is *almost* natural. It begins with a tiny quantity of commercial yeast, an amount that is so small that it doesn't change the flavor of either the starter or the bread it produces. This almost natural *biga* can be refreshed on a less demanding schedule than the natural *biga*.

Makes about 2 cups (16.6 oz / 475 g)

1/16 teaspoon active dry yeast

5 tablespoons (2.5 oz / 75 g) bottled spring water, warmed to about 100°F

3/4 cup (3.5 oz / 100 g) unbleached all-purpose flour, preferably steel-milled and organic

Stir the yeast into the water and let stand until creamy, 5 to 10 minutes. Stir in the flour with a wooden spoon or rubber spatula.

BY HAND

Mix with a rubber spatula or wooden spoon for 2 to 3 minutes.

BY MIXER

Mix with the paddle at the lowest speed for about 2 minutes.

First Rise. The dough, which will be roughly the size of a big orange, will be shaggy. You can knead it briefly to give it a somewhat smoother appearance. Transfer to a lightly oiled straight-sided transparent or translucent container in which you can measure how much the *biga* rises. Mark its point of departure with a pen or a piece of masking tape. Cover the container tightly with plastic wrap and let rise at room temperature for 8 to 16 hours. At that point the *biga* will have doubled and will look like tapioca, with its bubbles on the surface. If you leave it much longer, it will rise and then deflate, but you can safely leave it for 24 hours before refreshing it.

FIRST REFRESHMENT

5 tablespoons (2.5 oz / 75 g) bottled spring water, warmed to about 100°F

3/4 cup (3.5 oz / 100 g) unbleached all-purpose flour, preferably steel-milled and organic

Place the *biga* in a bowl or a mixer bowl and pour the water over it, stirring with a wooden spoon or rubber spatula and squeezing it through your fingers until the water is a milky white and the *biga* begins to break up. Stir in the flour and mix as on the first day. Return it to the plastic container, mark where it now stands, and cover it tightly with plastic wrap. Let it stand at room temperature for 8 to 16 hours.

SECOND REFRESHMENT

By now the dough should have numerous bubbles and be wet and sticky and noticeably elastic. Repeat the steps for the first refreshment, adding the same amount of flour and water. At this point you will have a bit more than a pound (about 475 g) of active starter. Cover it tightly with plastic wrap and let it sit at room temperature for about 1 hour.

Now the *biga naturale* is ready for baking, and you can use it to make a bread like *pane di Como antico* (page 76), which calls for a *biga* made with very little yeast.

If you're not ready to use it, you can refrigerate it for 24 hours and then bring it back to room temperature and refresh it. At this point you can choose to do what professional bakers do as they accumulate a large quantity of *biga*: divide it in half, refresh one half as described above (doing both the first and second refreshments), and either discard the other half or use it to bake with immediately. Continue repeating this process through the third day. After that, you only need to refresh your *biga* every 4 or 5 days. A *biga naturale* keeps in the refrigerator for 3 or 4 months with this method. You can also freeze it and bring it back to life at room temperature in a day or so.

Whenever you are ready to bake, take the starter out of the refrigerator, refresh it, and let it sit out for 4 hours to assure a fresh flavor.

If your *biga* doesn't seems to be responding as described here, try starting over, making sure that you use bottled spring water and steel-milled organic flour, if you can, and ensuring that your tools and implements are very clean, so that no unwanted bacteria can invade the mixture.

If your *biga* develops a vinegary smell or taste, oozes with a slick liquid, develops a stiff crust, or looks as inert as Play-Doh from being left in the refrigerator for too long, you can try to refresh the exhausted starter for several days. Don't give up hope. I have successfully brought back a *biga naturale* left for 12 days in the refrigerator. Scoop under the crust for the wet, elastic dough underneath and use it. Pour off any excess liquid or incorporate it into your refreshing liquid. Take 1 to 2 ounces (about 30 to 60 g) of the old dough, discard the rest, and refresh it as above, doing both the first and the second refreshments. Your *biga* should be active and ready to be used.

If at any time the *biga* seems less than lively, you can always add $1/16$ teaspoon of active dry yeast to the flour and water refreshment, as in the beginning of the recipe, and leave it out for 8 to 16 hours. If the *biga* overferments (it rises and falls, then remains flat, sticky, and lifeless), you can still use it, although the texture of the bread will be more consistent and have fewer big holes.

Pane di Como COMO BREAD

This is a spectacularly delicious white bread with a crunchy dome and a feathery, floury top that tastes of the sweetness of wheat. It is excellent for breakfast. The loaf is engraved with the delicate pattern of the basket in which it is given its final rise, and the interior is honeycombed with irregular holes.

The breads of Como are more than slightly confusing. The *pane francese*, the ciabatta, and the *ciabatta polesana* (recipes follow) are also breads from Como, but I discovered this Como bread in the early 1980s and still think it is irresistible.

Makes 2 round loaves

STARTER

1 teaspoon (0.1 oz / 3 g) active dry yeast

1 scant teaspoon (0.2 oz / 6 g) malt syrup or powder

1/3 cup (2.8 oz / 80 g) warm water

2/3 cup (5.7 oz / 163 g) milk, at room temperature

1 cup minus 1 tablespoon (4.7 oz / 135 g) unbleached all-purpose flour

Stir the yeast and malt, if you are using the syrup, into the water; let stand until foamy, about 10 minutes. Stir in the milk and beat in the flour and malt powder, if you are using it, with a rubber spatula or wooden spoon, about 100 strokes or until smooth. Cover with plastic wrap and let stand until bubbly, at least 4 hours but preferably overnight.

DOUGH

2 cups (16.8 oz / 480 g) water, at room temperature

About 6¼ cups (1 lb 14 oz / 860 g) unbleached all-purpose flour

1 tablespoon (0.5 oz / 15 g) salt

Cornmeal

BY HAND

Add the water to the starter; mix and squeeze it between your fingers until the starter is fairly well broken up. Mix the flour and salt together and add it, 2 cups at a time, into the starter mixer, stirring after each addition. When the dough is too stiff to mix with a wooden spoon, just plunge in with your hands. Mix until well blended, 4 to 5 minutes. Knead on a well-floured surface until elastic but still moist and tacky. Once it has come together nicely, slap it down vigorously on the work surface to develop the gluten.

BY MIXER

Mix the starter and the water with the paddle until the starter is well broken up. Add the flour and salt and mix for 2 to 3 minutes at low speed. The dough will be smooth but won't pull away from the sides of the bowl. Change to the dough hook and knead at medium speed, scraping down the sides of the bowl as necessary, until the dough is elastic but still slightly sticky, 3 to 4 minutes. Finish kneading by hand on a floured work surface.

BY PROCESSOR

Refrigerate the starter until cold. Unless you have a large processor, make the dough in two batches. Place the flour and salt in a food processor fitted with the dough blade and process with several pulses to sift. Place the starter on top of the flour mixture. With the machine running, pour the 2 cups of cold water through the feed tube and process until the dough comes together and gathers in a small ball. Process 30 to 45 seconds longer to knead. Finish kneading on a well-floured surface with well-floured hands. The dough will be sticky and moist.

First Rise. Place the dough in a well-oiled bowl, cover tightly with plastic wrap, and let rise until doubled, about 1$^1/_2$ hours.

The dough is ready when it is very bubbly and blistered.

Shaping and Second Rise. Cut the dough in half on a floured surface and shape it into two round loaves. Place in oiled and floured 8-inch round bannetons or in baskets lined with generously floured kitchen towels. Cover with towels and let rise until fully doubled and risen to the tops of the bannetons, about 1 hour.

Baking. Thirty minutes before baking, preheat the oven with a baking stone in it to 400°F. Just before baking, sprinkle the stone with cornmeal. Very carefully invert the loaves onto the stone and bake until the loaf sounds hollow when the bottom is tapped, about 1 hour. Cool on racks.

Pane di Como Antico o Pane Francese

COMO BREAD OF THE PAST, OR FRENCH BREAD

It is said that the legendary taste of Como bread owes a lot to the air and water of the famous lake, but even without those particular ingredients, this bread is a remarkable and delicious loaf with a crunchy crust and a chewy interior riddled with large holes. Today it is known all over Italy as *pane francese*, or French bread. When it was still called Como bread, it was the only food that brought about a rapprochement of sorts between the contentious regions of Lombardy and Piedmont. Each was fiercely proud of its culinary specialties, quarreling over every dish and gastronomic tradition, but they did relax their differences long enough to speed this bread from the Paduan plain where it was baked to the far reaches of both areas. I am told that it reached its pinnacle of tastiness on the Sunday bicycle ride from Milan to Como, when it was served as a snack after about twenty-five miles of pedaling.

I based this recipe on one from Giancarlo Grignani, a scholar and master baker in Milan, who researched the bread as it tasted in earlier centuries. He used a complicated natural yeast for which I have substituted a starter made with a minuscule amount of yeast and with a little whole wheat flour mixed into the unbleached flour to give it the authentic taste of a time when flours were less refined than today. You also might want to try using your *biga naturale* when you make this bread. I have often made this dough and refrigerated it overnight for the second rise; it only gets better with the long, cool development of the yeast.

Serve this bread with stews and meats with rich sauces, green salads, fresh cheeses, sliced salami, or smoked meats.

Makes 2 long loaves

³/₄ cup (6.3 oz / 180 g) biga (page 70) made with half the yeast

1¹/₂ cups (12.6 oz / 360 g) water, at room temperature (cold if using a processor)

Scant ¹/₂ cup (2.3 oz / 65 g) whole wheat flour

3 cups plus 1 tablespoon (15.2 oz / 435 g) unbleached all-purpose flour

2 teaspoons (0.3 oz / 10 g) salt

Cornmeal

BY HAND

Cut the *biga* into small pieces in a large mixing bowl. Add all but 1 to 2 tablespoons of the water and mix until the starter is in fine shreds and the liquid is chalky white. Stir in the whole wheat flour and most of the all-purpose flour, 1 cup at a time. When the dough is a fairly rough and shaggy mass, stir in the salt dissolved in the remaining water. Knead on a floured surface, sprinkling with up to

¹/₂ cup (2.5 oz / 70 g) of additional flour and using the dough scraper to scrape up the fine film of dough that will accumulate on the work surface, as well as to turn and lift the dough. After about 5 minutes of kneading, slam the dough down hard several times to help develop the gluten. Continue kneading until the dough is smooth, a total of 8 to 12 minutes. The dough should be soft, moist, and sticky.

BY MIXER

Mix the *biga* and all but 1 to 2 tablespoons of the water with the paddle. Mix in the flours and then the salt dissolved in the remaining water. Change to the dough hook and knead at medium speed until soft, moist, and sticky but obviously elastic, about 4 minutes. Finish kneading by hand on a floured surface, sprinkling with additional flour, until smooth but still soft.

BY PROCESSOR

Refrigerate the *biga* until cold. Process the *biga* and 1¹/₂ cups of cold water with the steel blade and move it to another bowl. Change to the dough blade and process the flours and salt with two or three pulses to sift. With the machine running, pour the *biga* mixture through the feed tube as quickly as the flour can absorb it. Process 30 to 45 seconds longer to knead. The dough will be moist and sticky. Finish kneading by hand on a floured surface, sprinkling with additional flour, until the dough is smooth but soft.

First Rise. Place the dough in a lightly oiled bowl, cover with plastic wrap, and let rise until doubled, 1¹/₂ to 2 hours. The dough is ready when it has numerous bubbles and blisters under the surface.

Shaping and Second Rise. Divide the dough in half on a floured surface without kneading it. Shape into two round loaves. Let them relax under a cloth for 20 minutes. Line baking sheets or peels with parchment paper and flour the paper generously. Roll each ball into a fat cylinder and place seam side down on the paper. Dimple the loaves all over with your fingertips or knuckles, as for focaccia, to keep the dough from springing up. The dough should feel delicate but extremely springy. Cover the loaves and let rise until doubled, with many visible air bubbles, 1¹/₄ to 1¹/₂ hours.

Baking. Thirty minutes before baking, preheat the oven to 425°F with a cast-iron frying pan inside on the bottom shelf and a baking stone on the shelf above it. Just before baking, sprinkle the baking stone with cornmeal. Carry the peel or baking sheet to the oven and very gently invert the dough onto the stone. Gently remove the parchment paper; if it sticks, wait 10 minutes and the paper will detach easily. Immediately put ¹/₂ cup of ice cubes into the pan, reduce the heat to 400°F and bake until golden, 35 to 40 minutes. Cool on racks.

Ciabatta SLIPPER-SHAPED BREAD FROM LAKE COMO

I can't think of a way to describe the fabulous and unusual taste of ciabatta except to say that once you've eaten it, you'll never think of white bread in the same way again. Everyone who tries this bread loves it. Ciabatta means "slipper" in Italian; one glance at the short, stubby bread will make it clear how it was named. Ciabatta is a remarkable combination of rustic country texture and elegant and tantalizing taste. It is much lighter than its homely shape would indicate, and the porous, chewy interior is enclosed in a slightly crunchy crust that is veiled with flour. Eat it for breakfast or slice an entire ciabatta horizontally and stuff it with salami and cheese.

This dough should be made in the mixer, although it can also be made in a food processor. I have made it by hand, but I wouldn't recommend it unless you are willing to knead the wet, sticky mass between your hands—in midair—turning, folding, and twisting it rather like taffy, your hands covered with dough. You can't put it on the table because the natural inclination is to add lots of flour to this very sticky dough, and pretty soon you wouldn't have a ciabatta. Resist the temptation to add flour, and follow the instructions. The dough will feel utterly unfamiliar and probably a bit scary. And that's not the only unusual feature: the shaped loaves are flat and look definitely unpromising. Even when they are puffed after the second rise, you may feel certain you've done it all wrong. Don't give up. The loaves rise nicely in the oven.

Makes 4 loaves, each about the width of a hand and the length of the arm from wrist to elbow

1 teaspoon (0.1 oz / 3 g) active dry yeast

5 tablespoons (2.7 oz / 76 g) warm milk

1 cup plus 3 tablespoons (10 oz / 285 g) water, at room temperature (cold if using a processor)

1 tablespoon (0.5 oz / 15 g) olive oil

2 very full cups (17.5 oz / 500 g) biga (page 70), made 12 hours before

3³/₄ cups (17.5 oz / 500 g) unbleached all-purpose flour

1 tablespoon (0.5 oz / 15 g) salt

Cornmeal

BY MIXER

Stir the yeast into the milk in a mixer bowl; let stand until creamy, about 10 minutes. Add the water, oil, and *biga* and mix with the paddle until blended. Mix the flour and salt, add to the bowl, and mix for 2 to 3 minutes. Change to the dough hook and knead for 2 minutes at low speed, then 2 minutes at medium speed. Knead briefly on a well-floured surface, adding as little flour as possible, until the dough is velvety, supple, very springy, and moist.

continued

Ciabatta, *continued*

BY PROCESSOR

Refrigerate the *biga* until cold. Stir the yeast into the milk in a large bowl; let stand until creamy, about 10 minutes. Add 1 cup plus 3 tablespoons of cold water, the oil, and the *biga* and mix, squeezing the *biga* between your fingers to break it up. Place the flour and salt in the food processor fitted with the dough blade and process with several pulses to sift. With the machine running, pour the *biga* mixture through the feed tube and process until the dough comes together. Process about 45 seconds longer to knead. Finish kneading on a well-floured surface until the dough is velvety, supple, moist, and very springy.

First Rise. Place the dough in an oiled bowl, cover with plastic wrap, and let rise until doubled, about $1^1/4$ hours. The dough should be full of air bubbles, very supple, elastic, and sticky.

Shaping and Second Rise. Cut the dough into four equal pieces on a well-floured surface. Roll each piece into a cylinder, then stretch each into a rectangle about 10 by 4 inches, pulling with your fingers to get each piece long and wide enough. Generously flour four pieces of parchment paper on peels or baking sheets. Place each loaf, seam side up, on a paper. Dimple the loaves vigorously with your fingertips or knuckles so that they won't rise too much. The dough will look heavily pockmarked, but it is very resilient, so don't be concerned. Cover loosely with dampened towels and let rise until puffy but not doubled, $1^1/2$ to 2 hours. The loaves will look flat and definitely unpromising, but don't give up; they will rise more in the oven.

Baking. Thirty minutes before baking, preheat the oven with baking stones in it to 425°F. Just before baking, sprinkle the stones with cornmeal. Carefully invert each loaf onto a stone. If the dough sticks a bit, just work it free from the paper gently. If you need to, you can leave the paper and remove it 10 minutes later. Bake for 20 to 25 minutes, spraying the oven three times with water in the first 10 minutes. Cool on racks.

Ciabatta Polesana CIABATTA FROM THE VENETO

Unlike France, which has long had its classic baguette, Italy didn't have a single iconic bread until this ciabatta came along. Like the *pane di Como antico* (page 76), the Como ciabatta (page 79), and the *pane di Como* (page 74), this ciabatta began in the Como area, where in 1982 Arnaldo Cavallari decided to give up his car racing career to use the flour made at his family's mills in Adria. And this is what he made: the ciabatta that conquered the country. It is singularly delicious, but it is also extremely challenging to make because of the very high ratio of water to flour. The dough is so wet that it cannot really be shaped.

Keeping in mind that the best bread is made by allowing the dough to rise slowly at a cool temperature, you have two choices when making this bread: you can let the *biga* rise at room temperature, or leave it in the refrigerator overnight. My preference is for the refrigerator.

Makes 2 loaves

BIGA

5 tablespoons (2.5 oz / 75 g) warm water

$^1/_4$ teaspoon active dry yeast

Scant $^3/_4$ cup (3.5 oz / 100 g) high-gluten flour

BY HAND ONLY

Pour the water into a small mixing bowl and whisk in the yeast. Let stand for 5 to 10 minutes. Stir in the flour with a rubber spatula for 1 to 2 minutes. Knead the rough dough on a lightly floured work surface for 1 to 2 minutes until it becomes a somewhat smooth ball. Put it in a lightly oiled bowl, cover tightly with plastic wrap, and let stand in the refrigerator until bubbly and lively, anywhere from 6 to 24 hours, or leave at room temperature for 1 to 2 hours, just until you see the *biga* has the beginnings of life, and then refrigerate it.

DOUGH

$^1/_4$ cup (2 oz / 60 g) warm water

$^1/_4$ teaspoon active dry yeast

2 cups minus 2 tablespoons (15.8 oz / 450 g) water, at room temperature

$3^3/_4$ cups (17.5 oz / 500 g) high-gluten flour

2 teaspoons (0.4 oz / 10 g) salt

BY MIXER ONLY

When you are ready to make the dough, whisk the yeast into the warm water and let stand for 5 to 10 minutes. Transfer this mixture and the rest of the water into a mixer bowl and add the *biga*, squeezing the starter through your fingers to break it up. Add the flour and salt and mix with the paddle until the dough comes together, about 3 minutes, and then mix 2 minutes longer.

Change to the dough hook and knead the dough on high speed for 15 to

continued

Ciabatta Polesana, *continued*

18 minutes. You must stay with the mixer the entire time because it can vibrate and walk right off the counter, and the motor can overheat. The dough will slap the sides of the bowl, then collapse toward the bottom, then clear the sides and collapse again. When it is ready, the dough will still be sticky but feel sturdy and elastic.

First Rise. Put the dough into a lightly oiled 3- or 4-quart translucent or clear straight-sided container and mark its volume. You can let it rise at room temperature until it has tripled, about $2^{1}/_{2}$ to 3 hours, or leave it at room temperature for 3 hours and then put it in the refrigerator, where it will continue to rise much more slowly over the next 18 to 24 hours. If you have refrigerated the dough, remove it from the refrigerator about 4 hours before continuing so that it warms up to room temperature.

Shaping and Second Rise. When you are ready to shape the dough, put two pieces of parchment paper on a baker's peel close to each other, but not touching. Sprinkle them lightly with flour.

Flour your work surface very well. Put a bowl of water nearby for your hands. Pour the wet, sticky dough onto the floured surface. Use your dough scraper to cut the dough into two equal pieces. Don't even imagine that you can shape them. Dip your hands into the water and then lift and move each half swiftly to the parchment paper on the peel, holding the parchment in one hand and using the dough scraper as an extension of your other hand to guide you as you place each piece on its parchment paper. Sprinkle the tops of the dough with a veil of flour. Lay a piece of plastic wrap over the top of each, drape lightly with a kitchen towel, and let the loaves rise briefly, no more than 45 minutes.

Baking. Forty-five minutes before baking, preheat the oven to 475°F with a cast-iron frying pan inside on the bottom shelf and a baking stone on the shelf above it. Theoretically you shouldn't have to sprinkle the stone with cornmeal because your loaves will stay on the parchment, but you can use the cornmeal as insurance, if you want. Slide one hand under the parchment paper with the dough on top, transfer it to the oven, and set it on one half of the baking stone. Repeat with the other piece of dough, making sure that no parchment hangs off the baking stone, because it will burn. Just before you close the oven door, put $^{1}/_{2}$ cup of ice into the cast-iron frying pan, and the steam will continue to mist the interior for 5 to 10 minutes. By the time the crust has set, the water will have evaporated and the rest of the baking will take place in a hot, dry oven. Bake until the loaves sound hollow when the bottom is tapped, about 30 minutes. Cool on racks.

Pane all'Olio OLIVE OIL BREAD

A little good olive oil makes a tasty white bread, especially when the top is sprinkled with granules of sea salt. I am charmed by this shape—little rolls connected in a wreath, each one to be broken off and eaten individually. I've also seen the bread made into *manini*, little hands, made by crossing two narrow cylinders of dough at a slight angle, so that it looks like a four-fingered hand. Serve with sliced salami, sausages, smoked meats, roast veal, ham, or antipasti.

Makes 2 rings of 6 or 7 rolls each or 12 to 14 individual rolls

2¼ teaspoons (1 package / 0.2 oz / 7 g) active dry yeast

1 cup plus 3 tablespoons (10 oz / 285 g) warm water (or 3 tablespoons / 1.6 oz / 45 g warm water plus 1 cup / 8.4 oz / 240 g cold water if using a processor)

3 tablespoons plus 1 teaspoon (1.75 oz / 50 g) olive oil

2 to 3 teaspoons (0.3 to 0.5 oz / 8 to 13 g) lard, at room temperature

3¾ cups (17.5 oz / 500 g) unbleached all-purpose flour

2 teaspoons (0.35 oz / 10 g) salt

Sea salt

BY HAND

Stir the yeast into the water in a large mixing bowl; let stand until creamy, about 10 minutes. Stir in the oil and lard and then the flour and salt until well blended. Knead on a floured surface until elastic and velvety, 8 to 10 minutes.

BY MIXER

Stir the yeast into the water in a mixer bowl; let stand until creamy, about 10 minutes. Stir in the oil and lard with the paddle, and then mix in the flour and salt. Change to the dough hook and knead about 5 minutes, half at low and half at medium speed. Scrape down the sides of the bowl as necessary. The dough should be elastic and velvety.

BY PROCESSOR

Stir the yeast into the 3 tablespoons of warm water; let stand until creamy, about 10 minutes. Place the flour and salt in a food processor fitted with the steel blade and process with several pulses to sift. Place the lard on top of the flour. With the machine running, pour the 1 cup of cold water, the oil, and the dissolved yeast through the feed tube and process until the dough gathers into a ball. Process about 40 seconds longer to knead. Finish kneading briefly by hand on a lightly floured surface. The dough should be elastic and velvety.

First Rise. Place the dough in a lightly oiled bowl, cover with plastic wrap, and let rise until doubled, about 2 hours. The dough should be very moist and velvety.

Shaping and Second Rise. Divide the dough into twelve to fourteen equal pieces, each about the size of a lime, and

continued

Pane all'Olio, *continued*

shape into small balls. Arrange the balls about 1¹/₂ inches apart in two free-form circles on oiled or parchment-lined baking sheets, or place in oiled ring molds that have been sprinkled with sea salt. Cover with plastic wrap and then a towel and let rise until doubled, about 1¹/₄ to 1¹/₂ hours.

Baking. Preheat the oven to 400°F. If you have made the free-form rings, brush the tops of the rolls with olive oil and then sprinkle lightly with sea salt. Bake 35 minutes for the wreath, 20 minutes for individual rolls. Cool on racks.

Variation. To make *manini*, divide the dough into twelve to fourteen pieces, each about the size of a lime. Roll out each piece lengthwise with a rolling pin into a thin strip, ³/₈ to ¹/₂ inch thick. Curve one strip into a bent half-circle. Arrange another strip across the first so that their centers meet, and curve the strip as you did the first. Roll each piece so that it looks like a four-fingered hand. Bake 20 minutes.

Pane Toscano o Pane Sciocco SALTLESS TUSCAN BREAD

Some cookbook authors insist that a bread made without salt could only be flat and insipid, but the Tuscans have been making this saltless bread for many centuries. Dante even referred to it in the *Divine Comedy*. Anticipating the difficulties of his exile from Florence, he speaks of them figuratively: "You shall learn how salty is the taste of another's bread." The big, flat rounds scored in tic-tac-toe patterns or the smaller crusty ovals of bread are sometimes rough and somewhat coarse, sometimes more compact inside, but they are always mellow and bland.

One explanation for the saltless bread from this region is that the Tuscans, well known for being tightfisted, couldn't bear the pay the government salt tax and chose instead to make bread without it. Perhaps, but gastronomes point out that the Tuscan bread is perfectly suited to their cuisine, which is full of strong flavors. Tuscans eat thick slabs of local prosciutto that is much stronger and saltier than that of other regions, and their *finocchiona* sausages are more highly flavored than other Italian varieties; the saltless Tuscan bread is a perfect foil for both. The sauces for Tuscan meats and stews are extremely spicy and flavorful, and the saltless bread sets a

continued

Pane Toscano o Pane Sciocco, *continued*

perfect balance when steeped in the gravies. Use Tuscan breads as the Tuscans do: for *fettunta*, a slice of bread grilled or broiled, rubbed with garlic, and then brushed with fruity olive oil of the first pressing; for crostini with chicken livers or game; for highly flavored Tuscan salami and prosciutto; for spicy sauces and gravies with meat. The bread dries out quickly, but it is very tasty soaked in a dressing or liquid for a salad or soup, such as *panzanella* or *minestrone toscana*.

Makes 1 large ruota, *or wheel, or 2 oval loaves*

STARTER

¹/₄ teaspoon active dry yeast

²/₃ cup (5.6 oz / 160 g) warm water

About 1¹/₄ cups (6.1 oz / 175 g) unbleached
    all-purpose flour

Stir the yeast into the water in a small bowl; let stand until creamy, about 10 minutes. Add the flour and stir with about 100 strokes of a wooden spoon, or stir with the paddle of an electric mixer for about 1 minute. Cover with plastic wrap and let rise until tripled, 6 hours to overnight.

DOUGH

1¹/₄ teaspoons (0.1 oz / 3.5 g) active dry yeast

¹/₃ cup (2.8 oz / 80 g) warm water

1 cup (8.4 oz / 240 g) water, at room temperature
    (cold if using a processor)

3³/₄ cups (17.5 oz / 500 g) unbleached
    all-purpose flour

Pinch of salt (optional)

Cornmeal

BY HAND

Stir the yeast into the warm water in a large bowl; let stand until creamy, about 10 minutes. Add the starter and the 1 cup of water and mix well, squeezing the starter between your fingers to break it up. Beat in the flour 1 cup at a time and continue beating until the dough is thoroughly mixed, about 4 to 5 minutes. Stir in the salt, if desired, in the last minutes. Turn out onto a well-floured surface and knead, using a dough scraper to begin with, until elastic, resilient, and somewhat velvety, 8 to 10 minutes.

BY MIXER

Stir the yeast into the warm water in a small bowl; let stand until creamy, about 10 minutes. Add the dissolved yeast and the 1 cup of water to the starter in a large mixer bowl and mix with the paddle. Beat in the flour and continue beating until thoroughly mixed, 1 to 2 minutes. Add the salt, if desired, and beat 1 more minute. Change to the dough hook and knead until the dough is elastic, resilient, and somewhat velvety, about 4 minutes. Finish kneading by hand on a floured surface.

BY PROCESSOR

If the capacity of your food processor is 7 cups or less, process this dough in two batches. Refrigerate the starter until cold. Stir the yeast into the warm water and let stand until creamy, about 10 minutes. Process the dissolved yeast, cold starter, and the 1 cup of cold water with the steel blade to the consistency of lumpy pancake batter. Pour the mixture into another container and change to the dough blade without cleaning the bowl. Add the flour and salt, if desired, to the bowl and process with two or three pulses to sift. With the machine running, pour the starter mixture through the feed tube as quickly as the flour can absorb it and process until the dough gathers into a ball. Process 20 seconds longer to knead. Don't worry if the dough never truly forms a ball, but it should hold its shape and not ooze. Finish kneading by hand on a lightly floured surface until elastic, resilient, and somewhat velvety.

First Rise. Place the dough in an oiled bowl, cover with plastic wrap, and let rise until doubled, about 1 hour.

Shaping and Second Rise. Turn the dough out onto a floured surface and lightly dust the top with flour. The dough will be very moist and soft, but don't punch it down. Flatten it with your hands and shape into a large flat round loaf, or cut it in half and shape each half into an oval. Place on a well-floured baking sheet or peel and gently turn the loaf over to collect some of the flour onto its surface. Turn it again, smooth side up, cover with a towel, and let rise until doubled, 45 minutes to 1¹/₄ hours.

Baking. Thirty minutes before baking, preheat the oven with a baking stone in it to 450°F. If you have shaped the dough into a single large wheel, score a tic-tac-toe pattern on top with a razor or sharp bread knife. Just before baking, sprinkle the stone with cornmeal and slide the loaf onto it. Bake 15 minutes. Reduce the heat to 400°F and bake 20 minutes for the smaller ovals, 25 to 30 minutes for the large *ruota*. Cool on a rack.

Pane Toscano Scuro DARK TUSCAN BREAD

A very common variation of the traditional saltless Tuscan bread is made with whole wheat. This recipe comes from Giovanni Galli, a wonderful Florentine baker, who showed me how Tuscan housewives made this bread. This is not a wet, sticky dough of the bakeries but a typical country loaf.

When it gets stale—and it will very quickly—use it for *panzanella* (page 164), the bread salad that starts with bread soaked in oil and vinegar, and for *pappa al pomodoro* (page 165), the vegetable soup thickened with bread and served in Tuscany in place of pasta.

Makes 1 large ruota, *or wheel, or 2 oval loaves*

STARTER

1 teaspoon (0.1 oz / 3 g) active dry yeast

²/₃ cup (5.6 oz / 160 g) warm water

1¼ cups (6.1 oz / 175 g) unbleached all-purpose flour

Stir the yeast into the water; let stand until creamy, about 10 minutes. Add the flour and stir with 100 strokes of a wooden spoon, or stir with the paddle of an electric mixer for 1 minute. Cover with plastic wrap and let rise until tripled, 6 hours to overnight.

DOUGH

1¼ teaspoon (0.1 oz / 3.5 g) active dry yeast

¹/₃ cup (2.8 oz / 80 g) warm water

1 cup (8.4 oz / 240 g) water, at room temperature

¹/₄ cup (1.1 oz / 30 g) unbleached all-purpose flour

4 cups (16.6 oz / 475 g) stone-ground whole wheat flour

Cornmeal

BY HAND

Stir the yeast into the warm water in a large mixing bowl; let stand until creamy, about 10 minutes. Add the 1 cup of water and the starter. Stir vigorously or squeeze the mixture between your fingers to break the starter up. Stir in the flours 2 cups at a time and continue stirring until thoroughly mixed. Flour a work surface well with all-purpose flour and knead the dough until firm and resilient, 8 to 10 minutes.

BY MIXER

Stir the yeast into the warm water in a mixer bowl; let stand until creamy, about 10 minutes. Add the 1 cup of water and the starter and mix with the paddle until the starter is broken up. Add the flours and mix until the dough comes together. Change to the dough hook and knead until firm and elastic, 3 to 4 minutes. Finish kneading briefly by hand on a surface floured with all-purpose flour.

First Rise. Place the dough in a lightly oiled bowl, cover tightly with plastic wrap, and let rise until doubled, 1 to 1¹/₂ hours.

Shaping and Second Rise. Turn the dough out onto a floured surface, flatten it gently to expel some of the air, and then shape into a flat round loaf or 2 oval loaves. Place on a cornmeal-sprinkled peel or an oiled baking sheet. Dust the top lightly with flour, cover with a very lightly dampened towel, and let rise until doubled, 45 minutes to 1 hour.

Baking. Preheat the oven to 450°F. If you are using a baking stone, turn the oven on 30 minutes before baking and sprinkle the stone with cornmeal just before sliding the loaf onto it. If making a single large loaf, score the top in a tic-tac-toe pattern with a razor or sharp knife. Bake the loaf or loaves for 15 minutes, then reduce the heat to 400°F. Continue baking a large *ruota* for 25 to 30 minutes, smaller loaves for 20 minutes. Cool on a rack.

Variation. For a lighter loaf, use 1 scant cup (4.4 oz / 125 g) of whole wheat flour and 2²/₃ cups (13.1 oz / 375 g) of all-purpose unbleached flour.

Pane di Terni TERNI BREAD

This wonderful rustic bread from Terni, a largish city in southern Umbria, is in such great demand that quantities of it are rushed to Rome daily. Traditionally a saltless bread, it tastes delicious with a bit of salt added. This is yet another exceptionally good country bread with a light crunchy crust, but the interior is a bit different from most breads because its close texture is honeycombed with larger holes. *Pane di Terni* makes wonderful toast and can be used in such Umbrian soups as *acquacotta* and *pancotto*.

Makes 4 round loaves

¹/₂ teaspoon (0.05 oz / 1.4 g) active dry yeast

¹/₃ cup (2.8 oz / 80 g) warm water

1 cup (8.4 oz / 240 g) water, at room temperature (cold if using a processor)

About 3 cups (26 oz / 750 g) biga (page 70), made with half the amount of yeast

1¹/₂ cups (6.3 oz / 180 g) whole wheat pastry flour

2¹/₃ cups (11.2 oz / 320 g) unbleached all-purpose flour

4 teaspoons (0.7 oz / 20 g) salt (optional)

Cornmeal

BY HAND

Stir the yeast into the warm water; let stand until creamy, about 10 minutes. Add the 1 cup of water and the *biga*; stir with a rubber spatula or wooden spoon or squeeze the mixture between your fingers to break up the *biga*. Stir in the whole wheat flour. Add the all-purpose flour and salt, if desired, and mix first with a spoon and then with your hands until the dough comes together. Knead on a floured surface until firm and elastic, 8 to 10 minutes.

continued

Pane di Terni, *continued*

BY MIXER

Stir the yeast into the warm water in a large mixer bowl; let stand until creamy, about 10 minutes. Add the 1 cup of water and the *biga* and mix with the paddle until the *biga* is fairly well broken up. Add the flours and salt, if desired. Mix until the dough comes together and then for 1 minute longer. Change to the dough hook and knead until the dough is firm and elastic, about 3 minutes. Finish kneading briefly by hand on a floured surface.

BY PROCESSOR

If your work bowl is 7 cups or smaller, process the dough in two batches. Refrigerate the *biga* until cold. Stir the yeast into the warm water; let stand about 10 minutes. Place the flours and salt, if desired, in a food processor fitted with the steel or dough blade and process with three pulses to sift. Mix the dissolved yeast and the 1 cup of cold water. With the machine running, quickly pour the yeast mixture and then the starter through the feed tube. Process 30 seconds longer to knead. Finish kneading by hand on a floured surface until firm and elastic, 1 to 3 minutes.

Rising. Place the dough in an oiled bowl, cover tightly with plastic wrap, and let rise until doubled, 2 to 3 hours.

Shaping and Second Rise. Divide the dough into four equal pieces on a floured surface and shape each piece into a round loaf. Cut four pieces of parchment paper and place on baking sheets; flour the paper. Place the loaves, rough side up, on the paper. Cover loosely with towels and let rest for 30 minutes. Dimple the loaves with your fingertips or knuckles, then oil the tops lightly and cover with plastic wrap. Let rise until very blistered with sizable air bubbles visible, about 2 hours. Remove the plastic wrap for the last 10 to 15 minutes of rising time to allow the loaves to develop a slight skin.

Baking. Thirty minutes before baking, preheat the oven with baking stones in it to 400°F. Just before baking, sprinkle the stones with cornmeal. Very gently invert each loaf onto a stone and remove the parchment paper. Bake until golden brown, 35 to 40 minutes, spraying the oven with water three times in the first 10 minutes. Cool on racks.

Coccodrillo CROCODILE BREAD

This bread, named for its shape, was dreamed up about thirty years ago by Gianfranco Anelli, then a baker in Rome. He called it his favorite bread and, judging by the number of people who came from all over the city to buy it, it may have been his most popular as well. At the bakery it takes two days to make. I suggest that you start in the morning, work at it again for 10 minutes in the evening, and finish the next day. I actually prefer to stretch the process over three days because the flavor is even better. Three days may seem formidable, but the working time of the first two days is only 5 to 10 minutes.

This is one dough that you will find difficult to make without an electric mixer, for it requires 30 minutes of continuous stirring for the final dough. Of course, you could enlist some help with hand kneading. The result is an extremely light bread with a crunchy dark-speckled crust and a very chewy interior. The bread stays fresh for an amazing number of days.

Makes 2 large loaves

FIRST STARTER

1/2 teaspoon (0.05 oz / 1.4 g) active dry yeast

1 cup (8.4 oz / 240 g) warm water

1/4 cup (1.2 oz / 35 g) durum flour

3/4 cup (3.2 oz / 90 g) unbleached stone-ground flour

The morning of the first day, stir the yeast into the water; let stand until creamy, about 10 minutes. Add the flours and stir with a wooden spoon about 50 strokes or with the paddle of an electric mixer about 30 seconds. Cover with plastic wrap and let rise 12 to 24 hours. The starter should be bubbly.

SECOND STARTER

1 1/4 teaspoons (0.1 oz / 3.5 g) active dry yeast

1/4 cup (2 oz / 60 g) warm water

1 1/4 cups (10.5 oz / 300 g) water, at room temperature

1/2 cup (2.5 oz / 70 g) durum flour

1 1/2 cups (6.3 oz / 180 g) unbleached stone-ground flour

The evening of the same day or the next morning, stir the yeast into the warm water; let stand until creamy, about 10 minutes. Add the water, flours, and dissolved yeast to the first starter and stir, using a spatula or wooden spoon or the paddle of the electric mixer until smooth. Cover with plastic wrap and let rise 12 to 24 hours.

continued

Coccodrillo, *continued*

DOUGH

¹/₄ cup (1.3 oz / 35 g) durum flour

1 to 1¹/₄ cups (4.2 to 4.9 oz / 120 to 140 g)
   unbleached stone-ground flour

1¹/₂ tablespoons (0.8 oz / 22.5 g) salt

BY MIXER

The next day, add the durum flour and
1 cup of unbleached flour to the starter
in the mixer bowl; mix with a paddle on
the lowest speed for 17 minutes. Add the
salt and mix 3 minutes longer, adding the
remaining flour if needed for the dough
to come together. You may need to turn
the mixer off once or twice to keep it
from overheating.

BY HAND

If you decide to make this dough by hand,
place the starter, durum flour, and 1 cup
of unbleached flour in a widemouthed
bowl. Stir with a rubber spatula or
wooden spoon for 25 to 30 minutes, then
add the salt and remaining flour if needed
and stir 5 minutes longer. The dough is
very wet and will not be kneaded.

First Rise. Pour the dough into a large
widemouthed bowl placed on an open
trivet on legs or on a wok ring so that air
can circulate all around it. Loosely drape
a towel over the top and let rise at about
70°F, turning the dough over in the bowl
every hour, until just about tripled, 4 or
5 hours.

Shaping and Second Rise. Pour the
wet dough onto a generously floured
surface. Have a mound of flour nearby
to flour your hands, the top of the oozy
dough, and the work surface itself.
This will all work fine—appearances to
the contrary—but be prepared for an
unusually wet dough. Make a big round
shape of it by just folding and tucking
the edges under a bit. Please don't try
to shape it precisely; it's a hopeless task
and quite unnecessary. Place the dough
on well-floured parchment paper placed
on a baking sheet or peel. Cover with a
dampened towel and let rise until very
blistered and full of air bubbles, about
45 minutes.

Baking. Thirty minutes before baking,
preheat the oven with a baking stone in
it to 475°F. Just before baking, cut the
dough in half down the center with a
dough scraper; a knife would tear the
dough. Gently slide the two pieces apart
and turn so that the cut surfaces face
upward. Sprinkle the stone with cornmeal. If you feel brave, slide the paper
with the dough on it onto the stone, but
the dough can also be baked directly on
the baking sheet. When the dough has
set, slide the paper out. Bake for 30 to
35 minutes. Cool on a rack.

Pane di Genzano GENZANO BREAD

When this bread is baked in the brick ovens of Genzano, a small city in the once castle-filled countryside just south of Rome, it has an almost black crust. Baked at home in a conventional oven, the fine dusting of bran that coats the dough gives it a golden to deep brown color. This is one of those good country breads made with a wet Italian dough, which is best left to the mixer, although you can use a food processor. Be sure to flour everything that comes in contact with the dough: the work surface, the dough scraper, and especially your hands. "The wetter the dough, the better the bread," one of the best bakers I know told me. Also, the longer the rise, the better the taste—let this bread develop slowly at a cool (70°F) room temperature. This bread is wonderful toasted, as well as served with salads, cheeses, and smoked meats.

Makes 1 round loaf

1 teaspoon (0.1 oz / 3 g) active dry yeast

1/3 cup (2.8 oz / 80 g) warm water

1 1/3 cups minus 1 tablespoon (10.7 oz /305 g) water, at room temperature (cold if using a processor)

Scant 3 cups (14 oz / 400 g) unbleached all-purpose flour

3/4 cup plus 1 tablespoon (3.5 oz / 100 g) white or whole wheat pastry flour

2 teaspoons (0.4 oz / 10 g) salt

1/2 cup (0.9 oz / 25 g) wheat bran

BY MIXER

Stir the yeast into the warm water in a mixer bowl; let stand until creamy, about 10 minutes. Stir in the remaining water. Add the flours and salt and mix with the paddle for 2 to 3 minutes. Change to the dough hook and knead for 5 to 6 minutes, half at low speed, then half at medium. You'll probably have to stop the machine and scrape down the dough from the collar of the hook several times. The dough should be extremely soft, velvety, and moist. You can pour the dough directly into an oiled bowl for the first rise, or first knead the dough briefly with well-floured hands and a dough scraper on a well-floured surface.

BY PROCESSOR

Stir the yeast into the warm water; let stand until creamy, about 10 minutes. Place the flours and salt in a food processor fitted with the dough blade and process with two or three pulses to sift. With the machine running, pour the cold water and the dissolved yeast through the feed tube as quickly as the flour can absorb it and process until the dough comes together. Process 45 seconds to knead. Finish kneading with well-floured hands and a dough scraper on a well-floured surface. The dough should be extremely soft, velvety, and moist.

continued

Pane di Genzano, *continued*

First Rise. Place the dough in a lightly oiled bowl, cover with plastic wrap, and let rise until tripled, 3 to 5 hours. While the dough is rising, grind the bran extremely fine in a blender. Lightly oil an 8- or 9-inch pie plate with sloping sides and coat the bottom with $^1/_4$ cup of the bran.

Shaping and Second Rise. Flour the work surface and your hands very well and pour the sticky dough onto the surface. Shape the dough loosely into a round loaf; don't worry if it is not perfectly shaped or tightly gathered. Place the dough in the prepared pie plate and gingerly pat the remaining bran around the sides and over the top of the dough so that it is completely covered. Cover the dough with a towel and let rise at a cool room temperature until at least doubled, $1^1/_2$ to 2 hours. Even when the dough has more than completely filled the pie plate and risen to a dome, it will shake like Jell-O when you jiggle it.

Baking. This is a perfect bread to bake in a La Cloche, if you have one. Thirty minutes before baking, preheat the oven to 425°F with the *cloche* top and bottom or a baking stone in it. If you are using the *cloche*, place the pie plate on the bottom and cover it with the top; if not, place the pie plate on the baking stone. Bake for 40 to 45 minutes. Remove the top for the last 10 to 15 minutes so the crust can brown. Because the bran makes it so difficult to test the bread for doneness (tapping the bottom gets you a handful of loose bran), try using a cake tester to see if it comes out clean, or insert an instant-read thermometer and check if the middle of the loaf has reached 200°F to 210°F. Immediately turn the loaf out of the plate onto a rack to cool.

Pane di Altamura DURUM FLOUR BREAD FROM ALTAMURA

The golden bread of Altamura, a handsome town in the region of Puglia on the heel of the Italian boot, is famous all over Italy. Made of the high-gluten durum that grows across the Tavoliere plain, the bread has a hard crust with a chewy interior that exudes the intense smell and taste of the wheat.

I had tasted a version of this bread elsewhere, but when I watched the bakers and ate the bread at the centuries-old Gesù Bakery in Altamura, I discovered a much chewier and more rustic loaf. I saw the oven fed with trunks of hard oak that result in a very high heat and saw the oven floor made of a very porous stone. I watched the men shape the bread into a round that swoops up into a second layer, resembling a pompadour. No wonder it is one of only two breads recognized with a Denominazione di Origine Protetta for its unique qualities.

It is not surprising that the golden bread of Altamura is famous all over Italy. Both the semolina grain, which is grown nearby and milled to the silky fineness of durum, and the water, rich in minerals and salts, are critical to its flavor. It may be the reason that the city is a national source of millers and has an exceptional number of bakeries, some more than a century old. Some years ago McDonald's came to Altamura and tried to woo the local populace, but when they ate the bread being served, they turned away. Ultimately the Golden Arches were defeated by the golden loaves of Altamura, and McDonald's was forced to close.

Do not try to make this bread with semolina flour, even if the label says "durum" in small print. Semolina is fine for pasta but is too coarsely ground for bread. Durum flour, the golden hard wheat used for making pasta, is hard to find, but it can be bought in some specialty shops. You can also order it on the web from the sources listed starting on page 401.

This bread keeps wonderfully and is splendid toasted. Eat it simply spread with butter, or serve it with fish or vegetable soups or meat with a gravy or sauce. This is made with a durum flour *biga*.

Makes 2 loaves

BIGA

¹/₂ teaspoon (0.5 oz / 14 g) active dry yeast

¹/₄ cup (2 oz / 60 g) warm water

³/₄ cup (6.3 oz / 180 g) water at room temperature

1³/₄ cups (8.8 oz / 250 g) durum flour

To make the *biga*, stir the yeast into the warm water and let stand until creamy, about 10 minutes. Stir in the remaining water and then the flour, 1 cup at a time.

continued

Pane di Altamura, *continued*

BY HAND

Mix with a wooden spoon for 3 to
4 minutes.

BY MIXER

Mix with the paddle at the lowest speed
for 2 minutes.

BY PROCESSOR

Mix just until a sticky dough is formed.

Rising. Remove to a lightly oiled bowl,
cover with plastic wrap, and let rise at a
cool room temperature for 6 to 24 hours.
The starter will triple in volume and still
be wet and sticky when ready. Cover and
refrigerate until ready to use.

DOUGH

1/2 teaspoon (0.05 oz /1.4 g) active dry yeast

1/4 cup (2 oz / 60 g) warm water

1 1/2 cups plus 2 teaspoons (13 oz / 370 g) water, at
    room temperature (cold if using a processor)

3 3/4 cups (17.5 oz / 500 g) durum flour, plus more
    for kneading

1 tablespoon (0.5 oz / 15 g) salt

BY HAND

Stir the yeast into the warm water; let
stand until creamy, about 10 minutes.
Measure out 7 ounces (200 g, or about an
ample 3/4 cup) of the *biga.* Mix the dissolved yeast, the remaining water, and the
biga in a large mixing bowl, squeezing the
biga between your fingers to break it up
and stirring vigorously with a wooden

spoon. Mix the durum flour and salt and
stir into the yeast mixture 2 cups at a time;
plunge in with your hands and mix vigorously until smooth. Knead on a surface
sprinkled with flour until the dough is
smooth, elastic, and slightly moist, about
10 minutes. Slam the dough on the surface
while kneading to develop the gluten.

BY MIXER

Stir the yeast into 2 cups of warm water in
a large mixer bowl; let stand until creamy,
about 10 minutes. Add the remaining
water and the *biga* and mix with the paddle
until the *biga* is broken up and the liquid is
chalky white. Add the flour and mix until
the dough pulls away from the sides of the
bowl, about 2 minutes. Don't add extra
water, although you will be tempted, for
this flour absorbs moisture slowly. If, after
mixing for about 2 minutes, it still seems
dry, mix in more water, 1 teaspoon at a
time, until the dough feels compact and
elastic. Change to the dough hook and
knead 2 minutes on low, then 8 to 10 minutes on medium speed. The dough should
be smooth, elastic, firm, and velvety. Knead
lightly by hand on a floured surface.

BY PROCESSOR

If the capacity of your food processor is
7 cups or less, process this dough in two
batches. Refrigerate the *biga* until cold. Stir
the yeast into the warm water; let stand
until creamy, about 10 minutes. Process
1 3/4 cups of cold water and the *biga* with

the steel blade to mix. Move the starter mixture to another bowl. Change to the dough blade and process the flour and salt with two or three pulses to sift. With the machine running, pour the dissolved yeast and *biga* mixture through the feed tube as fast as the flour can absorb it and process until the dough comes together. Process 45 seconds longer to knead. Finish kneading on a surface floured with durum flour. The dough should be elastic, slightly moist, and velvety.

First Rise. Place the dough in a lightly oiled container, cover with plastic wrap, and let rise until tripled, about 3 hours.

Shaping and Second Rise. Turn out the dough on a work surface lightly floured with durum flour and cut the dough in half. There are two ways to shape this bread. In either case, shape each piece first into a round, then to an oval that is higher and plumper in the center and slightly tapered at the ends. For the simpler shape make a deep slash down the middle of each loaf with a razor, and let rise, covered with a towel and cut side down, on a board or peel well-floured with durum or semolina flour until doubled with obvious big air bubbles, 45 minutes to 1 hour. Wait to form the other shape until just before baking.

Final Shaping and Baking. Thirty to forty-five minutes before baking, preheat the oven to 425°F with a cast-iron frying pan inside on the bottom shelf and a baking stone on the shelf above it. Turn the slashed dough over and slash again if it has closed during the rise. For the second

shape, flatten the oval into a rectangle, take the short end of the dough, and fold it two-thirds of the way up, as if you were folding a business letter. Use your fingers to press the seam down firmly. Then take the far edge of the dough and fold it up two-thirds of the way down toward you, making the traditional pompadour shape. Pat firmly around the end of the loaf so that it doesn't become unsealed. Sprinkle the stone with cornmeal and gently slide the loaves, cut or shaped side up, onto the stone. Just before you close the oven door, put $^1/_2$ cup of ice into the cast-iron frying pan, and the steam will continue to mist the interior for 5 to 10 minutes. By the time the crust has set, the water will have evaporated and the rest of the baking will take place in a hot, dry oven. Bake 50 to 55 minutes until deep golden brown. Cool on a rack.

Pane Pugliese BREAD OF PUGLIA

These big, crusty wheels of country bread originated from much darker loaves, a legacy of Turkish conquerors who baked their chewy porous bread in wood-burning stoves. In Italy today they still bow to tradition by making these loaves with less refined flours. To me they are the best of all possible rustic breads, perfect for picnics and informal eating. Baked in huge 1- or 2-kilo rounds, they are held against the chest and sliced toward the body with a sharp knife. The sizable hunks are dropped into soups or flavored with oil, salt, strong ricotta, and tomatoes. Because this is the bread of the poor, it is served with the typical food of the region: greens, fish from the sea, cheese, and fruit. More prosperous Italians eat it with stews and meat with strong-flavored sauces and gravies, steaks, and even carpaccio. Reverence for this bread still persists, as does the Pugliese legend that one who wasted even crumbs of this loaf would be condemned to purgatory for as many years as there were crumbs. One embellishment insists that the sinner would spend the time collecting the crumbs with his eyelids.

This bread is best made in the mixer, for the wet dough takes incredible skill and an extraordinary amount of flour when done by hand. Once you've made it—and please don't be daunted by the advice about the oozing dough; it is just meant to guide you realistically through the process—you'll find it isn't that difficult if you keep enough flour at hand. Begin by dipping your hands in a bowl of water so that the dough won't stick to them as much.

Makes 2 large round flat loaves or 3 smaller round loaves

1¹/₄ teaspoons (0.1 oz / 3.5 g) active dry yeast

¹/₄ cup (2 oz / 60 g) warm water

3 cups (25 oz / 720 g) water, at room temperature

³/₄ cup plus 1 tablespoons (7 oz / 200 g) biga (page 70)

7 cups plus 2 tablespoons (2 lb 3 oz / 1 kg) unbleached all-purpose flour

4 teaspoons (0.7 oz / 20 g) salt

BY MIXER ONLY

Stir the yeast into the warm water in a large mixer bowl; let stand until creamy, about 10 minutes. Add the 3 cups of water and the *biga* and mix with the paddle until well blended. Add the flour and salt and mix until the dough comes together and pulls away from the sides of the bowl, 1 to 2 minutes. The dough will be very soft and elastic but will never pull entirely away from the bottom of the bowl. If you want, finish kneading by hand on a floured surface with floured hands until the dough loses its stickiness and is soft and velvety, about 1 minute.

First Rise. Place the dough in a lightly oiled large bowl or plastic tub, cover tightly with plastic wrap, and let rise until tripled, about 3 hours. Do not punch down.

Shaping and Second Rise. Flour your work surface generously, flour a dough scraper, and have a mound of flour nearby for your hands. Pour the dough out of the bowl, flour the top, and cut into two or three equal pieces, depending on how many loaves you are planning. Flatten each piece of dough and roll it up lengthwise, using your thumbs as a guide for how tight the rolls should be. Turn the dough 90 degrees, pat it flat, then roll up again, still using your thumbs as a guide. Shape each piece into a ball by rolling the dough between your cupped hands and using the surface of the work table to generate tension and pull the dough taut across the skin of the dough. Place the loaves on floured parchment paper set on baking sheets or peels, cover with a heavy towel or cloth, and let rise until doubled, about 1 hour.

Baking. Thirty minutes before baking, preheat the oven with baking stones to about 450°F. Then, 5 to 10 minutes before baking, flour the tops of the loaves and dimple them all over with your fingertips. The imprints will disappear but will keep the bread from rising crazily in the oven. Let stand 5 to 10 minutes. The loaves will feel as soft as a baby's bottom when ready to bake, although you will notice a bit of resistance in the dough. Sprinkle the stones with cornmeal. Italian bakers turn the doughs over into the oven very carefully with a swooping motion that scoops

up some of the flour on the peel. You may prefer to slide the loaves onto the baking stones without turning them over, or, if they are on baking sheets, the loaves can be baked directly on the pans. Bake until golden brown and crusty, about 50 to 60 minutes for the larger loaves, 30 to 35 minutes for the smaller ones. Check by knocking on the bottom of each loaf and listening for the hollow ring that indicates it is cooked through; but if you're in doubt, bake for the longer time indicated. Cool on racks.

Variation. To make *puccia*, the traditional olive-studded bread of Puglia, knead a scant 8 ounces (220 g) of pitted small salty black olives into the dough after it has been mixed. Let the dough rise until tripled. Divide into pieces the size of a lemon (each 7 ounces or 200 grams) and roll each piece into a ball. Let rise again, covered, until doubled and bake at 425°F for 20 to 30 minutes.

Pane Siciliano SICILIAN BREAD

One of my favorite memories of Sicily is of the hill town of Erice, which is perched so far above the sea that the weather changes three times on the way up. We first found it on a fog-shrouded night when the only person visible was an ancient hunter carrying an even more ancient blunderbuss. Next morning the sun came out and people appeared in the shops and *piazze*. At breakfast we had the most wonderful golden semolina bread sprinkled with sesame seeds. We ventured out to the bakery, where we found that the bread came in an extravagant variety of forms. *Mafalda*, the most common, looks like a snake curled back and forth over itself with a baton laid across it; made without the baton, it's called a *scaletta*, or little ladder. *Occhi*, the shape that looks like a slightly askew pair of eyeglasses, is actually an homage to Santa Lucia, the patron saint of vision.

All the loaves have a golden crust with crunchy sesame seeds, which give a faint peanutlike taste to the bread. The Sicilians make it with a semolina flour milled especially for the bread, but because our semolina is coarser than theirs, I use durum flour, and you should do the same. Don't be tempted to use the coarse semolina, for it simply won't make bread. This bread is especially good with sausages, salami, oysters, and mussels.

Makes 2 loaves

2¼ teaspoons (1 package / 0.2 oz / 7 g) active
   dry yeast

¼ cup (2 oz / 60 g) warm water

1 tablespoon (0.5 oz / 15 g) olive oil

1 teaspoon (0.2 oz / 7 g) malt syrup or powder

1 cup (8.4 oz / 240 g) water, at room temperature
   (cold if using a processor)

About 2½ cups (12.3 oz / 350 g) durum flour

1 cup plus 1 tablespoon (5.3 oz / 150 g) unbleached
   all-purpose flour

2 to 3 teaspoons (0.3 oz to 0.5 oz / 10 to 15 g) salt

⅓ cup (1.4 oz / 40 g) sesame seeds

BY HAND

Dissolve the yeast in the warm water in a large mixing bowl; let stand until creamy, about 10 minutes. Whisk in the 1 cup of water, then the oil and malt syrup, if you are using it. Mix the flours and salt and malt powder, if you are using it, and whisk 1 cup at a time into the yeast mixture. Beat vigorously with a wooden spoon until smooth. Knead on a floured surface 8 to 10 minutes, occasionally slamming the dough down vigorously to develop the gluten.

BY MIXER

Stir the yeast into the warm water in a
large mixer bowl; let stand until creamy,
about 10 minutes. Mix in the 1 cup of
water, then stir in the oil and malt syrup, if
you are using it, with the paddle, then add
the flours and salt and malt powder, if you
are using it, and mix until smooth. Change
to the dough hook and knead on medium
speed until the dough is firm, compact,
and elastic, with lots of body, 4 to 5 minutes. Finish kneading by hand on a lightly
floured surface.

BY PROCESSOR

Stir the yeast and malt syrup, if you are
using it, into the warm water; let stand
until foamy, about 10 minutes. Place the
flours and salt and malt powder, if you are
using it, in a food processor fitted with
the steel blade; process with two or three
pulses to sift. Mix the 1 cup of cold water
and the oil. With the machine running,
pour the yeast and water mixtures and
malt syrup, if you are using it, through
the feed tube as quickly as possible and
process until the dough comes together.
Process 45 seconds longer to knead. Finish kneading briefly by hand on a lightly
floured surface.

First Rise. Place the dough in a lightly oiled
bowl, cover tightly with plastic wrap, and
let rise until doubled, about 1 1/2 hours.
The dough should be springy and blistered
but still soft and velvety.

Shaping and Second Rise. Punch the
dough down, knead it briefly, and let it rest
for 5 minutes. Flatten it with your forearm into a square. Roll it into a long, fairly
narrow rope, about 20 to 22 inches long.
The dough should be so elastic that it could
almost be stretched and swung like a jump
rope. Cut the dough in half and shape each
half into a loaf, choosing among the shapes
called *occhi*, *mafalda*, and *corona* (illustrated on
the next page).

Place the loaves on floured parchment paper, peels sprinkled with cornmeal,
or oiled baking sheets. Brush the entire
surface of each loaf lightly with water and
sprinkle with sesame seeds; pat the seeds
very gently into the dough. Cover with
plastic wrap and then a kitchen towel, and
let rise until doubled, 1 to 1 1/2 hours.

Baking. Thirty minutes before baking,
preheat the oven with baking stones to
425°F. Sprinkle the stones with cornmeal
just before sliding the loaves onto them.
Bake 10 minutes, spraying the oven three
times with cold water. Reduce the heat to
400°F and bake 25 to 30 minutes longer.
Cool on racks.

continued

Pane Siciliano, *continued*

THE EYE OR OCCHI:

Roll the dough into a 1¹/₂-inch-thick rope, then coil it into a figure that looks like an inverted "S."

Continue the coiling from each end until the ends meet.

The baked *occhi*.

THE CLASSIC MAFALDA:

Curl the rope back and forth on itself; leave a 5-inch tail for the baton.

Lay the baton over the top without stretching. Do not tuck it under or the loaf will not rise.

The baked *mafalda*.

THE CROWN OR CORONA:

Flatten the dough into a rectangle and score two times at equal intervals.

Pull apart slightly.

The baked *corona*.

Tastes of the Countryside

Pan Bigio RUSTIC WHEAT AND WHOLE WHEAT BREAD

When I hear bakers reminisce about rustic country bread before the flour became weak and overly refined and the water was treated with chemicals, this is the bread I think of. Big-holed and chewy, with a porous interior and a good firm crust, *pan bigio* is the classic bread of peasants. It is wonderful with everything from a green salad to soft fresh cheeses, from a handful of good salty olives to fresh tomatoes drizzled with olive oil and sprinkled with herbs. The brownish color comes from the whole wheat, and its earthy smell and taste are a result of the long, slow maturing of the dough. This wet dough is better left to the mixer, but is not impossible to make by hand.

Makes 2 large or 3 smaller round loaves

1¼ teaspoons (0.1 oz / 3.5 g) active dry yeast

¼ cup (2 oz / 60 g) warm water

2½ cups (21 oz / 600 g) water, at room temperature

1 full cup (8.8 oz / 250 g) biga (page 70)

2 cups (8.8 oz / 250 g) whole wheat flour, preferably stone-ground

3¾ cups (17.5 oz / 500 g) unbleached all-purpose flour

1 tablespoon (0.5 oz / 15 g) salt, plus 1 teaspoon (0.2 oz / 5 g) more (optional)

continued

Pan Bigio, *continued*

BY HAND

Stir the yeast into the warm water in a large mixing bowl; let stand until creamy, about 10 minutes. Add the 2^1/$_2$ cups of water and the *biga*; squeeze the *biga* between your fingers to break it up and stir vigorously. Mix the flours and salt and stir 2 cups at a time into the yeast mixture; beat with a wooden spoon for 4 to 5 minutes. Flour your work surface generously, flour a dough scraper, and have a mound of flour nearby for your hands. Turn the dough out onto the floured surface and, with the help of the dough scraper and extra flour, turn and knead the dough until it gradually loses its stickiness, although it will remain wet.

First Rise. Place the dough in a lightly oiled large bowl, cover tightly with plastic wrap, and let rise until tripled and full of air bubbles, about 3 hours. Do not punch down.

Shaping and Second Rise. Turn the dough out onto a well-floured surface and shape into two big, flat rounds or three smaller ones, pulling tight on the surface of the dough with your cupped hands to make a taut loaf (see page 106). Place the loaves, rough side up, on well-floured baking sheets, peels, or parchment paper set on baking sheets. Cover with a towel and let rise until there are lots of air bubbles under the surface, about 1 hour.

Baking. Thirty minutes before baking, preheat the oven with baking stones in it to 450°F. You can also use a cast-iron or aluminum griddle that is at least ^{3}/$_8$ inch thick, or preheated heavy baking sheets. Dimple the tops of the loaves all over with your fingertips or knuckles and let rest for 10 to 15 minutes. Just before baking, sprinkle the stones or griddle with cornmeal. Gently invert the loaves onto the stones. The bread will look deflated when you initially put it in, but it will puff up like a big pillow in no time. Bake 45 to 55 minutes. Cool on racks.

BY MIXER

Stir the yeast into the warm water in a mixer bowl; let stand until creamy, about 10 minutes. Add the 2^1/$_2$ cups of water and the *biga* and mix with the paddle until the water is chalky white and the *biga* is fairly well broken up. Add the flours and salt and mix until the dough comes together. You may need to add up to 2 tablespoons (1 oz / 15 g) more flour, but the dough will never pull away cleanly from the sides and bottom of the bowl. Change to the dough hook and knead a full 5 minutes at medium speed. Finish kneading the sticky, wet dough by hand on a well-floured surface, sprinkling the top with about 3 to 4 tablespoons more of flour.

Pan Bigio, *continued*

Shape each piece of dough into a ball by rolling between your cupped hands. Use the surface of the work table to generate tension and pull the dough taut.

Pan Giallo o Pan di Mais CORN BREAD FROM LOMBARDY

This Italian corn bread is not at all like the crumbly, rich bread of the American South, which is sweetened with sugar, enriched with butter, and leavened with baking powder. The Italian bread is dense and firm and is traditionally eaten with soups or rich broths after it has dried out for three or four days. Long ago, it was made in huge wheels of 1¹/₂ or 2 kilos, but now, even in Lombardy, where it is still popular, the dough is baked in much smaller loaves. Corn grows in the northern regions of Italy— the Veneto, Piedmont, and Lombardy—and the corn breads made here are quite heavy and rich with the taste of the corn. For a slightly less dense bread, the Italians use half cornmeal and half flour. This bread is often cut in big slices and dipped in beef broth with lots of Parmesan cheese or spread with Gorgonzola, warmed in the oven, and served with an aperitif.

Makes 2 round loaves

4¹/₂ teaspoons (2 packages / 0.5 oz / 14 g) active
   dry yeast

2 cups minus 2 tablespoons (15.8 oz / 450 g) warm
   water (or 6 tablespoons / 3 oz / 75 g warm water
   plus 1¹/₂ cups / 12.6 oz / 360 g cold water if using
   a processor)

¹/₂ cup (3.8 oz / 110 g) olive oil

3³/₄ cups (21 oz / 600 g) cornmeal, preferably
   stone-ground and not degerminated

Scant 3 cups (14 oz / 400 g) unbleached
   all-purpose flour

1 tablespoon (0.5 oz / 15 g) salt

BY HAND

This bread is just not worth the effort of making by hand, although it can be done if you have enormous patience. You must keep breaking the dough into little pieces, adding flour, then letting it rest, because it exudes water as it relaxes. Because it can take as long as 30 minutes, I strongly recommend the stand mixer.

BY MIXER

Stir the yeast into the water in a large mixer bowl; let stand until creamy, about 10 minutes. Stir in the oil, then mix in the cornmeal, flour, and salt with the paddle until the dough comes together. Change to the dough hook and knead for 3 to 4 minutes, stopping the machine several times to push down the dough that has climbed up the collar. Finish kneading the slightly sticky dough briefly by hand on a lightly floured work surface.

BY PROCESSOR

Process this dough in two batches. Stir the yeast into the ¹/₄ cup of warm water in a small bowl; let stand until creamy, about 10 minutes. Place the cornmeal, flour, and salt in a food processor fitted with the dough blade and process with several pulses to sift. Mix the oil and the cold water. With the machine running,

continued

Pan Giallo o Pan di Mais, *continued*

pour the dissolved yeast and the cold water mixture through the feed tube as fast as possible. Process 45 seconds to knead. Finish kneading by hand on a lightly floured surface. The dough should be soft but not wet; it will stick to your hands a bit.

First Rise. Place the dough in a lightly oiled bowl, cover tightly with plastic wrap, and let rise until doubled, about 1 hour.

Shaping and Second Rise. Cut the dough in half on a floured surface and shape each piece into a round loaf. Place in buttered 4-cup charlotte molds or soufflé dishes,

sprinkle the tops lightly with flour, cover with a towel, and let rise about 45 minutes. It must not double in volume or it will collapse in the oven.

Baking. Preheat the oven to 400°F. Just before baking, cut a pattern, either a tic-tac-toe or three parallel lines, on top of the loaves. Bake 30 minutes. (It will be slightly underdone but corn dries out as it cools.) You may bake the loaves out of the molds on a baking sheet or stone for the last 5 to 10 minutes to brown the bottoms and sides. Cool on racks.

Pane Nero RYE BREAD FROM BOLZANO

You can taste a strong German influence in the dark rye of Bolzano, just as the city, close against the high Alps near the border of the country, is still at least as Central European as it is Italian. Street signs and shop names are in both German and Italian, and the alpine look of the architecture is a continual reminder that the city was part of the South Tirol of Austria before World War I. Rye thrives in these cold northern regions where wheat cannot grow. This bread is traditionally flavored with caraway seed and put to rise in bannetons.

Rye breads are always made with some wheat flour so that they will rise nicely, for there isn't much gluten in rye flour to hold the bubbles of fermenting gases. Because rye always makes sticky doughs, be prepared with your dough scraper at hand. The traditional holes poked in the top of the dough let the loaf expand without cracking, as well as give it an interesting and characteristic look.

Italians serve rye breads with butter, fresh cheeses, game, mushrooms, caviar, smoked salmon, and oysters and other mollusks.

Makes 2 oval loaves

SPONGE

4¼ teaspoons (0.4 oz / 12 g) active dry yeast

1½ cups (12.6 oz / 360 g) warm water

2 cups plus 1 tablespoon (8.8 oz / 250 g) rye flour

Stir the yeast into the water in a large mixing bowl; let stand until creamy, about 10 minutes. Stir in the flour until blended. Cover with plastic wrap and let rise at room temperature at least 3 hours or overnight. The longer it is left, the stronger its taste will be.

DOUGH

1 cup (8.4 oz / 240 g) water, at room temperature (cold if using a processor)

1 tablespoon (0.7 oz / 21 g) malt syrup or powder

2 cups plus 1 tablespoon (8.8 oz / 250 g) rye flour

3¾ cups (17.5 oz / 500 g) unbleached all-purpose flour

1 tablespoon (0.5 oz / 15 g) salt

2½ teaspoons (0.2 oz / 6 g) caraway seeds or 1½ teaspoons (0.1 oz / 3 g) fennel seeds, crushed

BY HAND

Add the water and malt to the sponge and stir thoroughly. Stir in 1 cup of the rye and then the all-purpose flour, 1 cup at a time, until the dough is too stiff to stir. Using your hands, mix in the remaining all-purpose flour, then the remaining rye, the salt, and the caraway or fennel seeds. When the dough is no longer impossibly sticky, turn it out onto a well-floured surface and knead for 8 to 10 minutes.

The dough will be dense and sticky at first, but, as kneading proceeds, it will become more workable. Use the dough scraper and sprinkle with additional all-purpose flour as needed. When you are almost finished, slam the dough down hard four or five times while you are working it to help develop the gluten.

BY MIXER

Add the water and malt to the sponge in a large mixer bowl and mix well with the paddle. Add the flours, salt, and caraway or fennel seeds and mix until the dough pulls away from the sides of the bowl. Change to the dough hook and knead 3 to 4 minutes at low speed, then 2 minutes at medium speed. Finish kneading briefly by hand on a floured surface.

BY PROCESSOR

Process this dough in two batches. Refrigerate the sponge until cold. Place the flours, salt, and caraway or fennel seeds in a food processor fitted with the dough blade; process with several pulses to sift. Mix the cold starter, the 1 cup cold water, and the malt. With the machine running, quickly pour the mixture through the feed tube. If the dough seems too dry, add up to 2 tablespoons of cold water to each batch to get a workable dough. Process 45 seconds longer to knead. Finish kneading briefly by hand on a floured surface.

continued

Pane Nero, *continued*

First Rise. Place the dough in a lightly oiled bowl, cover tightly with plastic wrap, and let rise until doubled, about 1^1/$_2$ to 2^1/$_2$ hours. It will soften considerably and feel a bit like taffy.

Shaping and Second Rise. Cut the dough in half on a floured surface. Shape each half into a long oval loaf that is plump in the center and tapered at the ends. Place the loaves on lightly oiled baking sheets or peels sprinkled with cornmeal and let rise, covered, until doubled, about 1^1/$_4$ to 1^1/$_2$ hours.

Baking. Preheat the oven to 425°F. If you are using a baking stone, turn the oven on 30 minutes before baking and sprinkle the stone with cornmeal just before sliding the loaves onto it. Just before baking, poke 4 holes down the center of each loaf with the end of an instant-read thermometer or a chopstick. Bake 45 minutes. Cool on racks.

Other Shapes. Shape pieces of the dough, each the size of a lemon, into rolls. Bake 20 minutes.

L'Otto di Merano RYE BREAD FROM MERANO

This moist and slightly tangy rye gets its name from its shape: two balls of bread connected at the center look like a figure eight. Eat it with smoked meats, game, smoked salmon, caviar, fresh cheeses, or oysters.

Makes 1 large loaf

SPONGE

2^1/$_4$ teaspoons (1 package / 0.2 oz / 7 g) active dry yeast

1 tablespoon (0.7 oz / 21 g) malt syrup or powder

1^1/$_2$ cups (12.6 oz / 360 g) warm water

Scant 1 cup (3.5 oz / 100 g) stone-ground rye flour

^{3}/$_4$ cup (3.5 oz / 100 g) unbleached all-purpose flour

BY HAND

Stir the yeast and malt syrup, if you are using it, into the water in a large mixing bowl; let stand until foamy, 5 to 10 minutes. Stir in the flours with the malt powder, if you are using it. Cover tightly with plastic wrap and let rise until bubbly, 3 hours, until bubbly.

BY PROCESSOR

Dissolve the yeast and malt syrup, if you are using it, in the water and let stand until foamy, 5 to 10 minutes. Place the flours and the malt powder, if you are using it, in the food processor fitted with the steel blade and process with several pulses to sift. With the machine running, pour the yeast mixture through the feed tube as quickly as the flour can absorb it. Process 10 seconds longer and remove to a bowl. Cover tightly with plastic wrap and let rise for 3 hours.

DOUGH

2 tablespoons (1 oz / 28 g) lard

Scant 3 cups (14 oz / 400 g) unbleached all-purpose flour

2 teaspoons (0.4 oz / 10 g) salt

1¹/₄ teaspoons (0.1 oz / 3 g) caraway seeds

BY HAND

Stir the lard into the sponge. Combine the flour, salt, and caraway seeds and mix 1 cup at a time into the sponge. Stir until the dough comes together. Knead on a lightly floured surface until firm and elastic, 8 to 10 minutes.

BY MIXER

Add the lard to the sponge in a mixer bowl; mix with the paddle until blended. Add the flour, salt, and caraway seeds; mix until the dough comes together. Change to the dough hook and knead until firm and elastic, 3 to 4 minutes. If you want, finish kneading briefly by hand on a floured surface.

BY PROCESSOR (LARGER MACHINES ONLY)

Refrigerate the sponge until cold. Place the flour, salt, and caraway seeds in a food processor fitted with the dough blade. Place the lard in small bits on top of the dry ingredients. With the machine running, quickly pour the sponge through the feed tube and process until the dough gathers into a ball. Process 40 seconds longer to knead. Finish kneading by hand on a floured surface.

First Rise. Place the dough in a lightly oiled bowl, cover tightly with plastic wrap, and let rise until doubled, about 2 hours.

Shaping and Second Rise. Cut the dough in half on a floured surface and shape each piece into a round loaf. On a lightly oiled baking sheet or on floured parchment paper placed on cardboard or a peel, place the loaves next to each other so that they look like a figure eight. Cover with a towel and let rise until doubled, about 1 hour.

Baking. Preheat the oven to 400°F. If you are using a baking stone, turn on the oven 30 minutes before baking. Slide the parchment paper with the loaf onto the stone and remove the paper after the dough has set. Bake until the loaf sounds hollow when tapped, about 40 minutes. Cool on a rack.

Ciambelline Valtelline LITTLE RYE ROUNDS FROM VALTELLINA

High in the province of Sondrio in the further reaches of Lombardy lies the Valtellina, a valley that is usually covered with snow in the long months of winter. There people still make the rustic and charmingly uneven rings of rye bread that look like big, flat doughnuts. They were once all baked in communal wood-burning ovens and scored with marks that were so individual that each family could find its own baked rings. Today the necessity to bake bread at the beginning of winter that will last the entire season is not so great, but these little rye rounds are still made in every part of the area. Preserved in the cool, dry winter climate for months, the *ciambelline* are hung on long strings in the houses. When the need arises, they are snatched down, cracked on the table, and eaten like hardtack or dipped in soup to soften them. Long before the rounds become so hard, they are crisp and crunchy and are eaten as a snack with salami, sausages, aged cheeses, and wine from local cellars. Somewhat larger rings of rye are known as *brazadei,* and they are served at the table slipped onto the right arm while the left pours the local wine.

Makes 10 to 12 rings

SPONGE

2¼ teaspoons (1 package / 0.2 oz / 7 g) active
  dry yeast

2 cups (16.8 oz / 480 g) warm water

2¼ cups (10.7 oz / 300 g) dark rye flour or
  1¾ cup (8 oz / 225 g) dark rye flour and
  ½ cup plus 2 tablespoons (2.6 oz / 75 g)
  buckwheat flour

Stir the yeast into the water in a mixing bowl; let stand until creamy, about 10 minutes. Stir in the rye flour with a wooden spoon or the paddle of an electric mixer (it will be a very sticky mass). Cover tightly with plastic wrap and let rise about 2 hours.

DOUGH

3¾ teaspoons (0.4 oz / 10.6 g) active dry yeast

1½ cups (12 oz / 360 g) warm water

3¾ cups (17.5 oz / 500 g) bread flour

1½ cups (7 oz / 200 g) dark rye flour

⅓ cup (0.6 oz / 16 g) wheat bran

1 tablespoon (0.5 oz / 15 g) salt

BY HAND

Stir the yeast into the water in a large mixing bowl; let stand until creamy, about 10 minutes. Stir in the sponge, then the flours, 2 cups at a time, the bran, and the salt. Continue stirring until the dough is soft and light. Flour your work surface generously, flour a dough scraper, and have a mound of flour nearby for your hands.

Turn the very sticky dough out onto the floured surface and knead until the dough is the color of gingerbread and sticky inside but velvety against your palm on the outside.

BY MIXER

Stir the yeast into the warm water in a small bowl; let stand until creamy, about 10 minutes. Add the dissolved yeast to the sponge in a mixer bowl and mix with the paddle. Add the flours, bran, and salt and mix until the dough is soft and light. Change to the dough hook and knead until the dough is velvety to the touch but still sticky inside, about 5 minutes.

First Rise. Place the dough in a lightly oiled bowl, cover tightly with plastic wrap, and let rise until puffy, about 45 minutes.

Shaping and Second Rise. Divide the dough on a lightly floured surface into ten to twelve equal pieces. Roll each piece into a 12- to 14-inch rope and join the ends to make a circle. Flatten the tops of the dough circles with little karate chops delivered with the side of your hand. Place the dough circles on parchment paper set on baking sheets or on lightly oiled baking sheets (the rising will take longer). To capture the heat generated by the fermentation, prop up plastic wrap above the dough with juice glasses or spice jars and cover with a towel. You can preheat the oven to 150°F for 2 to 3 minutes, turn it off, and place the *ciambelline* inside to rise. The rings should rise to $1/2$ to $3/4$ inch in height and 10 inches in diameter.

Baking. Preheat the oven to 425°F. If you are using baking stones, turn the oven on 30 minutes before baking and sprinkle the stones with cornmeal just before sliding the rings on them. The rings can be baked on the parchment paper until set, and then the paper can be slipped out. Place the rings in the oven and reduce the heat to 375°F. Bake 15 to 20 minutes, spraying the oven with water three times in the first 10 minutes. Cool on racks.

Pane alle Olive OLIVE BREAD

Along the coast of the Italian Riviera near Genoa, the hillsides are covered with end-less ranks of silvery green olive trees interrupted only by tile-roofed pink villas, sharp outlines of palm trees, and flashes of brilliant geraniums. The strong sun and warm earth of the region produce the exceptional olives that find their way into the bread. In the past sailors took the bread to sea because the rich olive oil kept it fresh and the tiny pungent black and sweeter green olives gave it its flavor.

There are two ways to make this bread: mix Sicilian-style green olives, which are easy to pit, into the dough so that their moisture becomes part of the dough; or knead in half tiny black Ligurian olives and half green olives by hand. Serve with carpaccio, green salads, antipasti, and lamb. This bread makes wonderful sandwiches.

Makes 2 oval loaves or round rings

3¹/₂ teaspoons (0.4 oz / 10 g) active dry yeast

³/₄ cup (6 oz / 180 g) warm water (or ¹/₄ cup / 2 oz / 60 g warm water plus ¹/₂ cup / 4 oz / 120 g cold water, if using a processor)

3³/₄ cups (17.5 oz / 500 g) unbleached all-purpose flour

¹/₄ cup (1.9 oz / 55 g) olive oil

2 cups (12 oz / 340 g) Sicilian-style green olives; or 1¹/₄ cups (6 oz / 170 g) tiny black Ligurian olives, such as Ardoino or Crespi Olivelle plus 1¹/₃ cups (6 oz / 170 g) green olives, both types pitted and several whole olives reserved for garnish

1¹/₂ teaspoons (0.3 oz / 7.5 g) salt

This bread is difficult—if not impossible—to make by hand because the olives must be broken down enough to provide some of the liquid for the dough. The mixer and the food processor do the job nicely.

BY MIXER

Stir the yeast into the water in a large mixer bowl; let stand until creamy, about 10 minutes. Set aside ¹/₃ cup of the flour to add while kneading. Add the oil, pit-ted olives, the remaining flour, and the salt. Mix with the paddle for 2 minutes on low speed, then change to the dough hook and mix until the olives are well broken down, 4 to 5 minutes. The olives will exude their liquid, which will give the dough enough moisture. If necessary, add up to 1¹/₂ tablespoons of additional water. Finish kneading briefly by hand on a lightly floured surface, adding the reserved flour as needed, until the dough is firm. The dough will feel soft but never smooth.

continued

Pane alle Olive, *continued*

BY PROCESSOR

Stir the yeast into the $^1/_4$ cup of warm water; let stand until creamy, about 10 minutes. Stir the oil and the $^1/_2$ cup of cold water into the yeast mixture. Place the flour and salt in a food processor fitted with the steel blade; process with several pulses to sift. With the machine running, pour the yeast mixture through the feed tube in a steady stream. The flour will be moistened but will not yet make a dough. Sprinkle the olives over the top and process until the dough gathers into a ball and pulls away from the sides of the bowl. Process 30 seconds longer to knead. Knead briefly by hand on a floured work surface.

First Rise. Place the dough in an oiled bowl, cover with plastic wrap, and let rise until doubled, $1^1/_2$ to 2 hours.

Shaping and Second Rise. Cut the dough in half for 2 oval loaves or into sixteen to eighteen equal pieces for the rings. To make the oval loaves, flatten each half of the dough and fold into thirds, like a busi-

Set the balls in a circle 1$^1/_2$ inches apart. Press the olives very firmly into the tops.

ness letter. Roll the dough toward yourself, using your thumbs to guide the dough and create tension in the rolling process. Roll with both hands to a cigar shape that is plumper in the middle and tapered at the ends. Place the loaves on oiled baking sheets or peels sprinkled with cornmeal. To make the rings, roll each piece of the dough into a ball and arrange 1¹/₂ inches apart in two rings on oiled baking sheets or in two oiled ring molds. Press the reserved olives very firmly into the tops.

Cover with a towel and let rise in a warm spot for about 1 hour. The dough should relax and the skin should not be tight when it goes into the oven.

Baking. Preheat the oven to 450°F. If you are using a baking stone, turn the oven on 30 minutes before baking and sprinkle the stone with cornmeal just before sliding the loaves onto it. Place the loaves in the oven and reduce the heat to 400°F. Bake 35 to 40 minutes. Cool on racks.

Pane di Chiavari BREAD OF CHIAVARI

The unusual dark color of this bread comes from the shiny black olives of the Ligurian Riviera, where Chiavari is located. The olives have been ground into a paste, seasoned with herbs and salt, and left for six months to develop their full flavor. A mound of this paste in the dough creates a subtle, distinctive bread that is marbled with purplish black highlights and speckles. The bread keeps very well and seems to improve with age. It is especially good with lamb, chicken dishes, and fresh cheeses.

Makes 1 loaf

2¹/₄ teaspoons (1 package / 0.2 oz / 7 g) active dry yeast

1 cup plus 3 tablespoons (10 oz / 285 g) warm water (or ¹/₄ cup / 2 oz / 60 g warm water plus ³/₄ cup plus 3 tablespoons / 7.9 oz / 225 g cold water if using a processor)

6 tablespoons (3.5 oz / 100 g) olive paste

3³/₄ cups (17.5 oz / 500 g) unbleached all-purpose flour

1 teaspoon (0.2 oz / 5 g) salt

10 to 12 black olives, for garnish

1 large egg white, beaten, for glazing

Cornmeal

BY HAND

Stir the yeast into ¹/₄ cup of the water in a large mixing bowl; let stand until creamy, about 10 minutes. Stir in the remaining water and the olive paste. Mix the flour and salt and stir into the yeast mixture in two additions. Knead on a lightly floured surface, sprinkling with 2 to 4 tablespoons

continued

Pane di Chiavari, *continued*

of additional flour as needed, until shiny, elastic, and velvety, 5 to 7 minutes.

BY MIXER

Stir the yeast into the water in a large mixer bowl; let stand until creamy, about 10 minutes. Stir in the olive paste with the paddle. Combine the flour and salt and mix into the yeast mixture until well blended. Change to the dough hook and knead until shiny, elastic, and velvety, about 2 minutes. If you want, finish kneading by hand on a lightly floured surface.

BY PROCESSOR

Stir the yeast into the $^1/_4$ cup of warm water in a bowl; let stand until creamy, about 10 minutes. Stir in the olive paste and the $^3/_4$ cup plus 3 tablespoons of cold water. Place the flour and salt in a food processor fitted with the dough blade and process with several pulses to sift. With the machine running, pour the yeast mixture through the feed tube as quickly as the flour can absorb it. Process 45 seconds longer to knead. Finish kneading briefly by hand on a lightly floured surface.

First Rise. Place the dough in a lightly oiled bowl, cover tightly with plastic wrap, and let rise until doubled, about $1^1/_2$ hours.

Shaping and Second Rise. Turn the dough out onto a lightly floured surface, punch it down, and knead briefly. Shape the dough into one of the following: a large round loaf; an oval loaf, with both ends twisted so that it looks a bit like a large olive; a ring made by rolling the dough into a long thin rope and connecting the ends; two wreaths of six or seven rolls each. The ring or wreath can be baked free form or placed in an oiled ring mold. Place the shaped dough on a peel lightly sprinkled with cornmeal or on a lightly oiled baking sheet. Cover loosely with a towel and let rise until doubled, about 45 minutes.

Baking. Preheat the oven to 450°F. If you are using a baking stone, turn the oven on 30 minutes before baking and sprinkle the stone with cornmeal just before sliding the loaf onto it. Just before baking, press the whole olives very firmly into the loaf and brush the top with the egg white. Bake 10 minutes. Reduce the heat to 400°F and bake for 35 minutes more (10 minutes for rolls). Cool on a rack.

Piccia Calabrese CALABRIAN BREAD

I don't think there is a single southern Italian ingredient that hasn't found its way into this bread. To make it you can practically work your way through your pantry, opening jar after jar and chunking bits and pieces into this dough. If you don't have everything, just double an ingredient you do have or leave out an ingredient or two; it doesn't seem to make a big difference. The bread has a beautiful golden crust and an interior fragrant with all the tastes of the south, but it isn't nearly as overwhelming as the list of ingredients would lead you to believe. It tastes particularly good with fresh mozzarella, ricotta, Monterey Jack, or another smooth fresh cheese.

Makes 1 large or 2 smaller loaves

2¼ teaspoons (1 package / 0.2 oz / 7 g) active dry yeast

¼ cup (2 oz / 60 g) warm water

1¼ cups (10.5 oz / 300 g) biga (page 70)

2 tablespoons (.9 oz / 25 g) lard

2 tablespoons (0.5 oz / 15 g) sliced mushrooms

1 tablespoon (0.5 oz / 15 g) olive oil

3 tablespoons (2.6 oz / 75 g) chopped canned tomato with juice

½ large or 1 small anchovy, drained, boned if necessary, and chopped

1 tablespoon (0.4 oz / 10 g) capers, drained and chopped

6 small cocktail onions, chopped

2 tablespoons (1 oz / 28 g) drained and finely chopped artichoke hearts packed in oil

3 gherkin pickles, chopped

2 strips roasted red bell pepper, chopped

1 tablespoon (0.1 oz / 2 g) dried oregano

2 cups plus a scant 2 tablespoons (10.5 oz / 300 g) unbleached all-purpose flour, plus more as needed

1 teaspoon (0.2 oz / 5 g) salt

¾ teaspoon (0.1 oz / 3.5 g) freshly ground pepper

BY HAND

Stir the yeast into the water in a large mixing bowl; let stand until creamy, about 10 minutes. Add the *biga* and mix, squeezing the *biga* through your fingers to break it up. Stir in the lard until well blended. Sauté the mushrooms briefly in the oil and let cool. Stir the mushrooms into the starter mixture along with the tomato, anchovy, capers, onions, artichoke, pickles, bell pepper, and oregano, mixing the ingredients thoroughly. In a separate bowl, stir together the flour, salt, and pepper. Stir into the *biga* mixture 1 cup at a time. When the dough is too stiff for stirring, plunge in with your hands. Using a dough scraper and sprinkling with ½ to ⅔ cup (2.5 to 3.5 oz / 70 to 100 g) of additional flour as needed, knead the dough on a well-floured surface until velvety, moist, and elastic, 8 to 10 minutes.

continued

Piccia Calabrese, *continued*

BY MIXER

Stir the yeast into the water in a large mixer bowl; let stand until creamy, about 10 minutes. Add the *biga* and mix with the paddle until well blended. Add the lard and mix. Sauté the mushrooms briefly in the oil and let cool. Add the mushrooms, tomato, anchovy, capers, onions, artichoke, pickles, bell pepper, and oregano to the starter mixture and mix thoroughly. Add the flour, salt, and pepper, and mix slowly until the dough comes together. Change to the dough hook and knead at medium speed until velvety, moist, and elastic, about 3 minutes. If you want, finish kneading by hand on a floured surface, sprinkling with $^1/_2$ to $^2/_3$ cup (2.5 to 3.5 oz / 70 to 100 g) additional flour as needed.

BY PROCESSOR

Refrigerate the starter until cold. Stir the yeast into the water in a small bowl; let stand until creamy, about 10 minutes. Sauté the mushrooms briefly in the oil and let cool. Coarsely chop the mushrooms, tomato, anchovy, capers, onions, artichoke, pickles, and bell peppers in a food processor fitted with the steel blade. Remove to another bowl. Process the oregano, flour, salt, and pepper with five or six pulses to mix. Place the cold starter and the lard over the dry ingredients. With the machine running, pour the dissolved yeast through the feed tube as quickly as the flour can absorb it. Add the vegetable mixture and process just until combined. Finish kneading by hand on a well-floured surface, sprinkling with $^1/_2$ to $^2/_3$ cup (2.5 to 3.5 oz / 70 to 100 g) additional flour as needed, until elastic, moist, and velvety.

First Rise. Place the dough in an oiled bowl, cover with plastic wrap, and let rise until doubled, 1 to $1^1/_2$ hours.

Shaping and Second Rise. Shape the dough on a floured surface into one large or two smaller round loaves by rolling the dough first into a fairly taut log, then shaping it into a round loaf. The dough will be slightly sticky; sprinkle the dough and the work surface with flour while shaping it. Place each loaf on a peel sprinkled with cornmeal, cover with a slightly dampened towel, and let rise until doubled, about 50 minutes.

Baking. Thirty minutes before baking, preheat the oven with baking stones in it to 425°F. Just before baking, cut an even slash around the shoulder of the loaf or three slashes across the top with a razor. Sprinkle the stones with cornmeal and slide the loaf onto the stones. Bake, spraying the oven three times with water in the first 10 minutes, for 45 minutes. Cool on racks.

Casatiello NEAPOLITAN BREAD FOR EASTER MONDAY

This spicy cheese bread, flecked with chunks of salami and freshly ground pepper, was originally made for Easter in the countryside of Naples, but now it is eaten year-round except during the steamy months of summer. The traditional *casatiello* was a peppery rustic bread, shaped like a large doughnut and with eggs still in the shell held in place on top with two crossed bands of dough. This version can certainly be made with eggs set on the top. The Roman baker who taught me this variation has given it some of the richness of the *pizza di Pasqua* (page 217) that Romans ate for lunch on the Saturday before Easter.

Makes 2 round loaves

SPONGE

4¼ teaspoons (0.4 oz / 12 g) active dry yeast

4 teaspoons (0.7 oz / 20 g) sugar

1¼ cups (10.5 oz / 300 g) warm water

4 large egg yolks

2 cups plus a scant 2 tablespoons (10.5 oz / 300 g) unbleached all-purpose flour

1¼ teaspoon (0.2 oz / 6.5 g) salt

Stir the yeast and 1 teaspoon of the sugar into the water in a mixing bowl; let stand until foamy, about 10 minutes. Add the egg yolks and the remaining sugar and stir until smooth. Stir in half the flour and beat until smooth. Add the remaining flour and salt and stir until a soft dough is formed. Knead gently on a lightly floured surface for 3 to 4 minutes, or with the dough hook of an electric mixer at low speed for 1 to 2 minutes. Cover tightly with plastic wrap and let rise 45 minutes to 1 hour.

DOUGH

4 large eggs

½ cup plus 1½ tablespoons (4.2 oz / 120 g) sugar

1⅓ teaspoons (0.2 oz / 6.5 g) salt

About 4 cups (19.3 oz / 550 g) unbleached all-purpose flour

2 sticks plus 2 tablespoons (8.8 oz / 250 g) unsalted butter, at room temperature

½ cup (2 oz / 60 g) grated pecorino Romano cheese

½ cup (2 oz / 60 g) grated Parmesan cheese, preferably Parmigiano Reggiano

¼ cup (1 oz / 30 g) grated Gruyère cheese

½ cup (2 oz / 60 g) small cubes of provolone

½ cup (3.5 oz / 100 g) thinly sliced and finely chopped Milano salami

1 teaspoon (0.2 oz / 5 g) coarsely ground pepper

1 large egg white, beaten, for glazing

continued

Casatiello, *continued*

BY HAND

Beat the eggs, sugar, and salt together in a
large mixing bowl. Add 1 cup of the flour
and stir until smooth. Chop the sponge
into small pieces and add it to the egg mixture. Beat it together; then add the remaining flour and mix with your hands to a
shaggy mass. Mix in the butter. Sprinkle
the dough with the grated pecorino, Parmesan, and Gruyère and knead it in with
your hands. When the dough has come
together but is still fairly rough, knead it
on a flour surface until elastic, supple, and
fairly smooth, 5 to 7 minutes.

BY MIXER

Beat the eggs, sugar, and salt together
with the paddle in a large mixer
bowl. Add the sponge and mix until
blended. Add the flour and mix to a
shaggy mass. Add the butter and continue
beating with the paddle until a rough
dough is formed. Sprinkle the grated
pecorino, Parmesan, and Gruyère over
the dough and mix until it is roughly
blended. Change to the dough hook and
knead at medium speed until elastic,
supple, and fairly smooth, 3 to 4 minutes.

First Rise. Place the dough in a lightly oiled
bowl, cover with plastic wrap, and let rise
until almost tripled, 1 to $1^1/_2$ hours.

Shaping and Second Rise. Turn out onto
a lightly floured surface and pat and roll
the dough out to a large rectangle $^3/_4$ inch
thick. Sprinkle half the provolone, the
salami, and the pepper over the surface.
Fold into thirds, like a business letter (see
page 124); then roll the dough out again
$^3/_4$ inch thick. Sprinkle the dough with the
remaining provolone, the salami, and the
pepper, and fold again in thirds. Gently
knead for 2 to 3 minutes to distribute the
cheese and salami evenly. Cut the dough in
half and, with the cut side up, knead each
half gently into a round ball by rolling the
dough between cupped hands on the work
surface and pulling the skin of the dough
taut. Place each ball in a buttered 2-quart
charlotte mold or soufflé dish. The dough
should fill about half the mold. Cover with
a towel and let rise to the tops of the
molds, 1 to $1^1/_2$ hours.

Baking. Preheat the oven to 400°F.
Brush the top of each loaf with egg white.
Bake 45 minutes, then remove from the
molds and cool on racks.

continued

Casatiello, *continued*

Sprinkle half the provolone, the salami, and the pepper over the surface.

Fold over one-third of the dough.

Fold over the remaining dough, like a business letter.

The baked *casatiello.*

Crescia al Formaggio EASTER CHEESE BREAD

This is the bread that traditionally opens Easter lunch in Umbria. Eggs and cheese are beaten together to make a rich briochelike dough that has an intensely cheesy, lacy interior. When I watched it being made at Sandri in Perugia, the bakers cut right into a 50-pound wheel of three-year-old Parmigiano-Reggiano, the finest cheese the country offers. If you want the authentic bread, bake it in terra-cotta flowerpots (plug any holes in the bottom) and you'll see where the bread gets its name. *Crescia* refers to the sudden dramatic doming of the dough above the pots.

To season flowerpots, coat them with oil and set in a preheated 400°F oven for 20 minutes. Oil them again, then set them back in the 400°F oven for 20 minutes more. Cool them and be sure to grease them well before putting the dough inside.

Makes 2 tall round loaves

4¼ teaspoons (0.4 oz / 12 g) active dry yeast

1 tablespoon (0.5 oz / 13 g) sugar

⅓ cup (2.8 oz / 80 g) warm water

4 large eggs, at room temperature

4 large egg yolks, at room temperature

Scant 2 cups (8.8 oz / 250 g) unbleached all-purpose flour

1½ sticks (6 oz / 170 g) unsalted butter, at room temperature

Scant 2 cups (8.8 oz / 250 g) bread flour

1 teaspoon (0.2 oz / 5 g) salt

1⅔ cups (7 oz / 200 g) grated Parmesan cheese

1 cup (3.5 oz / 100 g) grated pecorino Romano

1 large egg white, beaten, for glazing

BY HAND

Stir the yeast and sugar into the water in a large mixing bowl; let stand until foamy, about 10 minutes. Beat the eggs and egg yolks together and beat into the yeast mixture. Add 1 cup of the all-purpose flour and beat until smooth. Add the butter in small pieces and mix well. Reserve ¼ cup of one of the flours for kneading. Stir in all the remaining flour and the salt. Knead on a floured surface, sprinkling with the reserved flour, 8 to 12 minutes; add the cheese in sprinkles in the last minutes of kneading. It will take a while, but it is the only way to get this much cheese evenly distributed.

BY MIXER

Stir the yeast and sugar into the water in a large mixer bowl; let stand until foamy, about 10 minutes. Mix in the eggs, egg yolks, and butter with the paddle. Add the flours and salt and mix until the dough comes together, about 2 minutes. Change to the dough hook and knead at medium speed for about 5 minutes, adding up to 2 tablespoons (0.8 oz / 13 g) more flour, until the dough pulls away from the sides of the bowl. If the dough climbs up to the

continued

Crescia al Formaggio, *continued*

collar, turn off the motor and push the dough down. Spread the dough out on a floured surface and gradually knead in sprinkles of cheese. The dough should be rich, springy, golden, and slightly gritty.

First Rise. Place the dough in a lightly buttered bowl, cover with plastic wrap, and let rise until doubled, 2 to 2^1/$_2$ hours.

Shaping. Turn the dough out onto a lightly floured surface and cut into two pieces, one twice as large as the other. Shape each piece into a tight ball and let rest under a towel for about 10 minutes. Reshape the balls firmly. Place the large ball, seam side down, in an oiled 2-quart terra-cotta flowerpot or charlotte mold, and the smaller ball in an oiled 1-quart pot or mold. The dough should fill the pots about halfway. Cover with plastic wrap held by a rubber band and let rise to the tops of the pots, 2 to 2^1/$_2$ hours.

Baking. Preheat the oven to 425°F. Brush the tops of the dough with the egg white. Bake until the tops have risen dramatically above the pots and are deep golden brown, about 45 minutes. Let the breads cool 10 to 15 minutes before unmolding. Cool on racks.

Pani Moderni
Modern Breads

In Italy, where *fantasia* is the rule and bakers are artists, there has been a real revolution in bread baking. Bakers have given their imaginations free rein and simply started kneading all the best products of the country's markets right into their doughs. Mounds of sweet bell peppers, fat bunches of basil, wheels of aged Parmesan cheese, nuts, and exotic grains have all found new homes in unusual loaves.

And that's not all. The Mediterranean diet is being touted as the healthiest way to eat, because it is rich in grains and vegetables, olive oil, and fresh fruit. The irony is that the best example of a healthy diet is probably what the poor people of Naples have always eaten—a diet of vegetables and grains (what are pizzas after all?), which they put together with dazzling colors and an abundant variety of flavors. For years you could not find whole wheat, graham flour, or multigrain breads at all, and bran was more likely to be fed to animals than to humans. Now bakers are really hitting their stride and are talking about a bread for every course and a course for every bread, hinting at a kind of culinary refinement and richness we Americans can hardly imagine.

Vegetable and Herb Breads

Pane al Pesto PESTO BREAD

Let's sing the praises of the unknown baker who first stirred fresh pesto into bread dough. When I was living with my family on the coast of Liguria in a tiny town above Lerici, the lady who helped us keep house was a wonderful cook who often arrived with bouquets of basil so recently picked that the leaves were still warm from the sun. She ground pine nuts and garlic with the basil leaves, then stirred in Parmesan cheese and beat in olive oil by drops, as if she were making mayonnaise. We ate it on fat ribbons of *trenette* pasta (our friends just over the border in Tuscany, not more than 30 kilometers away, served it on fusilli, which caught the sauce in its twists and turns), on potatoes, on grilled fresh fish, and sometimes just on our fingers, which we dipped surreptitiously into the bowl.

This recipe for pesto is stronger and more concentrated than most because it must retain its fragrance and taste even through the process of being baked. And it does! You must use fresh basil for the pesto; neither dried basil (which bears almost no relationship to the fresh), parsley, nor spinach will do. You may, however, substitute walnuts for the pine nuts.

Makes 2 round loaves

PESTO

1 firmly packed cup (2.5 oz / 75 g) fresh basil leaves

1/2 cup plus 2 tablespoons (2.6 oz / 75 g) grated Parmesan cheese

1/2 cup (3.8 oz / 110 g) olive oil

2 tablespoons (0.5 oz / 15 g) pine nuts or chopped walnuts

1 1/2 teaspoons (0.3 oz / 9 g) minced garlic

1/8 teaspoon salt

1/8 teaspoon freshly ground pepper

Purée all the ingredients in a food processor fitted with the steel blade or a blender. Measure 1/2 cup (3.5 oz / 100 g) for this recipe.

DOUGH

2 1/4 teaspoons (1 package / 0.2 oz / 7 g) active dry yeast

1 cup plus 2 tablespoons (9.5 oz / 270 g) warm water (or 1/4 cup / 2 oz / 60 g warm water plus 1 cup / 8.4 oz / 240 g cold water if using a processor)

Scant 2 tablespoons (1 oz / 30 g) olive oil

3 3/4 cups (17.5 oz / 500 g) unbleached all-purpose flour

2 teaspoons (0.4 oz / 10 g) salt

Cornmeal

BY HAND

Stir the yeast into the water in a mixing bowl; let stand until creamy, about 10 minutes. Stir in the oil and $^1/_2$ cup of pesto thoroughly. Mix the flour and salt and add to the yeast mixture. Stir until the dough comes together. Knead on a floured surface until soft, velvety, and elastic, 8 to 10 minutes.

BY MIXER

Stir the yeast into the water in a mixer bowl; let stand until creamy, about 10 minutes. Stir in the oil and $^1/_2$ cup of pesto thoroughly with the paddle. Mix the flour and salt and add to the yeast mixture. Mix until well moistened. Change to the dough hook and knead until the dough is velvety and medium soft, 3 to 4 minutes. Finish kneading briefly by hand on a lightly floured surface.

BY PROCESSOR

Stir the yeast into the $^1/_4$ cup of warm water in a small bowl; let stand until creamy, about 10 minutes. Place the flour and salt in a food processor fitted with the dough blade and process 10 seconds to sift. With the machine running, pour $^1/_2$ cup of pesto, the dissolved yeast, and the 1 cup of cold water through the feed tube as quickly as the flour can absorb it. Process 45 seconds longer to knead. Finish kneading by hand on a lightly floured surface for 1 minute.

First Rise. Place the dough in an oiled bowl, cover tightly with plastic wrap, and let rise until doubled, about 1$^1/_4$ hours.

Shaping and Second Rise. Cut the dough in half on a lightly floured surface. Punch each piece down and knead briefly to expel the air. Shape each piece into a round loaf. Place each loaf, seam side down, on an oiled baking sheet or a peel sprinkled with cornmeal. Cover with a towel and let rise until doubled, about 45 minutes to 1 hour. The dough must be very relaxed and fully risen before it is baked, so don't rush it.

Baking. Preheat the oven to 450°F. If you are using baking stones, turn the oven on 30 minutes before baking and sprinkle the stones with cornmeal just before sliding the loaves onto them. Place the loaves in the oven and immediately reduce the heat to 400°F. Bake 35 to 40 minutes, spraying the oven three times with water in the first 10 minutes, if you want. Cool completely on racks.

Ciabatta ai Funghi MUSHROOM BREAD

The two secrets of getting the most flavor into this bread are using the soaking water from the porcini and allowing the flavor to develop over long rises. You may find the bread growing powerfully in its second rise; if so, just dimple it gently to deflate it slightly, and allow the rise to go the full 3 hours.

Makes 2 large oval loaves

4 to 6 dried porcini mushrooms

1³/₄ cups (14.7 oz / 420 g) warm water

3 cups (8 oz / 225 g) sliced fresh mushrooms

1 teaspoon (0.2 oz / 5 g) minced garlic

1 to 2 tablespoons (0.5 to 1 oz / 15 to 30 g) olive oil

1¹/₄ teaspoons (0.1 oz / 3.5 g) active dry yeast

3³/₄ cups (17.5 oz / 500 g) unbleached all-purpose flour

1 tablespoon (0.5 oz / 15 g) salt

Cornmeal

Soak the porcini in the warm water for at least 1 hour, then drain, reserving the liquid. Strain the liquid through cheesecloth two or three times and measure out 1¹/₂ cups. Coarsely chop the porcini and pat dry. Sauté the fresh mushrooms and the garlic in as little of the oil as possible and set aside to cool. Warm the porcini liquid to 105°F to 115°F. If you are using the food processor, refrigerate 1¹/₄ cups of the liquid until cold and warm the remaining ¹/₄ cup. If making the dough by hand or with a mixer, warm all of the liquid.

BY HAND

Stir the yeast into the warm porcini soaking liquid in a large mixing bowl; let stand until creamy, about 10 minutes. Mix the flour and salt and stir into the yeast mixture in three additions; add the chopped porcini with the last of the flour. When the dough is too stiff to stir, plunge in with your hands. Knead on a lightly floured surface until the dough is as velvety as an earlobe, 5 to 7 minutes.

BY MIXER

Stir the yeast into the warm porcini liquid in a mixer bowl; let stand until creamy, about 10 minutes. Mix the flour and salt and add to the yeast mixture. Mix with the paddle until the flour is absorbed. Change to the dough hook and knead for 2 minutes at low speed and 2 minutes at medium. You will have to stop several times to adjust the dough in the bowl. Finish kneading briefly by hand on a floured surface, adding the porcini and a little extra flour to bring the dough together.

BY PROCESSOR

Stir the yeast into $1/4$ cup of warm porcini liquid in a small bowl; let stand until creamy, about 10 minutes. Place the flour and salt in a food processor fitted with the steel blade and process with two or three pulses to sift. Pour the dissolved yeast over the flour. With the machine running, pour the cold porcini liquid through the feed tube and process until the dough gathers into a ball. Process 45 seconds longer to knead. Finish kneading briefly by hand on a floured surface, adding the porcini. The dough should be soft, velvety, and very resilient.

First Rise. Place the dough in a lightly oiled bowl, cover tightly with plastic wrap, and let rise for 3 hours.

Shaping and Second Rise. Pour the dough onto a floured surface, punch it down, and knead briefly. Divide the dough in half and shape each half into a big flat oval. Scatter the sautéed mushrooms over both ovals and roll the dough up, tucking in the ends. Pat each loaf flat, roll it up again, and shape into an oval. The loaves will be compact and quite small initially, but they will rise. Dimple each loaf with your fingertips or knuckles, being careful not to expose the mushrooms. Place on a baking sheet or peel sprinkled with cornmeal, cover with a dampened kitchen towel or a heavy towel, and let rise for 3 hours.

Baking. Thirty minutes before baking, preheat the oven with baking stones in it to 400°F. Just before baking, sprinkle the stones with cornmeal. Slide the loaves onto the stones and bake 50 minutes to 1 hour, spraying the oven three times with water in the first 10 minutes. The loaves can also be baked on an oiled baking sheet, if you prefer. Cool completely on wire racks.

Pane di Patate POTATO BREAD

It's the rare person who even associates potatoes and Italy, but, in fact, they grow all over Puglia and Basilicata, two of the southern regions of Italy. It seems everyone there has enough potatoes in their gardens to make into dough for bread, focaccia, or pizza. This bread needs to be prepared by machine, either a processor or a mixer, because of its minimal water content. Because potatoes have a lot of starch, the bread browns quickly and you must keep an eye on it. It will split open dramatically as it bakes, and will come out looking like a big, crusty rosette. Potato bread is particularly good with stews or rich meat sauces into which slices of the bread can be dipped.

Makes 2 round loaves

1 1/2 pounds (675 g) baking potatoes

4 1/2 teaspoons (2 packages / 0.5 oz / 14 g) active dry yeast

3 to 4 tablespoons (1.5 to 2 oz / 45 to 60 g) warm water (or 1/4 cup / 2 oz / 60 g warm water plus 1/4 cup / 2 oz / 60 g cold water if using a processor)

1 1/2 to 2 tablespoons (0.75 to 1 oz / 22 to 30 g) olive oil

3 3/4 cups (17.5 oz / 500 g) unbleached all-purpose flour

1 1/2 teaspoons (0.3 oz / 8 g) salt

Cornmeal

Boil the potatoes in water to cover until tender; drain. Peel the potatoes and press them through a ricer or mash until very smooth. Keep warm until ready to use.

BY MIXER

Stir the yeast into 3 tablespoons of warm water; let stand until creamy, about 10 minutes. Place the potatoes, dissolved yeast, oil, flour, and salt in a mixer bowl. Beat with the paddle at low speed for 2 to 3 minutes. The dough will initially be very fine, like cornmeal, and then it will start to clump together. Add up to 1 tablespoon of water if necessary for the dough to come together. If you make a small ball of dough between your fingers, it should feel very slightly sticky. This is a hard dough that never gets very smooth. Knead by hand on a lightly floured surface for 3 to 4 minutes.

BY PROCESSOR

Stir the yeast into the 1/4 cup of warm water; let stand until creamy, about 10 minutes. Place the potatoes, flour, and salt in a food processor fitted with the dough blade, and process with several pulses to mix. With the machine running, pour the dissolved yeast, oil, and the 1/4 cup of cold water through the feed tube and process until the dough comes together. Process 45 seconds longer to knead. This is a hard dough that never gets very smooth. If you want, finish kneading briefly by hand.

First Rise. Place the dough in a lightly oiled bowl, cover tightly with plastic wrap, and let rise until doubled, 1 to 2 hours. The processor dough is sticky and delicate because of the extra water, and the mixer dough is slightly tacky and looks chunky.

Shaping and Second Rise. Cut the dough in half on a lightly floured surface and shape each half into a round loaf, using very light tension in shaping. Flatten slightly with the palm of your hand to encourage it to spread just a bit. Place the loaves, seam side down, on heavily floured peels or rimless baking sheets. Flour the tops lightly and cover with dampened kitchen towels. Let rise until doubled, about 45 minutes. When fully risen, the dough will feel somewhat soft.

Baking. Thirty minutes before baking, preheat the oven with baking stones in it to 450°F. Just before baking, sprinkle the stones with cornmeal. Very carefully invert the loaves onto the stones (the seam side will open dramatically in the baking). Bake 35 to 40 minutes, spraying the oven three times with water in the first 10 minutes. Cool completely on racks.

Pane al Pomodoro TOMATO BREAD

There is no question that this is an extravagant bread, but imagine an American hamburger on it, or slices of soft fresh cheese. You can throw caution to the wind and buy Italian sun-dried tomatoes packed in wonderful Ligurian olive oil, or you can be somewhat more restrained and buy domestic sun-dried tomatoes by the ounce at your local grocer. You can even dry and pack the tomatoes in oil yourself. The amount of tomatoes you use is up to you.

Makes 1 round loaf

1 clove garlic, minced

2 tablespoons (0.8 oz / 22 g) finely chopped onion

1 tablespoon (0.5 oz / 15 g) oil from oil-packed sun-dried tomatoes

2¼ teaspoons (1 package / 0.2 oz / 7 g) active dry yeast

¼ cup (2 oz / 60 g) warm water

1 cup (8.4 oz / 240 g) water, at room temperature (cold if using a processor)

⅓ cup to ½ cup (2.3 to 3.5 oz / 65 to 100 g) coarsely chopped sun-dried tomatoes packed in oil

3¾ cups (17.5 oz / 500 g) unbleached all-purpose flour

2 teaspoons (0.4 oz / 10 g) salt

1 large egg white, beaten, for glazing

continued

Pane al Pomodoro, *continued*

Lightly sauté the garlic and onion in the oil; let cool to room temperature.

BY HAND

Stir the yeast into the warm water in a large mixing bowl; let stand until creamy, about 10 minutes. Stir in the 1 cup of water and the garlic and onion with the oil; then stir in the tomatoes. Mix the flour and salt and stir 1 cup at a time into the yeast mixture. Knead on a lightly floured surface, sprinkling with 2 to 3 tablespoons of additional flour as needed, until the dough is soft, velvety, and slightly moist, 8 to 10 minutes.

BY MIXER

Stir the yeast into the warm water in a mixer bowl; let stand until creamy, about 10 minutes. Using the paddle, stir in the 1 cup of water and the garlic and onion with the oil; then stir in the tomatoes. Stir in the flour and salt. Change to the dough hook and knead until soft, velvety, and elastic, about 3 minutes. The tomatoes will be in distinct chunks.

BY PROCESSOR

Stir the yeast into the $^1/_4$ cup of warm water in a small bowl; let stand until creamy, about 10 minutes. Place the flour and salt in a food processor fitted with the steel blade or dough blade and process briefly to sift. Place the garlic and onion with the oil and the tomatoes on top of the flour. With the machine running, pour the dissolved yeast and the 1 cup of cold water through the feed tube as quickly as the flour can absorb it. Process until the dough comes together. Process 30 seconds longer to knead. The dough will be velvety, elastic, and salmon colored. Finish kneading by hand on a floured surface, if you want.

First Rise. Place the dough in a lightly oiled bowl, cover with plastic wrap, and let rise until doubled, about 1 hour.

Shaping and Second Rise. Punch the dough down on a lightly floured surface and knead briefly. Shape the dough into a ball. Place on a lightly oiled baking sheet or a peel sprinkled with flour, cover with a towel, and let rise until doubled, about 45 to 55 minutes.

Baking. Preheat the oven to 425°F. If you are using a baking stone, turn the oven on 30 minutes before baking and sprinkle the stone with cornmeal just before sliding the loaf onto it. Make three parallel slashes on the top of the loaf with a razor. Brush the top with the egg white. Bake 10 minutes, spraying the oven three times with water. Reduce the heat to 375°F and bake 25 to 30 minutes longer. Cool completely on a rack.

Pane agli Spinaci SPINACH BREAD

I watched bakers in Venice turn out hundreds of little spinach rolls all destined for elegant antipasti or the Italian variant of sandwiches for lunch. Why not make an entire loaf of this bread with a beautiful marbled green interior, I wondered, thus turning panini into *pane*. The bread is wonderful with roast chicken or lamb and tastes as good as it looks. Be certain to thaw the frozen spinach without cooking it further. Squeeze the spinach dry or, better yet, press out the liquid using a potato ricer, but save the liquid for the bread dough.

Makes 1 round loaf or 12 to 14 rolls

2 cloves garlic, minced

Scant 2 tablespoons (1 oz / 30 g) olive oil

2 packages (10 oz / 285 g each) frozen spinach, thawed, squeezed dry, and $^3/_4$ cup (6.3 oz / 180 g) of its liquid

$2^1/_4$ teaspoons (1 package / 0.2 oz / 7 g) active dry yeast

$^1/_4$ teaspoon sugar

$^1/_4$ teaspoon freshly grated nutmeg

$3^3/_4$ cups (17.5 oz / 500 g) unbleached all-purpose flour

$2^1/_2$ teaspoons (0.4 oz / 12.5 g) salt

Lightly sauté the garlic in the oil and cool to room temperature. Warm $^1/_4$ cup of the reserved spinach liquid to 105°F to 115°F. Leave the remaining $^1/_2$ cup of liquid at room temperature or, if using a food processor, refrigerate until cold.

BY HAND

Stir the yeast and sugar into the $^1/_4$ cup of warm spinach liquid in a mixing bowl; let stand until foamy, about 10 minutes. Add the $^1/_2$ cup of room temperature spinach liquid, the garlic with the oil, the spinach, and the nutmeg and stir thoroughly. Mix the flour and salt and stir into the spinach mixture. Knead on a floured surface, sprinkling with additional flour to absorb the moisture from the spinach, until the dough is well marbled, soft, and velvety, 8 to 10 minutes.

BY MIXER

Stir the yeast and sugar into the $^1/_4$ cup of warm spinach liquid in a mixer bowl; let stand until foamy, about 10 minutes. Add the $^1/_2$ cup of room temperature spinach liquid, the garlic with the oil, the spinach, and the nutmeg and mix with the paddle. Add the flour and salt and mix until the flour is absorbed. Change to the dough hook and knead until the dough is well marbled, soft, and velvety, 2 to 3 minutes.

BY PROCESSOR

If the capacity of your food processor is 7 cups or less, process this dough in two batches. Stir the yeast and sugar into the warm spinach liquid in a small bowl; let stand until foamy, about 10 minutes. Place the flour, salt, and nutmeg in a food processor fitted with the steel blade and

continued

Pane agli Spinaci, *continued*

process with two or three pulses to sift. Place the spinach in clumps on top of the flour mixture. Stir the $^1/_2$ cup of cold spinach liquid, the garlic with the oil, and 1 tablespoon of additional cold water into the dissolved yeast. With the machine running, pour the yeast mixture through the feed tube and process until the dough comes together. Add up to 1 tablespoon more water if needed for the dough to come together. Process 40 seconds longer to knead. Finish kneading briefly by hand on a lightly floured surface, if you want.

First Rise. Place the dough in an oiled bowl, cover tightly with plastic wrap, and let rise until doubled, $1^1/_4$ to $1^1/_2$ hours.

Shaping and Second Rise. The dough will be even wetter after rising, because the spinach will have exuded more liquid. Pour the dough onto a floured work surface and flour the top of the dough. Don't punch it down or try to knead it. Shape into a round loaf or rolls the size of a fat lemon and place on a lightly oiled baking sheet. Cover with a towel and let rise until doubled, about 45 minutes.

Baking. Thirty minutes before baking, preheat the oven with a baking stone in it to 425°F. Slash a big V on top of the loaf with a razor. Bake 10 minutes. Reduce the heat to 400°F and bake the rolls 20 minutes and the loaf 30 to 35 minutes. Cool completely on a rack.

Pane ai Peperoni SWEET PEPPER BREAD

Once bakers started letting their imaginations run free and using the whole range of ingredients the land produced, it was only a question of time before red bell peppers would find their way into the loaves of today. After all, slices of peppers have been baked on *focacce* and *schiacciate* for years. This bread is unexpectedly delicious and particularly appealing with its brilliant red color and the sweet bite of peppers, and it is very easy and straightforward to make. Serve this bread with soft and semisoft cheeses, roast chicken, lamb, or pork. It is easily made into rolls and makes a splendid vehicle for a sandwich.

Makes 2 long, thin loaves

1 large red bell pepper (8 oz / 225 g)

2 tablespoons (1 oz / 30 g) olive oil

$1^3/_4$ teaspoons (0.2 oz / 5 g) active dry yeast

$1^1/_4$ cups (10.5 oz / 300 g) warm water (or $^1/_4$ cup / 2 oz / 60 g warm water plus 1 cup / 8.4 oz / 240 g cold water if using a processor)

$3^3/_4$ cups (17.5 oz / 500 g) unbleached all-purpose flour

2 teaspoons (0.4 oz / 10 g) salt

Preheat the broiler, then broil the bell pepper 2 inches from the heat source until the skin on the exposed side is blackened and puffed. Turn the pepper and continue to broil until the pepper is blackened all over. While it is still warm, cut the pepper in half and scrape out the seeds. Cut into wide strips and pull off the blackened skin. Coarsely chop the pepper and sauté in the oil over low heat for 4 to 5 minutes, taking care not to let it brown.

BY HAND

Stir the yeast into the water in a large mixing bowl; let stand until creamy, about 10 minutes. Stir in the pepper with the oil. Mix the flour and salt together and stir 1 cup at a time into the yeast mixture. When the dough has roughly come together, knead on a lightly floured surface until soft and elastic, 8 to 10 minutes.

BY MIXER

Stir the yeast into the water in a mixer bowl; let stand until creamy, about 10 minutes. Stir in the pepper with the oil, then the flour and salt with the paddle. Mix until the dough comes together, about 2 minutes. Change to the dough hook and knead at medium speed for 2 to 3 minutes. Finish kneading briefly by hand on a floured surface. The dough should be soft and elastic.

BY PROCESSOR

Stir the yeast into the $1/4$ cup of warm water in a small bowl; let stand until creamy, about 10 minutes. Drain the oil

from the pepper and add the oil to the dissolved yeast. Place the flour, salt, and pepper in a food processor fitted with the dough or steel blade and process 10 seconds to mix. With the machine running, pour the dissolved yeast mixture and the 1 cup of cold water through the feed tube; process until the dough gathers into a ball. Process 45 seconds longer to knead. Finish kneading briefly by hand on a lightly floured surface. The dough should be soft and elastic.

First Rise. Place the dough in an oiled bowl, cover with plastic wrap, and let rise until doubled, about 1 hour.

Shaping and Second Rise. Punch the dough down on a floured surface and knead it briefly. Cut the dough in half. Shape each half into a long, round log, and then curve one end so that it looks like a J. Place the loaves on an oiled baking sheet or a peel sprinkled with cornmeal or flour, cover with a towel, and let rise until doubled, 45 minutes to 1 hour.

Baking. Preheat the oven to 450°F. If you are using a baking stone, turn the oven on 30 minutes before baking and sprinkle the stone with cornmeal just before sliding the loaves onto it. Place the loaves in the oven and immediately reduce the heat to 400°F. Bake 35 minutes, spraying the oven three times with water in the first 10 minutes. Cool completely on a rack.

Pane al Formaggio CHEESE BREAD

Take two of Italy's best cheeses—aged Parmesan and the saltier, more pungent pecorino—fold them into a dough enriched with eggs and a little olive oil, and you have a superb cheese bread to eat with smoked meats, soups, green salads, and even fresh fruit.

Makes 2 round or long, thin loaves

2¼ teaspoons (1 package / 0.2 oz / 7 g) active dry yeast

1 cup (8.4 oz / 240 g) warm water (or ¼ cup / 2 oz / 60 g warm water plus ¾ cup plus 2 tablespoons / 7.4 oz / 210 g cold water if using a processor)

2 large eggs, at room temperature

2 tablespoons (1 oz / 30 g) olive oil

3¾ cups (17.5 oz / 500 g) unbleached all-purpose flour

2 teaspoons (0.4 oz / 10 g) salt

½ cup plus 2 tablespoons (2.6 oz / 75 g) grated Parmesan cheese

Scant ½ cup (1.8 oz / 50 g) grated pecorino cheese

Cornmeal

1 large egg white, beaten, for glazing

BY HAND

Stir the yeast into the water in a large mixing bowl; let stand until creamy, about 10 minutes. Whisk in the eggs and oil. Mix the flour and salt and stir half into the yeast mixture; stir in the remaining flour with the cheese. Knead on a lightly floured surface, sprinkling with 2 to 3 tablespoons (0.6 to 1 oz / 18 to 26 g) of additional flour as needed, until firm, elastic, and silky, 8 to 10 minutes. The texture may be slightly gritty from the cheeses.

BY MIXER

Stir the yeast into the water in a mixer bowl; let stand until creamy, about 10 minutes. Mix in the eggs and oil with the paddle, and then the flour, salt, and cheeses. Change to the dough hook and knead until firm, velvety, and elastic, 3 to 4 minutes. The texture may be slightly grainy from the cheeses.

BY PROCESSOR

If the capacity of your food processor is 7 cups or less, process this dough in two batches. Stir the yeast into the ¼ cup of warm water in a small bowl; let stand until creamy, about 10 minutes. Place the flour, salt, and cheeses in a food processor fitted with the dough blade and process with several pulses to mix. Break the eggs and pour the oil on top of the flour mixture. With the machine running, pour the dissolved yeast and the ¾ cup plus 2 tablespoons of cold water through the feed tube as quickly as the flour can absorb it and process until the dough gathers into a ball. Process 45 seconds longer to knead. Knead briefly by hand on a lightly floured surface until elastic and silky.

First Rise. Place the dough in a lightly oiled bowl, cover with plastic wrap, and let rise until doubled, about 2 hours.

Shaping and Second Rise. Punch the dough down on a lightly floured surface and knead it briefly. Cut the dough in half and shape each piece into a round loaf or a log that is fatter in the middle and tapered at the ends. Place on a baking sheet or peel sprinkled with cornmeal, cover with a towel, and let rise until doubled, about 1 hour.

Baking. Thirty minutes before baking, preheat the oven with a baking stone in it to 425°F. Just before baking, brush the loaves with the egg white. Slash the long loaves with three parallel cuts, using a razor. Sprinkle the stone with cornmeal and slide the loaves onto it. Bake 40 minutes, spraying the oven three times with water in the first 10 minutes. Cool completely on a rack.

Panmarino ROSEMARY BREAD

The lovely pungent flavor of rosemary is often kneaded into the breads of Tuscany and Liguria, but this *panmarino* comes from Ferrara, and is the invention of an ebullient, mustachioed baker named Luciano Pancalde, whose surname aptly translates as "hot bread." Years ago, while reading a biography of the d'Este family who once ruled Ferrara, he discovered that one of the numerous spectacular court banquets featured a rosemary bread with a crust described as sparkling with diamonds. Luciano baked and baked again before he came up with this wonderful dome-shaped bread that is aromatic with fresh rosemary. But there's no need to go to Tiffany's for any of the ingredients. Just before baking, he slashes the top in the pattern of a star and sprinkles chunky crystals of sea salt into the crevices. The salt really does sparkle like diamonds. I make this bread all the time, not only because it is so easy and takes relatively little time from beginning to end, but also because it goes well with so many foods. It is wonderful with roast pork, chicken, or lamb and has an affinity with white fish, especially swordfish. Because the recipe makes two loaves, the second usually ends up sliced for sandwiches or a platter of cold meat.

If you use the 4^1/$_2$- or 5-quart KitchenAid stand mixer, you will have to stop the motor several times to push down the dough because the volume of the ingredients is just at the edge of the machine's capacity. Be sure not to let the dough fully double on its second rise or it won't spring to its full height in the oven. And there's no sense in not having a spectacular-looking bread to bring to the table.

continued

Panmarino, *continued*

Makes 2 round loaves

3³/₄ teaspoons (0.4 oz / 10.6 g) active dry yeast

1 cup (8.4 oz / 240 g) warm water (or ¹/₄ cup / 2 oz / 60 g warm water plus ³/₄ cup / 6.3 oz / 180 g cold water if using a processor)

1 cup (8.5 oz / 244 g) milk, at room temperature (cold if using a food processor)

¹/₄ cup plus 1 teaspoon (2 oz / 60 g) olive oil

3¹/₂ to 4 tablespoons (0.4 to 0.6 oz / 14 to 17 g) finely chopped fresh rosemary, or 1¹/₂ tablespoons (0.2 oz / 6 g) dried rosemary

4 teaspoons (0.7 oz / 20 g) salt

About 6²/₃ cups (2 lb / 900 g) unbleached all-purpose flour

1 to 1¹/₂ teaspoons (about 0.2 to 0.3 oz / 5 to 8 g) coarse sea salt

BY HAND

Stir the yeast into the water in a large mixing bowl; let stand until creamy, about 10 minutes. Stir in the milk and oil. Combine the rosemary, salt, and flour and stir into the yeast mixture in three or four additions. Stir until the dough comes together. Knead on a floured surface until velvety, elastic, and smooth, 8 to 10 minutes. It should be somewhat moist and blistered.

BY MIXER

This recipe is slightly large for the mixer, so that you'll have to stop and push the dough down frequently while the mixer is kneading it. Stir the yeast into the water

in a mixer bowl; let stand until creamy, about 10 minutes. Stir in the milk and oil with the paddle. Combine the rosemary, salt, and flour and add to the yeast mixture. Mix until the flour is absorbed, 1 to 2 minutes. Change to the dough hook and knead on medium speed until velvety, elastic, smooth, and somewhat moist, about 3 minutes. Finish kneading briefly by hand on a lightly floured surface.

BY PROCESSOR

Make sure your food processor can handle the volume of this dough. Even when done in two batches, there will be about 3¹/₂ cups of flour plus liquid to be processed. If you have a large-capacity machine, use the dough blade. Stir the yeast into the ¹/₄ cup of warm water in a small bowl; let stand until creamy, about 10 minutes. Place the rosemary, salt, and flour in a food processor fitted with the dough or steel blade and process briefly to mix and chop the rosemary. Stir the oil into the dissolved yeast. With the machine running, pour the yeast mixture, cold milk, and ³/₄ cup cold water in a steady stream through the feed tube and process until the dough gathers into a ball. Process 45 seconds longer to knead. Finish kneading by hand on a lightly floured surface until smooth, velvety, elastic, and slightly moist, 2 to 3 minutes.

continued

Panmarino, *continued*

First Rise. Place the dough in an oiled bowl, cover tightly with plastic wrap, and let rise until doubled, about 1¹/₂ hours.

Shaping and Second Rise. Gently punch the dough down on a lightly floured surface, but don't knead it. Cut the dough in half and shape each half into a round ball. Place the loaves on a lightly floured peel or a lightly oiled baking sheet, cover with a towel, and let rise 45 to 55 minutes (but not until truly doubled).

Baking. Preheat the oven to 450°F. If you are using a baking stone, turn the oven on 30 minutes before baking and sprinkle the stone with cornmeal just before sliding the loaves onto it. Just before you put the loaves in the oven, slash an asterisk into the top of each loaf with a razor blade and sprinkle half the sea salt into the cuts of each loaf. Bake 10 minutes, spraying the oven three times with water. Reduce the heat to 400°F and bake 30 to 35 minutes longer. Cool completely on racks.

Shape the dough into a round ball.

Slash a star on top.

Pane all'Erbe HERB BREAD

The first time our family lived in Italy, we rented a house in a tiny community where we were the sole foreigners. All the shopping was done in the five or six shops set along the only street in town. Every morning our children went to the grocery to get the bread that was delivered still hot from the nearby ovens, and, later in the morning, I would appear for the real shopping of the day with the other ladies, who gossiped, admired each other's children, and talked as the line moved sluggishly toward the reward of wonderful fresh fruits and vegetables. On one of our first days in town, I asked at the market for some parsley, only to feel the lady behind me tap me on the shoulder and ask me to save her place in line. "I'll be right back," she said, and she was, in a flash, with a lovely handful of parsley from her garden. In small Italian towns it seems everyone grows aromatic parsley with its flat green leaves. Elsewhere it is sometimes presented free with vegetables at the grocery or with meat at the butcher shop when it seems appropriate. If you can find Italian parsley, which has a full flavor, please use it in this bread; otherwise, the curly-leaf American variety will do. The piquant taste of the garlic, onions, and herbs give this bread a robust and earthy character, making it a particularly good choice to serve with roast meats and fish.

Makes 2 round loaves

1/2 cup (0.5 oz / 15 g) firmly packed fresh parsley leaves

3 tablespoons minced onion

1 large clove garlic, minced

2 1/4 teaspoons (1 package / 0.2 oz / 7 g) active dry yeast

1 cup plus 2 tablespoons (9.5 oz / 270 g) warm water (or 1/4 cup / 2 oz / 60 g warm water plus 3/4 cup plus 2 tablespoons / 7.4 oz / 210 g cold water if using a processor)

1 tablespoon (0.5 oz / 15 g) olive oil

3 3/4 cups (17.5 oz / 500 g) unbleached all-purpose flour

2 teaspoons (0.4 oz / 10 g) salt

Using a sharp knife or a food processor fitted with the steel blade, chop the parsley, onion, and garlic together until finely minced.

BY HAND

Stir the yeast into the water in a mixing bowl; let stand until creamy, about 10 minutes. Stir in the minced parsley mixture and the oil. Mix the flour and salt and stir 1 cup at a time into the yeast mixture. Stir until the dough comes together. Knead on a lightly floured surface, sprinkling with additional flour as needed, until silky and elastic, 8 to 10 minutes.

continued

Pane all'Erbe, *continued*

BY MIXER

Stir the yeast into the water in a mixer bowl; let stand until creamy, about 10 minutes. Mix in the oil and then the parsley mixture with the paddle. Mix the flour and salt and mix 1 cup at a time into the yeast mixture. Mix until the dough pulls away from the sides of the bowl. Change to the dough hook and knead until silky, elastic, and resilient, 2 to 3 minutes.

BY PROCESSOR

Stir the yeast into the $1/4$ cup of warm water in a small bowl; let stand until creamy, about 10 minutes. Place the flour and salt in a food processor fitted with the steel blade and process with two or three pulses to sift. Spoon the parsley mixture on top of the flour. With the machine running, pour the dissolved yeast and the $3/4$ cup plus 2 tablespoons of cold water through the food tube and process until the dough comes together. Process 40 seconds longer to knead. Finish kneading briefly by hand on a lightly floured surface.

First Rise. Place the dough in a lightly oiled bowl, cover tightly with plastic wrap, and let rise until doubled, about $1^1/2$ hours. The dough should be soft and pillowy.

Shaping and Second Rise. Punch the dough down on a lightly floured surface and knead it briefly. Cut the dough in half and shape each half into a round loaf. Place the loaves on a peel lightly sprinkled with cornmeal or on a lightly oiled baking sheet. Cover with a towel and let rise until doubled, about 45 minutes.

Baking. Thirty minutes before baking, preheat the oven to 400°F with a cast-iron frying pan inside on the bottom shelf and a baking stone on the shelf above it. Sprinkle the stone with cornmeal just before sliding the loaves onto it. Then, before you close the oven door, put $1/2$ cup of ice into the cast-iron frying pan. The steam will mist the interior for 5 to 10 minutes. Bake until the loaves sound hollow when you tap the bottoms, 40 to 45 minutes. Cool completely on racks.

Pane al Pepe Verde GREEN-PEPPERCORN BREAD

Italian artisan bakers lose no time in incorporating new ingredients into their breads. This bread is both imaginative and surprisingly delicate, much less overwhelming than it sounds. Use green peppercorns from Madagascar if you can find them. The bread goes well with mild cheeses, roast chicken, and vegetable salads.

Makes 1 long or round loaf

1³/₄ teaspoons (0.2 oz / 5 g) active dry yeast

1 cup (8.4 oz / 240 g) warm water (or ¹/₄ cup / 2 oz / 60 g warm water plus ³/₄ cup / 6.3 oz / 180 g cold water if using a processor)

1¹/₂ tablespoons (0.7 oz / 20 g) green peppercorns packed in brine, well drained

2 teaspoons (0.4 oz / 10 g) olive oil

2²/₃ cups (13.1 oz / 375 g) unbleached all-purpose flour

1 teaspoon (0.2 oz / 5 g) salt

BY HAND

Stir the yeast into the water in a large mixing bowl; let stand until creamy, about 10 minutes. Finely chop the peppercorns. If the peppercorns are not well chopped, they have an annoying way of popping out of the dough as you knead it. Stir the oil into the dissolved yeast; stir in the flour, salt, and peppercorns. Stir until the dough comes together. Knead on a floured surface, sprinkling with additional flour as needed, until moist, velvety, and elastic, 8 to 10 minutes. The dough should feel faintly like Silly Putty.

BY MIXER

Stir the yeast into the water in a mixer bowl; let stand until creamy, about 10 minutes. Lightly chop the peppercorns. Stir the oil into the dissolved yeast with the paddle. Add the flour, salt, and peppercorns and mix until the dough comes together. Change to the dough hook and knead at medium speed until the dough is elastic and velvety but still moist, 3 to 4 minutes. Finish kneading briefly by hand on a floured surface.

BY PROCESSOR

Stir the yeast into the ¹/₄ cup of warm water in a small bowl; let stand until creamy, about 10 minutes. Stir in the oil and the ³/₄ cup of cold water. Place the flour, salt, and peppercorns (drained but not chopped) in a food processor fitted with the steel blade and process with two or three pulses to coarsely chop the peppercorns. With the machine running, pour the yeast mixture through the feed tube as quickly as the flour can absorb it. Process 45 seconds longer to knead. Finish kneading briefly by hand on a lightly floured surface.

continued

Pane al Pepe Verde, *continued*

First Rise. Place the dough in a lightly oiled bowl, cover with plastic wrap, and let rise until doubled, about 1¹/₂ hours.

Shaping and Second Rise. Punch the dough down on a lightly floured surface and knead it briefly. Shape the dough into a long thin or a round loaf. The dough will be slightly moist. Place the loaf on a peel sprinkled with cornmeal or on a lightly oiled baking sheet. Cover with a towel and let rise until doubled, about 45 minutes to 1 hour. Flatten the bread slightly by pressing down firmly with the palm of your hand. Using a razor, slash three parallel wavy lines or, on the top of the round loaf, a star-shaped pattern.

Baking. Preheat the oven to 500°F. If you are using a baking stone, turn the oven on 30 minutes before baking and sprinkle the stone with cornmeal just before sliding the loaf onto it. Place the loaf in the oven and immediately reduce the heat to 400°F. Bake 35 minutes, spraying the oven three times with water in the first 10 minutes. Cool completely on a rack.

Breads of Various Grains

Segale con Pancetta RYE BREAD WITH PANCETTA

This is a dense, dark rye that is moist and velvety in texture. The pancetta gives it a slight bite, wonderful aroma, and good strong taste, but you can certainly substitute bacon or bake it as a regular rye without the pancetta. It is wonderful with cheese.

Makes 2 round loaves

SPONGE

4¹/₂ teaspoons (2 packages / 0.5 oz / 14 g) active dry yeast

3¹/₂ cups (29.4 oz / 840 g) warm water

3³/₄ cups (17.5 oz / 500 g) bread or unbleached all-purpose flour

Stir the yeast into the warm water in a large mixing bowl or mixer bowl, depending on your method; let stand until creamy, about 10 minutes. Stir in the flour and let stand until bubbly, 15 to 20 minutes.

DOUGH

$^{1}/_{4}$ cup (1.9 oz / 55 g) extra-virgin olive oil

4 cups plus 3 tablespoons (17.5 oz / 500 g) rye flour, preferably stone-ground, plus more as needed

4 teaspoons (0.9 oz / 25 g) sea salt

$1^{1}/_{2}$ cups (7 oz / 200 g) pancetta, cut into small cubes

BY HAND

Stir the oil into the sponge. Mix the rye flour and the salt; stir 1 cup at a time into the sponge. The dough should come together easily. Flour your work surface generously, flour a dough scraper, and have a small mound of flour nearby for your hands. Knead the dough for 8 to 10 minutes, using the dough scraper and sprinkling with $^{1}/_{4}$ to $^{1}/_{2}$ cup (1.3 to 1.8 oz / 35 to 50 g) of additional bread or all-purpose flour as needed. Although it hardly seems possible at the beginning, the dough will become firm, elastic, and consistent by the time you are through. Knead in the pancetta in two additions by sprinkling over the flattened dough, rolling up the dough, and repeating.

BY MIXER

Stir the oil into the sponge with the paddle. Add the rye flour and salt and mix until the dough comes together and is velvety to the touch. Change to the dough hook and knead at low speed until firm, consistent, and elastic, about 4 minutes. Knead in the pancetta in two additions as directed for mixing by hand.

BY PROCESSOR

Make sure your food processor can handle the volume of this dough. Even when done in two batches, there will be 4 cups of flour to be processed. Cover and refrigerate the sponge at least 30 minutes. Place the salt and rye flour in a food processor fitted with the dough blade and process with two or three pulses to sift. Stir the oil into the sponge. With the machine running, pour the sponge through the feed tube as quickly as the flour can absorb it and process until the dough gathers into a ball. Process 40 seconds longer to knead. Knead in the pancetta in two additions as directed for mixing by hand.

First Rise. Place the dough in an oiled bowl, cover tightly with plastic wrap, and let rise until doubled, about 1 hour.

Shaping and Second Rise. Turn the dough out onto a floured surface. Without kneading, cut the dough in half and shape each half into a round loaf, handling the dough gently. Place each loaf, seam side up, in an oiled and well-floured round banneton or basket lined with a tea towel that has been oiled and floured. Cover the loaves with heavy towels and let rise until the dough has doubled and thoroughly filled the baskets, about 1 hour. Like all ryes, the risen loaf will feel slightly tacky.

Baking. Thirty minutes before baking, preheat the oven with baking stones in it to 400°F. Just before baking, sprinkle the stones or baking sheets with cornmeal. Very gently invert the loaves onto the stones. Bake 40 to 45 minutes. Cool completely on racks.

Pan Completo o Pan Graham GRAHAM BREAD

Once it was almost impossible to find a loaf of whole wheat bread or a sack of whole wheat flour in Italy. But that was before the rediscovery of the highly prized Mediterranean diet, which is rich in whole grains, and it was certainly before the appearance of graham flour, which is actually whole wheat flour from which the bran and wheat germ have been extracted, finely powdered, and then reincorporated.

Graham flour is named for Sylvester Graham, the nineteenth-century reformer who was such a fanatic crusader for the benefits of whole grain that his name has become synonymous with whole wheat in some places. Graham bread is enjoying a vogue in the big cities of Italy, not only for its healthful properties, but also because it is a rich, nutty-tasting loaf with a lighter texture than might reasonably be expected. It is wonderful toasted. Variations of whole wheat breads include *pan graham* baked with yogurt, flax seeds, herbs, or soy flakes, which combine with the grain in a synergistic way so that the bread has the protein value of a sizable beef steak. If you can't find graham flour, substitute fine stone-ground whole wheat flour. Eat the bread with salami and smoked meat, mushrooms, or sliced salmon.

Makes two 9 by 5-inch loaves

STARTER

³/₄ teaspoon (0.1 oz / 2.1 g) active dry yeast

¹/₄ cup (2 oz / 60 g) warm water

1³/₄ cups (14.7 oz / 420 g) water, at cool room temperature

3³/₄ cups (17.5 ounces / 500 g) graham or stone-ground whole wheat flour

Stir the yeast into the warm water in a mixing or mixer bowl; let stand until creamy, about 10 minutes. Stir in the 1³/₄ cups of water and then the flour. Cover with plastic wrap and let rise overnight. The dough will initially be stiff, but it will have relaxed by morning.

DOUGH

¹/₂ teaspoon (0.05 oz / 1.4 g) active dry yeast

1 tablespoon (0.5 oz / 15 g) warm water

1³/₄ cups (8.8 oz / 250 g) graham or stone-ground whole wheat flour

1 teaspoon (0.2 oz / 5 g) salt

BY HAND

Stir the yeast into the water in a small bowl; let stand until creamy, about 10 minutes. Stir the dissolved yeast into the starter. Mix the graham flour and salt and stir ¹/₄ cup at a time into the starter, using strong strokes to work the stiff dough. Generously flour a work surface with all-purpose flour and knead the dough for 10 to 12 minutes. You will need to use about $^1/_3$ cup (1.8 oz / 50 g) of all-purpose flour in the kneading. Use a dough scraper to remove the film left on the work surface. Slam the dough down hard several times toward the end of the kneading to help develop the gluten.

BY MIXER

Stir the yeast into the water in a small bowl; let stand until creamy, about 10 minutes. Stir the dissolved yeast into the starter with the paddle. Mix the graham flour and salt and add to the starter. Mix until the dough comes together. Change to the dough hook and knead for 3 to 5 minutes at medium speed. Finish kneading briefly by hand on a floured work surface, sprinkling with all-purpose flour, until the dough is no longer sticky.

First Rise. Place the dough in a lightly oiled bowl, cover tightly with plastic wrap, and let rise until doubled, about $1^3/_4$ hours.

Shaping and Second Rise. Punch the dough down on a floured surface and cut it in half. Knead briefly and shape each half into an oval loaf to fit into a 9 by 5-inch loaf pan. Place the loaves, seam sides down, in the oiled loaf pans and cover with a towel. Let rise to one-and-a-half times their volume, about 40 minutes.

Baking. Preheat the oven to 375°F. Make several parallel slashes on the top of each loaf so that the sides won't split during baking. Bake 40 minutes. If you want, bake the last 10 minutes out of the pans on a baking sheet so that the bottoms and sides brown. Cool completely on racks.

Pane Integrale con Miele WHOLE WHEAT BREAD WITH HONEY

Whole wheat and a drizzle of honey make a wonderful full-flavored bread. Try it as delicious small dinner rolls; it's also a perfect breakfast or sandwich loaf.

Makes 1 round loaf

STARTER (*OPTIONAL*)

$^1/_4$ teaspoon active dry yeast

$^2/_3$ cup (5.6 oz / 160 g) warm water

$1^1/_2$ cups minus 1 tablespoon (7 oz / 200 g) unbleached all-purpose flour

If you are going to use the starter, which gives the bread a slightly lighter texture, stir the yeast into the water in a mixing bowl; let stand until creamy, about 10 minutes. Stir in the flour with 70 to 100 strokes of a wooden spoon. Let rise, covered, for 6 to 24 hours. Measure $^1/_4$ cup (50 g) for this recipe and discard the rest.

continued

Pane Integrale con Miele, *continued*

DOUGH

1³/₄ teaspoons (0.2 oz / 5 g) active dry yeast

1 tablespoon plus 2 teaspoons (1.2 oz / 35 g) honey

1¹/₂ cups (12 oz / 360 g) warm water

3³/₄ cups (17.5 oz / 500 g) whole wheat flour

1¹/₂ teaspoons (0.3 oz / 7.5 g) salt

BY HAND

Stir the yeast and honey into ¹/₄ cup of the water in a large mixing bowl; let stand until foamy, about 10 minutes. If you are using a starter, chop the starter into small pieces and add to the dissolved yeast. Pour in the remaining 1¹/₄ cups of water and squeeze the starter between your fingers until the starter is in little shreds and the water is chalky. Mix the flour and salt and stir 1 cup at a time into the yeast mixture. Stir until the dough comes together. Knead on a floured surface, sprinkling with additional whole wheat flour, until the dough is fairly smooth and has lost most of its stickiness, about 8 to 10 minutes.

BY MIXER

Stir the yeast and honey into the water in a mixer bowl; let stand until foamy, about 10 minutes. If you are using a starter, chop the starter into small pieces and add to the dissolved water. Stir with the paddle until the starter is in little shreds. Add the flour and salt and mix until the dough comes together. Change to the dough hook and knead 2 minutes at low speed and 2 minutes at medium speed. The dough should be fairly smooth and have lost most of its stickiness. Finish kneading briefly by hand on a floured surface, if you want.

First Rise. Place the dough in an oiled bowl, cover tightly with plastic wrap, and let rise until doubled, about 2 hours.

Shaping and Second Rise. Turn the dough out onto a well-floured surface and shape into a round loaf without punching the dough down. Place the loaf on a lightly oiled baking sheet or a peel sprinkled with cornmeal. Cover with waxed paper or a towel or lightly oil the top and cover with plastic wrap. Let rise until doubled, 45 minutes to 1 hour.

Baking. Preheat the oven to 450°F. If you are using a baking stone, turn on the oven 30 minutes before baking and sprinkle the stone with cornmeal just before sliding the loaf onto it. Bake 10 minutes, spraying the oven three times with water. Reduce the heat to 400°F and bake 25 minutes longer. Cool completely on a rack.

Pane Rustico RUSTIC WHOLE WHEAT PILLOWS

These pillow-shaped breads have a crisp crust and a nutty, crunchy interior with a robust flavor. They are wonderful sliced in half for sandwiches, but you can also make them much, much smaller for tiny hors d'oeuvres. The longer you soak your wheat berries, the more flavorful they will be. If you find they smell sour, add a little baking soda to the water and everything will be fine.

Makes 8 large rolls

¹/₂ cup (3.5 oz / 100 g) cracked hard wheat berries

³/₄ cup (3.5 oz / 100 g) unbleached all-purpose flour

2¹/₄ teaspoons (1 package / 0.2 oz / 7 g) active dry yeast

1 cup (8.4 oz / 240 g) warm water (or ¹/₄ cup / 2 oz / 60 g warm water plus ³/₄ cup / 6.3 oz / 180 g cold water if using a processor)

2¹/₄ cups (10.5 oz / 300 g) whole wheat flour

1 tablespoon (0.5 oz / 15 g) salt

Soak the wheat berries in cold water for 1 to 3 days or pour boiling water over the berries and let stand 6 to 8 hours. Drain the wheat berries and process the berries and the all-purpose flour in a food processor or blender just until coarsely chopped. If too finely chopped, the berries won't be crunchy.

BY HAND

Stir the yeast into the warm water in a mixing bowl; let stand until creamy, about 10 minutes. Stir in the berry mixture. Mix the whole wheat flour and salt and stir 2 cups at a time into the yeast mixture. Stir until the dough is stiff and sticky. Knead on a surface floured with all-purpose flour until firm and elastic but still slightly tacky, 8 to 10 minutes.

BY MIXER

Stir the yeast into the warm water in a mixer bowl; let stand until creamy, about 10 minutes. Stir in the berry mixture with the paddle and then the whole wheat flour and salt. Mix until the dough comes together and is stiff and sticky. Change to the dough hook and knead until firm and elastic but still slightly tacky, 3 to 4 minutes. If you want, finish kneading briefly by hand on a surface floured with all-purpose flour.

BY PROCESSOR

Stir the yeast into the ¹/₄ cup of warm water in a small bowl; let stand until creamy, about 10 minutes. Place the berry mixture, whole wheat flour, and salt in a food processor fitted with the steel blade. With the machine running, pour the dissolved yeast and the ³/₄ cup of cold water through the feed tube as quickly as the flour can absorb it and process until the dough comes together. Process 40 seconds longer to knead. Finish kneading briefly by hand on a surface floured with all-purpose flour until firm and elastic but still slightly tacky.

continued

Pane Rustico, *continued*

First Rise. Place the dough in a lightly oiled bowl, cover tightly with plastic wrap, and let rise until doubled, about 2 hours.

Shaping and Second Rise. Punch the dough down on a lightly floured surface and knead briefly. Shape into a long rectangle by flattening it with your forearm. Cut into eight 5-inch squares. Place on a lightly oiled baking sheet, cover with a towel, and let rise until well puffed and almost doubled, about 1³/₄ hours.

Baking. Preheat the oven to 450°F. Bake 10 minutes. Reduce the heat to 350°F and bake 15 minutes longer. Cool completely on racks.

Pane Integrale alle Erbe WHOLE WHEAT BREAD WITH HERBS

"Spiritoso," said the Roman baker, describing this bread—meaning it's witty and spirited, a bit out of the ordinary with its clever counterpoint of herbs played against the whole wheat. It's also straightforward and honest, with a crunchy top and soft interior, and it tastes wonderful with hearty beef and lamb dishes.

Makes 2 rings of 10 to 12 rolls each or 24 individual rolls

3¹/₄ teaspoons (0.3 oz / 9.2 g) active dry yeast

¹/₄ cup (2 oz / 60 g) warm water

¹/₄ cup (1.9 oz / 55 g) olive oil

2³/₄ cups (23 oz / 660 g) water, at room temperature (cold if using a processor)

2 tablespoons (0.2 oz / 7 g) chopped fresh rosemary or 2 teaspoons (0.1 oz / 3 g) dried rosemary

²/₃ cup (1 oz / 28 g) chopped fresh parsley

About 6 cups (1 lb 12 oz / 800 g) whole wheat flour

1¹/₂ cups (7 oz / 200 g) unbleached all-purpose flour

4 teaspoons (0.7 oz / 20 g) salt

BY HAND

Stir the yeast into the warm water in a large mixing bowl; let stand until creamy, about 10 minutes. Stir in the oil and the 2³/₄ cups of water. Stir in the rosemary and parsley. Mix the flours and salt and stir 1 cup at a time into the yeast mixture. Stir quickly to work into a dough. Knead on a lightly floured surface until firm and elastic, 8 to 10 minutes.

BY MIXER

Stir the yeast into the warm water in a mixer bowl; let stand until creamy, about 10 minutes. Stir in the oil and the

continued

Pane Integrale alle Erbe, *continued*

2³/₄ cups of water with the paddle. Add the rosemary, garlic, flours, and salt and mix until the dough pulls away from the sides of the bowl. Change to the dough hook and knead until firm and elastic, 2 to 3 minutes.

BY PROCESSOR

If the capacity of your food processor is 7 cups or less, process this dough in two batches. Stir the yeast into the ¹/₄ cup of warm water in a small bowl; let stand until creamy, about 10 minutes. Place the rosemary, parsley, salt, and flours in a food processor fitted with the steel blade and process with one or two pulses to mix. Pour the dissolved yeast and oil over the flour. With the machine running, pour the 2³/₄ cups of cold water through the feed tube as quickly as the flour can absorb it. Process until the dough gathers into a ball. Stop and then process 45 seconds longer to knead. Finish kneading briefly by hand on a lightly floured surface.

First Rise. Place the dough in a lightly oiled bowl, cover with plastic wrap, and let rise until doubled, about 1 hour and 20 minutes.

Shaping and Second Rise. Punch the dough down on a lightly floured surface. Cut the dough in half and cover the piece you are not working on with plastic wrap to keep the dough from drying out. Shape each piece into 10 to 12 balls and cover the shaped dough as you finish. Arrange the balls about ¹/₂ to ³/₄ inch apart on lightly oiled or parchment-lined baking sheets, forming two rings of 10 to 12 balls each. Cover with plastic wrap propped up on juice glasses or spice jars. Place a towel over the plastic wrap and let the dough rise until doubled, about 1¹/₄ hours. The risen rolls should look like big Swedish meatballs flecked with little pieces of parsley. You may make individual rolls instead of arranging them in rings, if you prefer.

Baking. Preheat the oven to 400°F. If you are using baking stones, turn the oven on 30 minutes before baking and sprinkle with cornmeal just before sliding the rolls onto them. Bake for 20 minutes. Cool completely on racks.

Pane ai Cinque Cereali con Noci

FIVE-GRAIN BREAD WITH WALNUTS

Walnuts are the brilliant touch in this bread. I've had more than my share of several-grain breads and have never been particularly knocked out by their taste. But when I bit into this and let the crunch and rich flavor of the roasted nuts race across my tongue, I knew I had left the world of health food for something a good deal more intriguing. Multigrain breads are popular in Italy, confirming what people living close to the earth have always known—the more genuine and natural the food, the better for the body. These natural grains may be tonic for the body, but it's those lovely nuts that make it a particularly tasty bread. Serve with smoked meats, smoked salmon, oysters and mussels, and sharp cheeses.

Makes two 9 by 5-inch loaves

1¼ cups (4.4 oz / 125 g) walnut pieces

3¾ teaspoons (0.4 oz / 10.6 g) active dry yeast

¼ cup (2 oz / 60 g) warm water

3 cups (25 oz / 720 g) water, at room temperature (cold if using a processor)

3¾ cups (17.5 oz / 500 g) unbleached all-purpose flour

1¼ cups (4.4 oz / 125 g) oat flour or finely ground rolled oats

1 cup plus 2 tablespoons (4.4 oz / 125 g) rye flour

1 cup minus 1 tablespoon (4.4 oz / 125 g) whole wheat flour

¾ cup (4.4 oz / 125 g) brown rice flour

4 teaspoons (0.7 oz / 20 g) salt

Preheat the oven to 375°F and toast the walnuts in the oven for 10 minutes. Let cool, then chop using a sharp knife or in a food processor fitted with the steel blade until the size of fat rice grains. Do not grind them finely.

BY HAND

Stir the yeast into the warm water in a large mixing bowl; let stand until creamy, about 10 minutes. Stir in the 3 cups of water. Mix the walnuts, flours, and salt and stir 2 cups at a time into the dissolved yeast, stirring vigorously with a wooden spoon or rubber spatula. The dough should come together easily. Knead on a floured surface, sprinkling with additional all-purpose flour as needed, until firm, elastic, and no longer sticky, 8 to 10 minutes.

BY MIXER

Stir the yeast into the warm water in a mixer bowl; let stand until creamy, about 10 minutes. Stir in the 3 cups of water. Stir in the flours, walnuts, and salt with the paddle. Mix until the dough comes together. Change to the dough hook and knead for 3 to 4 minutes at medium speed

continued

Pane ai Cinque Cereali con Noci, *continued*

until firm and elastic but still slightly sticky. Finish kneading briefly by hand on a surface floured with all-purpose flour.

BY PROCESSOR

Make sure your food processor can handle the volume of this dough. Even when done in two batches, there will be 4 cups of flour to be processed. Stir the yeast into the warm water in a small bowl; let stand until creamy, about 10 minutes. Place the flours and salt in a food processor fitted with the dough blade and process with several pulses to sift. With the machine running, pour the dissolved yeast and the 3 cups of cold water through the feed tube as quickly as the flours can absorb it; process until the dough gathers into a ball. Process 45 seconds longer to knead. Knead in the walnuts by hand on a surface floured with all-purpose flour.

First Rise. Place the dough in a lightly oiled bowl, cover with plastic wrap, and let rise until doubled, about 1 hour.

Shaping and Second Rise. Turn the dough out onto a lightly floured surface. The dough should be moist, firm, and noticeably elastic, if slightly sticky. Cut the dough in half and shape each half into an oval loaf to fit a 9 by 5-inch loaf pan. Place the loaves in the oiled pans (preferably glass), cover with a heavy towel, and let rise until truly doubled and fully above the tops of the pans, 1 to $1^{1}/_{4}$ hours.

Baking. Thirty minutes before baking, preheat the oven with baking stones to 400°F. Slash a pattern on the tops of the loaves. One baker in Milan cuts the shape of a stalk of grain on the top; elsewhere bakers make three parallel slashes. Bake 40 to 45 minutes, removing the loaves from the pans the last 5 to 10 minutes and placing on baking stones or baking sheets to brown the bottoms and sides. Cool completely on a rack.

Campagnolo COUNTRY BREAD WITH BRAN

There are Italians who jog and Italians who diet, and now there are more and more Italians who appreciate the importance of natural foods. Inspired by research extolling bran as an aid to digestion, a country baker dreamed up this bread. It gets its nutty crunch from the bran but maintains a lovely balance between heartiness and delicate flavor. Serve it with fresh cheeses.

Makes 2 loaves

2$^1/_4$ teaspoons (1 package / 0.2 oz / 7 g) active dry yeast

$^1/_3$ cup (2.8 oz / 80 g) warm water

2$^2/_3$ cups (22.4 oz / 640 g) water, at room temperature (or 2$^2/_3$ cups plus 1 tablespoon / 22.9 oz / 655 g cold water if using a processor)

2 tablespoons (1 oz / 30 g) olive oil

About 5$^1/_3$ cups (1 lb 10 oz / 750 g) unbleached all-purpose flour

2 cups (3.5 oz / 100 g) wheat bran

2$^1/_4$ teaspoons (0.4 oz / 12 g) salt

BY HAND

Stir the yeast into the warm water in a large mixing bowl; let stand until creamy, about 10 minutes. Stir in all but 2 table-spoons of the 2$^2/_3$ cups of water (you probably won't need it) and the oil. Mix the flour, bran, and salt and stir 2 cups at a time into the yeast mixture, reserving $^1/_4$ to $^1/_2$ cup of the flour mixture. When the dough is too stiff to stir, plunge in with your hands. Knead on a floured work surface, sprinkling with the reserved flour as needed, until firm and elastic but still slightly sticky, 8 to 10 minutes. Slam the dough down several times toward the end of the kneading to help develop the gluten.

BY MIXER

Stir the yeast into the warm water in a mixer bowl; let stand until creamy, about 10 minutes. Stir in the 2$^2/_3$ cups of water and the oil. Mix the flour, bran, and salt and reserve $^1/_4$ to $^1/_2$ cup for kneading. Add the remaining flour mixture to the yeast mixture and mix with the paddle for 2 to 3 minutes. Change to the dough hook and knead 3 to 4 minutes, half at low speed and half at medium. The dough should be creamy beige and feel stiff but elastic. If the dough is very stiff, let it rest a couple of minutes and then continue kneading. The dough will be sticky even when fully kneaded because of the bran. Finish kneading by hand, sprinkling with the reserved flour as needed, for 1 to 2 minutes.

BY PROCESSOR

Make sure your processor can handle the volume of this dough. Stir the yeast into the warm water in a small bowl; let stand until creamy, about 10 minutes. Place the flour, bran, and salt in a food processor fitted with the steel blade and process with two or three pulses to mix. Pour the oil

continued

Campagnolo, *continued*

and dissolved yeast over the flour mixture. With the machine running, pour the $2^2/_3$ cups plus 1 tablespoon of cold water through the feed tube and process until the dough comes together. Process 45 seconds longer to knead. Finish kneading very briefly by hand on a floured surface.

First Rise. Place the dough in a lightly oiled bowl, cover with plastic wrap, and let rise until doubled, about $1^1/_2$ hours.

Shaping and Second Rise. Turn the dough out on a lightly floured surface. Cut the dough in half and shape each piece into a ball and then into an oval loaf. Dip the flat edge of your hand, from little finger to wrist bone, into a bit of flour and press it down the center of each loaf to make a lengthwise cleft. Pinch the ends of the loaf tightly together and make a deep impression with your thumb at each end. It should resemble a pair of lips. Place the loaves, cleft sides down, on heavily floured peels or baking sheets. Cover with a towel and let rise for about 45 minutes. The dough will feel slightly less resilient then other doughs even when it is ready.

Baking. Thirty minutes before baking, preheat the oven with baking stones or oiled baking sheets in it to 425°F. If you are using baking stones, sprinkle the stones with cornmeal just before baking. Invert and firmly press the cleft again with the edge of your hand and emphasize the thumb impressions. Place the loaves onto the hot stones or baking sheets and bake 20 minutes. Reduce the heat to 375°F and bake 20 to 25 minutes longer. Cool on racks at least 30 minutes.

Gli Avanzi
Using Leftover Breads

Some of the best dishes in all Italy are the simplest and most rustic. They are the spontaneous creations of a peasant culture that has taken the tastiest ingredients of the countryside and turned then into comforting country food. Most of them begin with breads, those fat wheels and crusty ovals that are served at the table three times a day. These rustic dishes are a prime example of making a virtue of necessity. Because these regional breads go stale rather quickly, frugal peasants and thrifty housewives and cooks have dreamed up a whole poor people's cuisine that uses up every last crumb.

Many of the dishes are essentially moist breads turned into soups with the addition of a bit of broth and an egg or two or a handful of greens, or into salads with slices of tomato, bits of chopped onion and garlic, and perhaps a sprinkling of herbs and a few gratings of pepper. These homey regional recipes are savory and satisfying, the quintessential Sunday night supper. Some of them are absolutely basic to the region (*mozzarella in carrozza* is unmistakably Neapolitan and *pappa al pomodoro* is totally Tuscan, for example), while others are generic (you'll find bread puddings in more than one region), but all are the best of simple regional Italian cuisine, mixing leftover and stale bread with the freshest ingredients to make filling, tasty dishes.

Savory Dishes

Bruschetta o Fettunta GARLIC BREAD

Good chewy peasant bread grilled over a wood fire and drizzled with olive oil, sometimes rubbed with a clove of garlic and sometimes not, is known as bruschetta in Rome, *fettunta* in Tuscany, and *soma d'ai* in Piedmont. In all three places, it is the perfect way to taste rich, fruity olive oil just after it has been pressed. To make an authentic *fettunta*, use *pane toscano* (page 84) in this recipe.

Makes 6 servings

6 ³/₄-inch-thick slices (14 to 16 oz / 400 to 450 g) country bread

1 or 2 large cloves garlic cut in half

Salt and freshly ground pepper

¹/₄ cup (1.9 oz / 55 g) best-quality extra-virgin olive oil

Toast or grill the bread. When the slices are still warm, rub one side with half a garlic clove so that the flavor permeates the bread. Sprinkle with salt and pepper, and then drizzle with the oil. Serve immediately.

Variation. For bruschetta Pugliese, cook 2 chopped and seeded ripe tomatoes (12 oz / 310 g total) in 3 to 4 tablespoons of olive oil in a sauté pan over medium-low heat until it forms a rich concentrate, about 10 minutes. If you want, cook 1 minced garlic clove with the tomatoes. Toast 6 slices of *pane di Altamura* (page 95), rub with the garlic, sprinkle with salt and pepper, and drizzle with oil, as described above, before topping with the tomato concentrate.

Crostini LITTLE TOASTS WITH TOPPINGS

These traditional hors d'oeuvres are nothing more than croutons of saltless Tuscan bread topped with a particularly tasty chopped liver spread. The anchovies and capers are the perfect salty, piquant foil to the mellow but bland bread of the region. There are endless variations of crostini, but you can be sure that any assortment of antipasti you encounter at a Florentine restaurant will include one of them.

Makes 6 to 8 servings

8 ounces (225 g) chicken livers

2 tablespoons (1 oz / 30 g) unsalted butter

1 tablespoon (0.5 oz / 15 g) olive oil

1/4 cup (1.25 oz / 35 g) chopped onion

2 bay leaves

1/4 cup (2 oz / 60 g) Marsala

2 anchovies, drained and boned, if necessary

2 teaspoons (0.2 oz / 6.5 g) capers, drained

8 11/2- to 3/4-inch-thick slices (3 oz / 85 g) pane toscano (page 84)

Unsalted butter (optional)

Rinse the chicken livers and cut away any yellow spots. Heat the butter and oil in a sauté pan over medium-low heat. Add the livers and onions and sauté 3 to 5 minutes. Stir in the bay leaves and Marsala and cook over medium-high heat until the Marsala has almost evaporated. Remove the chicken livers to a cutting board. Very finely chop the livers, anchovies, and capers with a mezzaluna or a chef's knife. Don't use a food processor or blender; true Tuscan crostini should have a bit of texture to the liver. Return the mixture to the pan and cook 1 to 2 minutes.

Meanwhile, cut the bread into 2-inch squares or slightly larger rectangles for hors d'oeuvres, or cut the slices in half to serve as an antipasto. Toast the bread lightly in the oven or butter one side lightly and sauté, buttered side down, briefly in a skillet. Let the bread cool completely, then spread with the liver mixture or spoon it into a small bowl and let everyone spread his or her own. The chicken liver mixture can be served warm or at room temperature.

Crostoni con Taleggio o Gorgonzola

TOASTS WITH A CREAMY CHEESE TOPPING

What are *crostoni*? They are the perfect solution to a really quick first course or antipasto on a cold winter evening. Toast country bread, make a simple cheese topping, warm them together, and you have a splendid hors d'oeuvre that uses up your stale bread as well.

Makes 6 servings

3 to 3¹/₂ tablespoons (1.5 to 1.8 oz / 45 to 50 g) unsalted butter, at room temperature

6 thick slices (14 oz / 400 g) slightly stale country bread

6 ounces (180 g) Taleggio or Gorgonzola cheese, thinly sliced

4 to 6 teaspoons (0.8 to 1 oz / 20 to 30 g) water or milk

1 clove garlic, thinly sliced (optional)

Salt and freshly ground pepper

Preheat the oven to 425°F. Using 2 tablespoons of the butter, spread one side of each slice of bread with butter. Place buttered sides up on a baking sheet and bake until lightly browned.

Meanwhile, place the cheese, 4 teaspoons of water or milk, 1 tablespoon of butter, and the garlic, if desired, in a small saucepan. Heat over very low heat, mashing the cheese with a wooden spoon, until melted and creamy. Add the remaining water or milk and butter if the cheese mixture is too thick to spread.

Spread the cheese mixture on the lightly toasted bread and heat very quickly in the oven until golden. Season with salt and pepper and serve immediately.

Mozzarella in Carrozza MOZZARELLA IN A CARRIAGE

In Naples this sandwich of *mozzarella di bufala*, which sits handsomely in its carriage of bread, is almost as famous as pizza and is made in the same rustic pizzerias. It almost seems silly to write a recipe for two slices of bread enclosing buffalo mozzarella, which are then dipped into egg and flour and fried in hot oil. I particularly like this with a sliver or two of anchovy so that the saltiness of the fish plays against the crunch of the fried bread and the soft melting cheese.

Makes 4 servings

4 slices (2.8 oz / 80 g) fresh mozzarella, each about 1/2 inch thick

8 1/2-inch-thick slices (9.6 to 10.5 oz / 275 to 300 g) pane in cassetta (page 236), crusts trimmed

4 anchovies, drained, boned if necessary, and cut into thin slivers (optional)

Milk

2 large eggs

Pinch of salt

About 2 tablespoons (0.6 oz / 18 g) unbleached all-purpose flour

Olive oil for frying

Place one slice of the mozzarella on each of four slices of bread, making sure that the cheese doesn't extend beyond the edges of the bread. Place one or two anchovy slivers on the cheese, if using. Top with the remaining bread. Pour milk onto a platter and quickly dip both sides of each sandwich into it, just until moistened. Beat the eggs with the salt and pour into a wide platter; soak each sandwich to absorb the eggs for 2 to 10 minutes a side. Place the flour on a plate and dip each side of the sandwiches very lightly into the flour to coat. Shake off any excess flour.

Heat $3/8$ inch of olive oil in a large skillet over medium-high heat. When the oil is hot, add the sandwiches and fry until golden on both sides, turning once. Drain on paper towels and serve immediately.

Panzanella TUSCAN BREAD SALAD

Panzanella is one of the humblest Tuscan dishes, made merely of stale dark saltless bread moistened with water that is turned into a salad with slices of tomato, chopped basil, a few vegetables, and the best fruity olive oil. It is the perfect picnic food on a hot summer day and can be made on the spur of the moment. The bread should be rough and mellow—a good chewy *pane toscano*—and the olive oil the best peppery one you can find.

No one knows where the name for this salad comes from, although some say that *pan* (bread) and *zanella* (a little soup tureen) are easily enough deciphered. We do know that it has been popular for a long time, for, in the middle of the sixteenth century, the Mannerist painter Bronzino wrote a little rhyme in praise of a bread salad with chopped onions, cucumber, basil, *porcellana* (purslane), and *ruchetta* (arugula). The tomato hadn't yet made its debut in Italy, but there are words of praise for the pleasures of life enhanced by this lovely combination.

Makes 6 to 8 servings

6 to 8 thick slices (13 to 20 oz / 370 to 560 g) pane toscano (page 84)

6 ripe tomatoes (2 lb 2 oz / 1 kg), thinly sliced

3 large cucumbers (about 3 lb / 960 g), peeled and thinly sliced

2 red onions (about 14 oz / 400 g), thinly sliced

2 ribs celery (3.5 oz / 100 g), thinly sliced

10 to 12 fresh basil leaves

$^1/_2$ cup (3.8 oz / 110 g) olive oil

2 tablespoons (1 oz / 30 g) red wine vinegar

Salt and freshly ground pepper

Soak the bread in cold water to cover until very moist, about 15 minutes. Squeeze each bread slice dry between your hands and then tear into small chunks.

Place the bread in a large bowl and add the tomatoes, cucumbers, onions, celery, and basil. Mix the oil, vinegar, and salt and pepper to taste and pour over the salad. Toss to combine. Serve at room temperature.

Variation. The Romans like their *panzanella* spicier and add chopped capers, parsley, anchovies, garlic, and sometimes hard-cooked eggs.

Pappa al Pomodoro TOMATO AND BREAD SOUP

Here's a common enough Tuscan sort of soup: soften stale bread in good broth, whisk it all up, flavor it with a good peppery Tuscan oil and salt and pepper to taste, and add a bit of Tuscan pecorino cheese. There are countless recipes for *pappa al pomodoro*, because every Florentine considers it his heritage and has vivid memories of how it tasted at home. There are two schools of thought on how it should be cooked: either all the ingredients go in the pot cold and get boiled together, or the bread, garlic, and tomato are tossed into the hot broth. This recipe uses the traditional ingredients with a bit of extra garlic; it is full of flavor but isn't heavy or gummy. *Pappa* is never eaten with cheese.

Makes 6 servings

³/₄ to 1 cup (5.8 to 7.7 oz / 165 to 220 g) olive oil, plus more for garnish

2 large cloves garlic, chopped

1 teaspoon (0.2 oz / 5 g) tomato paste

2 cups (30 oz / 850 g) peeled, seeded, and chopped fresh ripe tomatoes

8 to 10 fresh basil leaves, torn into 3 or 4 pieces each

6 cups (49 oz / 1.4 kg) chicken broth, preferably homemade

Salt and freshly ground pepper

1 pound (450 g) stale pane toscano scuro (page 88) or pane toscano (page 84), thinly sliced or broken into small chunks

Heat the olive oil in a heavy 10-inch skillet over medium heat. Add the garlic and lightly sauté. Stir in the tomato paste and then the tomatoes and basil. Simmer over low heat for 5 minutes.

Combine the broth and salt and pepper to taste in a large saucepan and bring to a boil. Stir in the bread and the tomato mixture. Cook over medium heat for 2 to 3 minutes. Remove from the heat and let stand uncovered for 1 hour.

Just before serving, stir thoroughly. Serve hot, at room temperature, or cold. Drizzle a thin ribbon of olive oil over the top.

Minestrone Toscana TUSCAN BEAN SOUP

These days, simple is sophisticated and rustic is chic. All over Tuscany, trattorias are full of the most delicious peasant soups, which were initially created from simple necessity. Some say that during the Middle Ages bean soups were made from the bread that was used as a trencher for roasts. After the bread had served its purpose, it was given to the hungry servants, who put it in a big pot of water with vegetables and spices and turned it into minestrone or a similar soup. I've also heard that a bean soup such as this one was traditionally prepared in the country on a Friday; this would explain why it is meatless and doesn't have even a hint of prosciutto or a bit of pancetta. It is made of the most basic ingredients—bread, potatoes, chard, kale, and a few handfuls of cabbage. Most Tuscans do not serve Parmesan cheese with this bean soup.

Makes 6 servings

8 ounces (225 g) dried white cannellini beans, or 1¹/₂ cups canned cannellini beans with their liquid

³/₄ cup (5.8 oz / 165 g) olive oil

2 large yellow onions (about 1 lb / 450 g), finely chopped

3 ribs celery (5 oz / 150 g), diced

4 carrots (10 oz / 300 g), peeled and chopped

1 teaspoon (0.2 oz / 5 g) tomato paste

2 teaspoons (0.4 oz / 10 g) warm water

2 ripe tomatoes (12 oz / 310 g), chopped

2 bunches Swiss chard (about 2 lb / 900 g), stems trimmed and leaves chopped

2 firmly packed cups (about 6 oz / 175 g) lacinato or dinosaur kale, stems trimmed, leaves chopped (about 1 bunch)

3 cups (about 6 oz / 175 g) finely shredded Savoy cabbage

4 boiling potatoes (about 13 oz / 375 g), peeled and chopped

1 fresh small chile, seeded and chopped

2 cloves garlic, minced

2 teaspoons (0.1 oz / 2 g) chopped fresh thyme or 1 teaspoon dried thyme

Salt and freshly ground pepper

5 to 6 cups (42 to 49 oz / 1.2 to 1.4 kg) cold water

12 slices (about 1¹/₂ lb / 600 g) stale pane toscano scuro (page 88) or pane toscano (page 84)

Best-quality Tuscan olive oil, for garnish

If you are using dried beans, soak the beans overnight in water to cover, then drain. Bring the beans and fresh water to cover by 2 inches to a boil over high heat. Reduce the heat to medium-low and simmer, covered, until tender, about 1¹/₂ hours. Drain the beans but reserve the cooking liquid. Purée three-quarters of the cooked beans with a little of the cooking liquid or three-quarters of the canned beans in a little of their liquid in a food processor fitted with the steel blade or in a blender. Reserve the remaining whole beans.

Heat ¹/₂ cup of the oil in a large, heavy pot or Dutch oven over medium-high heat. Add the onions, celery, and carrots and sauté until the onions are soft, about 5 minutes. Thin the tomato paste with the warm water and add the thinned paste and the fresh tomatoes to the vegetables. Cook, stirring occasionally, for 5 to 10 minutes. Stir in the chard, kale, cabbage, potatoes, puréed beans, chile, garlic, thyme, and salt and pepper to taste. Add the remaining liquid from cooking the beans or from the can of beans and enough of the cold water to cover the vegetables. Heat to a boil. Reduce the heat to low and simmer, covered, for about 2 hours. Add the reserved beans 10 minutes before the soup is done.

Just before serving, grill or toast two slices of bread for every serving. You can sauté the bread in the remaining $1/4$ cup of oil, or brush one side of each slice with oil and bake on a baking sheet at 400°F until golden, or brush the bread with oil and grill under a broiler or over an open fire. Place the bread in the bottoms of wide soup bowls and ladle the soup over the bread. Drizzle a fine ribbon of olive oil over each serving.

Carabaccia FLORENTINE ONION AND PEA SOUP

This fabulous Florentine soup tastes so delicate and fresh with its infusion of puréed peas that it always amazes me that Italians think of it as an onion soup. It actually began life as *carabazada* in the Renaissance, when, according to the great cookbook writer Cristoforo da Messisbugo, it numbered almonds, cinnamon, and sugar among its ingredients. Needless to say, those sweet tastes have been banished from the modern version, which I have modified further by adding chicken broth to make it a true soup instead of the thicker original *minestra* that is served under a blanket of poached eggs. I have found in serving this *carabaccia* to Italians that it evokes the most remarkable memories in my guests of springtime lunches in the Tuscan countryside or wonderful meals in tiny little hill towns with several generations of Italian family, baskets of bread on the table, and a pervasive sense of well-being.

Makes 4 servings

$1/3$ cup (2.8 oz / 75 g) olive oil, plus more for sautéing the bread (optional)

3 large yellow onions (about 8 oz / 225 g each), finely diced

4 ribs celery (7 oz / 200 g), finely diced

2 carrots (about 5 oz / 145 g), peeled and finely diced

Salt and freshly ground pepper

12 ounces (340 g) fresh peas, shelled, or 1 package (10 oz / 285 g) frozen peas, thawed

2 cups (16.8 oz / 480 g) chicken broth

4 $1/2$-inch-thick slices (about 8.5 oz / 245 g) stale country bread

Grated Parmesan cheese

continued

Carabaccia, *continued*

Heat the oil in a heavy, large pot or Dutch oven over low heat and add the onions, celery, carrots, and salt and pepper to taste. Cook, uncovered, over very low heat, stirring occasionally, for at least 1 hour but preferably 1 1/2 hours. Don't add any water; the vegetables will render enough liquid to keep them sufficiently moist.

Meanwhile, if using fresh peas, cook them in 1/2 cup of the broth until just tender. If using frozen peas, thaw them in the warmed broth. Drain the peas, reserving the broth. Purée half of the cooked or thawed frozen peas in a food processor fitted with the steel blade or in the blender.

Toast the bread or sauté it in oil until golden and place 1 slice in the bottom of each soup bowl. Stir all the broth, including the broth used to cook or thaw the peas, into the vegetable mixture and heat to a boil. Immediately reduce the heat, add the whole and puréed peas, and heat until warmed through, about 5 minutes. Ladle the soup over the bread in the bowls. Pass the Parmesan cheese at the table.

Soupe Paysanne Val d'Aosta
PEASANT SOUP WITH FONTINA CHEESE FROM THE VAL D'AOSTA

The hearty soups of the Val d'Aosta in the mountains of Piedmont are meals in themselves. All of them start with rustic country bread—sometimes it is black and sometimes a coarse, chewy wheat bread—and they are usually layered with the Fontina cheese for which the valley is so famous. This particular soup is so rich that it is very filling, perfect after a day of skiing or hiking. It is best if you use a good homemade beef stock. The local residents start with a bouillon left from boiling meat (if you make *bollito misto*, this soup would be a perfect use for the stock), then flavor it with any number of herbs and seasonings, and cook it very slowly to concentrate the flavors. Don't be bewildered by the name; French is the language of the valley, and the bread-and-cheese-thickened soup is absolutely indigenous to the area. If you can't find Toma Valdostana or Taleggio, simple double the amount of Fontina.

Makes 6 servings

6 to 9 thick slices (13 to 19 oz / 365 to 540 g)
stale rustic country bread

8 ounces (225 g) Italian Fontina cheese,
thinly sliced

8 ounces (225 g) Toma Valdostana or Taleggio
cheese, thinly sliced

4 oz (115 g) grated Parmesan cheese

6¼ cups (50 oz / 1.5 kg) beef broth, preferably
homemade

Freshly ground pepper

Place a third of the bread in a single layer in the bottom of a deep casserole or baking dish, cutting the slices to fit. Top with a third of the sliced cheeses and sprinkle with a third of the Parmesan. Repeat the layers two more times. Heat the broth to boiling and pour over the bread and cheeses.

Baking. Preheat the oven to 400°F. Bake, uncovered, for 20 to 30 minutes. Grind pepper over the top and serve immediately.

Zuppa di Verdure all'Agliata GARLICKY VEGETABLE SOUP

Liguria lies on the shores of the Mediterranean, stretching in a thin band from the French border at Provence to Tuscany. It is famous for its fabulous vegetables, the garlic that seems to suffuse the whole region, its basil (as well as the pesto that it becomes), and the olive oil from the trees of its hillsides. This soup is quintessentially Ligurian. It is more delicate in taste than its ingredients might suggest. Don't try to reheat it, as the peas won't stand up to a second appearance. In winter the Ligurians use turnips instead of peas.

Makes 4 servings

¼ cup (1.9 oz / 55 g) olive oil, plus more for the
bread (optional)

1 large yellow onion (about 8 oz / 225 g), very
thinly sliced

About 8 ounces (225 g) kale, stems removed and
leaves finely chopped or shredded

2 zucchini (about 8 oz / 225 g), finely chopped

2 ribs celery (3.5 oz / 100 g), finely chopped

2 large carrots (about 10 oz / 300 g), peeled and
finely chopped

1 large potato (8 oz / 225 g), peeled and finely
chopped

2 tomatoes (about 12 oz / 310 g), peeled, seeded,
and chopped

Salt and freshly ground pepper

4½ cups (36 oz / 1 kg) chicken broth or a
combination of chicken and beef broths

12 ounces (340 g) fresh peas, shelled, or 1 package
(10 oz / 285 g) frozen peas, thawed

2 or 3 large cloves garlic, finely minced

2 to 3 tablespoons (about 0.2 oz / 6 g) finely
chopped fresh parsley

4 to 6 slices (about 9 to 14 oz / 245 to 400 g)
country bread

Olive oil for the bread (optional)

Grated Parmesan cheese

continued

Zuppa di Verdure all'Agliata, *continued*

Heat the oil in a heavy, large pot or Dutch oven over medium heat. Add the onion and sauté until pale golden. Stir in the kale, zucchini, celery, carrots, potato, tomatoes, and salt and pepper to taste. Sauté until lightly browned. Pour the broth over the vegetables and cook, uncovered, over medium heat for 20 to 30 minutes. If you are using fresh peas, add them with the garlic and parsley after 15 minutes of cooking and cook 15 minutes longer. If you are using thawed frozen peas, add them with the garlic and parsley after 25 minutes of cooking and cook briefly, no more than 3 or 4 minutes.

Lightly toast the bread in the oven or sauté in oil and place 1 slice in the bottom of each soup bowl. Ladle the hot soup over the bread and serve immediately. Pass the Parmesan cheese at the table.

Minestra Mariconda

BEEF BROTH WITH EGGS, CHEESE, AND CHEESE BREAD

This soup is a special dish of the town of Brescia, which sits in the lovely countryside of Lombardy north of Milan. It dates as far back as the Renaissance and belongs to the fine old tradition of cooking bread with eggs and cheeses in homemade broth. Many cooks chop up leftover chicken or meat and add it with the leftover bread. In Mantua, families add minced cooked chicken livers to the mixture. *Squisito*, as the Italians say.

Although it is no way traditional, I like making this soup with a cheese bread because it has such a rich and wonderful taste. You could also try using *pan giallo* (page 107)—a typical Lombard cornbread—or any rustic country loaf, either white or mixed grain.

Makes 6 to 8 servings

8 ounces (225 g) stale bread, crusts removed

1¼ cups (10.6 oz / 300 g) milk

1 stick (4 oz / 115 g) unsalted butter

4 large eggs, beaten

Scant 1 cup (3.5 oz / 100 g) grated Parmesan cheese

Freshly grated nutmeg

Salt and freshly ground pepper

6½ cups (about 52 oz / 1.5 kg) homemade beef broth

Crumble the bread into a bowl and pour the milk over it. Let stand 30 minutes. Squeeze the bread dry with your hands and tear into small pieces. Melt the butter in a small skillet over low heat. Add the bread and sauté gently until dry but still soft.

Beat the eggs, 1/4 cup of the Parmesan, the nutmeg, and salt and pepper to taste in a mixing bowl. Add the bread and stir until thoroughly blended. Let stand, covered, for 1 hour.

About 10 minutes before serving, heat the broth in a large saucepan to a rolling boil. Shape the bread mixture between your hands into even balls, using 1/2 to 1 tablespoon of the mixture for each ball. Slide the balls into the broth and cook, uncovered, over medium heat for about 5 minutes.

Serve the soup steaming hot. Pass the remaining Parmesan cheese at the table.

Panada di Milano RICH EASTER SOUP

Every region has its *pancotto* (literally, "cooked bread"), which is simply a soup made with crumbs of leftover loaves, but this *panada* is particularly rich and filling, having been traditionally served for Easter lunch in Milan. Because the eggs and cheese are beaten in the tureen before the hot broth and bread crumbs are added, it looks quite a lot like *stracciatella*, with its lovely ribbons of egg. Your guests will be surprised when their spoons bring up lightly crunchy bread crumbs floating in their bowls.

Makes 6 servings

1/2 cup plus 2 tablespoons (7 oz / 210 g) fine stale bread crumbs

6 1/2 cups (52 oz / 1.5 kg) homemade beef broth

1/4 cup (2 oz / 55 g) unsalted butter

3 large eggs

3 tablespoons (0.8 oz / 22 g) grated Parmesan cheese

Place 1/2 cup of the bread crumbs in a small bowl and pour 1/4 cup of the broth over the bread. Heat the remaining broth in a large saucepan to a rolling boil.

About 10 minutes before serving, heat the butter in a small skillet over low heat. Add the moistened bread crumbs and sauté until golden, about 5 minutes.

Place the remaining 2 tablespoons of dry bread crumbs in a soup tureen and break the eggs into the bottom of the tureen. Add the cheese and beat with a fork or whisk until well blended. Pour the boiling broth into the tureen and add the sautéed bread crumbs. Beat vigorously for 1 to 2 minutes. Serve immediately.

Canederli BREAD DUMPLINGS

Canederli are wonderfully flavored bread dumplings made in the mountainous Italian-speaking part of the Trentino region, north of Venice. Because they originate from the Austro-Hungarian culinary tradition, and because the word is really a translation of *Knödel*, you might think of them as northern gnocchi. I like to serve them floating in a good homemade chicken or turkey broth, but there are many other possibilities. You can also use stale rye bread instead of white bread, as they do in the Alto Adige. They often turn up at Italian tables with a ragout, gravy, or, at their most Teutonic, a big helping of sauerkraut.

Makes 6 servings

10 ounces (300 g) stale white bread, crusts trimmed

About 1 cup (8.5 oz / 240 g) milk

2 to 3 tablespoons (1 to 1.5 oz / 30 to 45 g) olive oil

³/₄ cup (3.5 oz / 100 g) diced pancetta

¹/₂ cup (2 oz / 60 g) diced salami

1 small yellow onion (about 4 oz / 115 g), minced

1 clove garlic, minced

2 large eggs, 1 of them separated

1 tablespoon (0.1 oz / 2.5 g) chopped fresh parsley

Grated zest of 1 lemon

Freshly grated nutmeg

Salt and freshly ground pepper

¹/₂ cup (2.5 oz / 65 g) unbleached all-purpose flour

6 to 7 cups (49 to 60 oz / 1.4 to 1.6 kg) homemade chicken broth

Cut the bread into rough 1-inch cubes and place in a large mixing bowl. Pour the milk over the bread. There should be enough milk to moisten the bread but not enough to make it really wet. Let stand for about 1 hour.

Heat 2 tablespoons of the oil in a small skillet over medium-high heat. Add the pancetta and salami and sauté 3 to 4 minutes. Remove with a slotted spoon to a mixing bowl. Add 1 tablespoon of oil, if needed, to the skillet and heat. Add the onion and garlic and sauté just until translucent. Add to the pancetta. Squeeze the bread dry with your hands and tear it into small pieces. Add the bread, one whole egg, the egg yolk, parsley, lemon zest, nutmeg, and salt and pepper to taste to the pancetta mixture and stir thoroughly. Add enough of the flour so that the mixture will hold its shape. If it is too dry, you may need to add a little of the egg white from the separated egg. Before you make all the dumplings, shape a small amount of the mixture into a ball the size of a walnut and slide it into a small pan of boiling water. If it holds its shape and doesn't disintegrate, shape the remaining mixture; if it does fall apart, add a little more flour and test again. The mixture should be slightly moist and sticky.

Heat the broth in a large saucepan to a slow boil. Slide the dumplings into the broth and simmer, uncovered, for about 15 minutes. Serve immediately with the broth.

Passatelli FAT NOODLES IN SOUP

Passatelli are fat little noodles of bread, eggs, and cheese that got their name from the kitchen tool, called a *passatello*, that gives them their shape. Don't worry about the utensil. You can use a ricer or the coarse disk of a food mill to make the delicate little strands that flow into the hot broth. They are a specialty of Romagna and the cities of the Marche on the Adriatic coast.

Makes 6 servings

6 cups (48 oz / 1.4 kg) homemade beef broth

³/₄ cup (3 oz / 75 g) dry bread crumbs, preferably from grated stale pasta dura (page 225)

¹/₂ cup plus 2 tablespoons (2.6 oz / 75 g) grated Parmesan cheese

1 or 2 large eggs, beaten

Grated zest of ¹/₂ lemon

¹/₄ to ¹/₂ teaspoon freshly grated nutmeg

¹/₂ teaspoon (0.1 oz / 2.5 g) salt

Heat the broth in a large saucepan to a gentle boil.

Mix the bread crumbs, Parmesan, one egg, lemon zest, nutmeg, and salt in a mixing bowl. The mixture should be firm enough to put through a ricer, but not too stiff. If necessary, mix in the second egg, a little at a time, until the mixture is the desired consistency.

Spoon the bread mixture into a ricer, a food mill fitted with the coarsest disk, or a coarse sieve. Press the mixture through your utensil into the slowly boiling stock. Little strands of the bread mixture should float in the stock like tiny wiggly bits of pasta. Remove from the heat and let stand for a minute or two before serving.

Bread-Based Desserts

Torta Nicolotta BREAD PUDDING

This old and very popular cake gets its name from the inhabitants of the poorest neighborhood in Venice, i Nicolotti, who live by begging. They make this very simple dessert with leftover bread, milk, and a few sweeteners.

Makes 8 to 10 servings

3 to 4 cups (12 to 14 oz / 350 to 400 g) stale white bread or raisin bread, crusts trimmed, cubed

4¼ cups (36 oz / 1 kg) milk

5 tablespoons (2.5 oz / 70 g) unsalted butter

¾ cup (5.3 oz / 150 g) sugar

1 cup (6 oz / 175 g) raisins

2 tablespoons (1 oz / 30 g) rum

5 large eggs, beaten

Grated zest of 1 lemon

¾ cup (3.5 oz / 100 g) chopped candied citron (page 39, optional)

¼ teaspoon ground cinnamon

1 teaspoon (0.1 oz / 4 g) vanilla extract

Unsalted butter and fine bread crumbs for the baking dish

Place the bread cubes in a large mixing bowl. Heat the milk, butter, and sugar in a saucepan just to a low boil and pour over the bread cubes. Let stand 2 hours.

Place the raisins and rum in a small bowl; add warm water to cover. Let stand at least 15 minutes to plump the raisins. Drain, squeeze the raisins to eliminate excess liquid, and pat dry. Squeeze the bread dry and break it up with your hands to a soft, crumbly mass. Stir the raisins, eggs, lemon zest, and citron, if using, into the bread. Add the cinnamon and vanilla and stir thoroughly. Butter a 2-quart baking dish and lightly coat it with fine bread crumbs. Pour the bread mixture into the dish.

Baking. Preheat the oven to 375°F. Bake until the top is the golden color of a hazelnut, 45 to 55 minutes.

Torta di Mele APPLE CAKE

Apples grow in the north of Italy, especially in Trentino, where the orchards extend for miles along roads that wind toward the border and the Alps. This apple cake is an adaptation of an old recipe from the Brianza, the region above Milan, and it is rather like an apple charlotte in the way it combines leftover stale bread with cooked apples.

Makes 6 to 8 servings

2 pounds (900 g) apples, preferably Granny Smiths or pippins, peeled and sliced

1/2 cup (4 oz / 120 g) Riesling, Gewürztraminer, or other slightly sweet white wine

1/2 cup (4 oz / 120 g) water

3/4 cup (5.3 oz / 150 g) sugar

Grated zest of 1 lemon

1/4 cup (2 oz / 55 g) unsalted butter, or as needed

About 4 ounces (100 to 125 g) homemade bread, crusts trimmed

1 large egg

3/4 cup (6.3 oz / 180 g) milk

1/2 teaspoon (0.07 oz / 2 g) vanilla extract

3/4 teaspoon (0.07 oz / 2 g) grated nutmeg

3/4 teaspoon (0.07 oz / 2 g) ground cinnamon

2/3 cup (3.5 oz / 100 g) raisins

2 tablespoons (1 oz / 28 g) apricot jam

Place the apples, wine, water, 1/2 cup plus 2 tablespoons of the sugar, and the lemon zest in a heavy saucepan. Cook, covered, stirring occasionally, until roughly the texture of applesauce, 25 to 30 minutes.

Preheat the oven to 350°F. Butter the bread on both sides and bake on a baking sheet until lightly toasted. Mix the egg, milk, vanilla, nutmeg, the remaining 2 tablespoons of sugar, and 1/4 teaspoon of the cinnamon and pour over the bread in a large bowl. Let stand about 30 minutes.

Place the raisins in a small bowl and add warm water to cover; let stand 15 minutes. Drain the raisins, squeeze out the excess liquid, and pat dry. Add the raisins, apricot jam, and the remaining 1/2 teaspoon of the cinnamon to the applesauce and stir thoroughly.

Butter a 2-quart soufflé dish and line the bottom and sides with the soaked bread. Pour the apple mixture into the dish and smooth the top. Trim the bread even with the apple mixture.

Baking. Bake at 350°F until set and lightly golden on top, 45 to 50 minutes. If you want, unmold the *torta* onto a serving platter. Serve hot or warm.

Torta di Pere e Pan Giallo
RUSTIC PEAR AND CORNBREAD DESSERT

Sometimes rustic food made with leftovers is irresistible. Bake a little leftover corn-bread with pears poached in wine with lemon peel, cinnamon, cloves, and sugar for a perfect family dessert.

Makes 6 servings

3 or 4 slices (4 to 6 oz / 120 to 170 g) leftover pan giallo (page 107), crusts trimmed

2 tablespoons (1 oz / 28 g) unsalted butter, at room temperature

$^1/_2$ cup (4 oz / 120 g) dry white wine

$^1/_3$ to $^1/_2$ cup (2.5 to 3.5 oz / 70 to 100 g) granulated sugar

Grated zest of 1 lemon

$^1/_4$ teaspoon ground cinnamon

2 whole cloves

2 pounds (900 g) ripe pears, peeled and sliced

$^1/_4$ cup (1.8 oz / 50 g) turbinado or granulated sugar

Preheat the oven to 350°F. Cut the bread into 3-inch pieces and butter each piece. Bake on a baking sheet until lightly toasted. Place the bread in a buttered 1-quart baking dish and spread evenly.

Heat the wine, $^1/_3$ to $^1/_2$ cup of granulated sugar, depending on the sweetness of the pears, and the zest, cinnamon, and cloves in a 2-quart saucepan over medium heat and simmer for 10 minutes; add the pears and enough water to just cover the pears, if necessary. Poach the pears, uncovered, over medium heat until just tender, about 15 minutes. Spoon the pears and whatever liquid is left over the bread in the baking dish and sprinkle the top with the turbinado sugar.

Baking. Bake at 350°F for 40 to 45 minutes. Let cool to room temperature.

Pani Festivi
Celebration Breads

Fruit and nut breads are among the oldest country loaves, invented by poor Italians who used raw and dried fruits and nuts to give sweetness to their doughs in the days when sugar was unavailable. I like the thought of medieval peasants, whose lives were difficult at best, adding a bit of sweetness to their days with special breads bursting with fat raisins or figs or studded with walnuts. It was common in those times and much later as well to make regular doughs during the week and then enrich them on Sunday with a splash of milk, an egg or two, and a few handfuls of candied fruits and nuts. Of course, such exotic ingredients as chocolate did not make an appearance until the seventeenth century.

Many of these rich, eggy doughs are very similar. The *colomba pasquale* has more butter and is sprinkled with almonds, the *pizza Civitavecchia* is flavored with port and anise, and the panettone is studded with raisins, citron, and candied orange peel, but all are essentially variations on a theme of flour, eggs, butter, and yeast. In Italy every bakery has bottles of powerful essences labeled *aroma di panettone, aroma di colomba, aroma di limone,* and *aroma di arancia dolce,* which give the breads their memorable tastes, but some of the finest bakers I met prefer using freshly grated lemon and orange zests or a splash of vanilla extract for flavoring, which is the approach I have used to replicate the mysterious essence of these Italian holiday breads.

The doughs are delicate and complex, and almost all need fairly long rises to create the high, airy loaves. But that does not mean that they cannot be made in a day. I like to start baking right after breakfast and work out a schedule for the first and second rises that fits into the rest of my day. The dough can go in the refrigerator if you have other things to do; the action of the yeast will be slowed down, but the dough will develop more flavor.

Actually, it isn't putting the ingredients together that is time-consuming, but rather the time required for the yeast to do its magical work, which is true for all breads but especially for these loaves, which are heavy with eggs and butter as well as fruits and nuts. I have found several ways to encourage the process, however. Covering the bowl tightly with plastic wrap for the dough's first rise traps the heat given off as the yeast begins to work. I never place the dough directly over the pilot of my gas stove, but it can certainly be set near the source of heat. I also have taken note of the warm, moist proofers in bakeries and approximated the method by turning the oven on at 150°F for three minutes and then immediately placing the shaped loaves in the oven along with a pan of steaming water. The warm moisture is a wonderful incentive for the expansion of the dough.

The holiday bread doughs (pages 199–222) must be made by hand or by mixer, for the food processor simply will not create the right airy texture. Don't be daunted by their seeming complexity. After you've tried one recipe, you'll find that the process is not as complicated as it reads. And, when you take a bite of the finished bread, close your eyes and you'll find you're tasting the true flavor of Italy.

Fruit and Nut Breads

Pane di Noci WALNUT BREAD

The first time I tasted this bread, I was certain that its rich, almost mahogany-colored interior came from freshly milled whole wheat, which shows how much I knew. The lovely dark color comes entirely from the walnuts that saturate the bread with their irresistibly delicate and nutty flavor. Be sure to toast your walnuts lightly to bring out the flavor before you chop and knead them into the dough. Baking the bread in a little ring mold with a few whole walnuts on the bottom makes an appetizing loaf when it is unmolded. The Italians particularly enjoy eating this bread with soft fresh cheeses.

Makes 1 ring or round loaf

- 2 cups (7 oz / 200 g) walnut pieces, plus 4 to 6 perfect halves for the ring loaf
- 2¼ teaspoons (1 package / 0.2 oz / 7 g) active dry yeast
- ¼ cup (3 oz / 85 g) honey
- 1⅓ cups (11.2 oz / 320 g) warm water (or ⅓ cup / 2.8 oz / 80 g warm water plus 1 cup / 8.4 oz / 240 g cold water if using a processor)
- 2 tablespoons (1 oz / 30 g) olive oil
- 3¾ cups (17.5 oz / 500 g) unbleached all-purpose flour, plus up to ⅓ cup (scant 2 oz / 56 g) extra for kneading
- 1½ teaspoons (0.3 oz / 7.5 g) salt

Preheat the oven to 400°F. Toast the walnuts on a baking sheet for 10 minutes. Let cool, then chop the walnuts to coarse crumbs with a sharp knife or in a food processor fitted with the steel blade. Reserve the perfect halves for the ring mold, if using.

BY HAND

Stir the yeast and honey into the water in a large mixing bowl; let stand until foamy, about 10 minutes. Stir in the oil. Combine the flour, salt, and walnuts and stir 1 cup at a time into the yeast mixture. Mix until the dough looks like whole wheat. Using a dough scraper, knead on a floured surface 8 to 10 minutes, sprinkling with up to ⅓ cup of additional flour to keep the dough from sticking. The dough should be soft, moist, and fairly dense but easy to work, although it is not particularly elastic.

BY MIXER

Stir the yeast and honey into the water in a mixer bowl; let stand until foamy, about 10 minutes. Stir in the oil with the paddle. Add the flour, salt, and walnuts and mix until the dough comes together. Change to the dough hook and knead until soft, moist, and fairly dense, 4 to 5 minutes.

continued

Pane di Noci, *continued*

Knead briefly by hand on a lightly floured surface.

BY PROCESSOR

Stir the yeast and honey into the $^1/_3$ cup warm of water in a small bowl; let stand until foamy, about 10 minutes. Coarsely chop the nuts in a food processor fitted with the steel blade. Add the flour and salt and process with two or three pulses to sift. Stir the oil into the dissolved yeast. With the machine running, pour the yeast mixture and the 1 cup of cold water through the feed tube as quickly as the flour can absorb it and process until the dough comes together. Process 45 seconds longer to knead. If you want, finish kneading briefly by hand on a lightly floured surface.

First Rise. Place the dough in an oiled bowl, cover tightly with plastic wrap, and let rise until doubled, about $1^1/_4$ hours.

Shaping and Second Rise. Turn the dough out onto a lightly floured surface. Without punching it down or kneading it, shape it into a log and join the ends to make a ring. You may place the ring in an oiled ring mold with the reserved walnut halves set on the bottom, so that when the bread is baked and turned out of the mold the nuts are on the top. The dough can also be baked in a free-form ring, oval loaf, or round loaf. Place the free-form loaf on a floured peel or oiled baking sheet. Cover the dough with plastic wrap and let rise until doubled, about 1 hour.

Baking. Preheat the oven to 400°F. If you are using a baking stone, turn the oven on 30 minutes before baking and sprinkle the stone with cornmeal just before sliding the loaf onto it. Bake for 10 minutes. Reduce the heat to 350°F and bake 40 minutes longer. If you are baking the bread in a ring mold, bake the loaf out of the pan on a baking sheet or stone for the last 10 minutes to brown the bottom and sides. Cool completely on a rack.

Pane di Fichi FIG BREAD

The first thing to be said about this bread is that it is succulent and delicious as well as very easy to make. The second thing to be noted is that a bread like this has a lot of history behind it. This bread undoubtedly dates back at least to the early Middle Ages, a time when cities like Perugia, Florence, and Siena were dotted with towers that gave warring families and factions a good view of their neighbors and enemies. Even though bakers were busy making the daily bread, they made a point of transforming the dough for Sundays and special celebrations by sweetening it with honey and enriching it with nuts or dried fruits, such as figs.

Makes 1 loaf

2 1/4 teaspoons (1 package / 0.2 oz / 7 g) active dry yeast

1 cup (8.4 oz / 240 g) warm water (or 1/4 cup / 2 oz / 60 g warm water plus 3/4 cup / 6.3 oz / 180 g cold water if using a processor)

1 1/2 tablespoons (0.8 oz / 22 g) olive oil

2 3/4 cups (13.1 oz / 375 g) unbleached all-purpose flour, plus 2 tablespoons (0.6 oz / 18 g) for the figs

1 teaspoon (0.17 oz / 5 g) salt

1 cup (7 oz / 200 g) figs, preferably Calimyrna or Greek string figs, cut into about 12 pieces each

BY HAND

Stir the yeast into the water in a large mixing bowl; let stand until creamy, about 10 minutes. Stir in the oil. Mix the 3 cups of flour and the salt and stir into the yeast mixture. Stir until the dough comes together. Knead on a floured surface, sprinkling with additional flour, until velvety and moist, 7 to 10 minutes.

BY MIXER

Stir the yeast into the water in a mixer bowl; let stand until creamy, about 10 minutes. Stir in the oil with the paddle and then the 3 cups of flour and the salt. Mix until the dough comes together. Change to the dough hook and knead until velvety and moist, 3 to 4 minutes.

BY PROCESSOR

Stir the yeast into the 1/4 cup of warm water in a small bowl; let stand until creamy, about 10 minutes. Place the 3 cups of flour and the salt in a food processor fitted with the steel blade and process with several pulses to sift. Stir the 3/4 cup of cold water and the oil into the dissolved yeast. With the machine running, pour the yeast mixture through the feed tube as quickly as the flour can absorb it. Process 40 to 45 seconds longer to knead. Finish kneading briefly by hand on a floured surface.

First Rise. Place the dough in a lightly oiled bowl, cover tightly with plastic wrap, and let rise until doubled, about 1 hour.

Filling. Toss the figs in the 2 tablespoons of flour to coat the surfaces. Turn the dough out onto a floured surface. Without punching it down, pat the dough into an oval and spread half of the figs evenly over the surface; roll up the dough. Pat the dough into an oval again and sprinkle evenly with the remaining figs; roll it up again. Shape into a round loaf, being gentle but, at the same time, pulling the dough taut over the figs. Place the loaf, rough side down, on a lightly floured peel or oiled baking sheet, cover with a towel, and let rise until doubled, $1^{1}/_{4}$ to $1^{1}/_{2}$ hours.

Baking. Thirty minutes before baking, preheat the oven with a baking stone in it to 450°F. Sprinkle the stone with cornmeal just before sliding the loaf onto it. Bake 15 minutes. Reduce the heat to 375°F and bake 15 minutes longer. Cool completely on a rack.

Pan Tramvai o Pane all'Uva RAISIN BREAD

This outrageously delicious bread is so crammed with raisins that it actually has equal amounts of raisins and flour. A look at its knobby, slightly gnarled form gives no hint of the sweetness inside, but, once you've eaten it, you'll understand why the Milanese gave it such importance in their lives. It was originally made in the nineteenth century by a bread baker at the tramway station in Monza, where commuters caught the horse-drawn tram for Milan, hence its name, *tramvai*, or go by tram. Over time the loaf became as fat, crusty, and long as a French bread loaf, and the old-fashioned trams were replaced by sleek modern trains, but the Milanese continued to eat it as their special breakfast bread, and schoolchildren or anyone forced to eat away from home at midday depended on it as a lunchtime snack.

This raisin bread makes delicious focaccia (see Variation) and is wonderful for making *torta di mele* (page 175). It keeps extremely well, although most people love the bread so much they never find that out.

Makes 1 large or 2 smaller loaves

About 3 cups (17.5 oz / 500 g) golden or dark raisins

$3^{3}/_{4}$ teaspoons (0.4 oz / 10.6 g) active dry yeast

1 teaspoon (0.3 oz / 7 g) malt syrup or powder

1 tablespoon (0.5 oz / 13 g) sugar

2 teaspoons (0.3 oz / 9.5 g) unsalted butter, at room temperature

$3^{3}/_{4}$ cups (17.5 oz / 500 g) unbleached all-purpose flour, plus 2 to 3 tablespoons (0.6 to 1 oz / 18 to 27 g) for the raisins

$1^{1}/_{2}$ teaspoons (0.3 oz / 7.5 g) salt

continued

Pan Tramvai o Pane all'Uva, *continued*

Soak the raisins in water to cover (cool water for the golden raisins, warm water for the dark) at room temperature for $1^1/2$ hours. Drain the raisins, squeezing out any excess liquid. Reserve the raisin soaking water. Warm $1^1/3$ cups of the raisin water for the yeast, or, if using a food processor, warm $^1/4$ cup and refrigerate the remaining 1 cup plus 3 tablespoons until cold.

BY HAND

Stir the yeast, malt, and sugar into the raisin water in a large mixing bowl; let stand until foamy, about 10 minutes. Stir in the butter. Mix the $3^1/2$ cups of flour and the salt. Stir the flour mixture, 2 cups at a time, into the yeast mixture. Knead on a lightly floured surface until firm, elastic, and silky, 4 to 5 minutes. You will find that the dough comes together quickly.

BY MIXER

Stir the yeast, malt, and sugar into the raisin water in a mixer bowl; let stand until foamy, about 10 minutes. Stir in the butter with the paddle. Add the $3^1/2$ cups of flour and the salt and mix until the dough comes together. Change to the dough hook and knead until firm, elastic, and silky, 2 to 3 minutes.

BY PROCESSOR

Dissolve the yeast, malt, and sugar in the $^1/4$ cup of warm raisin water in a small bowl; let stand until foamy, about

10 minutes. Place the $3^1/2$ cups of flour and the salt in a food processor fitted with the dough blade and process with several pulses to sift. Stir the butter and 1 cup plus 2 tablespoons of the cold raisin water into the dissolved yeast mixture. With the machine running, pour the yeast mixture through the feed tube as quickly as the flour can absorb it and process until the dough gathers in to a ball, adding the remaining 1 tablespoon of water if necessary. Process 30 to 40 seconds longer to knead. If you want, finish kneading briefly by hand on a lightly floured surface.

First Rise. Place the dough in a lightly oiled bowl, cover tightly with plastic wrap, and let rise until doubled, $1^1/2$ to 2 hours.

Filling. Turn the dough out onto a lightly floured surface. Without punching the dough down or kneading it, pat it gently with your palms or roll with a rolling pin into a circle about 14 inches in diameter. The dough will be slightly sticky and tacky. Pat the raisins dry and toss them with 2 to 3 tablespoons of flour. Work the raisins into the dough in three additions: sprinkle a third of the raisins over the dough, turn in the sides, and roll it up. Flatten the dough with your palms and sprinkle with half the remaining raisins. Roll up and let the dough rest under a towel until relaxed and easy to work again, about 15 minutes. Pat the dough as flat as you can and sprinkle with the remaining raisins. Try to get as many in as you can but don't worry if you can't incorporate them all—this is an extraordinary amount of raisins.

Shaping and Second Rise. Roll up the dough into a long, slightly tapered loaf. You may either bake it as one long loaf or cut in half for two shorter loaves. Tuck the ends of the loaf under and try to keep the raisins under the taut surface of the dough. Place the loaf on a lightly floured peel, a lightly oiled baking sheet, or a baking sheet lined with parchment paper. Cover with a towel and let rise until well puffed and almost, but not quite, doubled, about 1 hour. Roll the loaf gently back and forth to set the shape before baking and check that the ends are tucked under.

Baking. Preheat the oven to 450°F. If you are using a baking stone, turn the oven on 30 minutes before baking and sprinkle the stone with cornmeal just before sliding the loaf onto it. Bake 5 minutes. Reduce the heat to 400°F and bake 40 minutes longer. Cool completely on a rack.

Variation. Transform raisin bread into focaccia by following this recipe through filling, and then following the basic focaccia recipe starting with shaping and second rise (page 269) and sprinkling the top with turbinado sugar.

Dolce Milanese MILAN SWEET BREAD

Despite the name, this buttery, sweet fantasy was actually dreamed up by a Venetian baker, who based it on *pan tramvai*, the famous raisin bread of Milan that is essentially half bread and half raisins. This version is fragrant with rum and orange as well.

Makes 1 large or 2 small loaves

FILLING

About 3 cups (17.5 oz / 500 g) golden or
  dark raisins

4 cups (34 oz / 960 g) cool water

Soak the raisins in the water for 1 to 2 hours. Drain, reserving the liquid. Warm $1^1/4$ cups of the soaking liquid for the sponge.

SPONGE

$3^3/4$ teaspoons (0.4 oz / 10.6 g) active dry yeast

$2^1/2$ teaspoons (0.4 oz / 12 g) sugar

1 cup plus 1 tablespoon (5.3 oz / 150 g)
  unbleached all-purpose flour

Stir the yeast and sugar into the warm raisin soaking water in a large mixing or mixer bowl; let stand until foamy, about 10 minutes. Add the flour and stir until smooth. Cover with plastic wrap and let rise until doubled, about 45 minutes to 1 hour.

DOUGH

2 tablespoons (1 oz / 30 g) dark rum

1 tablespoon (0.2 oz / 6 g) grated orange zest

About $2^1/2$ cups (12.3 oz / 350 g) unbleached
  all-purpose flour, plus 3 to 4 tablespoons
  (1 to 1.3 oz / 26 to 35 g) for the raisins

2 sticks (8 oz / 225 g) unsalted butter, at
  room temperature

1 large egg white, beaten, for glazing

BY HAND

Stir the rum, orange zest, and $2^1/2$ cups of flour into the sponge. Stir until well blended. Stir in the butter 2 tablespoons at a time. Knead on a lightly floured surface until velvety and very soft but not sticky, 8 to 10 minutes. The surface will be quite smooth, although you will notice a number of blisters. It smells wonderful.

BY MIXER

Mix the rum, orange zest, and $2^1/2$ cups of flour into the sponge with the paddle. Mix in the butter 2 tablespoons at a time. Change to the dough hook and knead at medium speed until velvety and very soft but not sticky, about 4 minutes. The surface will be quite smooth, although you will notice some blisters under the skin.

First Rise. Place the dough in a lightly oiled bowl, cover with plastic wrap, and let rise until doubled, about 1 hour.

Filling. Pat the raisins dry and toss with 3 to 4 tablespoons of flour. Work the raisins into the dough in four additions: Spread the dough out on a lightly floured surface, cover with a quarter of the raisins, tuck the sides in, and roll it up. Flatten the dough and repeat. Cover the dough with a towel and let it relax for about 10 minutes. Flat-

ten the dough again and repeat the procedure twice, incorporating the remaining
raisins. Let rest 10 minutes.

Shaping and Second Rise. Shape the
dough into a large oval or round loaf, a
free-form ring, or two smaller loaves. To
make the two small loaves, cut the dough
in half and pat each piece into a 9-inch
square and roll it up, tucking in the sides
so that the raisins don't fall out. It is easier
to pat the dough out with the cut side

closest to you. I personally prefer the
larger loaf because it has more crumb and
less crust, but it is huge. Place the loaf on
an oiled baking sheet, cover with a towel,
and let rise until not quite doubled, 35 to
45 minutes.

Baking. Preheat the oven to 425°F.
Brush the top of the loaf with the egg
white. Bake the smaller loaves 45 minutes
and the large loaf 1 hour. Cool completely
on a rack.

Bolzanese FRUIT BREAD OF BOLZANO

These fat buns, stuffed with fruits and nuts and studded with whole almonds, bear
more than slight atavistic traces of Bolzano's Austrian origins. They make a robust and
tasty breakfast or teatime snack and are big enough to be a meal in themselves if you
have a sweet tooth and are on the run.

Makes 5 fat buns

DOUGH

3³/₄ teaspoons (0.4 oz / 10.6 g) active dry yeast

¹/₂ cup plus 2 teaspoons (3.8 oz / 110 g) sugar

³/₄ cup (6.3 oz / 180 g) warm water

2 large eggs

1 large egg yolk

1 stick (4 oz / 115 g) unsalted butter,
    at room temperature

3³/₄ cups (17.5 oz / 500 g) unbleached
    all-purpose flour

1¹/₂ teaspoons (0.3 oz / 7.5 g) salt

BY HAND

Stir the yeast and 2 tablespoons of the
sugar into the water in a large mixing
bowl; let stand until foamy, about 10 minutes. Stir in the remaining sugar, the eggs,
and the egg yolk; stir in the butter until
blended. Add the flour and salt and stir
until the dough comes together. Knead
on a floured surface until soft and elastic,
8 to 10 minutes.

continued

Bolzanese, *continued*

BY MIXER

Stir the yeast and 2 tablespoons of the sugar into the water in a mixer bowl; let stand until foamy, about 10 minutes. Add the remaining sugar, the eggs, and the egg yolk and mix with the paddle. Mix in the butter. Add the flour and salt and mix until the dough comes together. Change to the dough hook and knead until soft and elastic, 3 to 4 minutes.

First Rise. Place the dough in a lightly oiled bowl, cover tightly with plastic wrap, and let rise until soft and puffy but not quite doubled, about 2 hours.

FILLING AND TOPPING

²/₃ cup (3.5 oz / 100 g) halved hazelnuts, toasted and skinned (page 32)

²/₃ cup (3.5 oz / 100 g) chopped candied fruit

²/₃ cup (3.5 oz / 100 g) firmly packed raisins

1 large egg, beaten

1 tablespoon (0.5 oz / 15 g) water

³/₄ cup (4.3 oz / 120 g) blanched whole almonds

Flatten the dough on a lightly floured surface into a large circle. Mix the hazelnuts, candied fruit, and the raisins and work the mixture into the dough in three additions: Sprinkle the dough with a third of the nut mixture, fold the four sides of the dough into the center, and flatten. Repeat the process twice more, flattening the dough as much as you can.

Shaping and Second Rise. Cut the dough into five equal pieces (each weighs about 11 ounces or 300 g) and shape each piece into a ball, rolling the dough between your cupped hands and pulling the skin of the dough taut over the fruits and nuts. Place the buns on an oiled or parchment-lined baking sheet. Mix the egg and water in a small bowl. Brush the buns with the egg wash and cover with the almonds. Let rise until doubled, about 5 hours.

Baking. Preheat the oven to 400°F. Bake until golden, about 30 minutes. Cool completely on a rack.

Schiacciata con l'Uva TUSCAN SWEET BREAD WITH RAISINS

There are two ways of making this traditional Tuscan sweet bread: the bread baker adds a little sugar and olive oil to regular bread dough, but the pastry baker makes up an eggy briochelike dough that bakes into a more delicate bread much like coffeecake. Traditionally, this dish is made at grape harvest time with Sangiovese grapes, which are the basis of Chianti wines; I have tried it with Thompson red flame seedless grapes, which made a piquant, tart *schiacciata*. But, because grapes are in season so briefly, I decided to make it with raisins—something that is actually done in the tiny town of Conegliano, in the Veneto—by pressing them between the layers of dough and then covering the dough with a hailstorm of sugar. It tastes delicious, and you will not have to wait for grape season to make it.

Makes 1 loaf

SPONGE

1³/₄ teaspoons (0.2 oz / 5 g) active dry yeast

3 tablespoons (1.5 oz / 45 g) sugar

1 cup (8.4 oz / 240 g) warm water

2 large eggs

1³/₄ cups (8.8 oz / 250 g) unbleached
  all-purpose flour

BY HAND

Stir the yeast and sugar into the water in a large mixing bowl; let stand until foamy, about 10 minutes. Beat in the eggs with a wooden spoon. Stir in the flour in two or three additions and mix thoroughly with a wooden spoon or your hands. Cover tightly with plastic and let stand until bubbly, about 30 minutes.

BY MIXER

Stir the yeast and sugar into the water in a mixer bowl; let stand until foamy, about 10 minutes. Beat in the eggs with the paddle. Add the flour and mix well. Cover tightly with plastic wrap and let stand until bubbly, about 30 minutes.

DOUGH

2 tablespoons (1 oz / 28 g) lard or olive oil,
  at room temperature

1³/₄ cups (8.6 oz / 250 g) unbleached all-purpose
  flour

1 teaspoon (0.17 oz / 5 g) salt

¹/₄ cup (2 oz / 55 g) unsalted butter, at room
  temperature

BY HAND

Beat the lard into the sponge. Stir in the flour and salt, then beat in the butter 1 tablespoon at a time. Knead on a lightly floured surface for 6 to 7 minutes. The

continued

Schiacciata con l'Uva, *continued*

dough should be stiff enough so that, when you pinch the surface, the little peak you make holds its shape.

BY MIXER

Beat the lard into the sponge with the paddle. Add the flour and salt and mix until the dough comes together. Mix in the butter. Change to the dough hook and knead about 3 minutes. The dough should be stiff enough so that, when you pinch the surface, the little peak you make holds its shape.

First Rise. Place the dough in an oiled bowl, cover tightly with plastic wrap, and let rise until doubled, about 1 1/2 hours.

FILLING

3 cups (17.5 oz / 500 g) raisins

3/4 cup (5.3 oz / 150 g) sugar

While the dough is rising, soak half the raisins in cool water to cover 1 hour; drain, squeezing out any residual liquid.

Turn the dough out onto a lightly floured surface and cut in half, without punching the dough down. The dough will be soft and stretchy. Stretch one piece on the work surface to a rectangle to fit the bottom of a 16 by 11-inch buttered or oiled baking pan. Place the dough in the pan and sprinkle first with the raisins that haven't been soaked in water and then with half the sugar. Stretch the remaining dough to fit the pan and place over the raisins and sugar. Pat the dough flat and poke holes in it with the tip of a small knife or a skewer to let the trapped air escape. Pat dry the raisins that have been soaked and sprinkle over the dough. Sprinkle with the remaining sugar.

Second Rise. Cover the baking pan tightly with plastic wrap and let rise until puffy and doubled, about 1 hour.

Baking. Preheat the oven to 400°F. Bake 40 minutes. Cool a few minutes in the pan, then remove from the pan and cool completely on a rack.

Note. Should you try making this with wine or table grapes, tilt the pan after 20 minutes of baking and pour the sweet sugar syrup into a small bowl; brush the syrup over the top of the dough and finish baking.

Lightly Sweetened Breads

Pane alla Cioccolata CHOCOLATE BREAD

The secret of this chocolate bread is that it isn't too sweet. It is wonderful eaten with a mild fresh cheese, such as mascarpone, a glass of red wine, or a cup of coffee. You can form it into big loaves, perfect for slicing, or you can layer or braid it with sweet milk bread (recipe follows).

Makes 2 round or oval loaves

2^1/$_4$ teaspoons (1 package / 0.2 oz / 7 g) active dry yeast

^{1}/$_2$ teaspoon (0.1 oz / 2.5 g) sugar

^{1}/$_3$ cup plus 1 tablespoon (3.5 oz / 95 g) warm water

4^1/$_4$ cups (21 oz / 600 g) unbleached all-purpose flour

^{1}/$_2$ cup plus 2 tablespoons (4.4 oz / 125 g) sugar

^{1}/$_3$ cup (1.1 oz / 31 g) unsweetened cocoa powder, preferably Dutch process

2 teaspoons (0.4 oz / 10 g) salt

1^1/$_4$ cups (10 oz / 285 g) water, at room temperature (cold if using a processor)

1 large egg yolk

1 tablespoon (0.5 oz / 14 g) butter, at room temperature (cold if using a processor)

1 cup (6 oz / 170 g) semisweet chocolate chips

BY HAND

Stir the yeast and the ^{1}/$_2$ teaspoon of sugar into the warm water in a large mixing bowl; let stand until foamy, about 10 minutes. Mix the flour, the ^{1}/$_2$ cup plus 2 tablespoons of sugar, the cocoa, and the salt. Stir the 1^1/$_4$ cups of water, the egg yolk, and the butter into the dissolved yeast; then stir in the flour mixture 1 cup at a time. Stir in the chocolate chips last. Knead on a lightly floured surface until velvety, elastic, and moist, 8 to 10 minutes.

BY MIXER

Stir the yeast and the ^{1}/$_2$ teaspoon of sugar into the warm water in a small bowl; let stand until foamy, about 10 minutes. Mix the flour, the ^{1}/$_2$ cup plus 2 tablespoons of sugar, and the cocoa, salt, and chocolate chips in a mixer bowl. Stir the 1^1/$_4$ cups of water, the egg yolk, and the butter into the dissolved yeast. Pour the yeast mixture into the flour mixture and mix with the paddle until well blended. Change to the dough hook and knead 2 minutes at low speed, then 2 minutes at medium speed. The dough should be velvety, moist, and elastic.

BY PROCESSOR

Stir the yeast and the ^{1}/$_2$ teaspoon of sugar into the warm water in a small bowl; let stand until foamy, about 10 minutes. Place the flour, the ^{1}/$_2$ cup plus 2 tablespoons of

continued

Pane alla Cioccolata, *continued*

sugar, the cocoa, and the salt in a food processor fitted with the dough blade and process with several pulses to mix. Stir the 1¼ cups of cold water and the egg yolk into the dissolved yeast. Cut the cold butter into four pieces and place on top of the dry ingredients. With the machine running, pour the yeast mixture through the feed tube as quickly as the flour can absorb it and process until the dough gathers into a ball. Process 40 to 45 seconds longer to knead, pouring the chocolate chips through the feed tube in the last 10 seconds.

First Rise. Place the dough in a lightly oiled bowl, cover tightly with plastic wrap, and let rise until doubled, about 2 hours.

Shaping and Second Rise. Punch the dough down and cut in half on a lightly floured surface. Shape each piece into a round or oval loaf and place on oiled baking sheets. Cover with a towel and let rise until doubled, about 1 hour.

Baking. Preheat the oven to 450°F. Bake 15 minutes. Reduce the heat to 375°F and bake 30 minutes longer. Cool completely on a rack.

Pane al Latte MILK BREAD

Lightly sweetened, *pane al latte* is perfect for breakfast with butter or jam, or for a snack. The addition of rum is the fantasy of one Italian baker, who also gave it this charming shape, but it is often made into a fat golden roll with a touch of honey in the dough. This bread has a light, eggy interior and a glazed surface.

Makes 3 loaves

SPONGE

1¾ teaspoons (0.2 oz / 5 g) active dry yeast

1 tablespoon (0.5 oz / 13 g) sugar

½ cup (4.2 oz / 120 g) warm milk

1 cup minus 1 tablespoon (4.7 oz / 135 g) unbleached all-purpose flour

Stir the yeast and sugar into the milk in a large mixing or mixer bowl; let stand until foamy, about 10 minutes. Add the flour and whisk vigorously to make a thick batter. Cover and let stand until doubled, less than 1 hour.

DOUGH

2 large eggs

1 tablespoon (0.5 oz / 15 g) rum

1 cup (8.5 oz / 244 g) milk, at room temperature (cold if using a processor)

1/4 cup (2 oz / 55 g) unsalted butter, at room temperature (cold if using a processor)

2²/₃ cups (13.1 oz / 375 g) unbleached all-purpose flour

1 teaspoon (0.2 oz / 5 g) salt

BY HAND

Stir one of the eggs, the rum, and the milk into the sponge and then stir in the butter. Mix the flour and salt and stir into the sponge mixture in two additions. Stir for about 3 minutes. Knead on a floured work surface, sprinkling with additional flour as needed, until soft, silky, and elastic, 8 to 10 minutes.

BY MIXER

Add one of the eggs and the rum, milk, and butter to the sponge and mix with the paddle for about 1 minute. Add the flour and salt and mix on low speed. Change to the dough hook and knead until soft, silky, and elastic, 3 to 4 minutes. Finish kneading briefly by hand on a lightly floured surface.

BY PROCESSOR

Place the flour and salt in the food processor fitted with the dough blade and process with two or three pulses to sift.

Place the sponge and the cold butter on top of the flour mixture. Mix one of the eggs, the rum, and the 1 cup of cold milk. With the machine running, pour the milk mixture through the feed tube and process until the dough gathers into a ball. Process 30 to 45 seconds to knead. The dough should be elastic and moist. Knead briefly by hand on a lightly floured surface, if you want.

First Rise. Place the dough in a lightly oiled bowl, cover tightly with plastic wrap, and let rise until doubled, 1 to 2 hours. The dough should be very soft but slightly tacky, and if you pinch the surface, the little peaks of dough should hold their shape.

Shaping and Second Rise. Cut the dough into fifteen pieces the size of a small lemon (about 2 ounces or 60 grams each) and shape into balls. Roll five of the balls with your palms into five 6-inch-long cigars, plumper in the center and tapered at the ends. Keep the remaining dough covered while you are working. Place the five cigars next to each other on an oiled baking sheet and pinch the ends together; you will have to stretch the first and fifth cigars so that they will meet at the ends. Repeat twice with the remaining ten balls. Cover with a towel and let rise until doubled, about 45 minutes.

Baking. Preheat the oven to 400°F. Beat the remaining egg and brush over the loaves. Bake 25 minutes. Cool on racks.

Pane al Latte e Cioccolata MILK AND CHOCOLATE BREAD

You'd never know it from a quick glance, but this is a bread with something for everyone. Hidden inside its fat chocolate exterior is a secret vein of lightly sweetened milk bread.

Makes 1 large loaf

Pane alla cioccolata (page 191), prepared through the first rise

14 ounces (400 g) pane al latte (¹/₃ recipe, page 192), prepared through the first rise

1 large egg white, beaten, for glazing

Shaping and Second Rise. Punch down the chocolate dough and shape into a big ball on a lightly floured surface. Let rest 10 to 15 minutes. Cut the dough in half, and flatten each half into a 12 by 6-inch rectangle. Punch down the milk dough and shape into a rectangle of the same size. Sandwich the milk dough between the two pieces of chocolate dough and roll up, starting from one long edge, like a jelly roll. Tuck the edges under so that the bread looks like a long log and roll it back and forth to set the shape. Place the loaf on an oiled baking sheet, cover with a towel, and let rise until doubled, about 1 hour.

Baking. Preheat the oven to 425°F. Brush the loaf with the egg white. Bake 1 hour. Reduce the heat to 350°F and bake 35 minutes longer.

Pane del Marinaio SAILOR'S BREAD

A dome-shaped sweet bread full of raisins, spices, and nuts is popular in Genoa, a seaport town on the Italian Riviera. No wonder the sailors liked it so much—it keeps for weeks.

Makes 2 round loaves

1¹/₂ sticks (6 oz / 170 g) unsalted butter, at room temperature

¹/₃ cup (2.5 oz / 70 g) sugar

2 large eggs, beaten

1 heaping cup (5.8 oz / 165 g) raisins

¹/₃ cup (1.8 oz / 50 g) chopped candied citron (page 39)

¹/₃ cup (1.8 oz / 50 g) chopped candied orange peel (page 39)

2 tablespoons (0.5 oz / 14 g) pine nuts

1¹/₂ tablespoons (0.3 oz / 9 g) fennel seeds

2 cups plus 2 tablespoons (10.5 oz / 300 g) unbleached all-purpose flour

1¹/₂ teaspoons (0.25 oz / 7.5 g) baking powder

1 tablespoon (0.5 oz / 15 g) milk

2 tablespoons (1 oz / 30 g) Marsala

BY HAND

Using a wooden spoon, cream the butter and sugar together in a large mixing bowl. Beat in the eggs, adding just a little at a time so the batter doesn't curdle, and reserving a quarter of the eggs for the egg wash. Combine the raisins, candied citron and orange peel, 1 tablespoon of the pine nuts, and the fennel seeds and stir into the flour and baking powder. Stir half the flour mixture into the butter mixture. Stir in the milk and Marsala, and then the remaining flour mixture. Knead on a floured surface until the dough holds its shape, about 2 minutes.

BY MIXER

Cream the butter and sugar together in a mixer bowl with the paddle. Increase the speed to high and add the eggs a little at a time, reserving a quarter of the eggs for the egg wash. Beat until well blended. Combine the raisins, candied citron and orange peel, 1 tablespoon of the pine nuts, and the fennel seeds and stir into the flour and baking powder. Add half the flour mixture to the butter mixture and mix thoroughly. Mix in the milk and Marsala, and then the remaining flour mixture. Knead on a floured surface until the dough holds its shape, about 2 minutes.

Shaping. Cut the dough in half. Flour your hands well and gently shape the dough into two thick logs; then pat each log into a ball, patching over any cracks as you shape. Sprinkle each ball lightly with flour. Place the loaves on an oiled baking sheet. Make a tic-tac-toe pattern in each top with a razor or dough scraper.

Glazing. Brush the tops with the reserved egg, filling in the cracks as you brush. Sprinkle each loaf with half the remaining pine nuts.

Baking. Preheat the oven to 360°F. Bake until a toothpick inserted in the center comes out clean, about 40 minutes. Cool on racks.

Meini o Pani de Mei SWEET CORN BUNS

These sweet buns are a very delicate cross between a corn muffin and a scone. They are particularly appealing because the covering on the top cracks into a pattern that looks like the land after a long, dry summer. *Meini* are definitely a Lombard specialty, and the Milanese traditionally eat them on April 24 to celebrate the liberation of their countryside from the assaults of a ferocious highwayman and his brigands during the Middle Ages.

Makes 15 buns

2 sticks plus 2 tablespoons (8.8 oz / 250 g)
    unsalted butter, at room temperature

1¼ cups (8.8 oz / 250 g) plus ⅓ cup (2.5 oz / 70 g)
    granulated sugar

2 tablespoons plus 1 teaspoon (1.8 oz / 50 g) honey

1 large egg

1 large egg yolk

½ cup plus 1 teaspoons (4.6 oz / 130 g) milk

3¼ cups (15.8 oz / 450 g) unbleached
    all-purpose flour

2⅓ cups (10.5 oz / 300 g) fine yellow cornmeal

3½ teaspoons (0.6 oz / 17.5 g) baking powder

2 drops almond oil, or ⅛ teaspoon almond extract

½ cup (2 oz / 60 g) confectioners' sugar

BY MIXER ONLY

Using the whisk attachment, if you have one, beat the butter, the 1¼ cups of granulated sugar, and the honey for 1 to 2 minutes at low speed until combined. Increase the speed to medium–high and beat until light and fluffy. Add the egg, egg yolk, and 2 teaspoons of the milk and continue beating for 1 minute. Mix in the flour, cornmeal, and baking powder. Add the remaining ½ cup of milk and the almond oil and mix at the lowest speed until blended. The dough should be stiff but not heavy. Knead briefly by hand or mixer, sprinkling with additional flour as needed, until buttery, soft, pliable, and slightly sticky.

Shaping. Line baking sheets with parchment paper or buttered brown paper. Cut the dough into fifteen equal pieces (3 oz / 90 g each). Flour your hands and roll each piece into a ball. Flatten each ball into a ½-inch-thick patty the size of a hamburger and the width of a woman's hand. Place on the paper-lined baking sheets.

Glazing. Brush the tops with water and then sprinkle with the remaining

$^1/_3$ cup of granulated sugar, making sure a thin layer of sugar covers each bun. You can shake off the excess sugar by holding onto the paper and shaking the sugar up and over the edge of the pan. Place the confectioners' sugar in a sifter or sieve and sift the sugar heavily over the buns so that they look as if they're lost in a blizzard of sugar. The excess powdered sugar can stay on the paper, because it will not caramelize.

Baking. Preheat the oven to 375°F. Bake until the sugar on top has cracked into an irregular design, 15 to 20 minutes. Cool on racks.

Pan de Mej o Pan Mein Dolce SWEET CORN BREAD

Pan de mej was originally a coarse millet bread of the poor people of Milan, made by mixing wheat and millet (*meg* in the Milanese dialect). The nobles had first choice of the grains the peasants and farmers harvested, leaving the lesser grains for the peasant loaves. In time, the millet in this bread was replaced with corn, which became the grain of the common people, and sugar was added along with the delicate flavor of the *sambuco* flower. The bread was regularly made on April 24, the feast day of San Giorgio, the patron saint of dairymen. Until a short time ago, the day was celebrated by milk workers whose contracts ran from April 24 to April 24, or from San Giorgio to San Giorgio, as they say. On that day they used to eat this rough bread with rich double cream. The bread is usually shaped into individual English muffin–size buns, but, because I have included a similar sweet corn bread, *meini o pani de mei* in this chapter (preceding recipe), I have written this recipe for a single large loaf. The herb *sambuco,* European black elderberry, is next to impossible to find in America, but sambuca liqueur is a good substitute, so use some as a glaze for the top of the bread and put a little in the dough as well.

Makes 1 large loaf

SPONGE

2$^1/_4$ teaspoons (1 package / 0.2 oz / 7 g) active dry yeast

$^1/_4$ cup (2 oz / 60 g) warm water

2 tablespoons (1 oz / 30 g) milk

$^3/_4$ cup (3.5 oz / 100 g) unbleached all-purpose flour

Stir the yeast into the water and milk in a mixing or mixer bowl; let stand until creamy, about 10 minutes. Stir in the flour until smooth. Cover with plastic wrap and let rise 2 hours.

continued

Pan de Mej o Pan Mein Dolce, *continued*

DOUGH

³/₄ cup (3.5 oz / 100 g) corn flour or yellow
    cornmeal finely ground in the blender

¹/₂ cup plus 2 tablespoons (3.5 oz / 100 g)
    coarsely ground yellow cornmeal

1 cup (7 oz / 200 g) granulated sugar

3 large eggs

2¹/₂ tablespoons (1.4 oz / 40 g) sambuca liqueur

Pinch of salt

7 tablespoons (3.5 oz / 100 g) unsalted butter,
    at room temperature

Turbinado sugar

BY HAND

Stir both the fine and coarse cornmeals,
granulated sugar, eggs, 1¹/₂ tablespoons of
the liqueur, and the salt into the sponge.
Stir in the butter. Knead on a lightly floured
surface until soft and tender but slightly
springy, 8 to 10 minutes.

BY MIXER

Mix both fine and coarse cornmeals,
granulated sugar, eggs, 1¹/₂ tablespoons of
the liqueur, and the salt into the sponge

with the paddle. Add the butter and mix
until the dough comes together. Change
to the dough hook and knead until soft
and tender but slightly springy.

Rising. Place the dough in a buttered
6-cup baking dish. You may want to line
the dish with parchment paper so that it
will be easier to unmold the baked loaf.
Cover with a heavy towel and let rise until
doubled, about 4 hours.

   Baking. Preheat the oven to 375°F.
Brush the top of the loaf with the remaining 1 tablespoon of liqueur and sprinkle
with a handful of turbinado sugar, which
will give the crust a nice crunch. Bake
50 to 55 minutes. The loaf need not be
totally dry inside, because the cornmeal
will dry more when it is out of the oven.
Cool completely on a rack and turn out
of the baking dish.

Sweet and Holiday Breads

Panettone CHRISTMAS BREAD OF MILAN

Traditionally eaten by the Milanese on Christmas, panettone is a delicate and porous rich egg bread studded with raisins and bits of candied citron and orange. These days it can be found all over Italy and America as well, and not only during the holidays. Many panettones from Italy are made with a special natural yeast, and they seem to last almost forever. I once received one that had been two months in transit and still tasted fresh and delicious. Panettones made at home probably will not keep for such a long time, but I have never had panettone around long enough to see.

No bread has more stories of its origins. The most reasonable explanation of the name is that the Milanese passion for terms of affection led them to call regular bread *panett*, so that when a larger or richer bread was made, it was inevitably called panettone. Some point instead to the Middle Ages, when bakers were divided into two groups: those who baked for the poor with millet and other inexpensive grains, and those who baked for the rich with wheat flour. Only at Christmas could bakers for the poor make an enriched bread with butter, eggs, sugar, raisins, and candied fruit, which became known as *pan di tono*, or rich and fancy bread.

The most famous story of the origins of panettone involves a wealthy young Milanese noble in the fifteenth century who fell in love with the daughter of a poor baker named Tony. He wanted to marry the girl, and so he put at her father's disposal the means to buy the best flour, eggs, and butter, as well as candied orange peel and citron and fat sultana raisins. The bread he created, known as *pan di Tonio*, was a great success. It made Tony's reputation as well as his fortune (and, as a dividend, Tony's backer got the baker's daughter).

If the beginnings of panettone are clouded with mystery, it is well known that panettone was politicized after the uprisings of 1821, when red candied cherries were substituted for raisins and green citron was added so that the bread symbolized the tricolored Italian flag and liberty itself.

Panettone was a much shorter and less dramatic bread until 1921, when Angelo Motta founded a company that used natural yeast and his own tall cylindrical form to make a dazzlingly tall, domed panettone. The soft and delicate bread was such an immediate success that the following year Motta's friend Giacchino Allemagna set up a rival company making equally light and airy panettones. Today both of those two firms are owned by Bauli. Panettone is more popular in central and southern Italy

continued

Panettone, *continued*

than in the north, and Italian bakers today turn out more than 117 million *panettoni* and *pandori* a year, making porous, delicately sweetened breads synonymous with Italy and Christmas. There is nothing better with coffee or cappuccino for breakfast or with tea at midday, but the Milanese insist that it is best at Christmas with cream or, even better, fresh mascarpone. And they traditionally put aside a piece to eat on February 3, the feast day of Saint Biagio, the protector of the throat.

Makes 2 panettoni

SPONGE

2¼ teaspoons (1 package / 0.2 oz / 7 g) active dry yeast

⅓ cup (2.8 oz / 80 g) warm water

½ cup (2.5 oz / 70 g) unbleached all-purpose flour

Stir the yeast into the water in a small bowl; let stand until creamy, about 10 minutes. Stir in the flour. Cover tightly with plastic wrap and let rise until doubled, 20 to 30 minutes.

FIRST DOUGH

2¼ teaspoons (1 package / 0.2 oz / 7 g) active dry yeast

3 tablespoons (1.5 oz / 45 g) warm water

2 large eggs, at room temperature

1¼ cups (6.3 oz / 180 g) unbleached all-purpose flour

¼ cup (1.8 oz / 50 g) sugar

1 stick (4 oz / 115 g) unsalted butter, at room temperature

BY HAND

Stir the yeast into the water in a mixing bowl; let stand until creamy, about 10 minutes. Add the sponge and beat thoroughly together. Add the eggs, flour, and sugar and mix well. Stir in the butter thoroughly. The entire process will take 5 to 6 minutes. Cover with plastic wrap and let rise until doubled, 1 to 1¼ hours.

BY MIXER

Stir the yeast into the water in a mixer bowl; let stand until creamy, about 10 minutes. Add the sponge, eggs, flour, and sugar and mix with the paddle. Add the butter and mix until the dough is smooth and consistent, about 3 minutes. Cover with plastic wrap and let rise until doubled, 1 to 1¼ hours.

SECOND DOUGH

2 large eggs

3 large egg yolks

¾ cup (5.3 oz / 150 g) sugar

2 tablespoons (1.5 oz / 42 g) honey

1½ teaspoons (0.2 oz / 6 g) vanilla extract

1 teaspoon (0.2 oz / 5 g) salt

2 sticks (8 oz / 225 g) unsalted butter, at room temperature

3 cups (14.7 oz / 420 g) unbleached all-purpose flour, plus up to ¾ cup (3.5 oz / 100 g) for kneading

BY HAND

Place the first dough in a large mixing
bowl, if it isn't already. Add the eggs, egg
yolks, sugar, honey, vanilla, and salt and mix
well. Add the butter and stir until blended.
Stir in the flour and keep stirring until
smooth. The dough will be soft, a bit like
cookie dough. Knead gently on a well-
floured surface with well-floured hands
until it is smooth and holds its shape. You
may need as much as ³/4 cup of additional
flour during the kneading.

BY MIXER

Add the eggs, egg yolks, sugar, honey,
vanilla, and salt to the first dough and mix
thoroughly with the paddle. Add the butter
and mix until smooth. Add the flour and
mix again until smooth. The dough will be
soft, a bit like cookie dough. Change to the
dough hook and knead until smooth and
soft, about 2 minutes. Finish by kneading
on a lightly floured work surface, using a
little additional flour as necessary.

First Rise. Place the dough in a lightly oiled
bowl, cover with plastic wrap, and let rise
until tripled, 2¹/2 to 4 hours. The dough
can also rise overnight at a cool room temperature (65°F to 68°F).

FILLING

1²/3 cups (8.8 oz / 250 g) golden raisins

¹/2 cup (2.7 oz / 75 g) chopped candied citron
   (page 39)

¹/2 cup (2.7 oz / 75 g) chopped candied orange
   peel (page 39)

Grated zest of 1 orange

Grated zest of 1 lemon

2 to 3 tablespoons (0.6 to 1 oz / 18 to 26 g)
   unbleached all-purpose flour

At least 30 minutes before the end of the
first rise, soak the raisins in cool water.
Drain and pat dry. Cut the dough in half
on a floured surface. Combine the raisins,
candied citron and orange peel, and orange
and lemon zest and dust with the flour.
Pat each piece of dough into an oval and
sprinkle with a quarter of the fruit mixture. Roll up into a log. Gently flatten the
dough again to create as much surface as
possible, sprinkle with the remaining fruit
mixture, and roll up again.

Shaping and Second Rise. Shape each
piece into a ball and slip into two well-
buttered 6 by 4-inch paper panettone molds
or 6-inch-high 2-pound coffee cans lined
on the bottom with a parchment paper. For
this panettone, which is as light and airy as
the traditional bakery panettone, the pan is
very important; if you use a 2-quart charlotte mold, springform pan, or soufflé dish,
you will not get the same spectacular height
or delicate porous texture.

Cut an X in the top of each loaf with a
razor. Cover with a towel and let rise until
doubled, about 2 hours. If your kitchen is
cold, warm the oven at the lowest possible
setting for 3 minutes, place a large pan of
hot water on the lowest rack, and let the
dough rise in the warm, slightly moist
atmosphere. With a gas oven, the heat of
the pilot light may be enough.

continued

Panettone, *continued*

Baking. Preheat the oven to 400°F. Just before baking, cut the X in each loaf again. Some bakers insert a nut of butter into the cut. Bake 10 minutes. Reduce the heat to 375°F and bake 10 minutes. Reduce the heat to 350°F and bake until a tester inserted in the center comes out clean, 30 minutes. Cool on racks for 30 minutes.

If you have used paper molds, place the loaves on their sides on pillows to cool. If you place warm panettone on a rack to cool, it will collapse. If you have used coffee cans, remove gently after 30 minutes and set on pillows as above. For all other pans, carefully remove from the molds after 30 minutes.

Mataloc CHRISTMAS BREAD OF LAKE COMO

You won't find a *mataloc* anywhere but at Lake Como. It is made much the same as panettone; sometimes, in fact, the figs, raisins, walnuts, and hazelnuts are simply added to panettone dough before its last rise. The name seems to come from the Arab through the Spanish, for whom *matalauga* means "anise." The Spanish evidently brought their *matalauga* with them to Como, where it met with such an enthusiastic reception that its name was domesticated and its shape transformed into a panettone-like sweet bread. It most resembles a panettone from Genoa with its fennel seeds, nuts, raisins, and candied fruits, but, even so, how this exotic sweet came to Como during Spanish rule is still a mystery, although it continues to be made and eaten there today.

Makes 1 tall round loaf

SPONGE

1³/₄ teaspoons (0.2 oz / 5 g) active dry yeast

¹/₂ cup (4.2 oz / 120 g) warm water

¹/₂ cup plus 1 tablespoon (2.8 oz / 75 g) unbleached all-purpose flour

Stir the yeast into the water in a small bowl; let stand until creamy, about 10 minutes. Stir in the flour. The dough will be rough and shaggy. Cover with plastic wrap and let rise until doubled, about 30 minutes to 1 hour.

DOUGH

¹/₂ teaspoon (0.05 oz / 1.4 g) active dry yeast

1 tablespoon (0.8 oz / 21 g) honey

¹/₄ cup (2 oz / 60 g) warm water

1 cup (7 oz / 200 g) sugar

3 large eggs

2¹/₂ cups (12.3 oz / 350 g) unbleached all-purpose flour, plus up to 3 tablespoons (1 oz / 26 g) more, as needed

¹/₄ teaspoon salt

¹/₈ teaspoon crushed fennel seeds

Grated zest of 2 oranges

Grated zest of 2 lemons

1 stick plus 3 tablespoons (5.5 oz / 155 g) unsalted butter, at room temperature

BY HAND

Stir the yeast and honey into the water in a large mixing bowl; let stand until foamy, about 10 minutes. Stir in the sugar and eggs. Beat in the sponge, then beat in the flour, salt, fennel seeds, and orange and lemon zests. Work in the butter. Knead on a floured surface until soft, sticky, and delicately elastic, about 8 to 10 minutes.

BY MIXER

Stir the yeast and honey into the water in a mixer bowl; let stand until foamy, about 10 minutes. Add the sugar, eggs, and sponge and mix thoroughly with the paddle. Mix in the flour and salt. Change to the dough hook and add the butter, fennel seeds, and orange and lemon zests. Knead at high speed for 4 minutes. Finish kneading briefly by hand on a floured surface, adding up to 3 tablespoons more flour as needed, until the dough is sticky, soft, buttery, and delicately elastic.

First Rise. Place the dough in an oiled or buttered bowl, cover with plastic wrap, and let rise overnight at a cool room temperature, 65°F to 68°F. The dough will more than double; it might even triple.

FILLING

1 cup (5 oz / 140 g) hazelnuts

1¹/₂ cup (5.3 oz / 150 g) walnut pieces

4 dried figs, chopped

1 heaping cup (5.6 oz / 160 g) raisins

1 tablespoon (0.3 oz / 9 g) unbleached all-purpose flour

Preheat the oven to 375°F. Toast the hazelnuts on a baking sheet in the oven for 10 minutes. Rub the skins from the hazelnuts in a kitchen towel and chop both the hazelnuts and walnuts. Coat the figs and raisins with the flour and combine with the nuts. Flatten the dough on a lightly floured surface. Spread a quarter of the fruits and nuts over the top and roll up. Flatten again and repeat the process three more times, letting the dough rest for 10 to 15 minutes after rolling up the dough the second time.

Shaping and Second Rise. Shape the dough into a ball and place in a well-buttered 2-quart charlotte mold, soufflé dish, or 8-inch springform pan whose sides you have built up with aluminum foil. Cover with a towel and let rise until the dough doubles and fills the mold, about 3 hours.

Baking. Preheat the oven to 400°F. Bake 10 minutes. Reduce the heat to 350°F and bake 40 to 45 minutes longer. Unmold very carefully and cool on a rack. Cut into wedges to serve.

Panettone con Datteri e Noci

PANETTONE WITH DATES AND WALNUTS

Before I was taken to the bakery where this phenomenal panettone was made, I had to promise not to divulge anything about our intended destination. Carlo Veggetti, who had more than five hundred bakeries under his protective wing at that time, did not blindfold me, but he did take me on a roundabout route through Milan so that I would not be able to find it again. If he'd thought of it, he probably would have inked out the shop's name from the front of the bakery boxes. I don't blame him for trying to keep it a secret, although two Milanese who really care about such things had already slipped me its name and whispered superlatives about everything in that bakery. The great baker, Don Carlo Oldani, made his panettone exactly like *pasta sfogliata* (puff pastry). I've adapted his method to the panettone dough on page 200. The dough is then cut into three pieces before one is covered with dates and one with walnuts, and one is left plain. The pieces are then stacked in layers, rolled up into a ball, and baked just like regular panettone.

Makes 1 panettone

2¹/₂ sticks (10 oz / 285 g) cold unsalted butter

¹/₃ cup plus 1 tablespoon (2 oz / 56 g) unbleached all-purpose flour

Panettone dough (page 200) made, without butter or the filling, through the first rise and refrigerated 2 to 3 hours

1 cup (5 oz / 150 g) chopped dates

1¹/₂ cups (5 oz / 150 g) chopped toasted walnuts

BY HAND

Place the butter between 2 sheets of waxed paper and beat with a rolling pin to soften slightly. Sprinkle the flour on top of the butter and work it into the butter with a dough scraper. The flour shouldn't be thoroughly worked in, and the butter should be cold but malleable, so that it forms a dry but firm butter packet.

BY MIXER

Beat the butter and flour in a mixer bowl with the paddle until smooth. The flour shouldn't be thoroughly worked in and the butter should still be cold.

The dough is turned four times as for *cornetti dolci* (page 285). Lightly flour the work surface. Roll the cold dough into an 18 by 12-inch rectangle, ¹/₂ inch thick, so that one short side is nearest you. Break the butter into small (¹/₂-inch) pieces and dot over two-thirds of the dough rectangle nearest you, leaving a 1¹/₂-inch border around the edges. Fold as if you were folding a business letter, folding the unbuttered third over the middle and the remaining third over the top. Pinch the edges together so that the butter does not fall out. Tap the surface of the dough with a rolling pin to evenly distribute the butter.

First Set of Two Turns. Keep the work surface clean and lightly dusted with flour at all times. Place the dough on the surface so that the top flap faces your right (like a book). Roll the dough into a 24 by 8-inch rectangle, $^1/_2$ inch thick. Fold the two short ends to meet in the middle. Then fold in half, as if closing a book, and turn the dough so that the open folded edge is facing away from you toward the top of the table. Tap the dough with the rolling pin from one end to the other to consolidate it, and brush off all the excess flour. Roll the dough out once again to approximately the same size rectangle and fold into thirds, like a business letter. Lightly tap the dough to consolidate it, brush off the excess flour, and place the dough in a plastic bag. Refrigerate 30 to 45 minutes. If the dough is refrigerated too long, the butter will break or crack instead of rolling out smoothly.

Second Set of Two Turns. Place the dough on a lightly floured surface so that the top flap faces to your right. Roll the dough into the same size rectangle and fold once again into thirds. The surface should be blistered and the dough springy,

elastic, and very smooth. Refrigerate the dough 30 to 45 minutes to let it relax. Roll the dough out a final time and fold again. Let it relax at room temperature for about 15 minutes.

Filling and Shaping. Roll the dough out $^1/_2$ inch thick. Cut the dough into three equal rectangles. On one rectangle, sprinkle the dates, and on the second sprinkle the walnuts; leave the third rectangle plain. Place the walnut dough on top of the date dough and cover both of them with the plain dough. Pinch the edges to seal and gently shape into a ball by pulling the dough taut and pinching it together at the bottom. Place in a paper panettone mold, a buttered panettone mold, a 2-pound coffee can lined with a round of parchment paper, or a 2-quart springform mold with sides built up with aluminum foil. Cover with a towel and let rise until doubled, 3 to 4 hours.

Baking. Preheat the oven to 400°F. Bake 10 minutes. Reduce the heat to 375°F and bake 40 to 50 minutes. If the top starts to get too brown, cover it with aluminum foil. Cool completely in the mold, laying it on a pillow in the case of the paper mold, and then unmold onto a rack.

Veneziana VENETIAN HOLIDAY BREAD

This sweet bread from Venice, made for Christmas and especially for New Year's Eve, is very much like panettone but has no citron or candied fruits. The top is dusted with confectioners' sugar and studded with whole almonds.

Makes 2 round loaves

SPONGE

3¹/₂ teaspoons (0.4 oz / 10 g) active dry yeast

¹/₄ cup (1.8 oz / 50 g) sugar

³/₄ cup (6.3 oz / 180 g) warm water

3 large egg yolks

Scant 2 cups (8.8 oz / 250 g) unbleached all-purpose flour

¹/₄ cup (2 oz / 55 g) unsalted butter, at room temperature

Stir the yeast and sugar into the water in a mixing bowl; let stand until foamy, about 10 minutes. Stir in the egg yolks, and then mix in the flour to form a soft dough. Beat in the butter thoroughly. Cover with plastic wrap and let rise until tripled, about 2 hours.

DOUGH

1 teaspoon (0.1 oz / 3 g) active dry yeast

1 tablespoon (0.7 oz / 21 g) honey

3 tablespoons (1.5 oz / 45 g) warm water

¹/₂ cup (3.5 oz / 100 g) sugar

3 large egg yolks

1 cup plus 2 tablespoons (4.4 oz / 125 g) cake flour

1 cup (4.9 oz / 140 g) unbleached all-purpose flour

1 stick (4 oz / 115 g) unsalted butter, at room temperature

2 teaspoons (0.3 oz / 8 g) vanilla extract

Grated zest of 2 oranges

Grated zest of 1 lemon

1 teaspoon (0.2 oz / 5 g) salt

BY HAND

Stir the yeast and honey into the water in a large mixing bowl; let stand until foamy, about 10 minutes. Stir in the sugar and egg yolks; add the sponge and mix until smooth. Stir in the flours 1 cup at a time. The dough should be soft. Stir in the butter, vanilla, and orange and lemon zests, and then the salt. Knead on a lightly floured surface until smooth but still soft and slightly sticky, 8 to 10 minutes.

BY MIXER

Stir the yeast and honey into the water in a large mixer bowl; let stand until foamy, about 10 minutes. Add the sugar, egg yolks, and sponge and mix with the paddle until smooth. Add the flours and mix until the dough comes together. Mix in the butter, vanilla, orange and lemon zests, and salt. Change to the dough hook and knead until smooth but still soft and slightly sticky, about 3 minutes.

First Rise. Place the dough in a lightly buttered bowl, cover tightly with plastic wrap, and let rise until doubled, about 2 hours. The dough should be full of air bubbles.

Shaping and Second Rise. Pour the dough out onto a floured surface, punch it down, and knead lightly. Cut the dough in half and shape each piece into a ball. Because the dough is very sticky, shape the ball in your hands, holding it in the air and stretching the skin taut as you turn it and pinch the dough together on the bottom. Place each ball in a buttered 2-quart charlotte mold or soufflé dish. Cover with plastic wrap and let rise until doubled, about 2$^1/_2$ hours.

TOPPING

$^1/_4$ cup (1.4 oz / 40 g) blanched almonds, plus 10 to 12 whole almonds for the top

$^1/_2$ teaspoon (0.07 oz / 2 g) bitter almond oil or almond extract (optional)

$^3/_4$ cup (5.3 oz / 150 g) granulated sugar

1 to 2 large egg whites

1$^1/_2$ tablespoons (0.7 oz / 20 g) turbinado sugar

Confectioners' sugar

Process $^1/_4$ cup of the almonds and the sugar in a food processor fitted with the steel blade, or grind the nuts in a nut grinder, then add the sugar. Move to a small bowl, add the bitter almond oil or extract if you are using it, and stir in enough of the egg whites to make the mixture easily spreadable but not runny. When the loaves have fully risen, delicately brush the topping all over the surfaces. Dot each loaf with whole almonds and then sprinkle with the turbinado sugar. Finish with a heavy dusting of confectioners' sugar.

Baking. Preheat the oven to 400°F. Bake 10 minutes. Reduce the heat to 350°F and bake 35 to 40 minutes longer. Let cool 10 minutes and unmold very carefully onto racks to cool completely.

Focaccia Veneziana Infarcita con Crema di Zabaglione
VENETIAN FOCACCIA LACED WITH ZABAGLIONE CREAM

One morning I walked through the streets of Venice at 2 A.M. to join the bread bakers of Il Fornaio at San Luca at their work. The bakery itself was huge, but it took only three men to turn out a prodigious selection of regional breads, rolls in any number of forms, and big *pani in cassette* for sandwich loaves. As they worked, they joked, told stories, and tossed the dough at the worktables with abandon before shaping it. Around 5 A.M. the pastry bakers started to arrive along with a second crew to tend the ovens. By eight o'clock, as I was wondering how anyone could keep up the relentless pace, there suddenly appeared a tray of espressos and cappuccinos and the most extravagant dome of sweet bread laced with hidden veins of zabaglione cream. It was every bit as wonderful as it sounds. Although the recipe looks complicated because of the three initial steps in putting the dough together, if you can plan to do it on a day when you will be home and have other things to do, it shouldn't be a problem. I suggest baking the focaccia on one day and making the filling and injecting it the next day.

Makes 1 round loaf

SPONGE

1¼ teaspoons (0.1 oz / 3.5 g) active dry yeast

½ teaspoon (0.1 oz / 2.5 g) sugar

¼ cup (2 oz / 60 g) warm water

2 large eggs

1 cup plus 1 tablespoon (5.3 oz / 150 g) unbleached all-purpose flour

Stir the yeast and sugar into the warm water in a large mixing or mixer bowl; let stand until foamy, about 10 minutes. Stir in the eggs and then the flour to make a soft dough. Cover with plastic wrap and let rise until bubbly and doubled, about 45 minutes.

FIRST DOUGH

½ teaspoon (0.05 oz / 1.4 g) active dry yeast

1 tablespoon (0.5 oz / 15 g) warm water

2 tablespoons (0.7 oz / 20 g) nonfat dry milk

Scant ¼ cup (1.6 oz / 45 g) sugar

2 tablespoons (1 oz / 28 g) unsalted butter, at room temperature

1 large egg

3 large egg yolks

1 cup plus 1 tablespoon (5.3 oz / 150 g) unbleached all-purpose flour

1 teaspoon (0.2 oz / 5 g) salt

Stir the yeast into the water in a bowl; let stand until creamy, about 10 minutes. Stir in the milk. Beat the sugar, butter, egg, and egg yolks together until blended, stir into the yeast mixture, and then stir into the sponge. Add the flour and salt and stir just until the dough comes together. Cover with plastic wrap and let rise until doubled, $1^1/_2$ to $2^1/_2$ hours.

SECOND DOUGH

1 tablespoon (0.7 oz / 21 g) honey

Scant $^1/_2$ cup (3.2 oz / 90 g) sugar

$4^1/_2$ teaspoons (0.8 oz / 22 g) rum

$1^1/_2$ teaspoons (0.2 oz / 6 g) vanilla extract

Grated zest of 1 orange or $^1/_2$ teaspoon (0.07 oz / 2 g) best-quality orange oil

4 large egg yolks, beaten

2 cups plus 2 scant tablespoons (10.5 oz / 300 g) unbleached all-purpose flour

$^1/_3$ cup (2.6 oz / 75 g) unsalted butter, at room temperature

BY HAND

Add the honey, sugar, rum, vanilla, and orange zest to the first dough and beat until blended. Add the egg yolks and stir vigorously. The dough will look stringy and lumpy, but it will smooth out later. Stir in the flour 1 cup at a time, and beat vigorously until the dough is stretchy and smooth. Beat in the butter 1 tablespoon at a time, and continue stirring until the dough comes together. Knead vigorously on a floured surface until smooth and elastic, 10 to 12 minutes.

BY MIXER

Add the honey, sugar, rum, vanilla, and orange zest to the first dough and beat with the paddle until blended. Beat in the egg yolks. The dough will look stringy and lumpy, but it will smooth out later. Beat in the flour 1 cup at a time, then beat in the butter 1 tablespoon at a time at medium speed. Beat until the dough comes together, although it will never pull entirely away from the bottom of the bowl. Change to the dough hook and knead at medium speed until smooth and elastic, about 4 minutes.

Shaping. Shape the dough into a ball and place in a buttered 2-quart charlotte mold or soufflé dish. Cut a Y in the top of the loaf with a razor. Cover with a towel and let rise until doubled, about $2^1/_2$ to 3 hours.

GLAZE

2 to 3 tablespoons (1 to 1.5 oz / 30 to 45 g) amaretto liqueur

$^1/_4$ cup (1.8 oz / 50 g) turbinado sugar

2 to 3 tablespoons (0.5 to 0.8 oz / 16 to 24 g) confectioners' sugar

Brush the top of the loaf with the liqueur, sprinkle with turbinado sugar, and then sift the confectioners' sugar over the top. Recut the Y to be sure it is open.

Baking. Preheat the oven to 350°F. Bake 1 hour 10 minutes. It will puff up dramatically in the oven, rising over the top of the form to almost twice its original height. Let cool completely in the mold.

Filling. Make the zabaglione cream (recipe follows). Use the special long-nosed (Bismarck) pastry tip for injecting the zabaglione cream into the focaccia. First spoon the cream into a pastry bag fitted with the tip. Make eight to ten small indentations in the focaccia with the tip

continued

Focaccia Veneziana Infarcita con Crema di Zabaglione, *continued*

and then squirt little rivulets of filling into the interior and into the Y-shaped opening. If you don't have the special tip, use a sharp bread knife to cut the focaccia into three horizontal layers and fill with the cream as you would a layer cake.

ZABAGLIONE CREAM

I think this Marsala-flavored cream is so good I would happily dip my fingers in it and eat it unaccompanied. The origins of zabaglione, one of the most famous desserts in Piedmont, have been credited to two different sources. One of them was a Franciscan priest, Pasquale de Baylon, who became the patron saint of cooks. The story is told that during his funeral rites, at the moment of the elevation of the host, the Franciscan suddenly reopened his eyes to see the bread and wine of the Eucharist, which members in the church interpreted as the ultimate testimony of his love for the divine sacrament. Since Baylon was also known to be a fine cook, the worshipers around him suggested honoring him with a dish made with eggs and wine. When Baylon was elevated to sainthood during the papacy of Alexander VIII, he became San Bayon, which became zabaglione (pronounced zah-buy-YOH-nay). And thus, one story goes, was born zabaglione.

2 tablespoons (0.6 oz / 18 g) unbleached all-purpose flour

6 tablespoons (2.6 oz / 75 g) sugar

1¹/₃ cups (11.4 oz / 325 g) milk

1 large egg

3 large egg yolks

Grated zest of ¹/₂ lemon

3 tablespoons (1.5 oz / 45 g) Marsala

Mix the flour and sugar in a small, heavy saucepan. Stir in the milk. Heat to a simmer, stirring constantly, until as thick as hot cereal, about 5 minutes. Beat the egg and egg yolks in a mixing bowl. Pour half of the milk mixture into the eggs and beat until smooth; add the rest of the milk and beat again. Return to the saucepan and heat just until it comes to a boil. Return to the bowl and dot the butter over the top. Stir in the lemon zest. Cool to lukewarm. Add the Marsala and beat until smooth.

Colomba Pasquale EASTER BREAD

Everyone agrees that the *colomba pasquale* is a sweet bread made at Easter from a dough almost identical to panettone; it is shaped like a dove and veiled with crystallized sugar and studded with toasted unpeeled almonds. There are, however, two very different stories about its origins. One traces the *colomba* of Milan to the victory of Legnano in 1176 when the cities of the Lombard League finally defeated Frederick Barbarossa, who was intent on capturing Italy for the Holy Roman Empire. It is said that two doves, symbolizing the Holy Ghost, appeared during the battle on the altar of the chariot carrying the battle standards and that the *colomba* memorializes that event and victory. Others say that, while the panettone comes from Milano, the *colomba* clearly derives from nearby Pavia during the time when Alboin, King of the Lombards, conquered the city. As tribute, they say, he exacted an enormous number of precious jewels as well as twelve girls to do with as he pleased. All except one girl wept and sobbed at her fate, but the one who used her head took some eggs, yeast, sugar, flour, candied fruits, and spices and made a sweet cake in the shape of a dove. When the king called her to his bed, the story goes, she brought him her *colomba*, which he ate with pleasure and then allowed her to go free. Yet another story says that she baked him a sweet cake shaped like a dove, the symbol of peace, and Alboin made Pavia his capital and spared it from destruction.

Makes 1 shaped loaf

SPONGE

3¹/₂ teaspoons (0.4 oz / 10 g) active dry yeast

1 tablespoon (0.5 oz / 13 g) sugar

¹/₂ cup (4.2 oz / 120 g) warm water

3 large egg yolks

¹/₂ cup (2.5 oz / 70 g) unbleached all-purpose flour

Stir the yeast and sugar into the water in a large mixing bowl or mixer bowl; let stand until foamy, about 10 minutes. Vigorously stir in the egg yolks and flour and continue stirring until smooth. Cover tightly with plastic wrap and let rise until doubled, about 30 minutes.

FIRST DOUGH

1 teaspoon (0.1 oz / 3 g) active dry yeast

5 tablespoons (2.5 oz / 75 g) warm water

3 tablespoons (1.6 oz / 45 g) unsalted butter, at room temperature

1¹/₂ cups (7.4 oz / 210 g) unbleached all-purpose flour

Stir the yeast into the water in a small bowl; let stand until creamy, about 10 minutes. Stir the dissolved yeast into the sponge. Stir in the butter and then the flour. The dough should be stiff but sticky. Cover tightly with plastic wrap and let rise until doubled, 1 to 2 hours.

continued

Colomba Pasquale, *continued*

SECOND DOUGH

1/2 cup plus 3 tablespoons (5 oz / 145 g) sugar

1 tablespoon (0.7 oz / 21 g) honey

3 large egg yolks

1 1/2 teaspoons (0.2 oz / 6 g) vanilla extract

Grated zest of 2 oranges

1 stick (4 oz / 115 g) unsalted butter, at room temperature

Scant 2 cups (8.8 oz / 250 g) unbleached all-purpose flour

1 teaspoon (0.2 oz / 5 g) salt

1 cup (5.3 oz / 150 g) chopped candied orange peel (page 39)

BY HAND

Add the sugar, honey, and egg yolks to the first dough and stir thoroughly. Stir in the vanilla, orange zest, and butter. Mix the flour and salt and stir into the dough, 1 cup at a time. Continue stirring until a soft dough is formed. Knead on a floured surface until soft but elastic, 7 to 10 minutes.

BY MIXER

Add the sugar, honey, egg yolks, vanilla, orange zest, and butter to the first dough in the mixer bowl. Mix with the paddle until smooth. Add the flour and salt and beat until a soft dough is formed. Change to the dough hook and knead briefly. Knead gently by hand on a floured surface until elastic.

First Rise. Place the dough in an oiled bowl, cover tightly with plastic wrap, and let rise until tripled, about 3 1/2 hours. The dough will have lots of air bubbles beneath the surface when it is fully risen.

Shaping and Second Rise. Cut the dough in half on a lightly floured surface. Pat each piece flat and sprinkle the candied orange peel over the surface. Roll up each piece into a log. Pat the dough flat again and roll up one piece into a 10-inch log with slightly tapered ends, the other into a fatter 7-inch log also with slightly tapered ends. Place the shorter log across the other, shaping them into a stylized dove, on a lightly oiled or buttered baking sheet. Make a slight indentation in the bottom log where the top log crosses it. Cover with a towel and let rise until doubled, 2 to 3 hours. If your kitchen is very cold or dry, let rise in a slightly warm oven (85°F to 90°F) over a pan of steaming water.

TOPPING

5 tablespoons (1.6 oz / 48 g) blanched almonds

1/2 cup plus 2 tablespoons plus 1 teaspoon (4.6 oz / 130 g) granulated sugar

1 or 2 large egg whites

1/4 cup (1.3 oz / 37 g) whole unpeeled almonds

1 to 2 tablespoons (0.5 to 1 oz / 13 to 28 g) turbinado sugar

Confectioners' sugar

Process the blanched almonds and granulated sugar in a food processor fitted with the steel blade. Alternatively, grind the almonds in a nut grinder until fine; transfer to a small bowl and add the sugar. Stir in enough of the egg whites to make the mixture easily spreadable but not runny.

continued

Colomba Pasquale, *continued*

Delicately brush the topping over the fully risen dough. Dot with the whole almonds and then sprinkle with the turbinado sugar. Sift the confectioners' sugar lightly over the top.

Baking. Preheat the oven to 400°F. Bake 10 minutes. Reduce the heat to 350°F and bake 40 minutes longer. Cool completely on a rack.

Other Shapes. The dough can also be shaped into a round loaf and baked in a buttered 2-quart mold or soufflé dish. Bake 10 minutes at 400°F. Reduce the heat to 350°F and bake for 55 minutes longer.

Pandoro CHRISTMAS BREAD OF VERONA

This buttery golden bread is the Christmas specialty of Verona and is always baked in a star-shaped mold beneath a hail of confectioners' sugar. Although the name suggests *pan d'oro* (golden bread), *pandoro* is actually a dialect word for a Veronese dessert made more than two centuries ago. The bread is not complicated to make, but it needs plenty of time for each one of the rises, which are the secret of its delicate, buttery texture. If you start around breakfast time, you can easily have the *pandoro* out of the oven by supper, and you will not have spent much time with the dough itself. This dough is difficult, but not impossible, to make by hand. By all means, use the mixer, if you have one, for this dough. Serve *pandoro* with fresh mascarpone whipped with sugar and egg yolks, flavored with good rum, and sprinkled with chopped toasted almonds.

Makes 2 tall round loaves

SPONGE

4¼ teaspoons (0.4 oz / 12 g) active dry yeast

½ cup (4.2 oz / 120 g) warm water

1 large egg

2 tablespoons (1 oz / 28 g) sugar

¾ cup (3.5 oz / 100 g) unbleached all-purpose flour

Stir the yeast into the water in a large mixing or mixer bowl; let stand until creamy, about 10 minutes. Add the egg, sugar, and flour and beat until smooth. Cover tightly with plastic wrap and let rise until doubled, about 30 minutes.

FIRST DOUGH

Scant 3 cups (13.3 oz / 380 g) pastry flour

3 cups plus 4 teaspoons (15.2 oz / 435 g) unbleached all-purpose flour

1 teaspoon (0.1 oz / 3 g) active dry yeast

1 tablespoon (0.5 oz / 15 g) warm water

¼ cup (1.8 oz / 50 g) sugar

2 large eggs

¼ cup (2 oz / 55 g) unsalted butter, at room temperature

Mix the pastry and all-purpose flours; measure 2¹/₂ cups for this dough and reserve the remaining flour for the second dough. Stir the yeast into the water in a small bowl; let stand until creamy, about 10 minutes. Add the dissolved yeast, sugar, the 2¹/₂ cups of mixed flour, and the eggs to the sponge and stir vigorously. Add the butter and beat until blended. Cover with plastic wrap and let rise until doubled, about 45 minutes.

SECOND DOUGH

4 large eggs

2 large egg yolks

1 cup (7 oz / 200 g) sugar

Reserved mixed pastry and all-purpose flours from the first dough

1 teaspoon (0.2 oz / 5 g) salt

2 teaspoons (0.3 oz / 8 g) vanilla extract

1 teaspoon best-quality lemon extract (0.15 oz / 4 g), or grated zest of 1 lemon

2¹/₂ sticks (10 oz / 285 g) unsalted butter, at room temperature

¹/₂ cup (2.7 oz / 75 g) chopped candied citron (page 39)

4 tablespoons (1.3 oz / 35 g) unbleached all-purpose flour, plus ¹/₂ cup (2.5 oz / 70 g) for kneading, as needed

BY HAND

Add the eggs, egg yolks, sugar, reserved flour mixture, salt, and vanilla and lemon extracts to the first dough and stir until blended. Stir in the butter gradually. Toss the citron and 1 tablespoon of the all-purpose flour together and stir into the dough. Knead on a floured surface, sprin-kling with additional flour (a generous ¹/₂ cup), until soft, light, and delicately elastic, 10 to 12 minutes.

BY MIXER

Add the eggs, egg yolks, sugar, and vanilla and lemon extracts to the first dough and beat thoroughly with the paddle. Toss the citron and 1 tablespoon of the all-purpose flour together and mix into the dough. Mix in the butter gradually and then the reserved flour and the salt. Change to the dough hook and knead at low speed for 4 to 6 minutes, adding the additional ¹/₂ cup of flour as necessary and stopping occasionally to scrape the dough down from the hook. The dough should be soft, buttery, and delicate.

First Rise. Place the dough in a buttered bowl, cover tightly with plastic wrap, and let rise at warm room temperature (75°F to 80°F) until doubled, 2 to 3 hours. The rise may take as long as 4 hours in a cold kitchen; you may place the bowl in a warm water bath (about 90°F) and cover it with a towel to encourage the rising.

Shaping and Second Rise. Sprinkle the top of the dough with the remaining 3 tablespoons of flour. Pour the very buttery and sticky dough onto a well-floured surface. Flour your hands as well. Cut the dough in half with a dough scraper and gently shape each piece into a ball. Place in buttered *pandoro* molds, 2-quart springform pans, or 2-pound coffee cans

continued

Pandoro, *continued*

that have been lined with parchment paper. Cover with a towel and let rise until doubled, about 2¹/₂ to 4 hours, depending on the size of the mold and the warmth of the room.

Baking. Preheat the oven to 350°F. Bake 30 minutes. Reduce the heat to 300°F and bake 20 to 30 minutes longer. Let cool completely before removing the loaves from the molds.

Pizza Civitavecchia EASTER SWEET BREAD FROM CIVITAVECCHIA

The sweet Easter bread of the port of Rome is distinguished not only by its slanting domed top but also by its unusual taste derived from the port, ricotta, and aniseeds that flavor it. This makes extraordinary French toast.

Makes 2 tall domed loaves

SPONGE

3¹/₂ teaspoons (0.35 oz / 10 g) active dry yeast

¹/₂ cup (4 oz / 120 g) warm water

³/₄ cup (3.5 oz / 100 g) bread flour

Stir the yeast into the water in a small bowl; let stand until creamy, about 10 minutes. Add the flour and stir vigorously to make a thick batter. Cover tightly with plastic wrap and let rise until doubled, about 1 hour.

DOUGH

3 cups (14.7 oz / 420 g) unbleached all-purpose flour

¹/₄ cup (1.8 oz / 50 g) sugar

1 teaspoon (0.2 oz / 5 g) salt

4 large eggs

9 large egg yolks

¹/₃ cup (2.6 oz / 75 g) ricotta, pressed through a fine-mesh sieve

¹/₂ cup (4.2 oz / 120 g) port or rum

2 tablespoons plus 2 teaspoons (0.5 oz / 15 g) crushed aniseeds

Grated zest of 1 lemon

¹/₂ teaspoon (0.04 oz / 1 g) ground cinnamon

2 sticks (8 oz / 225 g) unsalted butter, at room temperature

1 large egg white, beaten, for glazing

BY MIXER ONLY

Beat the flour, salt, sugar, eggs, and egg yolks in a mixer bowl with the paddle until blended. Add the sponge and beat 6 to 7 minutes, half at medium speed and half at high. The dough should be golden, springy, and stretchy. Mix the ricotta, port, aniseeds, lemon zest, and cinnamon and beat into the dough. Cut the butter into seven or eight pieces and place on top of the dough.

First Rise. Cover the dough, leaving the butter on top, with plastic wrap, and let rise until doubled, 1 to 1¹/₂ hours. The risen dough should be soft and very elastic. Beat in the butter by hand or with the dough hook until the dough is quite smooth and no longer ropy, 3 to 4 minutes for the mixer.

Shaping and Second Rise. This sticky dough seems more like pound-cake batter than bread dough. You can simply pour it into two well-buttered 2-quart charlotte molds or soufflé dishes, or, if you want to shape it before you place it in the molds,

flour the work surface and your hands well, place a small mound of flour nearby, and shape the dough into two round loaves. Cover with a towel and let rise to the tops of the molds, 1 to 1¹/₂ hours.

Baking. Preheat the oven to 400°F. Brush the tops of the loaves with the egg white. Bake 15 minutes. Reduce the heat to 350°F and bake 1 hour longer. The loaves will rise high above the baking dishes like panettones, and the dome will be tilted.

Note. To double the recipe, double all the ingredients, but use twenty egg yolks and seven eggs in the dough.

Pizza di Pasqua EASTER PIZZA, A SWEET BREAD

This sweet bread made only for Easter comes from an old Roman recipe. Even though it is rich with eggs and butter, it is airy, light, and flavored delicately with orange and lemon. Because it is made with bread flour, it must be beaten at a high speed for a long time. Unless you have phenomenal muscles and remarkable stamina and are willing to beat by hand for 25 to 30 minutes, you will have to use an electric mixer.

Makes 2 tall domed loaves

SPONGE

3¹/₂ teaspoons (0.4 oz / 10 g) active dry yeast
¹/₂ cup (4.2 oz / 120 g) warm water
¹/₂ cup (2.5 oz / 70 g) bread flour

Stir the yeast into the water in a large mixer bowl; let stand until creamy, about 10 minutes. Add the flour and stir until smooth. Cover tightly with plastic wrap and let rise until the sponge has enormous bubbles, is very soupy, and has doubled, about 1 hour.

continued

Pizza di Pasqua, *continued*

DOUGH

3¼ cups (15.8 oz / 450 g) bread flour

10 large egg yolks

½ cup plus 2 tablespoons (4.4 oz / 125 g) granulated sugar

½ cup (4.3 oz / 122 g) milk

3 oranges

2 lemons

1½ teaspoons (0.2 oz / 6 g) vanilla extract

1 stick plus 1 tablespoon (4.5 oz / 130 g) unsalted butter, at room temperature

1 large egg white, beaten, for glazing

2 to 3 tablespoons (1 to 1.5 oz / 28 to 45 g) turbinado sugar

BY MIXER ONLY

Add the flour to the sponge and beat with the paddle until smooth. Beat in the egg yolks, one at a time. Mix in the granulated sugar. Add the milk and mix until well blended. Grate the zest from the oranges and lemon directly into the bowl, so that none of the oils are lost. Add the vanilla and mix until blended. Beat in the butter 2 tablespoons at a time. Beat at medium and medium-high speeds for at least 10 minutes. You may want to turn the mixer off once or twice to be sure that it doesn't overheat. The dough should be very, very soft and extremely elastic.

First Rise. Flour your work surface generously before you pour the dough out. Depending on the wetness of the dough and your ease in handling it, you may need to have a mound of flour nearby to sprinkle on top as you work the dough. Cut the dough in half and shape into two round loaves. Place in two well-buttered 2-quart soufflé dishes or charlotte molds. Cover with a towel and let rise until doubled, 2½ to 3 hours. The dough should fill the entire baking dish.

Baking. Preheat the oven to 400°F. Just before baking, brush the top of each loaf with the egg white and then sprinkle with the turbinado sugar. Bake 35 to 40 minutes. The tops will puff into big domes like panettones. Because the dough is very eggy and porous, it will need the entire baking time. Cover the tops with aluminum foil when they are baked to a golden brown. Let cool 15 minutes and unmold very carefully onto a rack to cool completely. If the loaves seem very delicate to you, you may let them cool completely in the baking dishes.

Gubana EASTER BREAD OF FRIULI

Almost everyone has heard of panettones and *colombe,* but even many Italians are unaware of the *gubana,* the Easter bread of Friuli, the region east of Venice that sits close against the Slovenian and Austrian borders. As soon as I tasted this dense, complicated nut and raisin bread, I was a convert, ready to convince the world of the allure of its bittersweet tastes. I've even tried to import *gubane,* which keep very well even for a journey by sea if they are made with natural yeast. *Gubana* actually exists in two versions, one wrapped in puff pastry, and this one from Cividale, made according to a genuine recipe given to me by Dottore Angelo Albini, a fourth-generation baker. It is essentially equal amounts of dough and filling, which consists of raisins, walnuts, hazelnuts, pine nuts, and almonds moistened with the robust flavors of five different wines and liqueurs. The sweet briochelike dough is rolled up like a strudel, twisted around itself like a snail, and generously showered with crunchy sugar. Some say the *gubana* dates back to the sixth to eighth centuries, when the Lombards settled on Cividale as the capital of their duchy. The first documentary evidence dates it to 1700, but that hardly makes it an upstart.

Its name presumably comes from the Slavic *guba,* which describes the shape of a snail, although there are those who say the name is derived from *bubane,* Friulian dialect for "abundance." You can certainly taste the Slavic influence in the dense, chewy, nut- and fruit-filled interior and in the bittersweet bite of its liqueurs. In Italy, *gubana* is made with the local grappa, a rustic kind of brandy, but you may choose from the amazing variety of grappas available in the United States or substitute plum brandy, aquavit, slivovitz, or marc. Because it is laced with liqueurs, *gubana* is usually eaten for dessert and is especially good with sweet white wines, such as the Verduzzo of Friuli.

Makes 2 round loaves

SPONGE

2 tablespoons plus 2 teaspoons (0.8 oz /22.6 g) active dry yeast

³/₄ cup (6.3 oz / 180 g) milk, warmed to 110°F and then cooled to 75°F to 80°F

1 cup plus 1 tablespoon (5.3 oz / 150 g) unbleached all-purpose flour

Stir the yeast into the milk in a large mixing or mixer bowl; let stand until creamy, about 10 minutes. Stir in the flour with a wooden spoon until smooth. Cover with plastic wrap and let rise 30 minutes to 1 hour.

continued

Gubana, *continued*

DOUGH

2 large eggs

2 large egg yolks

²/₃ cup (4.9 oz / 140 g) sugar

3 to 4 tablespoons (1.5 to 2 oz / 45 to 60 g) milk

3³/₄ cups (17.5 oz / 500 g) unbleached
all-purpose flour

1¹/₄ teaspoons (0.2 oz / 6.5 g) salt

Grated zest of 2 lemons

2¹/₂ teaspoons (0.4 oz / 10 g) vanilla extract

1 stick (4 oz / 115 g) unsalted butter, at room
temperature

BY HAND

Add the eggs, egg yolks, sugar, and
3 tablespoons of the milk to the sponge
and stir until smooth. Stir in the flour, 1 cup
at a time, and the salt and keep stirring
until smooth. Stir in the lemon zest, vanilla,
and 1 more tablespoon of milk, if needed.
Finally stir in the butter (the butter also
can be cut into eight pieces and set on top
of the kneaded dough for the first rise).
Flour your work surface generously, flour
your hands, and have a dough scraper
ready to help knead the dough, which
will be sticky at first. Knead until velvety,
supple, and blistered, 8 to 10 minutes.

BY MIXER

Add the eggs, egg yolks, sugar, and 3 tablespoons of the milk to the sponge and mix
with the paddle until smooth. Mix in the
flour and salt until smooth. Mix in the
lemon zest, vanilla, and 1 more tablespoon
of milk, if needed. Change to the dough

hook and knead until velvety, supple, and
blistered, 3 to 4 minutes. Cut the butter
into eight pieces and set on top of the
dough for the first rise.

First Rise. Place the dough in a lightly buttered bowl, cover with plastic wrap, and
let rise at warm room temperature until
doubled, 2 to 3 hours. You can speed up
the rising a bit by placing the bowl in a
warm water bath (90°F).

FILLING

2³/₄ cups (10.5 oz / 300 g) toasted, skinned, and
chopped hazelnuts

Generous ³/₄ cup (3.2 oz / 90 g) walnuts, toasted
and chopped

¹/₃ cup (1.3 oz / 37 g) pine nuts, lightly toasted

2 tablespoons (0.7 oz / 20 g) blanched almonds,
chopped

1¹/₂ cups (5.6 oz / 160 g) crumbs from leftover
sweet breads, cookies, or homemade breads

Generous 1 cup (6.3 oz / 180 g) raisins

¹/₂ cup plus 1 tablespoon (4.5 oz / 130 g) apricot jam

¹/₂ cup (2.6 oz / 75 g) chopped candied orange peel
(page 39)

Grated zest of 1 lemon

1¹/₂ tablespoons (0.3 oz / 8 g) unsweetened cocoa
powder

1 teaspoon (0.08 oz / 2.5 g) ground cinnamon

3 tablespoons (1.5 oz / 45 g) Marsala

2 tablespoons plus 1 teaspoon (1.2 oz / 35 g) grappa

2 tablespoons (1 oz / 30 g) rum

1 tablespoon (0.5 oz / 15 g) amaretto liqueur

1 teaspoon (0.2 oz / 5 g) maraschino liqueur

1 large egg

2 teaspoons (0.4 oz / 10 g) water

1 large egg white, beaten, for glazing

continued

Gubana, *continued*

Combine the nuts, bread crumbs, raisins, jam, orange peel, lemon zest, cocoa, cinnamon, Marsala, grappa, rum, and liqueurs. Work the butter into the dough, if necessary. Cut the dough in half on a lightly floured surface. Roll out each piece into an 18 by 12-inch rectangle. Spread the filling over the dough rectangles, leaving a 2-inch border on all sides. Mix the egg and water in a small bowl and brush the edges of the dough with the egg wash.

Shaping and Second Rise. Starting at one long edge, roll up each dough rectangle and pinch the ends. Shape each log into a spiral so that it looks like a big snail. Place each dough spiral in a well-buttered 2- to 3-quart baking or soufflé dish. The *gubana* can also be baked free form on a buttered baking sheet, but the dish will help it keep its shape. Cover with plastic wrap or a towel and let rise until well puffed but not doubled, 2 to 2$^{1}/_{2}$ hours.

Baking. Preheat the oven to 375°F. Just before baking, brush the tops of the loaves with the egg white and poke several holes in the tops with a skewer to let air escape from any air pockets. Bake 25 minutes. Reduce the heat to 325°F and bake until deep golden, about 25 minutes longer. Unmold very carefully and cool completely on racks.

Panini e Grissini
Rolls and Breadsticks

Panini

If anything indicates the changing pace of Italian life, it's the explosion of panini, the little rolls that appear in numerous shapes and sizes all over Italy. Walk into any *caffè* bar in Milan, Rome, or another good-size city after 10:30 A.M. and you will find glass cases full of rolls bursting with the most extraordinarily inventive combinations. Here's lunch between two slices of bread, eaten standing at a counter elbow to elbow with masses of other Italians, who can no longer spend several hours in a restaurant or at home for the midday meal.

The possibilities seem endless, limited only by the variety of rolls, the ingredients on hand, and the imagination of the person behind the counter. In addition to soft panini or crisp, crunchy rolls filled with the obvious prosciutto and cheese are rolls thickly studded with olives and filled with tuna and artichoke hearts, sesame seed–topped golden bread with spicy local salami and sweet red and yellow peppers; spinach rolls with Gorgonzola cheese melted on top; braids of *pasta dura* moistened with tomatoes and fresh mozzarella; fat panini stuffed with mozzarella, anchovies, and parsley.

Panini are every bit as regional as breads, and Italians develop fierce loyalties to the panini they grew up with. Plump, soft *biove* come from Piedmont; small cleft *spaccatini* are made at

Lugano and Como; extravagant *coppiette*, shaped like starfish, artichokelike *carciofi*, and scroll-like *montasù* come from Emilia; and crunchy *ciriole*, with their soft interiors, are the classic Roman roll.

There's absolutely no question that the *michetta* is the quintessential bread of Milan. With its five-sided central button and a design that looks like a flower opening, the *michetta* has a crisp crunchy crust and an interior that is almost entirely hollow, which makes it the perfect vehicle for a sandwich. These big, empty rolls appear on breakfast, lunch, and dinner tables all over Lombardy. Some Americans confronting their first *michetta* let it be known that they feel certain they've been cheated. The *rosetta* of Florence, Rome, and points south and the *michetta* are almost identical, although sometimes the central shape of the *rosetta* has only three sides and it can be somewhat puffier and sometimes not quite as hollow. Moot points, perhaps, to outsiders, but sources of controversy and regional pride to Italians. These two particular rolls cannot be made at home because they must be cut with special machines and baked in very hot ovens. These facts are evidently not known to all bakers, for a baker in Rimini assured a knowledgeable Italian cook that they are made by inserting a syringe inside the rolls as they expand in the oven to draw out the air and create the cavity.

There are numerous breads in this book that can be made into excellent rolls. Try particularly the *pane alle olive* (page 115), *pane di Chiavari* (page 117), *pane agli spinaci* (page 135), *pan bigio* (page 103), *pane siciliano* (page 100), and any of the vegetable, herb, and cheese breads. The *pane all'olio* (page 83) and the *pane integrale alle erbe* (page 152) are simply a number of rolls set in a ring; the olive breads and some of the vegetable and herb breads can be shaped in the same way. A particularly delicious treat is to spread a cooled spinach roll with a tablespoon or two of Gorgonzola that has been beaten to a buttery consistency and heat in the oven just long enough for the cheese to melt and brown slightly.

Pasta Dura VARIOUS ROLLS FROM EMILIA-ROMAGNA

If you have ever been to Bologna or Modena or Ferrara and were served a roll that had a hard, matte crust and a dense, stark white, slightly cottony interior, you've eaten *pasta dura*. You may have had it as a *coppietta*, whose characteristic form was already known in the sixteenth century, when it was served at banquets at the Este court in Ferrara. Its double croissant shape with the connecting ends knotted in the center can look rather like a starfish. Or you may have had it shaped like an open hand, a scroll (*montasù*), or an artichoke or open flower (*carciofo*). *Baulette* from Mantua are thick cylinders of the dough slashed open at the top, while *banane* from Lombardy look more than slightly phallic and may seem at first to be croissants made of flat dough.

Pasta dura is one of the oldest breads in the world. Long before there were machines to mix and knead the dough, the Egyptians and Romans made it with their feet or by pounding it with a wooden bar. Bakeries, of course, have machines to mix the dough and form the cylinders that are the basis of many traditional *pasta dura* shapes; you'll have to use an electric mixer to put the dough together, because it has so little water that it is extremely difficult to make by hand. You'll also need a rolling pin or pasta machine to give the dough the correct density.

Pasta dura is a rather controversial bread; there are as many who praise it as the tastiest and most typical bread of Italy as there are those who are mystified by the appeal of its dense interior. It is traditionally eaten with sliced and smoked meats, veal roasts, sausages, and stews. You can use it to make sandwiches with salami or mozzarella and tomatoes, or put slightly stale slices into vegetable soups.

Makes 7 coppietta, montasù, or bauletta or 15 carciofo rolls

1¼ teaspoons (0.1 oz / 3.5 g) active dry yeast

¼ cup (2 oz / 60 g) warm water

1¾ cups plus 2 tablespoons (15.8 oz / 450 g) very cold water

About ¼ cup (2 oz / 60 g) lard or olive oil, at room temperature

7 cups plus 2 tablespoons (2 lb 3 oz / 1 kg) enriched bleached all-purpose flour, or 5⅓ cups (1 lb 10.3 oz / 750 g) enriched bleached all-purpose flour plus 2 cups pastry flour (8.8 oz / 250 g)

2 teaspoons (0.4 oz / 10 g) salt

BY HAND

Stir the yeast into the warm water in a large mixing bowl; let stand until creamy, about 10 minutes. Stir in the cold water and lard. Add 3 cups of the flour and the salt and beat vigorously with a wooden spoon, whisk, or rubber spatula until smooth. Stir in the remaining flour 1 to 2 cups at a time. When the dough is too stuff to stir, plunge in with your hands and mix until the dough is no longer sticky. Knead firmly on a floured surface until stiff, resistant, and satiny, 6 to 8 minutes. (If it is too hard to

continued

Pasta Dura, *continued*

knead, let it rest, covered, for about 5 minutes and try again.) To get the characteristic dense, smooth crumb, beat the dough with a rolling pin without stopping, folding and turning the dough from time to time, until smooth, compact, and dense, about 5 minutes.

BY MIXER

Stir the yeast into the warm water in a large mixer bowl; let stand until creamy, about 10 minutes. Stir in the cold water and lard with the paddle. Add the flour and salt and mix at low speed for 2 to 3 minutes, then briefly at a slightly faster speed. Change to the dough hook and knead at medium speed for 4 to 5 minutes. Knead by hand on a lightly floured surface until stiff, resistant, and satiny. (If it is too hard to knead, let it rest, covered, for about 5 minutes.) To get the characteristic dense, smooth crumb, beat the dough with a rolling pin without stopping, folding and turning the dough from time to time, until smooth, compact, and dense, about 5 minutes.

Resting. Let the dough rise under a towel until it softens slightly, about 30 minutes. The dough should feel cold and clammy like modeling clay.

Shaping. To keep this dough elastic, cover any pieces you aren't working under plastic wrap. First cut the dough into the appropriate size, either seven pieces (7 oz / 200 g each, for *coppietta*, *montasù*, or *bauletta*

rolls) or fifteen pieces ($3^{1}/_{2}$ oz / 100 g each, for *carciofo*). Roll each piece into a tight ball. With a rolling pin, roll each ball into a thick ribbon. Grasping the end nearest you in your left hand, use your right hand to roll up the ribbon at a slight angle into a tightly graduated cylinder that looks like a fat cigar. With the rolling pin, roll each cylinder into a long, thin strip of dough, about 9 to 10 inches long and $1^{1}/_{2}$ to 2 inches wide. Shape the dough into any of the following shapes.

Coppietta (see photo opposite). Place one strip of dough, short end facing you, on a work surface. Turn over a small edge of the dough at the top. Holding the bottom edge with your left hand, stretch the dough as you roll it toward you from the opposite end. The way to get the dough properly stretched and thin is to push the dough down and away as you roll it up. Push down hard and roll fast so the dough spreads out into long thin rolls. When the roll is about 5 inches wide, lessen the pressure so that it will narrow as you continue to stretch and roll it into a shape fatter in the center and narrower at the edges. Roll to about 1 inch from the center. Turn the strip around and repeat on the other end, leaving a 2-inch bridge. Twist one roll completely around the other in two 360-degree turns to make a double twist in the center. Place the roll on a lightly oiled baking sheet with the twisted bridge piece on top. Pinch the two

continued

Pasta Dura, *continued*

pieces together from the middle beneath the bridge.

Montasù (Scroll Shape). Place one strip of dough, short end facing you, on a work surface. Fold over a small edge of dough at each end; then roll up the two short ends toward the middle, leaving a 2-inch gap in the middle. Use less tension in pressing and rolling the dough than in the *coppietta*, as these rolls should be short and fat. Press down firmly as you roll and, at the same time, stretch the dough away from the center. When both ends are rolled up, hold the dough up and, with your finger under the stretched center, twist one roll at a 90-degree angle and place it on top of the other. With your thumb, press hard at the center where they meet so that the roll holds its shape. Place on lightly oiled baking sheets.

Carciofo (Artichoke Shape, see photos opposite). Roll each strip a bit wider, to 3 inches. Using a razor or dough scraper, make 1-inch-deep cuts every $^1/_2$ inch along one long edge. Starting at the short end, roll the dough up and pinch the seam closed. Stand each roll on end on an oiled baking sheet and carefully pull open the "petals" so that it looks like a flower or the leaves of an artichoke. Place on lightly oiled baking sheets.

Bauletta (Little Trunk from Mantua). Roll up each strip from the short end into a tightly graduated cylinder, as you did in the *coppietta* initial shaping. Use your left hand to create tension, and, with your right hand, push down hard on the dough to spread it out as quickly as possible until it is 5 inches wide. At that point, decrease the pressure so that the strip narrows as you continue to stretch and roll it into a tapered form that is narrower at the tips and fatter in the middle. Place on lightly oiled baking sheets.

Rising. To capture the heat generated by the fermentation, prop up plastic wrap above the dough with juice glasses or spice jars. Cover with a towel and place the dough in a 90°F gas oven or an electric oven that you have heated at 150°F for 3 minutes only. Let the rolls stand 1 to $1^1/_2$ hours, or until they puff about $^1/_4$ inch. They will never double, but the small rise is important. Let the thicker *baulette* stand about $2^1/_2$ hours. Just before baking the *baulette*, slash each one with a razor in a long, narrow cut that is deeper at the center than at the ends.

Baking. Preheat the oven to 425°F. Five minutes before baking, place $1^1/_2$ cups of boiling water in a pan on the bottom rack of the oven. Bake the rolls for 20 minutes, spraying the oven three times with hot water in the first 10 minutes. Cool on racks.

Variation. To make *streghe*, a wonderful crunchy, crackly snack or hors d'oeuvre, roll out the dough very, very thin and cut it into diamond shapes. Place on oiled baking sheets, brush the diamonds with oil, and sprinkle with salt. Bake at 425°F until lightly golden, about 10 minutes.

THE CARCIOFO:

Beat the dough with a rolling pin in one hand.

Make cuts into one edge.

Roll the dough up.

Open the "petals."

Semelle LITTLE ROLLS FROM FLORENCE

The names of rolls in Italy are even more confusing than the names of breads. Bakers in Florence use this dough to make *rosette*, the flower-shaped panini that are similar to the *michette* of Milan. Both the *rosetta* and the *michetta* get their height and almost empty interior from the combination of a special cutter and very high oven temperatures. When made by hand, these rolls become *semelle* and are shaped in this simple form. Of course, they don't have the empty interior, but they are crunchy and have a lovely fragrance. I think they are the perfect dinner rolls.

Makes 10 rolls

2¼ teaspoons (1 package / 0.2 oz / 7 g) active dry yeast

1¼ cups (10.5 oz / 300 g) warm water

3¾ cups (17.5 oz / 500 g) unbleached all-purpose flour

2 teaspoons (0.4 oz / 10 g) salt

Olive oil for brushing

BY HAND

Stir the yeast into the water in a mixing bowl; let stand until creamy, about 10 minutes. Stir in the flour, 1 cup at a time, and the salt. When the dough is too stiff to stir, plunge in with your hands. Knead on a lightly floured work surface until solid and elastic, 8 to 10 minutes.

BY MIXER

Stir the yeast into the water in a mixer bowl; let stand until creamy, about 10 minutes. Add the flour and salt and mix with the paddle until the dough pulls away from the sides of the bowl. Change to the dough hook and knead until solid and elastic, 3 to 4 minutes.

First Rise. Place the dough in a lightly oiled bowl, cover tightly with plastic wrap, and let rise until doubled, about 1 hour.

Shaping and Second Rise. Cut the dough into ten equal pieces and shape each piece into a ball. Brush a little oil over each and let rest 10 minutes under a towel. With the edge of your hand, make a deep indentation down the center of each ball; be sure to press down firmly. Place the rolls, cleft side down, on floured parchment or brown paper. Cover with a towel and let rise until doubled, about 1 hour.

Baking. Preheat the oven to 425°F. Just before baking, turn each roll over and reemphasize the cleft. Place the rolls, cleft side up, on an oiled baking sheet. Bake 15 to 18 minutes, spraying the oven three times with water in the first 10 minutes. Cool on a rack.

Rosette Veneziane ROSETTES OF VENICE

Rosette are extremely popular in Venice, perhaps because the tender rolls are shaped delicately to look like a flower with all its petals neatly tucked into the center. When *rosette* are made by hand, they look a lot like *Kaisersemmel* rolls. This recipe is my variation of the Venetian rolls.

Makes 12 to 14 rolls

1 teaspoon (0.1 oz / 3 g) active dry yeast

2 tablespoons (1 oz / 30 g) warm water

Scant ¼ cup (1.8 oz / 50 g) lard

¼ cup (1.9 oz / 55 g) olive oil

3 tablespoons (1.5 oz / 45 g) sugar

2 cups (17.5 oz / 500 g) biga (page 70)

2 cups plus 2 tablespoons (10.5 oz / 300 g) unbleached all-purpose flour

1 teaspoon (0.2 oz / 5 g) salt

1 or 2 large egg whites, beaten, for glazing

BY HAND

Stir the yeast into the water in a large mixing bowl; let stand until creamy, about 10 minutes. Stir in the lard, oil, sugar, and *biga* and mix until the *biga* is broken up. Add the flour and salt and stir until the dough comes together. Knead on a floured surface until moist, elastic, and slightly blistered, 8 to 10 minutes.

BY MIXER

Stir the yeast into the water in a mixer bowl; let stand until creamy, about 10 minutes. Add the lard, oil, sugar, and *biga* and mix with the paddle until the

biga is broken up. Add the flour and salt and mix until the dough comes together. Change to the dough hook and knead at low speed until moist, elastic, and slightly blistered, 3 to 4 minutes.

First Rise. Place the dough in a lightly oiled bowl, cover tightly with plastic wrap, and let rise until doubled, about 2 hours.

Shaping and Second Rise. Rosette, which look like flowers, are somewhat complicated to shape. Turn the soft, springy dough out onto a floured surface and pat or roll out ³/₄ inch thick. Using a cookie cutter, cut out 5¹/₂-inch circles. Mark the enter of each circle lightly. You will shape five equidistant points of dough around the circle, using your left thumb as an anchor and guide throughout the process, if you are right-handed. Place your left thumb in the center of the dough from the 9 o'clock position. With your other hand, pick up the dough at 12 noon and roll the edge over (on top of the dough), turning and twisting it to set the point at the center of the dough. (You can cover your thumb, if that's easier, and then pull it out.) Be sure to roll the dough with a good turn

continued

Rosette Veneziane, *continued*

to create a three-dimensional roll. Turn the circle of dough clockwise so that the rolled point is at 12 noon and continue to shape three more points, placing your left thumb in the center of the dough from the 9 o'clock position and starting the roll at 12 noon, but ending with the point covering your thumb in the center of the dough. The last point should be tucked into the last pocket. If all this sounds complicated and you make mistakes, don't worry: this dough is very forgiving. Take apart any rosettes you aren't pleased with, let the dough rest briefly, and shape again. Place on lightly oiled baking sheets, cover with a towel, and let rise until doubled, about 1 1/2 to 1 3/4 hours.

Baking. Preheat the oven to 400°F. Brush the rolls with the egg white. Bake until golden, about 20 minutes. Cool on racks.

Spaccatini LITTLE CLEFT ROLLS

These wonderful rolls from Lugano are really something to sink your teeth into. With a light, chewy crust and full-bodied, soft crumb, they add a mellow wheat flavor to a meal. If you are willing to wait slightly longer, you can cut the amount of yeast for these rolls in half, and the flavor will be even mellower.

Makes 16 rolls

3/4 teaspoon (0.07 oz / 2.1 g) active dry yeast

1/2 cup (4.2 oz / 120 g) warm water

2 cups (17.5 oz / 500 g) biga (page 70)

Scant 2 cups (8.8 oz / 250 g) unbleached all-purpose flour

1 teaspoon (0.2 oz / 5 g) salt

BY HAND

Stir the yeast into the water in a large mixing bowl; let stand until creamy, about 10 minutes. Add the *biga*, stir vigorously with a wooden spoon, and squeeze the *biga* between your fingers to break it up. Add the flour, 1 cup at a time, and the salt and stir until the dough comes together. Knead on a well-floured surface, sprinkling with 1 to 2 tablespoons of additional flour, until elastic and supple, 4 to 5 minutes.

BY MIXER

Stir the yeast into the water in a mixer bowl; let stand until creamy, about 10 minutes. Add the *biga* and mix with the paddle until the *biga* is broken up. Add the flour and salt and mix until the dough comes

together. Change to the dough hook and knead at low speed 2 minutes, then at medium speed 1 minute. If you want, finish kneading briefly on a floured surface; you will probably need 1 to 2 tablespoons of additional flour.

First Rise. Place the dough in a lightly oiled bowl, cover tightly with plastic wrap, and let rise until doubled, 1 1/2 to 2 hours.

Shaping and Second Rise. Cut the dough into sixteen pieces, each about the size of a lemon. Shape each piece into a ball on a floured surface, then, with the edge of your hand, a dowel, or the floured handle of a wooden spoon, make a deep indentation down the center of each ball. Place the rolls, cleft side down, on a well-floured surface. Cover with a towel and let rise until doubled, about 1 hour.

Baking. Preheat the oven to 425°F. Just before baking, turn each roll over and reemphasize the cleft. Place the rolls, cleft side up, on lightly oiled or parchment-lined baking sheets. Bake 20 to 25 minutes, spraying the oven three times with water in the first 10 minutes. Cool on a rack.

Biovette PLUMP ROLLS FROM PIEDMONT

The golden crust and soft light interior of *biove* are among the happiest memories of many people who grew up eating them in the Piedmont region. They are, however, as difficult to reproduce as they are wonderful, so this recipe is just a fragrant memory of the real thing.

Makes 8 rolls

1¼ teaspoons (0.1 oz / 3.5 g) active dry yeast

1½ teaspoons (0.4 oz / 10.5 g) malt syrup or powder

1 cup plus 3 tablespoons (10 oz / 285 g) warm water

2 tablespoons (0.9 oz / 26 g) lard

2½ tablespoons (1.3 oz / 37 g) olive oil

3¾ cups (17.5 oz / 500 g) unbleached all-purpose flour, plus up to ¼ cup (1.3 oz / 35 g) more, if needed

2 teaspoons (0.4 oz / 10 g) salt

BY HAND

Stir the yeast and the malt, if you are using the syrup, into the water in a large mixing bowl; let stand until foamy, about 10 minutes. Stir in the lard and oil, and then the flour, 1 cup at a time, and the salt and malt powder, if you are using it. Stir until a soft dough is formed. Knead on a floured surface, sprinkling with up to ¼ cup of additional flour, until velvety, soft, and elastic, 8 to 10 minutes.

BY MIXER

Stir the yeast and malt, if you are using the syrup, into the water in a mixer bowl; let stand until foamy, about 10 minutes. Mix in the lard and oil with the paddle, and then the flour, salt, and malt powder, if you are using it. Mix until the dough comes together. Change to the dough hook and knead at medium speed until velvety, soft, and elastic, about 4 minutes.

First Rise. Place the dough in a lightly oiled bowl, cover tightly with plastic wrap, and let rise until doubled, 1 to 1¼ hours.

Shaping and Second Rise. Cut the dough into eight equal pieces (about 4 oz / 120 g each). Let the dough rise under a towel for 10 minutes. Flatten each piece into a rectangle, 10 to 12 inches long and 4 inches wide. Roll up from one short side into a fat log or lozenge shape. Place the rolls, seam side down, on a well-floured surface, cover with a towel, and let rise until almost doubled, 1 to 1½ hours.

Final Shaping. Turn the rolls over. In Italy a special knife is used to cut the *biove*, but a wooden dowel or even the edge of a dough scraper will do fine. Cut each roll lengthwise through the center, pressing down hard and then pushing with a single snapping motion to open and almost cut through the dough. Place the rolls, cut sides up, on oiled baking sheets.

Baking. Preheat the oven to 425°F. Bake about 25 minutes. Cool on racks.

Other Shapes. Biove in Italy are characteristically larger than these rolls, which are *biovette,* the size of dinner rolls. To make true *biove,* shape the dough into four rolls and cut them almost in half in the final shaping.

Panini al Pomodoro TOMATO ROLLS

This is my version of the tomato rolls I saw being made by the dozens in Venice. The decoration of tomato paste and rosemary leaves makes the rolls look a bit like jaunty, rosy tomatoes.

Makes 12 rolls

2¼ teaspoons (1 package / 0.2 oz / 7 g) active dry yeast

1 teaspoon (0.2 oz / 5 g) sugar

1 cup plus 3 tablespoons (10 oz / 285 g) warm water (or ¼ cup / 2 oz / 60 g warm water plus ¾ cup plus 3 tablespoons / 7.9 oz / 225 g cold water if using a processor)

¼ cup (1.9 oz / 55 g) olive oil

½ cup (4.4 oz / 125 g) biga (page 70; optional)

3¾ cups (17.5 oz / 500 g) unbleached all-purpose flour

2 teaspoons (0.4 oz / 10 g) salt

¼ cup (1.3 oz / 35 g) finely chopped onion

1½ tablespoons (0.8 oz / 22.5 g) tomato paste, slightly thinned with warm water

Tomato paste for dabbing

24 fresh rosemary or oregano leaves

BY HAND

Stir the yeast and sugar into the water in a large mixing bowl; let stand until foamy, about 10 minutes. Add 2 tablespoons of the oil and the *biga,* if you are using it; stir vigorously and squeeze the *biga* between your fingers to break it up. Stir in the flour, 1 cup at a time, and the salt and stir until the dough comes together. Knead on a floured surface until silky and elastic, 8 to 10 minutes.

BY MIXER

Stir the yeast and sugar into the water in a mixer bowl; let stand until foamy, about 10 minutes. Add 2 tablespoons of the oil and the *biga,* if you are using it, and mix with the paddle until the *biga* is broken up. Add the flour and salt and mix until the dough comes together. Change to the dough hook and knead at medium speed until silky and elastic, 2 to 3 minutes.

BY PROCESSOR

Refrigerate the *biga,* if you are using it, until cold. Sir the yeast and sugar into ¼ cup of warm water in a small bowl; let

continued

Panini al Pomodoro, *continued*

stand until foamy, about 10 minutes. Place the flour and salt in a food processor fitted with the dough blade and process with several pulses to sift. Place the cold *biga*, if you are using it, on top of the flour. With the machine running, pour the dissolved yeast, 2 tablespoons of the oil, and the cold water through the feed tube and process until the dough gathers in a ball. You may need to add up to 2 tablespoons more cold water. Process 30 seconds longer to knead.

First Rise. Place the dough in a lightly oiled bowl, cover tightly with plastic wrap and let rise until doubled, about 45 minutes to 1 hour.

Shaping and Second Rise. While the bread is rising, sauté the onion in the remaining oil until softened and set aside to cool. Do not drain. Knead the onion and thinned tomato paste into the dough on a lightly floured surface. Cut the dough into twelve pieces and roll each piece into a round ball. Place on a lightly oiled baking sheet, cover with a towel, and let rise until doubled, about 45 minutes.

Baking. Preheat the oven to 400°F. Just before baking, spoon a dab of tomato paste on top of each roll, and place a couple of rosemary leaves on the paste. Bake 20 minutes. Cool on a rack.

Pane in Cassetta SANDWICH BREAD

Pane in cassetta is nothing other than *pain carré*, the equivalent of good old American sandwich bread. It became chic in Italy as part of *il sandwich* boom, for more and more people are eating lunch between two slices of bread at the local *caffè* rather than lingering over a long meal at home or in restaurants. Its fillings and functions sometimes determine its name or where it comes from: *tartine* are filled with chicken salad, creamy pastes, or pâté, while *tramezzini*, the generic word for sandwich in Rome, often hold even softer fillings, such as *insalata russa*. Toast may have a slice of prosciutto and a slice of cheese and be topped with artichoke hearts, sliced red bell peppers, or mushrooms preserved in oil. Open-faced sandwiches can turn into canapés (you may notice an international theme to this bread), spread with mayonnaise and topped with a variety of tastes limited only by the imagination of the person putting them together. The bread is also used for *mozzarella in carrozza* (page 163) and for the base of apple charlottes and fruit tarts. It is named *cassetta* for the boxlike shape of the Pullman loaf pan in which it is baked.

The only trick to making *pane in cassetta* is rolling the dough out with a rolling pin, folding it, and then flattening it firmly with your rolling pin to make it strong and compact. Don't forget to butter the inside of the lid of the pan before you slide it in place. The crust of *pane in cassetta* is very fine, and the bread is best eaten very fresh, preferably the day it is baked.

Makes 1 loaf

4 teaspoons (0.4 oz / 11.3 g) active dry yeast

1 tablespoon (0.5 oz / 13 g) sugar

^{1}/$_4$ cup (2 oz / 60 g) warm water

1^1/$_4$ cups plus 3 tablespoons (12.1 oz / 345 g) water, at room temperature (cold if using a processor)

Scant ^{1}/$_4$ cup (1.8 oz / 50 g) lard

About 5^1/$_3$ cups (1 lb 10 oz / 750 g) unbleached all-purpose flour

1^1/$_3$ teaspoons (0.2 oz / 6.5 g) salt

BY HAND

Stir the yeast and sugar into the warm water in a large mixing bowl; let stand until foamy, about 10 minutes. Stir in the 1^1/$_4$ cups plus 3 tablespoons of water and the lard; then stir in the flour, 2 cups at a time, and the salt. Knead vigorously on a floured surface until silky and very dry with a powdery feel to the surface, 8 to 10 minutes.

BY MIXER

Stir the yeast and sugar into the warm water in a mixer bowl; let stand until foamy, about 10 minutes. Stir in the 1^1/$_4$ cups plus 3 tablespoons of water and the lard with the paddle. Add the flour and salt and mix until the dough comes together. Change to the dough hook and knead at medium speed until very stiff, silky, and dry, about 4 minutes.

BY PROCESSOR

If the capacity of your food processor is 7 cups or less, process this recipe in two batches. Stir the yeast and sugar into the warm water in a small bowl; let stand until foamy, about 10 minutes. Place the flour, salt, and lard in a food processor fitted with the steel blade and process with several pulses to mix. With the machine running, pour the dissolved yeast plus the cold water through the feed tube and process until the dough gathers into a ball. If the dough is too dry, add up to 3 tablespoons more cold water. Process 30 seconds longer to knead.

First Rise. Place the dough in a lightly oiled bowl, cover tightly with plastic wrap, and let rise until doubled, about 1 to 1^3/$_4$ hours.

Shaping and Second Rise. Flatten the dough on a lightly floured surface to break up the air bubbles. Roll out the dough with a rolling pin to a 24 by 12-inch rectangle. Either fold in thirds, like a business letter, or fold the top and bottom edges to meet in the center and then fold the top half over the bottom (into fourths). Flour

continued

Pane in Cassetta, *continued*

the dough and work surface again, roll out the dough, and repeat the same folds. Then flatten the dough well to fit into a 13-inch-long Pullman pan and place in the well-buttered pan. The compact dough should fill the pan about halfway. Butter the lid and slide it into place. Let the dough rise until 1 inch short of the top of the pan, about 1 to 1¹/₂ hours.

Baking. Preheat the oven to 400°F. Bake 1 hour. Carefully unmold onto a rack and cool completely.

Panini Dolci

Maritozzi ROMAN SWEET BUNS

These fat buns, which are bursting with raisins, appear in Rome today as they did in medieval times, when they were a traditional Lenten sweet bread made with sugar and spices. Now Romans have them all year long and are as likely to eat them for breakfast or tea as with a glass of white wine.

Makes 16 to 18 buns

SPONGE

1¹/₂ cups (8 oz / 225 g) raisins

Water to cover

3¹/₂ teaspoons (0.4 oz / 10 g) active dry yeast

¹/₂ cup plus 2 tablespoons (5.3 oz / 150 g) warm milk

¹/₂ cup (2.5 oz / 70 g) unbleached all-purpose flour

Soak the raisins in cool water to cover at least 30 minutes, then drain, reserving ¹/₄ cup of the soaking liquid. Stir the yeast into the warm milk in a small bowl; let stand until creamy, about 10 minutes. Add the flour and the reserved raisin soaking water and stir until smooth. Cover with plastic wrap and let rise until doubled, 20 to 30 minutes.

DOUGH

3 cups plus 1 tablespoon (15.1 oz / 430 g) unbleached all-purpose flour

1/2 cup (3.5 oz / 100 g) sugar

1 teaspoon (0.2 oz / 5 g) salt

2 large eggs

1 large egg yolk

Grated zest of 1/4 lemon

Grated zest of 1/4 orange

1/4 teaspoon vanilla extract

1 stick (4 oz / 115 g) unsalted butter, at room temperature

1/4 cup (1.3 oz / 35 g) unbleached all-purpose flour for the raisins

BY HAND

Place the flour, sugar, and salt in a large mixing bowl. Stir in the sponge and eggs, egg yolk, lemon and orange zests, and vanilla, then stir in the butter. Knead on a lightly floured surface until soft, springy, and very smooth, 8 to 10 minutes.

BY MIXER

Place the flour, sugar, salt, sponge, eggs, egg yolk, lemon and orange zests, and vanilla in a mixer bowl and mix with the paddle until blended. Add the butter and mix thoroughly. Change to the dough hook and knead at medium speed until soft, springy, and smooth except for a few blisters, 3 to 4 minutes.

First Rise. Place the dough in a lightly oiled bowl, cover tightly with plastic wrap, and let rise until doubled, about 1 hour.

Shaping and Second Rise. Pat the raisins dry and toss with the 1/4 cup of flour. Add the raisins to the dough in one or two additions by flattening the dough, patting the raisins over the surface, and rolling up the dough. Cut the dough into sixteen to eighteen pieces and roll each piece into a ball. Place the rolls on lightly buttered or parchment-lined baking sheets. Cover with a towel and let rise half their original volume, about 30 minutes.

Baking. Preheat the oven to 400°F. Bake 18 minutes. The rolls should double in size and puff up into fat buns as they bake. Cool on racks.

Pan di Ramerino ROSEMARY AND RAISIN BUNS

Pan di ramerino resembles a hot cross bun flavored with rosemary. It was traditionally eaten in Tuscany only on Holy Thursday of Easter week, but now you can find it all year long in Florence, where its glossy crosshatched top is instantly recognizable. This recipe comes from Giovanni Galli, an imaginative baker in Florence, who has made the very lightly sweetened bread richer by adding eggs. The combination of raisins, rosemary-scented oil, and a sprig of rosemary sounds strange to Americans, who would never think of putting them together, but there is something intangibly wonderful about the taste. Florentines speak with real nostalgia about these buns, whose crosses on top are reminders that the buns are permeated with religious meaning, as well as the taste of the past.

Makes 12 buns

3¹/₂ teaspoons (0.4 oz / 10 g) active dry yeast

³/₄ cup (6.3 oz / 180 g) warm water

2 large eggs

1 large egg yolk

¹/₄ cup (1.9 oz / 55 g) olive oil, plus more
   for brushing

2¹/₂ tablespoons (1.3 oz / 36 g) sugar

3³/₄ cups (17.5 oz / 500 g) unbleached
   all-purpose flour

1 teaspoon (0.2 oz / 5 g) salt

3 to 4 sprigs fresh rosemary

²/₃ cup (3.5 oz / 100 g) golden or monukka raisins

¹/₃ cup (2 oz / 75 g) apricot glaze (page 325)

BY HAND

Stir the yeast into the warm water in a large mixing bowl; let stand until creamy, about 10 minutes. Whisk in the eggs, egg yolk, 2 tablespoons of the oil, and the sugar thoroughly. Stir in the flour, 1 cup at a time, and the salt; keep stirring until the dough is no longer sticky. Knead on a lightly floured surface until elastic and supple, 7 to 9 minutes.

BY MIXER

Stir the yeast into the warm water in a large mixer bowl; let stand until creamy, about 10 minutes. Add the eggs, egg yolk, 2 tablespoons of the oil, and the sugar and mix thoroughly with the paddle. Add the flour and salt and mix until the dough pulls away from the sides of the bowl. Change to the dough hook and knead at low speed 2 minutes, then at medium speed for 2 minutes more. The dough should be elastic and supple.

First Rise. Place the dough in a lightly oiled bowl, cover tightly with plastic wrap, and let rise until doubled, about 1 hour.

   Shaping and Second Rise. While the dough is rising, sauté 2 or 3 sprigs of fresh rosemary very briefly in the remaining

continued

Pan di Ramerino, *continued*

2 tablespoons of oil. Toss the rosemary out after it has flavored the oil. Add the raisins and sauté very briefly in the oil. Remove from the heat and add 1 chopped fresh rosemary sprig to the raisins, if you want. Cool to room temperature. Knead the raisins into the dough; it is much easier to do by mixer than by hand if you have the choice.

Cut the dough into twelve pieces and roll each piece into a ball. Place on lightly oiled baking sheets, cover with a towel, and let rise until doubled, about 1 hour.

Reshape the buns, which will have slumped a bit, into definite balls. Flatten each ball with your hand and brush the tops with oil. Using a razor, slash a deep tic-tac-toe pattern in the top of each bun. Let the buns rest under a towel 10 to 15 minutes.

Baking. Preheat the oven to 400°F. Bake 20 minutes. Remove the buns to racks to cool, let cool slightly, and brush with the apricot glaze.

Grissini

Grissini Torinesi BREADSTICKS FROM TURIN

Most Americans know *grissini* as those pale breadsticks in the long waxen envelopes that appear on the tables of Italian restaurants, but those bear about as much resemblance to authentic *grissini* as packaged industrial white bread does to true country loaves. Real *grissini* are made of yeast, flour, water, and either olive oil, lard, or butter. They are shaped between the hands by gently vibrating and stretching the dough to about the span of the baker's arms, and are then baked directly on the floor of a wood-burning oven. They are as thick and irregular as knobby fingers and look like cordwood when stacked. They have crunch and an earthy taste. Even when made at home with the methods and recipes that follow, they are still redolent of the countryside and the old ways.

Although there is some dispute about who came up with the first *grissini*, there is no question that they first appeared in Turin sometime in the seventeenth century. Some say that a baker in Turin invented them in 1668 in response to inquiries from the doctor of the young duke Vittorio Amadeo II, who had stomach disturbances, for a bread that would be good for the duke's digestion. The baker stretched out the traditional local bread dough so long that it became a long, thin, crunchy stick that was essentially all crust. Although there is no word on their effect on the patient's health, it is safe to assume that they met with great success, because *grissini* were well known all over Italy by the next century, when Napoleon discovered *"les petits batons de Turin."* Napoleon was so enthusiastic about the breadsticks that he instituted a fast postal service expressly for transporting them to court every day. The most popular rival story to that of the young duke credits a Florentine abbot on a diplomatic mission near Turin in 1643 with the discovery of "a thin bread as long as an arm and very, very fine."

Serve *grissini* with eggs, green salad, prosciutto, and smoked beef, as well as with any kind of antipasti. Some Italians eat them for breakfast with milk or coffee, an old custom that was once widespread.

continued

Grissini Torinesi, *continued*

Makes 20 to 22 breadsticks

1³/₄ teaspoons (0.2 oz / 5 g) active dry yeast

1 tablespoon (0.7 oz / 21 g) malt syrup

1¹/₄ cups (10.5 oz / 300 g) warm water (or ¹/₄ cup / 2 oz / 60 g warm water plus 1 cup / 8.4 oz / 240 g cold water if using a processor)

2 tablespoons (1 oz / 30 g) olive oil, plus more for brushing

3³/₄ cups (17.5 oz / 500 g) unbleached all-purpose flour

1¹/₂ teaspoons (0.3 oz / 7.5 g) salt

¹/₂ cup (3 oz / 85 g) semolina flour

BY HAND

Stir the yeast and malt into the warm water in a large mixing bowl; let stand until foamy, about 10 minutes. Stir in the oil. Add the flour and salt and stir until the dough comes together. Knead on a lightly floured surface until smooth, soft, velvety, and elastic, 8 to 10 minutes.

BY MIXER

Stir the yeast and malt into the water in a mixer bowl; let stand until foamy, about 10 minutes. Mix in the oil with the paddle. Add the flour and salt and mix until the dough comes together. Change to the dough hook and knead at low speed about 3 minutes. Finish kneading briefly by hand on a lightly floured surface.

BY PROCESSOR

Stir the yeast and malt into the ¹/₄ cup of warm water in a small bowl; let stand until foamy, about 10 minutes. Place the flour and salt in a standard food processor fitted with the dough blade or a large (over 7-cup capacity) processor fitted with the steel blade and process with several pulses to sift. Mix the 1 cup of cold water and the oil. With the machine running, pour the water mixed with oil and the dissolved yeast through the feed tube and process until the dough comes together. Process 45 seconds longer to knead. Finish kneading by hand on a lightly floured surface.

First Rise. Pat the dough with your hand into a 14 by 4-inch rectangle on a well-floured surface. Lightly brush the top with oil. Cover with plastic wrap and let rise until doubled, about 1 hour.

Shaping. Sprinkle the dough with semolina flour before cutting and stretching. The baker's method of shaping breadsticks is ingenious, simple, and quick, for he certainly doesn't have time to roll out individual *grissini*. Cut the dough crosswise into four equal sections and then cut each section crosswise again into five strips, each about the width of a fat finger. The dough is so elastic that you can simply

continued

Grissini Torinesi, *continued*

pick up each piece, hold each end with your fingers, and pull and stretch to fit the width (or length) of a baking sheet. Place the breadsticks several inches apart on lightly oiled baking sheets (I find it easier to use the backs of the baking sheets, unless you have rimless sheets). There is no need to let them rise.

Baking. Preheat the oven to 450°F. If you are using a baking stone, turn the oven on 30 minutes before baking. Bake the breadsticks for 20 minutes. If you like crunchy breadsticks, bake directly on the baking stone, which has been sprinkled with cornmeal or coarse semolina, for the last 5 minutes. Cool on racks.

Variations. For *grissini siciliani*, sprinkle the dough with ½ cup (2 oz / 60 g) of sesame seeds instead of semolina flour before cutting and shaping.

For *grissini al papavera*, sprinkle the dough with ½ cup (1 oz / 28 g) of poppy seeds instead of semolina flour before cutting and shaping.

Grissini Integrali WHOLE WHEAT BREADSTICKS

Makes 20 to 22 breadsticks

1¾ teaspoons (0.2 oz / 5 g) active dry yeast

1¼ cups (10.5 oz / 300 g) warm water

1 tablespoon (0.7 oz / 21 g) malt syrup

¼ cup (1.9 oz / 55 g) olive oil, plus more for brushing

2¼ teaspoons (0.4 oz / 10 g) lard

1 cup minus 2 tablespoons (4.4 oz / 125 g) unbleached all-purpose flour

2¾ cups (13.1 oz / 375 g) whole wheat flour

1½ teaspoons (0.3 oz / 7.5 g) salt

Follow the directions for *grissini torinesi* (page 243), adding the lard with the oil. Omit sprinkling the dough with semolina flour.

Grissini alle Cipolle ONION BREADSTICKS

Makes 20 to 22 breadsticks

1 large yellow onion (8 oz / 225 g), finely diced

¼ cup (1.9 oz / 55 g) olive oil, plus more for brushing

1¾ teaspoons (0.2 oz / 5 g) active dry yeast

1¼ cups (10.5 oz / 300 g) warm water

1 tablespoon (0.7 oz / 21 g) malt syrup

2 tablespoons (0.9 oz / 26 g) lard

3¾ cups (17.5 oz / 500 g) unbleached all-purpose flour

2 teaspoons (0.4 oz / 10 g) salt

Sauté the onion in 2 tablespoons of the oil over low to medium heat until golden and almost dry roasted, 10 to 15 minutes. Watch carefully to make sure that the onion doesn't burn. Allow to cool.

Follow the directions for *grissini torinesi* (page 243), adding the lard with the remaining 2 tablespoons of oil. Work the onion into the dough at the very end of the kneading. Omit sprinkling the dough with semolina flour.

Grissini al Formaggio CHEESE BREADSTICKS

Makes 20 to 22 breadsticks

1¾ teaspoons (0.2 oz / 5 g) active dry yeast

1⅓ cups (11.2 oz / 320 g) warm water

2 tablespoons (1 oz / 30 g) olive oil, plus more for brushing

3¾ cups (17.5 oz / 500 g) unbleached all-purpose flour

1½ teaspoons (0.3 oz / 7.5 g) salt

½ cup (2 oz / 60 g) grated Parmesan cheese

Follow the instructions for *grissini torinesi* (page 243). Work the cheese into the dough at the very end of the kneading. Omit sprinkling the dough with semolina flour. Bake at 450°F for 12 to 15 minutes.

Grissini Cric-Crac alla Salvia
SAGE BREADSTICKS FROM COMO

I suppose you could call this recipe and the variations that follow *grissini nuovi*, for they are imaginative departures from the classical breadsticks of Turin. *Cric-crac* is really a musical bit of onomatopoeia.

Makes 20 to 22 breadsticks

1³/₄ teaspoons (0.2 oz / 5 g) active dry yeast

1 tablespoon (0.7 g / 21 g) malt syrup

1¹/₄ cups (10.5 oz / 300 g) warm water

¹/₄ cup (1.9 oz / 55 g) olive oil, plus more for brushing

3³/₄ cups (17.5 oz / 500 g) unbleached all-purpose flour

1¹/₂ teaspoons (0.3 oz / 7.5 g) salt

¹/₄ cup (0.2 oz / 5 g) chopped fresh sage

Follow the instructions for *grissini torinesi* (page 243). Work in the sage at the very end of the kneading. Omit sprinkling the dough with semolina flour.

Variations. Cric-crac alla Pancetta. Substitute ¹/₂ cup (2 oz / 60 g) of diced pancetta for the sage.

Cric-crac al Salame. Substitute ¹/₂ cup (2 oz / 60 g) of diced salami for the sage.

Cric-crac alla Gorgonzola. Substitute ¹/₃ cup (2 oz / 60 g) of softened Gorgonzola for the sage.

Cric-crac agli Spinaci. Substitute ¹/₂ cup (2 oz / 60 g) of frozen chopped spinach, thawed and well drained, for the sage.

Pizze e Focacce
Pizzas and Focaccias

What are pizzas and *focacce* but primitive, rustic food made of the tastiest ingredients harvested from the fields, the vines of the hillside, and the seas? These crisp or chewy country breads are the food of peasants and wily city dwellers with little money but lots of imagination. Flavored with oils from local olives, cheeses from herds that graze neighboring pastures, tomatoes planted in the nearby countryside, and herbs that grow in wild tangles or are cultivated in gardens and the window boxes that punctuate the facades of houses all over the country, pizza and focacce represent the triumph of *fantasia* and strategy over a scarcity of ingredients, the instinct for survival transformed into an infinite variety of tastes. Clever Italians simply take a little dough, sprinkle it with the products of the countryside, and turn it into a delicious and edible plate. Flat or slightly raised with rims, these breads are easier to eat out of hand than with a knife and fork. In one of those delicious bits of irony, these most basic of rustic breads have become popular and chic, symbols of the relaxed easy pleasures of eating with friends.

Perhaps it has always been so. The thin, chewy bread that Italians call focaccia may have been the first national dish of the country. Remains of carbonated *focacce* as old as Neolithic man indicate that, even before recorded time, Italians were grinding grain between stones, mixing it with water, and boiling it into a mush not unlike polenta. This mush was probably left out one night, and an adventurous Neolithic baker must have decided to cook it under the embers or roast it, pancake style, over the stones.

Although we are still in the realm of educated guessing, we know that Egyptians discovered the miracle of fermentation, but we don't know how. It is probable that flour and water mixed together to make bread was left out and trapped the wild yeasts of the air, which transformed yesterday's ingredients into a puffy mass. Cooks and scholars surmise that someone—perhaps an insolent slave, or an angry one—tossed a bit of this risen mass into the fresh dough and, through this inspired offhand gesture, discovered the process of leavening dough. This is all a long preamble to the fact that pizza and focaccia are simply branches of the bread family. Once made without leavening but now a part of the baker's repertoire, both are flat, round breads seasoned with oil and cooked in the oven or over embers, and they are called pizza in the south and focaccia in the north.

Pizza seems to date to the era when the Greeks settled the region in the south of Italy that has become known as Magna Graecia because it was so purely Greek. The Greeks taught the Romans the secrets of their trade, for they were very inventive bakers who made breads with many flavorings and baked them in a variety of forms. At about the time that the Etruscans, who settled initially in the north of Italy, were baking flat *focacce* and *schiacciata*-like breads, the Italians of the south, including the early Neapolitans of that time, were probably eating an ancestor of pizza called *laganum* by the poet Horace. Virgil, who lived in Augustan Rome and went to Naples to visit, wrote a poem celebrating *moretum*, a flat disk of dough that was baked on a griddle and covered with an herb sauce of garlic, parsley, rue, coriander, and a dry cheese, all ground together in a mortar and bound with olive oil and a few drops of strong vinegar. The topping certainly sounds very much like pesto without the basil. Had the rustic *moretum* been leavened, it would be a direct relative of pizza, even though it was cooked first and sprinkled with the herb mixture just before eating.

Another ancestral flatbread, the *piadina* of Romagna, still appears at every country festival and rustic celebration in the area between the low hills east of the Apennines and the quiet coast of the Adriatic Sea. The thin tortillalike circle of dough that was originally baked not in an oven but on a thick piece of terra-cotta called a *testo* is yet one more flat peasant bread that can claim an early ancestry. Today you can still find *piadine*, folded over fat slices of country salami or wrapped around boiled or sautéed greens, in restaurants as well as at local *sagre* (festivals) all over the countryside. All these unleavened rustic breads reach far back in the history of Italy and are predecessors of the *focacce* and pizzas we eat today.

The focaccia of today derives its name from *focus*, the Latin word for "hearth," for focaccia, which began life long before ovens were common, was made by patting the dough into a flat round and cooking it directly on a hot stone or under a mound of hot ashes on the hearth itself. *Schiacciata*, the term still used in Tuscany, simply means "flattened" or "crushed." One look at these low, crisp, crunchy rounds is convincing evidence that the word was well chosen. The word *pizza* may simply mean "pie"; it can be sweet or savory, flat or risen, although it is most frequently encountered in the circle of dough with a raised edge that has conquered America. There are many different stories about the origins of the word, although the *Italian Encyclopedia of Science, Literature, and Art* virtually shrugs its shoulders and says only "uncertain etymology." It might come from the Roman *placenta*, a flat focaccialike dish made, as Cato described it, of wheat flour, cheese, and honey and baked over a low fire, but it could also come from *picea*, a Greek adjective that describes the dark black coating left on the bottom of dough by the burning ashes of early ovens. According to many sources, pizza is simply the Neapolitan dialect word for *picea*, denoting both the pie and the black color of the ash that cooked it.

Now that that is clear, perhaps it would be better not to acknowledge the fact that stuffed doughs such as *calzoni, pizze rustica,* and fried stuffed turnovers also go by the name of pizza. There is method in the madness, but it helps to know the history to understand, for instance, how the half-moon-shaped turnovers that are today's *calzoni* got their name. *Calzoni,* meaning "pant legs," were originally long, narrow tubes of dough enclosing sausages or salamis; they looked very much like the baggy pants Neapolitan men wore in the eighteenth and nineteenth centuries. *Panzarotti,* fat envelopes of pizza dough stuffed with various fillings, are named from the Neapolitan dialect word for "stomach," because when they are fried in extremely hot oil they suddenly swell up just like big full bellies.

It wasn't until the mid-1700s that pizza became a common dish in Naples, although pizza as we know it didn't really come into its own until the introduction of the tomato, that strange globe of red fruit brought to Italy from Peru and Mexico in the wake of Columbus's voyage. Initially the Italians were extremely suspicious of this foreign invader, which they called *pomodoro,* or "golden apple" (the first tomatoes were, in fact, yellow). It took two centuries for them to overcome their reluctance and accept it. In the middle of the eighteenth century, tomatoes were still considered an optional ingredient in pizzas. It was only when the particular synergy between the dough and the tomato sauce began to be appreciated that pizza achieved its incredible popularity.

"The word *pizza* is not found in the [official Italian] dictionary because it is made with flour and because it is a specialty of the Neapolitans and of the very city of Naples itself. If you want to know what a pizza is, take a piece of dough, roll it out, then pull or spread it a bit with a rolling pin or push it out with the palm of your hand, put whatever comes into your head on it, season it with oil or lard, bake it in the oven, eat it, and you will know what pizza is. Though more or less the same, the focaccia and the *schiacciata* are but embryos of the art." So said Sir Emanuele Rocco in the anthology *Usi e Costumi di Napoli,* compiled in 1850 by a Frenchman named De Bourcard, whose chauvinistic convictions reflect his attachment to the pizzas of Naples baked at the little stalls and shops of his day.

A few years previously Alexandre Dumas, author of *The Three Musketeers*, had written in his *Grand Dictionnaire de la Cuisine*, "Pizza is a sort of bun like the ones made at Saint-Denis; it is round in shape and made with the same bread dough. It seems simple enough, but on closer inspection it is really very complicated." Enumerating its ingredients, he continues, "Pizza is made with oil, bacon, lard, cheese, tomato, or small fish. It is the yardstick by which the whole food market is measured; prices rise and fall according to the prices of these ingredients and their relative availability." Imagine what a vast public pizza must have had to make such an impact on the price of its flavorings; did hamburgers ever influence the price paid for beef on the hoof in the stockyards of Chicago, or did fried chicken change the economy of the south? Dumas's appreciation for pizza was great, but, as any number of eminent authorities have pointed out, he was off-base in one of his observations. Dumas thought that *pizza oggi a otto* was made eight days before it was eaten; actually it was (and still is) eaten hot out of the oven but paid for eight days later—easy financial terms provided then, as now, by neighborhood *pizzaioli* to local residents who as likely as not are a bit strapped. Not only is the arrangement easy on the wallet, but it also guarantees that your last pizza is free if you die before the eight days have elapsed. In another bit of financial strategy, canny Neapolitans frequently use anchovies on pizzas because the little fish can easily be cadged from the sea for very little money, but they also spare the pizza maker the expensive tax the government levies on salt, the most basic of all seasonings.

The first pizzas as we know them today were probably flavored very simply with oil, garlic, mozzarella, and anchovies or tiny local fish called *ciciniella*. The wit of Neapolitan bakers soon spawned a much greater variety of combinations. The single most famous story of toppings and pizza concerns Queen Margherita, who traveled with King Umberto I to Naples in 1889 when he was on a visit to the lands of his kingdom. The queen, who had heard about pizza, was anxious to sample the dish, but, because she could hardly go off to an open-air pizza stand or pizzeria, the premier pizza maker of the time called upon her. Don Raffaele Esposito, owner of the pizzeria Pietro il Pizzaiuolo, and his wife went to the Capodimonte Palace, with several varieties for the queen to taste. She was most enthusiastic about the pizza made with mozzarella, tomatoes, and fresh basil, which was red, white, and green, the colors of the Italian flag. In the flush of success, Don Raffaele christened it pizza Margherita in her honor. It didn't take long for word to spread throughout the kingdom and make pizza Margherita an instant success. Whether the tale is apocryphal or not, pizza Margherita helped put pizza on the national culinary map of Italy.

Today pizza is so varied and widespread that *pizza alla napoletana, pizza alla romana* (thin, crunchy, and rimless, with only salt and oil on the top), *pizza di Pasqua* (sweet and risen), and *pizza rustica* (filled and risen) only hint at its protean forms. From the *sfinciuni* of Sicily—pizza dough covered with tomato sauce, cheeses, onions, oil, and bread crumbs and baked in the oven—to the *sardenaria* of San Remo, named for its topping of local sardines or sardine paste, pizza expresses the extraordinary diversity of regional tastes. The focaccia of Recco, which has put the little town outside Genoa on the gastronomic map, is made with a strudellike dough, while the pizza named for the admiral Andrea Doria is made with durum flour and covered with the inevitable tomatoes, anchovies, garlic, onion, and black olives.

Some of the most basic pizzas and variations from south to north are included here, but you should use your own imagination and be guided by your own taste buds when choosing your toppings. Formal recipes are much less important than having flavorful ingredients on hand. Follow the lead of the Neapolitans, who start with the sun and the fish of the Gulf of Naples and add strong local flavors that are neither intricate nor mysterious. You can add anchovies to one pizza or mozzarella to another; you can use Fontina instead of mozzarella or add prosciutto, mushrooms, clams, pesto, or mussels. Pizza is really only a platter of bread topped with the provender of the countryside and made with passion and imagination.

Pizza

Pizza alla Napoletana PIZZA OF NAPLES

Like the discoverer of fire or the maker of the wheel, the creator of pizza remains unknown. We do know that by the eighteenth century pizza was the food of Naples, an extravagantly delicious dish combining the simplest and cheapest of ingredients with fabulous imagination. The crisp, slightly smoky tang of the pizza, made as it should be, depends on the hands and secrets of the *pizzaioli locali*, heirs of a tradition passed orally from one baker to the next; and heirs, as well, of the oils of their olives and lard of their pigs, the waters of their hills, the tomatoes of their vines, the leaves of basil ripened by their sun, the mozzarella of their buffalo, and the wood-burning fires of their brick-lined ovens.

These pizzas are as big as a plate, with rings of dough raised at the outer edges (all the better to grasp them with). Ask a Neapolitan and he'll tell you that pizza is a grace note of life, a subtle piece of magic transmuted by the alchemy of fire into a delicacy for the nose, the mouth, and the eyes.

Numerous pizzerias dot the streets, the narrow curling *vicoli*, and the mazes of tiny dark lanes that wind through the labyrinthine heart of the city, but once pizza vendors wandered through Naples carrying dozens of pizzas, each folded in half in the shape called a "libretto" because it looked like a pocketbook, and calling out phrases describing their wares in ringing tones, in rhyming couplets, in double entendres, and in simple descriptive phrases. Though few of these troubadours with the slang and song and come-ons are left, the circle of dough, holding within it a world of southern Italian tastes, still dazzles the taste buds and remains the remarkable rustic treat that conquered the world.

A couple of tips: To shape the dough, you may use either a rolling pin (the easiest) or your fists, draping the dough over them and then moving them apart to within an inch of the rim, slowly and gently turning them and stretching the dough $1/4$ to $1/8$ inch thick. The experts get it even thinner. The edge, called the *cornicione* (like a big picture frame), is a favorite of babies and gastronomes, and it should be a bit thicker to keep the sauce and ingredients in their place. Always brush the rim of the pizza with a bit of olive oil when it is still hot from the oven so that the entire dish glistens.

After mixing and resting at room temperature for 60 to 90 minutes, pizza dough can be refrigerated for baking later. Use it within 2 days. Bring the dough to room temperature for about 2 hours before baking.

PIZZA AGLIO E OLIO TOPPING

The simplest and most traditional topping of all.

Makes enough to top pizza alla napoletana
dough

3 tablespoons (1.5 oz / 45 g) fruity olive oil

3 to 6 cloves garlic, very thinly sliced

1 tablespoon (0.1 oz / 3 g) chopped fresh oregano
   or 1¹/₂ teaspoons (0.04 oz / 1 g) dried oregano

1¹/₂ teaspoons (0.3 oz / 7.5 g) salt

Freshly ground pepper

Drizzle the oil over the dough and sprinkle with the garlic, oregano, salt, and pepper to taste.

PIZZA ALLA NAPOLETANA TOPPING

Makes enough to top pizza alla napoletana
dough

2 to 3 tablespoons (1 to 1.5 oz / 30 to 45 g) olive oil

5 tomatoes (1¹/₂ lb / 650 g total), peeled, seeded
   and coarsely chopped, or 1 can (14 oz / 400 g)
   San Marzano plum tomatoes, drained
   and coarsely chopped

2 large cloves garlic, very thinly sliced

1¹/₂ teaspoons (0.04 oz / 1 g) dried oregano, or
   8 fresh oregano leaves, minced, or 8 fresh
   basil leaves, roughly torn

1 teaspoon (0.2 oz / 5 g) salt

1 teaspoon (0.2 oz / 5 g) freshly ground pepper
   (optional)

Drizzle a little of the oil over the dough and spread the tomatoes over the top. Sprinkle with the garlic, oregano or basil, salt, and pepper if desired; then drizzle with the remaining oil.

PIZZA MARGHERITA TOPPING

Makes enough to top **pizza alla napoletana dough**

2 to 4 tablespoons (1 to 1.9 oz / 30 to 55 g) olive oil

4 or 5 tomatoes (1 to 1½ lb / 450 to 650 g total), peeled, seeded, and cut into strips, or 1 can (14 oz / 400 g) San Marzano plum tomatoes, drained and cut into strips

8 ounces (225 g) sliced fresh mozzarella or Italian Fontina cheese

3 tablespoons (0.9 oz / 25 g) grated Parmesan or pecorino cheese

7 to 10 fresh basil leaves

1 teaspoon (0.2 oz / 5 g) salt

Lightly moisten the dough with a bit of the oil. If you are making medium or individual-size pizzas, spread the dough with the tomatoes, cheeses, and basil (in that order) and sprinkle with the salt. Drizzle the remaining oil over the top. If you are making one large pizza, top it with all the ingredients except the mozzarella and a few of the basil leaves. Bake 10 to 15 minutes, then top with the mozzarella and bake until done. Because mozzarella is high in butterfat, it tends to burn before the crust is done, but this baker's secret solves the problem. Dapple the cheese with the remaining basil leaves before serving.

PIZZA ALLA MARINARA TOPPING

Makes enough to top **pizza alla napoletana dough**

¼ cup (1.9 oz / 55 g) olive oil

4 or 5 tomatoes (1 to 1½ lb / 450 to 650 g total), peeled, seeded and cut into strips, or 1 can (14 oz / 400 g) San Marzano plum tomatoes, drained and cut into strips

2 cloves garlic, very thinly sliced

4 to 6 salt-packed anchovies, washed, boned, and patted dry

Brush a little of the oil onto the dough. Spread the tomatoes and garlic on top, then sprinkle with small pieces of anchovy, or use the whole fillet, or cut them in half to make a sunburst pattern of them on top. Drizzle with the remaining oil.

PIZZA PUGLIESE TOPPING

Makes enough to top **pizza alla napoletana** *dough*

2 eggplants (2 lb 4 oz / 1 kg), peeled and sliced crosswise

$^{3}/_{4}$ to 1 teaspoon (about 1.2 oz / 5 g) salt

Vegetable oil for frying

6 ounces (170 g) provolone cheese, sliced

1 or 2 anchovies, boned, if necessary, and cut crosswise into slices

$^{1}/_{3}$ to $^{1}/_{2}$ cup (about 0.5 oz / 15 g) chopped fresh basil

3 fresh tomatoes (about 13 oz / 375 g total), peeled, seeded, and diced

$^{1}/_{2}$ to $^{3}/_{4}$ cup (2 to 3 oz / 60 to 85 g) pitted black olives

1 tablespoon (0.5 oz / 15 g) olive oil

Freshly ground black pepper

Place the eggplant slices in a colander, sprinkle liberally with the salt, and toss to distribute. Let stand 1 hour and pat the eggplant dry. Heat $^{1}/_{2}$ inch of vegetable oil in a heavy skillet over high heat. Fry the eggplant in a single layer in the oil until creamy but not golden. Drain on paper towels. Arrange about half of the eggplant in a single layer over the dough; top with the cheese, then the anchovy pieces. Arrange the remaining eggplant on top in a single layer, then sprinkle the basil on top. Cover with the tomatoes and olives. Drizzle the olive oil over the top and sprinkle with salt and pepper to taste.

Pizza alla Romana PIZZA BY THE METER

Americans invariably envision pizza as a thick- or thin-crusted round of dough that is covered with toppings, cut into wedges, and eaten out of hand. Italians, who go to bakeries to buy pizza by the meter, know another way. This extraordinary recipe comes from Gianfranco Anelli in Rome. He allows the soft, supple dough a very long rest—up to 7 1/2 hours, and the longer the better—and then places it on a baker's peel 2 1/2 feet long before he rhythmically pounds it with such vigor that it dances beneath his fingers. He paints the dough with oil and then sets the peel in the oven, where the totally unforeseen occurs; the baker slowly, slowly withdraws the peel, stretching the remarkably elastic dough to a thin, incredibly light crust that is an astonishing 6 feet long.

Romans eat *pizza bianca*, white pizza sprinkled only with oil and salt, in the morning the way Florentines eat *schiacciata* and other northern Italians snack on *focaccia*. You'll know just what I mean if you have ever been in a Roman bakery in the middle of the morning when a flood of schoolchildren at recess tumbles through the doors, queues up at the counter for individual lengths of *pizza bianca* still steaming from the oven, and then washes out again, snacks wrapped in waxed paper clutched in their hands. The rest of the day there is always a crowd of people at the counter at the moment the pizza is about to emerge from the oven; they seem to have a sense of just when the next long plank of pizza will arrive, hot, its fragrance scenting the warm air.

Because 6-foot-long wood-burning ovens are hardly standard equipment, I've adapted the recipe for traditional round pizza shapes. Each round of dough can be set in a 14- or 15-inch pan, and you can dimple and pummel and stretch it until it becomes very fine. Give it time to recover and then go back with those fingers and work it some more. If you keep oil on your hands and on the top of the dough, it will not develop a skin. You can try to make long strips of pizza, Roman style, which can then be cut with scissors into any length you want, but be sure to put the flour on parchment paper on your peels or baking sheets, for once the dough is shaped and topped, it is virtually impossible to move it.

A final secret from Rome: The pizza is washed with oil and sauce, if there is one, and, halfway through the baking, it is pulled out of the oven, dappled with shreds of mozzarella, and baked a few more minutes in the extreme heat of the fire. When it reappears, it is quickly brushed with oil and rushed to the front counter, where the inevitable press of hungry Romans is waiting impatiently for its arrival.

Because this dough uses so little yeast and wants a long rising, you can work it into a busy American schedule by making the dough at night with cool water, letting it rest for 30 minutes, and then refrigerating it. Next morning, place it in a cool spot to rise slowly at room temperature (65°F to 70°F is optimal). The cooler the spot, the longer you can wait to shape and bake it for dinner.

Makes three 14- or 15-inch pizzas

2¼ teaspoons (1 package / 0.2 oz / 7 g) active dry yeast

¼ cup (2 oz / 60 g) warm water

5⅓ cups (26 oz / 750 g) unbleached all-purpose flour

1 teaspoon (0.2 oz / 5 g) salt

1¾ cups plus 1 tablespoon (15.2 oz / 435 g) water, at room temperature (cold if using a processor)

1 tablespoon (0.5 oz / 15 g) olive oil, plus more for shaping the dough

4 teaspoons (0.6 oz / 17 g) lard or olive oil

BY HAND

Stir the yeast into the warm water in a small bowl; let stand until creamy, about 10 minutes. Mix the flour and salt in a large widemouthed bowl. Make a well in the center of the flour; then pour the dissolved yeast, the 1¾ cups plus 1 tablespoon of water, the 1 tablespoon of oil, and the lard into the well. Gradually stir the flour into the liquid and work to a soft dough that can be gathered into a ball. Knead on a floured surface, or in the bowl if it is large enough, until soft, smooth, and elastic, 10 to 15 minutes, sprinkling with additional flour as needed. Slam the dough down hard from time to time to help develop the gluten.

BY MIXER

Stir the yeast into the warm water in a mixer bowl; let stand until creamy, about 10 minutes. Add the 1¾ cups plus 1 tablespoon of water, the 1 tablespoon of oil, and the lard, and mix with the paddle. Add the flour and salt and mix until the dough comes thoroughly together (it can take as long as 5 minutes). Change to the dough hook and knead until soft and sticky but smooth, 5 to 6 minutes. Finish kneading by hand on a floured surface, sprinkling with additional flour as needed. Slam the dough down hard from time to time to help develop the gluten.

BY PROCESSOR

If the workbowl of your processor holds less than 8 cups, make the dough in two batches. Stir the yeast into the warm water in a medium-size bowl; let stand until creamy, about 10 minutes. Stir in the 1¾ cups plus 1 tablespoon of cold water, the 1 tablespoon of oil, and the lard. Place the flour and salt in a food processor fitted with the steel or dough blade and process with several pulses to sift. With the machine running, pour the liquid mixture through the feed tube and process until

continued

Pizza alla Romana, *continued*

the dough is smooth and moist. Process the soft dough 10 to 15 seconds longer to knead. Don't allow the dough to gather in a ball. Finish kneading with well-floured hands on a floured surface, sprinkling with up to ¼ cup (1 oz / 30 g) of additional flour as needed, until delicate, velvety, and somewhat elastic, 2 to 3 minutes. Slam the dough down hard from time to time to help develop the gluten.

First Rise. Place the dough in a lightly oiled bowl, cover tightly with plastic wrap and let rise at a cool room temperature until doubled, at least 4 hours but preferably 8 hours. If the dough looks as if it is rising too fast, simply punch it down.

Shaping. The trick in dealing with this delicate dough is to keep oil on your hands and on the top of the dough at all times. Turn the elastic, bubbly dough out onto a floured surface and cut into three equal pieces. Shape each piece into a rough ball. Oil the tops and let rest under a kitchen towel 30 minutes.

Oil three 14- or 15-inch pizza pans or flour three pieces of parchment paper that have been set on baker's peels or the backs of baking sheets. Place the balls of dough on the peels or pizza pans and dimple them vigorously, stretching each to a 14- or 15-inch circle, ⅛ inch thick, and leaving a thick edge.

If you want, you can place the dough over your oiled fists and gradually pull them apart, while at the same time turning and stretching the dough. Keep moving your hands to the outside to avoid tearing the center. For both methods, you will need to let the dough rest several times when it becomes unmanageable. The process may demand a bit of patience, but it makes an outstanding crust. When you have finished the shaping, carefully place each dough circle on floured parchment paper or the prepared pizza pan.

The dough can stand, covered, for 30 minutes to 1 hour before being spread with toppings. The Italian baker insists that the internal temperature of the dough must be 78°F for 12 minutes before it can go into the oven.

Topping. Select one of the topping recipes that follow, use one of the toppings for *pizza alla napoletana* (double or triple the recipe for three pizzas), or, if you have gotten into the spirit of Italian baking, use whatever combinations of mushrooms, cheeses, greens, onions, anchovies, and herbs that strike your imagination. Remember to add any fresh cheese halfway through the baking so that it doesn't burn.

Baking. Preheat the oven to 500°F, or as hot as you can get it. Using baking stones is really important for this recipe. Place them in the oven to heat for 45 to 60 minutes before baking. Place the pizza pans directly on the preheated stones, or use a peel to slide the pizzas, still on the parchment paper, onto the stones, taking care that no paper hangs over the stones' edges. You can take the paper out after a few minutes. As you get used to sliding the pizzas off the peel and onto the stones, this will become easier. Bake until the edge of the dough is golden and bubbly, 20 to 30 minutes. Immediately brush the crust with oil and drizzle a bit more oil over the pizza. Serve very hot.

PIZZA BIANCA TOPPING

Makes enough to top **pizza alla romana** *dough*

About ¹/₂ cup (3.8 oz / 110 g) best-quality olive oil

10 to 12 cloves garlic (about 0.5 oz / 20 g total), very, very thinly sliced

2 to 3 tablespoons (about 0.3 oz / 9 g) coarsely chopped fresh rosemary or 2 to 3 teaspoons dried rosemary (about 0.1 oz / 3 g) (optional)

Salt and freshly ground pepper

Brush the dough with some of the oil and sprinkle with the garlic and rosemary, then salt and pepper to taste. Brush the top liberally with the remaining olive oil.

PIZZA ROSSA TOPPING

Makes enough to top **pizza alla romana** *dough*

About 4 pounds (1.75 kg) fresh, ripe plum tomatoes, peeled, seeded, and coarsely chopped, or 3 cans (14 oz / 400 g each) San Marzano plum tomatoes, drained and chopped

¹/₄ cup (1.9 oz / 55 g) olive oil

2 teaspoons (0.4 oz / 10 g) salt

Freshly ground pepper

1 pound (450 g) best-quality whole-milk fresh mozzarella, thinly sliced

Sauté the tomatoes in the oil over medium heat for 7 to 8 minutes. Drain in a sieve or colander and then force through the coarsest blade of a food mill. Brush the dough with a thin layer of the tomatoes and sprinkle lightly with the salt and pepper to taste. About halfway through baking, distribute the cheese evenly over the dough.

Pizza alla Siciliana SICILIAN PIZZA

If you come to Palermo and explore the long curving streets of its fascinating market, the Vucciria, you'll see all the ingredients that give this fat pizza its typically Sicilian flavor. Sharp, tangy anchovies and a tomato sauce that is rich, sweet, and full of flavor play against the herbs and cheeses in this juicy, light pizza.

Makes one 15- to 16-inch round pizza or one 12 by 17-inch pizza

DOUGH

2¼ teaspoons (1 package / 0.2 oz / 7 g) active dry yeast

1½ teaspoons (0.2 oz / 6.3 g) sugar

1½ cups plus 1 tablespoon (13.1 oz / 375 g) lukewarm water (or ½ cup / 4.2 oz / 120 g warm water plus 1 cup plus 1 tablespoon / 9 oz / 255 g cold water if using a processor)

2 tablespoons (1 oz / 30 g) olive oil or lard

1½ teaspoons (0.3 oz / 7.5 g) salt

About 4 cups (19.3 oz / 550 g) unbleached all-purpose flour

BY HAND

Stir the yeast and sugar into the water in a large mixing bowl; let stand until foamy, about 10 minutes. Stir in the lard. Whisk in the salt and 2 cups of the flour, 1 cup at a time; add the remaining flour and stir until the dough comes together. Knead on a lightly floured surface until soft and velvety, 10 to 12 minutes..

BY MIXER

Stir the yeast and sugar into the water in a mixer bowl; let stand until creamy, about 10 minutes. Mix in the lard with the paddle. Add the salt and flour and mix 1 to 2 minutes. Change to the dough hook and knead at medium speed until soft and velvety, 3 to 4 minutes.

BY PROCESSOR

Stir the yeast and sugar into the warm water in a small bowl; let stand until creamy, about 10 minutes. Place the flour and salt in a food processor fitted with the dough blade and process with several pulses to sift. With the machine running, pour the dissolved yeast, the 1 cup plus 1 tablespoon of cold water, and the lard through the feed tube and process until the dough gathers into a ball. Process no longer than 20 seconds to knead. Finish kneading by hand on a lightly floured surface until smooth, soft, and velvety.

Rising. Place the dough in a lightly oiled bowl, cover tightly with plastic wrap, and let rise until almost doubled, about 1 hour. Punch it down, cover again, and let rise just 20 minutes.

Shaping. Turn the dough out onto a lightly floured surface and shape into a thick disk. Roll it out with a rolling pin to a 12-inch circle about ¼ inch thick, leaving a thick edge. Turn the dough over several times as you roll it so that it won't shrink back later. Place on an oiled baking sheet, a peel sprinkled with cornmeal, or a 12-inch oiled pizza pan.

TOPPING

3 large anchovies, rinsed, boned if necessary, and finely chopped

3 to 4 tablespoons (about 0.8 oz / 25 g) grated fresh caciocavallo or mild provolone cheese

1 cup (4 oz / 120 g) drained and coarsely chopped artichoke hearts packed in oil

Sfinciuni tomato sauce (page 266)

2 to 2¹/₂ teaspoons (0.05 oz / 1.5 g) dried oregano

¹/₂ teaspoon (0.08 oz / 2.5 g) salt

Freshly ground pepper

About 1 tablespoon (0.5 oz / 15 g) olive oil, plus more for brushing

¹/₂ cup (2 oz / 60 g) coarsely chopped prosciutto

¹/₂ cup (3 oz / 85 g) finely sliced fresh mozzarella

Sprinkle the anchovies, half of the caciocavallo, and three-quarters of the artichokes over the dough. Spread with half the tomato sauce and then sprinkle with 1¹/₂ teaspoons of the oregano, the salt, and pepper to taste. Drizzle with the olive oil and spread with the remaining tomato sauce.

Baking. Preheat the oven to 425°F. Use a baking stone if you have one (turn the oven on 45 minutes before baking). Sprinkle the stone with cornmeal just before sliding the pizza onto it, or place the baking sheet directly on the stone. Bake until the crust is crisp and crunchy, 20 to 25 minutes. Remove the pizza and sprinkle the prosciutto, the remaining artichoke hearts, the mozzarella, the remaining oregano, and the remaining caciocavello on top. Bake until the cheese is completely melted, 5 to 10 minutes. Immediately brush the crust with oil.

Sfinciuni alla Palermitana SFINCIUNI FROM PALERMO

Sfinciuni is the quintessential pizza of Palermo. Some versions, like this one that uses Sicilian pizza dough, are rustic and countrified, while others, such as the one made famous by the nuns of the monastery of San Vito, which encloses a meat filling between two very fine layers of dough, are much more elegant. People pick up a slice or two at bakeries or fast-food shops to eat as they walk around the city, and sometimes you'll even see a vendor in a piazza selling *sfinciuni* right off the cart. They are usually baked in big rectangular pans and cut to whatever size matches the buyer's appetite.

Makes one 15-inch round pizza or one 12 by 17-inch pizza

TOMATO SAUCE

2 large yellow onions (about 1 lb / 450 g), chopped

4 cups (33.6 oz / 960 g) water

4 or 5 ripe tomatoes (1¹/₂ lb / 650 g), peeled and chopped

2 tablespoons (1 oz / 30 g) tomato paste

2 tablespoons (1 oz / 30 g) olive oil

1 anchovy, drained, boned if necessary, and chopped

Simmer the onions in the water in a covered heavy saucepan for at least 30 minutes and preferably 1 hour. Stir in the tomatoes, tomato paste, oil, and anchovy and simmer, covered, at least 1 hour more; the longer you cook the sauce, the lighter and sweeter its taste will be. Cool to room temperature.

SFINCIUNI

Pizza alla siciliana dough (page 264), made through the first rising

3 to 4 tablespoons (0.8 to 1 oz / 22 to 30 g) grated fresh caciocavallo or mild provolone cheese

³/₄ cup (3 oz / 85 g) artichoke hearts packed in oil, drained and chopped

¹/₄ cup (0.4 oz / 10 g) plain fresh bread crumbs, lightly toasted

1 to 2 tablespoons (0.5 to 1 oz / 15 to 30 g) olive oil, plus more for brushing

Shaping. Knead the dough briefly on a lightly floured surface and shape it into a thick disk. Roll it out to fit a 15-inch round pizza pan, leaving a thick edge. Lightly oil the pan and place the dough in the pan. Cover with a towel and let rise for 30 minutes.

Sprinkle the cheese and artichoke hearts over the dough, then spoon on the tomato sauce and sprinkle with the bread crumbs. Drizzle the oil over the surface.

Baking. Preheat the oven to 400°F. Using a baking stone if you have one (turn the oven on 30 minutes before baking), place the pan directly on the preheated stone. Bake until the dough is golden, 20 to 25 minutes. Immediately brush the crust with oil. Serve hot.

Calzoni Pugliese HALF-MOON-SHAPED FILLED PIZZAS FROM PUGLIA

Makes 6 to 7 calzoni

DOUGH

2¹/₄ teaspoons (1 package / 0.2 oz / 7 g) active
    dry yeast

4 teaspoons (0.6 oz / 20 g) sugar

3 to 4 tablespoons (1.5 to 2 oz / 45 to 60 g)
    warm water

1 cup plus 1 tablespoon (9.1 oz / 259 g) milk
    (cold if using a processor)

1 large egg

3³/₄ cups (17.5 oz / 500 g) unbleached
    all-purpose flour

1¹/₂ teaspoons (0.3 oz / 7.5 g) salt

BY HAND

Stir the yeast and sugar into 3 tablespoons warm water in a small bowl; let stand until foamy, about 10 minutes. Whisk the milk and egg together. Mix the flour and salt, make a mound of it in a large bowl or on a well-floured work surface, and then make a large well in the center. Gradually pour the dissolved yeast and milk mixture into the well, working the flour from the inside of the well into the liquid with your fingers. Continue until the flour is absorbed, adding 1 tablespoon water, if needed. Knead until soft, velvety, strong, and elastic, 10 to 15 minutes.

BY MIXER

Stir the yeast and sugar into 3 tablespoons warm water in a mixer bowl; let stand until foamy, about 10 minutes. Mix in the milk and egg with the paddle. Add the flour and salt and mix until the dough comes together, adding 1 tablespoon water, if needed. Change to the dough hook and knead at medium speed until soft, velvety, strong, and elastic, 3 to 4 minutes.

BY PROCESSOR

Stir the yeast and sugar into 3 tablespoons warm water in a small bowl; let stand until foamy, about 10 minutes. Place the flour and salt in a food processor fitted with the dough blade and process with several pulses to sift. With the machine running, pour the dissolved yeast, cold milk, and egg through the feed tube and process until the dough comes together in one or two balls on top of the blade. You may need to add a bit more water. Finish kneading by hand on a lightly floured surface, 4 to 5 minutes.

Rising. Place the dough in a lightly oiled bowl, cover with plastic wrap, and let rise until doubled, about 2 hours.

continued

Calzoni Pugliese, *continued*

Shaping. Knead the dough briefly on a well-floured surface. Cut into six or seven pieces (about 4 oz / 110 g each). Shape each piece into a ball, flatten each firmly with your hand, and roll it with a rolling pin into a 1/4-inch-thick oval.

TOPPING

1 teaspoon (0.07 oz / 2 g) minced garlic

1/4 cup (1.9 oz / 55 g) olive oil

About 2 1/2 cups (12 oz / 340 g) finely sliced fresh mozzarella

2 cups (13.1 oz / 375 g) peeled, seeded, and chopped fresh tomatoes or drained canned Italian plum tomatoes

2 to 3 tablespoons (0.5 to 0.8 oz / 15 to 22 g) grated Parmesan cheese

1/4 cup (0.3 oz / 10 g) chopped fresh basil leaves

Salt

1 large egg, beaten

1 tablespoon (0.5 oz / 15 g) water

Warm the garlic in the oil in a small, heavy skillet over low heat for 4 to 5 minutes. Remove from the heat and set aside. Place 1 1/2 to 2 ounces (a scant 1/3 cup) of the mozzarella and about 1/3 cup of chopped tomato in the center of each dough oval. Sprinkle with a little Parmesan, basil, and salt to taste. Mix the egg and water in a small bowl. Brush the egg wash on the edge of each oval and let rest 10 minutes covered by a towel. Fold each oval in half and press the edges together with your fingertips. Brush the tops with some of the garlic-scented olive oil. Place the *calzoni* on an oiled baking sheet if you don't have a baking stone.

Baking. Preheat the oven to 450°F. If you are using a baking stone, turn the oven on 30 minutes before baking and sprinkle with cornmeal just before sliding the *calzoni* onto it. Bake 20 to 25 minutes. Brush again with the garlic-scented oil and serve hot.

Focaccia

Focaccia alla Genovese FOCACCIA FROM GENOA

Focaccia has become a national dish. This disk or large rectangle of leavened dough is found from the tiny towns of the Italian Riviera to Naples on the Mediterranean and Ostuni on the Adriatic, but its true home is Genoa, which is to focaccia what Naples is to pizza. It is called focaccia in Genoa and much of Liguria, but it changes names elsewhere. It is known as *sardenaira* in Provence and as *sardenara* or *sardinaire* in the most western parts of Liguria, which feel a magnetic attraction to the French tradition just over the border; it is known as *schiacciata* in Florence and pockets of Puglia; and it is called *pinze* in the south. The *fougasse* of France and hearth cakes of England share the same ancestry, for as the Romans extended their empire they brought with them not only their carefully reasoned city plans, their temples, and their amphitheaters, but also their *focacce* and flat disks of bread as well.

Focacce are simplicity itself; herbs of the countryside and the golden oils of Liguria flavor the interior, while a little local garlic or tiny savory olives stud its surface. In Puglia a variety called *puddica* is enriched with the ingredients of a pastoral people— tomatoes, garlic, oregano, capers, and oil, and variations on the theme. Anchovies and cheeses from herbs tended by local shepherds flavor other southern specialties. The bakers of Italy, never willing to rest on their laurels, are always using their fertile imaginations to create other possibilities; you, too, should combine appealing ingredients— pancetta, grated cheeses, shreds of basil, or sweet onions sweated in oil—according to your own desires. *Focacce* are usually savory, seasoned with oil or other fats, but there are sweet ones as well, such as the focaccia from Bologna made from simple brioche-like dough that becomes the envelope for ice cream sandwiches, Italian style. Try making *pan tramvai* (raisin bread) as a focaccia with a hail of crystallized or turbinado sugar on top; this innovative departure makes a sensational breakfast bread.

Focacce can be soft or crisp, thick or thin, light and almost plain or topped with any number of condiments, but they are always rustic, a convivial treat eaten as a snack. When I bake them at home, the entire house is lightly perfumed by their cooking, bringing the flavors of the countryside dancing in the air, tickling the nose, and encouraging the taste buds to prepare for a treat.

Bakers sometimes tuck flavoring right into the dough, while other times they only dapple the top. The dough is always stretched in a well-oiled pan, then dimpled with

continued

Focaccia alla Genovese, *continued*

the fingertips, leaving little indentations to collect the oil and salt on top. Sprinkle water, oil, and salt over the surface just before baking so that the focaccia emerges golden, moist, and perfectly cooked from the oven. When this rustic dish is ready for eating, you'll undoubtedly be inspired to take it on country outings and picnics, to slip it to children for lunch and snacks, and to keep it for eating with salads, cheeses, roast chickens and meat along with a glass of good earthy wine.

Makes enough dough for three 9- or 10-inch round focacce or two $10^{1}/_2$ by $15^{1}/_2$-inch thinner rectangular focacce

2$^1/_4$ teaspoons (1 package / 0.2 oz / 7 g) active dry yeast

$^1/_4$ cup (2 oz / 60 g) warm water

2$^1/_4$ cups plus 1 to 2 tablespoons (19.4 to 20 oz / 555 to 570 g) water, at room temperature (cold if using a processor)

2 tablespoons (1 oz / 30 g) olive oil

Scant 7$^1/_2$ cups (2 lb 3 oz / 1 kg) unbleached all-purpose flour or half all-purpose flour and half bread flour

1 tablespoon (0.5 oz / 15 g) fine sea salt or table salt

BY HAND

Stir the yeast into the warm water in a large mixing bowl; let stand until creamy, about 10 minutes. Stir in 2$^1/_4$ cups plus 1 tablespoon of the water and the oil. Add 2 cups of the flour and the salt and whisk or stir until smooth. Stir in the remaining flour, 1 cup at a time, until the dough comes together. Knead on a floured surface until velvety and soft, about 8 to 10 minutes.

BY MIXER

Stir the yeast into the warm water in a mixer bowl; let stand until creamy, about 10 minutes. Stir in 2$^1/_4$ cups plus 1 tablespoon of the water and the oil with the paddle. Add the flour and salt and mix until the dough comes together, 1 to 2 minutes, adding 1 more tablespoon of water if needed. Change to the dough hook and knead at low speed for 1 to 2 minutes, then at medium speed for another 3 minutes, stopping to push the dough down from the collar. The dough should be velvety and elastic.

BY PROCESSOR

Process this dough in two batches. Stir the yeast into the warm water in a small bowl; let stand until creamy, about 10 minutes. Place the flour and salt in a food processor fitted with the steel blade and process with two or three pulses to sift. With the machine running, pour 2$^1/_4$ cups plus 1 tablespoon of the cold water, the dissolved yeast, and the oil through the feed tube and process until the dough gathers into a rough mass. Process 20 seconds longer to knead. Finish kneading by hand on a floured surface until the dough is velvety and elastic, 2 to 3 minutes.

First Rise. Place the dough in a lightly oiled bowl, cover tightly with plastic wrap, and let rise until doubled, about $1^1/2$ hours.

Shaping and Second Rise. For round *focacce*, cut the dough into three equal pieces on a lightly floured surface. Shape each piece into a thick disk; roll out each disk to a 9- or 10-inch circle and place in the bottom of an oiled 9- or 10-inch plate. For rectangular *focacce*, cut the dough in half and shape to fit two oiled $10^1/2$ by $15^1/2$-inch pans. Cover the dough with towels and let rise for 30 minutes.

Dimpling and Third Rise. Dimple the dough vigorously with your fingertips, leaving indentations that are as deep as $1/2$ inch. The bakers of Genoa do this to trap the little pools of oil and salt that flavor the surface. Cover the tops with moist towels and let rise until doubled, about 2 hours.

Topping. Select one of the topping recipes that follow. One baker of Genoa told me that the great secret of keeping these doughs so moist while cooking them thoroughly is to cover the tops with equal amounts of olive oil and water mixed with salt; the water evaporates slowing during the cooking, allowing the interior of the focaccia to cook fully without drying out. Alas, home ovens don't get hot enough to make use of this wonderful piece of advice, but you can paint the tops with oil and sprinkle them with salt, and, when you place the *focacce* in the oven, spray them with water.

Baking. Preheat the oven to 400°F. Use baking stones if you have them (turn the oven on 30 minutes before baking) and place the pans directly on the preheated stones. Bake 20 to 25 minutes, spraying with water three times in the first 10 minutes. When finished baking, immediately remove the *focacce* from the pans and place the *focacce* onto racks to cool so that the bottoms do not get soggy. Eat *focacce* warm or at room temperature the same day you bake them. No matter what, don't refrigerate them; they simply won't taste right.

Focaccia col Sale FOCACCIA WITH SEA SALT

Makes three 9- or 10-inch round focacce *or two 10¹/₂ by 15¹/₂-inch rectangular* focacce

Focaccia alla genovese dough (page 270), made
    through the third rise

2 to 3 tablespoons (1 to 1.5 oz / 30 to 45 g) olive oil

1¹/₂ to 2 teaspoons (0.3 to 0.4 oz / 8 to 10 g) coarse
    sea salt

Brush the doughs with the oil and sprinkle with the salt. Bake as directed for *focaccia alla genovese.*

Focaccia alla Salvia FOCACCIA WITH SAGE

Makes three 9- or 10-inch round focacce *or two 10¹/₂ by 15¹/₂-inch rectangular* focacce

Focaccia alla genovese dough (page 270)

24 to 30 fresh sage leaves chopped, or
    1¹/₂ teaspoons dried sage leaves, crumbled
    (not powdered, which is much too pungent)

2 tablespoons (1 oz / 30 g) olive oil

1¹/₂ tablespoons (0.8 oz / 22.5 g) salt

Whole fresh sage leaves, for garnish (optional)

Work the chopped sage leaves into the dough in the first kneading. Follow the directions for *focaccia alla genovese* through the third rise. Just before baking, brush the dimpled dough with oil and sprinkle with the salt. Decorate the tops with the whole sage leaves. Bake as directed for *focaccia alla genovese.*

Variation. To make *focaccia al rosmarino,* substitute 1¹/₂ tablespoons of chopped fresh rosemary or 2 teaspoons of dried rosemary for the chopped sage. Decorate each focaccia with several sprigs of fresh rosemary, if you want.

Focaccia alle Olive FOCACCIA WITH OLIVES

Makes three 9- or 10-inch round focacce *or two 10¹/₂ by 15¹/₂-inch rectangular* focacce

Focaccia alla genovese dough (page 270), made through the third rise

About 1²/₃ cups (8 oz / 225 g) black Ligurian olives, or a combination of black and green olives, preferably Ponentine, Ardoino, or Niçoise

2 tablespoons (1 oz / 30 g) olive oil

Pit the olives and push them into the dimpled doughs just before baking. Brush the doughs with olive oil. Bake as directed for *focaccia alla genovese.*

Focaccia al Gorgonzola GORGONZOLA FOCACCIA

This focaccia is very appealing to look at as well as to eat. It is about 1¹/₂ to 2 inches high, and the Gorgonzola covering settles slightly unevenly on the surface, creating irregular valleys with deep golden patches and higher raised sections lightly brushed with the topping.

Makes two 9- or 10-inch round focacce *or one 12 by 17-inch focaccia*

DOUGH

3¹/₂ teaspoons (0.4 oz / 10 g) active dry yeast

1¹/₂ cups (12.6 oz / 360 g) warm water (or ¹/₄ cup / 2 oz / 60 g warm water plus 1¹/₄ cups / 10.5 oz / 300 g cold water if using a processor)

¹/₄ cup (1.9 oz / 55 g) olive oil

3³/₄ cups (17.5 oz / 500 g) unbleached all-purpose flour

2¹/₂ teaspoons (0.4 oz / 12.5 g) salt

BY HAND

Stir the yeast into the warm water in a large mixing bowl; let stand until creamy, about 10 minutes. Stir in the oil, then the flour and salt. Knead on a lightly floured surface until smooth and elastic, 8 to 10 minutes.

BY MIXER

Stir the yeast into the water in a mixer bowl; let stand until creamy, about 10 minutes. Stir in the soil with the paddle, then the flour and salt. Change to the dough hook and knead until smooth and elastic, about 3 minutes.

BY PROCESSOR

Stir the yeast into the ¹/₄ cup of warm water in a small bowl; let stand until creamy, about 10 minutes. Place the flour

continued

Focaccia al Gorgonzola, *continued*

and salt in a food processor fitted with the dough blade and process briefly to sift. With the machine running, slowly pour the dissolved yeast, oil, and the $1^1/4$ cups of cold water through the feed tube and process until the dough gathers into a ball. Process 40 seconds longer to knead. Finish kneading by hand on a lightly floured surface for 2 to 3 minutes.

First Rise. Place the dough in a lightly oiled bowl, cover tightly with plastic wrap, and let rise until doubled, 1 to $1^1/2$ hours.

Shaping. Cut the dough in half and place each piece in a lightly oiled 9- or 10-inch pie plate; or, if you prefer, keep the dough in one piece and instead use a lightly oiled 12 by 17-inch rimmed baking sheet. Flatten and stretch the dough to cover as much of the bottom as possible; then dimple the tops quite vigorously with your fingertips to stretch it some more. Cover with a towel and let it relax 10 minutes. Dimple and stretch the dough more, so that it really covers the bottom. Let rise under a towel another 20 to 25 minutes.

TOPPING

$1/4$ cup (2 oz / 60 g) heavy cream

8 ounces (225 g) Gorgonzola cheese

$1/2$ teaspoon (0.3 oz / 7 g) dried thyme

Olive oil for brushing

Mix the cream, cheese, and thyme in a food processor fitted with the steel blade or in a stand mixer with the paddle, or mash the cheese in a mixing bowl with a wooden spoon and beat in the cream and

thyme. Spread the cheese mixture equally over the doughs with a rubber spatula or wooden spoon.

Second Rise. Brush the tops lightly with oil, cover with a towel, and let rise until well puffed, 50 minutes to 1 hour.

Baking. Preheat the oven to 425°F. Bake 10 minutes. Reduce the heat to 375°F and bake until the topping is golden brown and just starting to bubble, about 10 minutes. Unmold immediately onto a rack. This focaccia is best hot but can also be served warm or at room temperature. Do not refrigerate.

Variations. To make *focaccia alle cipolle*, substitute 2 yellow onions (about 7 oz / 200 g each), thinly sliced and sautéed, for the topping. Sprinkle with salt and brush with olive oil. Brush again with oil after baking.

To make *focaccia ai peperoni*, sauté 2 to 3 finely sliced red and yellow bell peppers (1 to 1.5 lb / 450 to 680 g total) in 3 tablespoons (1.5 oz / 45 g) of olive oil and $1^1/2$ tablespoons (0.8 oz / 21 g) of butter over medium-low heat until soft, about 15 minutes. Substitute the sautéed pepper mixture for the Gorgonzola topping. Brush the *focacce* with oil after baking.

To make *focaccia alla ricotta*, mix 1 cup (8 oz / 225 g) of ricotta, $1/2$ cup (3 oz / 85 g) of diced prosciutto, $1/3$ cup (1.2 oz / 35 g) of grated pecorino or Parmesan cheese, 5 tablespoons (2.7 oz / 76 g) of milk, and $1/8$ teaspoon of freshly grated nutmeg and substitute for the Gorgonzola topping.

Schiacciata alla Fiorentina FLATBREAD FROM FLORENCE

Schiacciata, which simply means "squashed" or "crunched," is the word Florentines use for the flatbreads that other Italians call focaccia or pizza. At an Il Fornaio bakery in Florence, I watched as the bakers shaped *schiacciate* as big as a small pizza and as small as an hors d'oeuvre, but to me they were at their most appealing as six-inch disks topped with brilliant strips of red and yellow peppers, ribbons of zucchini, or almost translucent slices of ripe tomatoes dusted with tiny basil leaves, and all glossy from a wash of local olive oil. They are wonderful eaten cold for lunch with a salad; you can also take them on picnics or serve them with a platter of cold meats.

Makes six 6-inch schiacciate *or two 10-inch and one 8-inch* schiacciate

DOUGH

2¼ teaspoons (1 package / 0.2 oz / 7 g) active dry yeast

Dash of malt syrup (optional)

1½ cups (12.6 oz / 360 g) warm water (or ¼ cup / 2 oz / 60 g warm water plus 1¼ cups / 10.5 oz / 300 g cold water if using a processor)

2 tablespoons (1 oz / 30 g) olive oil

2½ tablespoons (1.1 oz / 30 g) lard, at room temperature

2½ tablespoons (0.9 oz / 26 g) nonfat dry milk

3¾ cups (17.5 oz / 500 g) unbleached all-purpose flour

1½ teaspoons (0.3 oz / 7.5 g) salt

Olive oil for brushing

Salt for sprinkling

BY HAND

Stir the yeast and malt, if using, into the water in a bowl; let stand until creamy, about 10 minutes. Stir in the oil, lard, and dry milk. Mix the flour and salt in a wide-mouthed bowl and make a well in the center. Pour the yeast mixture into the well and gradually stir the flour into the liquid. Stir until well combined. Knead on a floured surface or in the big bowl until velvety and smooth, 8 to 10 minutes. The dough should be soft, so add any extra flour sparingly.

BY MIXER

Stir the yeast and malt, if using, into a mixer bowl; let stand until creamy, about 10 minutes. Stir in the oil, lard, and dry milk with the paddle. Add the flour and mix at low speed about 2 minutes. Change to the dough hook and knead 4 to 5 minutes. Add the salt and knead another 1 to 2 minutes. The dough will climb up the collar of the hook, and you will have to stop several times to push it down. The dough should be smooth, velvety, and softer than bread dough but firmer than croissant dough.

BY PROCESSOR

Unless you have a food processor with an enormous capacity, process this recipe in two batches. Stir the yeast and malt, if using, into the ¼ cup of warm water in a

continued

Schiacciata alla Fiorentina, *continued*

small bowl; let stand until creamy, about 10 minutes. Place the flour and dry milk in a food processor fitted with the dough blade and process with several pulses to mix. Place the lard on top of the flour. With the machine running, pour the 1¼ cups of cold water, the dissolved yeast, and oil through the feed tube and process until the dough comes together. Add the salt and process briefly to incorporate it. Finish kneading by hand on a lightly floured surface, 3 to 5 minutes.

First Rise. Place the dough in a lightly oiled bowl, cover tightly with plastic wrap, and let rise until doubled, 1 to 2 hours.

Shaping Large Schiacciate. Flatten the dough firmly on a lightly floured work surface and divide into two 8-ounce (225 g) and one 10½-ounce (300 g) pieces. Roll each piece into a ball and let rest under a towel for 15 minutes. Dimple and spread the balls with your fingers to cover the bottoms of two oiled 8-inch pie plates and one oiled 10-inch pie plate, or shape free form on floured peels. Brush the tops with oil and sprinkle with salt.

Shaping 6-inch Schiacciate. Cut the dough into six pieces (5 oz / 140 g each) on a lightly floured surface and shape into balls. Let rest under a towel for 15 minutes. Dimple the doughs, spreading each into a circle, and let rest under a towel for another 15 minutes. Dimple the dough again, stretching each piece into a 6-inch circle. Brush the tops with oil and sprinkle

lightly with salt. Place the dough circles on parchment-lined or oiled baking sheets or baker's peels sprinkled with cornmeal.

Second Rise. Cover with a towel and let rise until doubled, about 1 hour.

Topping. Dimple the dough again with your fingertips, stretching it as you go. Sprinkle with salt and brush with oil. Mist water very lightly over the top to cover and trap the oil and then cover with one of the following toppings:

2 red onions (14 oz / 200 g), thinly sliced and sautéed in 2 tablespoons (1 oz / 28 g) of oil and 1 tablespoon (0.5 oz / 14 g) of unsalted butter over low heat for 15 to 20 minutes; sprinkle with 1 tablespoon (0.1 oz / 2.5 g) of torn fresh basil leaves

or 3 to 4 fresh tomatoes (about 1 lb / 450 g), thinly sliced; sprinkle with chopped fresh basil leaves and ¾ teaspoon (0.1 oz / 3.5 g) of salt

or 2 yellow and/or red sweet peppers (1 lb / 450 g), thinly sliced and lightly sautéed with a large garlic clove in 2 to 3 tablespoons (about 1.5 oz / 45 g) of olive oil for 15 minutes; discard the garlic

or 1 or 2 eggplants (about 1 lb / 450 g), peeled and very thinly sliced, salted, drained, and lightly sautéed with 1 or 2 whole cloves of garlic in ¼ cup (2 oz / 55 g) of olive oil until creamy, 10 to 15 minutes; drain on paper towels and layer with 2 fresh, ripe tomatoes

(12 oz / 340 g), thinly sliced, or 1 can (14 oz / 400 g) of San Marzano plum tomatoes, drained and chopped

or about 3 cups (1 lb/ 450 g) thinly sliced stracchino or Taleggio cheese

or 4 to 6 small zucchini (20 oz / 575 g), cut lengthwise into thin slices and lightly sautéed with 2 whole cloves of garlic in 3 to 4 tablespoons (about 2 oz / 55 g) of olive oil; discard the garlic; sprinkle with 2 tablespoons (0.15 oz / 5 g) of chopped fresh basil.

Brush the tops with oil, sprinkle with salt, and brush or mist lightly with water.

Baking. Preheat the oven to 425°F. Use baking stones if you have them (turn the oven on 30 minutes before baking) and place the baking pans directly on the preheated stones. Bake the 10-inch *schiacciata* 25 to 30 minutes, the 8-inch ones 22 to 25 minutes, and the 6-inch ones 18 to 20 minutes. Immediately brush the surface with oil. You may bake the larger *schiacciate* out of their pans directly on the stones for the last 10 minutes. Serve hot, or cool on racks to room temperature.

Pizzette Florentine LITTLE PIZZAS OF FLORENCE

Pizzette **are much thinner than pizzas and are wonderful little rounds for snacks.**

Makes eight 5-inch pizzette

Schiacciata alla fiorentina dough (page 275), made through the first rising

2 to 2$^{1}/_{2}$ tablespoons (1 to 1.3 oz / 30 to 37 g) olive oil

$^{3}/_{4}$ to 1 teaspoon (0.1 to 0.2 oz / 3.5 to 5 g) salt

Choice of topping for schiacciata alla fiorentina (page 276)

Shaping and Second Rise. Cut the dough into eight pieces (4 oz / 110 g each) on a lightly floured surface; flatten each piece with your palms (not fingertips) and brush with oil. Let rest on a floured surface under a towel for 15 minutes. Spread the pieces with your fingertips into very, very thin 5-inch circles. Brush with oil, set on cornmeal-sprinkled peels or oiled baking sheets, cover with a towel, and let rise to half their original volume, about 30 minutes.

Topping. Sprinkle salt over the tops and brush with oil. Top with your choice of lightly sautéed, thinly sliced vegetables, as for *schiacciate*. Drizzle oil over the topping and mist or brush lightly with water.

Baking. Preheat the oven to 425°F. Use baking stones if you have them (turn the oven on 30 minutes before baking) and place the baking pans directly on the preheated stones. Bake 15 minutes. Immediately brush the *pizzette* thoroughly with oil to give them a luscious finish. Serve hot or at room temperature. Do not refrigerate.

Schiacciate Integrali WHOLE WHEAT FLATBREADS

These Florentine *schiacciate* are simply tasty flatbreads made of whole wheat flour. Top them with sweet red onions flavored with thyme or wash the tops with garlic-scented olive oil. If you bake them without toppings, these make wonderful buns for sandwiches; just cut them in half, stuff with slices of prosciutto and cheese, and warm them briefly. Whether you make them as big as pizzas or as small as hors d'oeuvres, you can be sure you're making the Tuscan equivalent of *focacce* in the stylish whole wheat variation.

Makes 5 to 6 pizzette; *two 10-inch* schiacciate; *or about 60* focaccette

2¹⁄₄ teaspoons (1 package / 0.2 oz / 7 g) active dry yeast

1¹⁄₂ cups (12.6 oz / 360 g) warm water (or ¹⁄₄ cup / 2 oz / 60 g warm water plus 1¹⁄₄ cups / 10.5 oz / 300 g cold water if using a processor)

4 teaspoons (0.7 oz / 20 g) lard

About 2²⁄₃ cups (13.1 oz / 375 g) unbleached all-purpose flour

1 cup minus 1 tablespoon (4.4 oz / 125 g) whole wheat flour

1¹⁄₂ teaspoons (0.3 oz / 7.5 g) salt

Olive oil for brushing

BY HAND

Stir the yeast into the water in a large mixing bowl; let stand until creamy, about 10 minutes. Stir in the lard. Mix the flours and salt and whisk the first 2 cups, a cup at a time, into the yeast mixture; stir in the remaining flour mixture thoroughly with a wooden spoon. Knead on a lightly floured surface until velvety and elastic, 8 to 10 minutes.

BY MIXER

Stir the yeast into the water in the mixer bowl; let stand until creamy, about 10 minutes. Stir in the lard with the paddle. Mix in the flours thoroughly; add the salt and mix until incorporated. Change to the dough hook and knead until velvety and elastic, 2 to 3 minutes. If you want, finish kneading by hand on a floured surface.

BY PROCESSOR

Stir the yeast into the ¹⁄₄ cup of warm water in a small bowl; let stand until creamy, about 10 minutes. Place the flours and salt in a food processor fitted with the dough blade. Process with several pulses to sift. Place the lard on top of the flour. With the machine running, pour the 1¹⁄₄ cups of cold water and the dissolved yeast through the feed tube and process until the dough gathers into a rough mass. Add the salt. Process 25 seconds longer to knead. Finish kneading by hand, 2 to 3 minutes.

First Rise. Place the dough in a lightly oiled bowl, cover tightly with plastic wrap and let rise until doubled, 1 to 1¼ hours.

Shaping. Knead the dough briefly on a lightly floured surface. Cut the dough in half for two 10-inch *schiacciate* or into five or six pieces for *pizzette*. Shape each piece into a ball. Roll out each ball on a lightly floured surface or stretch the dough over your fists to a 10-inch circle for *schiacciate* or a 5-inch circle for *pizzette*, leaving a thick edge. Place on floured baker's peels or lightly oiled pizza pans, pie plates, or baking sheets. You may need to stretch the dough, let it relax for a few minutes under a towel, then stretch it again. Brush the tops with oil.

To Make Focaccette. Roll the dough out thin on a floured surface and cut out circles with a 1¼- to 1½-inch cookie cutter. Place on lightly oiled baking sheets. Do not oil the tops. Cover with towels and let rise without any topping.

Topping for Schiacciate or Pizzette. Sauté 2 large red onions (1 lb / 450 g total), thinly sliced, in 2 tablespoons (1 oz / 30 g) of olive oil and 1 tablespoon (0.5 oz / 14 g) of unsalted butter over very low heat for 15 to 20 minutes; spread the onions over the dough and sprinkle with a fat pinch of dried thyme. Or sauté 2 thinly sliced cloves of garlic in 2 to 2½ tablespoons (about 1 oz / 30 g) of olive oil over medium heat for 4 to 5 minutes; brush the dough with the oil and sprinkle with 2 tablespoons of chopped fresh sage or rosemary or 1 tablespoon (0.7 oz / 20 g) of sea salt.

Second Rise. Cover the dough with towels and let rise until puffy but not doubled, about 45 minutes. Dimple and stretch the dough again with your fingers. Before baking and after the second rise, dimple the *focaccette* with your index fingers, then oil the tops and sprinkle with a bit of fine sea salt.

Baking. Preheat the oven to 400°F. Use baking stones if you have them (turn the oven on 30 minutes before baking) and place the baking pans directly on the preheated stones. Bake the *schiacciate* 22 to 25 minutes, the *pizzette* 15 to 18 minutes, and the *focaccette* 12 to 15 minutes. Serve hot, or cool on racks to room temperature.

Focaccia alla Pugliese POTATO FLATBREAD FROM PUGLIA

I discovered this unusual kind of focaccia in Puglia, the region on the heel of the boot in southern Italy, where huge well-kept farms with great green and golden fields of grain are interrupted only by stands of olive trees, stone walls, and *trulli*, charming whitewashed round houses with conical roofs. Of course we stopped in the town of Alberobello to enter the *trulli* that were actually open to the countryside, and then set out for Mia Casa, a restaurant patronized by local people who know good regional food when they taste it. We began a large lunch with an antipasto of wonderful homemade sausages, salami, olives, and this special version of focaccia made with potatoes that grow throughout the entire region. About $1^1/_4$ inches high with what looks like a dense breadlike texture, this focaccia is actually as light as cake when you eat it. The tomato-scented oil painted across the top leaves a veil of red sprinkled with a dusting of oregano.

Makes two 9-inch focacce

DOUGH

$1^3/_4$ teaspoons (0.2 oz / 5 g) active dry yeast

1 cup plus 3 tablespoons (10 oz / 285 g)
  warm water

$3^3/_4$ cups (17.5 oz / 500 g) unbleached
  all-purpose flour

$1^1/_3$ cups (9.6 oz / 275 g) lightly packed peeled,
  boiled, and riced potatoes

2 teaspoons (0.4 oz / 10 g) salt

BY HAND

Stir the yeast into $^1/_3$ cup of the water in a small bowl; let stand until creamy, about 10 minutes. Mix the flour, potatoes, and salt in a large bowl; mound the mixture in the bowl and make a well in the center. Pour the dissolved yeast into the well and gradually add the rest of the water, stirring the dry ingredients from the side of the well into the liquid. Stir until the dough comes together. Knead on a floured surface until soft and elastic, 8 to 10 minutes.

BY MIXER

Stir the yeast into the water in a mixer bowl; let stand until creamy, about 10 minutes. Add the flour, potatoes, and salt and mix with the paddle until the mixture comes together. Change to the dough hook and knead at medium speed until soft and elastic, about 3 minutes.

First Rise. Place the dough in a lightly oiled bowl, cover tightly with plastic wrap, and let rise until doubled, about $1^1/_2$ hours.

Shaping and Second Rise. Cut the dough in half on a lightly floured surface and shape each piece into a ball. Place in two lightly oiled 9-inch pie plates; stretch the dough out toward the edges.

Cover with a damp towel and let rise until the dough has doubled and completely filled the pans, about 45 minutes.

TOPPING

2 to 3 tablespoons (1 to 1.5 oz / 30 to 45 g) oil from a jar of sun-dried tomatoes, or 2 to 3 tablespoons (1 to 1.5 oz / 30 to 45 g) olive oil mixed with 1 tablespoon (0.5 oz / 15 g) mashed plum tomatoes or 1/2 teaspoon (0.08 oz / 2.5 g) tomato paste

2 teaspoons (0.05 oz / 1.5 g) dried oregano

Dimple the tops of the doughs, letting your fingertips dance across the surface and leave little indentations in the dough. Using a pastry brush, lightly brush the tops of the *focacce* with the oil and sprinkle with the oregano.

Baking. Preheat the oven to 400°F. Use baking stones if you have them (turn the oven on 30 minutes before baking) and place the pie plates directly on the preheated stones. Bake until the edges are golden, 25 to 30 minutes; if you want, bake the *focacce* out of the pans directly on the stones for the last 10 minutes. Cool to room temperature.

Focaccia di Patate e Cipolle POTATO AND ONION FOCACCIA

There's nothing ordinary about this focaccia, for it is made not only without yeast but also without flour. The secret is that the dough really isn't a dough at all but a mixture based on potatoes, which make a wonderful foil for the intriguing onion, olive, and caper filling. I happened upon it in Lecce, the city in Puglia that is sometimes called "the Florence of Baroque Art." No wonder—the façade of almost every cathedral, palazzo, and building is awash with voluptuous cupids, elegant virgins, grinning monkeys, gargoyles, and demons clearly up to no good. Lecce had its centuries of privilege and influence under the Normans and Spanish, but this focaccia reflects a much humbler tradition. The potato is part of a rustic style of cooking and eating and enjoys a popularity in Puglia that isn't matched anywhere else in Italy.

Makes 1 focaccia

SAUCE

1/4 cup (2 oz / 55 g) olive oil

4 large yellow onions (2 lb / 900 g), coarsely chopped

1 crumbled bay leaf

1/4 cup (2 oz / 60 g) dry white wine

1 1/2 teaspoons (0.3 oz / 7.5 g) salt

Freshly ground pepper

3 cups (25.2 oz / 720 g) water

4 black olives, preferably Gaeta or Kalamata, pitted and chopped

Scant 1 tablespoon (0.3 oz / 9 g) capers, drained or washed free of salt

continued

Focaccia di Patate e Cipolle, *continued*

Pour the oil into a Dutch oven or heavy saucepan; it should cover the bottom of the pan. Add the onions, bay leaf, wine, salt, and pepper to taste and pour in the water. Cook, uncovered, over medium heat, stirring occasionally, until all the water is evaporated. The mixture must be really dry or the interior of the focaccia will be gummy. Remove from the heat and stir in the olives and capers.

DOUGH

About 2 large boiling potatoes (20 oz / 560 g total), peeled, boiled, and riced or mashed

2 tablespoons (0.5 oz / 15 g) grated Parmesan cheese

1¹/₂ teaspoons (0.3 oz / 7.5 g) salt

Freshly ground pepper

3 to 4 tablespoons (1.5 to 2 oz / 45 to 60 g) dry white wine

5 to 7 tablespoons (0.5 to 0.8 oz / 14 to 22 g) coarsely ground fresh bread crumbs

Olive oil for rubbing

Place the hot potatoes in a mixing bowl; beat in the Parmesan, salt, pepper to taste, and enough of the wine to make a consistent dough.

Oil a 9-inch pie plate and coat with 2 to 3 tablespoons of the bread crumbs, enough for a thin layer to keep the potatoes from sticking. Spread slightly more than half the potato mixture in a layer about ³/₄ inch thick in the pie plate. Spread with the onion sauce and cover with a second layer of the remaining potatoes. Spread a little olive oil on your hand and rub it over the top. Sprinkle with the remaining bread crumbs so that the top is completely covered.

Baking. Preheat the oven to 350°F. Bake until the top is golden and the crumbs are crisp, about 45 minutes. Serve warm or at room temperature.

Pani Raffinati
Elegant Breads

It may be stretching the term just a bit to think of croissants and puff pastries, those two supreme accomplishments of the baker's art, as *pani raffinati*, refined breads, although, of course, that is exactly what they are. A bit of flour, a bit of water, a little yeast, and salt layered with butter and suddenly—or slowly—you have incredibly flaky and tender doughs that can be sweet or savory. These *pani raffinati* are very versatile, as well as more than a little tricky. Even in Italy they are considered the more rarified expression of the cook's art, so it's no wonder that many cookbooks simply suggest that their readers buy *pasta sfogliata* already prepared.

I hope a few tastes of these Italian treats will immediately convince you to make them yourself. Fragrant, delicate doughs flavored with any number of ingredients are turned into *mignon* hors d'oeuvres and sweets, tiny little mouthfuls permeated with a flash of cheese, a crunch of caraway, a bit of anchovy, or a whiff of sweet apple and nut. Their delicacy and elegance simply have no rival; so, while these wonderful discoveries for every course of every meal may take more than a bit of work, you can make dozens at a time, freeze them with ease, and pull them out any time to dazzle your guests.

Sweet Croissants

Cornetti Dolci ITALIAN CROISSANTS

In big cities, such as Milan and Rome, hot *cornetti* were once all the rage. Kids used to flock to the back doors of bakeries at one and two o'clock in the morning to buy them still steamy from the ovens. It was slightly tricky, because it was against the law to sell bread until it was cool, but that probably only made these delicate, flaky pastries all the more appealing. *Cornetti* come plain or filled with apricot jam, almond paste, or pastry cream, which is a particular favorite all over the south.

What makes Italian *cornetti* different from French croissants? Certainly not their heritage, for both are descendants of a pastry devised by a Viennese baker to celebrate the city's liberation from the Turkish siege in 1793. The shape is the same—it comes from the crescent on the Turkish flag—but the sweet yeast dough of *cornetti* is enriched with egg and sometimes even has a bit of butter tucked into it. This particular recipe makes *cornetti* that are delicate, tender, and amazingly light and airy. It is inspired by the Venetian baker's *cornetti*, which are sugary and full of butter, and uses high-gluten bread flour to produce the spectacularly light and delicious effect.

Makes enough for 20 cornetti

DOUGH

5 teaspoons (0.5 oz / 15 g) active dry yeast

1¹⁄₂ cups (12.6 oz / 360 g) warm water

1 stick (4 oz / 115 g) unsalted butter, at room temperature

¹⁄₃ cup plus 1 teaspoon (2.6 oz / 75 g) sugar

2 large eggs

2¹⁄₃ cups (11.4 oz / 325 g) unbleached all-purpose flour

2¹⁄₃ cups (11.4 oz / 325 g) bread flour

2¹⁄₂ teaspoons (0.4 oz / 12.5 g) salt

BY HAND

Stir the yeast into the water in a large mixing bowl; let stand until creamy, about 10 minutes. Beat in the butter, sugar, and eggs until blended. Mix the flours and the salt and stir, 1 cup at a time, into the yeast mixture until the soft dough comes together. Turn out onto a lightly floured surface. Knead lightly until smooth, about 1 minute (eighteen to twenty times). Do not overknead or the dough will become too elastic.

continued

Cornetti Dolci, *continued*

BY MIXER

Stir the yeast into the water in a mixer bowl; let stand until creamy, about 10 minutes. Beat in the butter, sugar, and eggs with the paddle until blended. Mix the flours and salt into the yeast mixture just until the dough comes together, about 30 seconds. Mix at medium speed for 1 minute. Knead on a lightly floured surface, lightly dusting the top with additional flour, until smooth, about 1 minute. Do not overknead or the dough will become too elastic.

First Rise. Place the dough in a lightly oiled bowl, cover tightly with plastic wrap, and let rise until doubled, 1 to $1^{1}/_{2}$ hours.

   Chilling. Turn the dough out onto a lightly floured surface and sprinkle the top of the dough lightly with flour. Knead five or six times, or just enough to expel some of the air without developing the gluten. Flatten the dough with your hand, sprinkle the top with flour, wrap in plastic wrap, and refrigerate until the dough is cold throughout, 4 to 6 hours or overnight.

BUTTER BLOCK

4 sticks (1 lb / 450 g) cold unsalted butter

1 cup minus 2 tablespoons (4.4 oz / 125 g) unbleached all-purpose flour

BY HAND

Place the butter on a work surface. Holding a rolling pin by one handle, beat the butter until malleable and creamy. Sprinkle $^{1}/_{2}$ cup of the flour on top of the butter. Scrape the softened butter from the work surface with a dough scraper, and, using the scraper, cut the flour into the butter. Sprinkle the remaining flour over the mixture. Working quickly, smear the butter and flour together with the dough scraper and the heel of your hand until smooth. Scrape the mixture together into a smooth block about $^{1}/_{2}$ inch thick. Wrap in plastic wrap; refrigerate until cold but not hard, 15 to 20 minutes.

BY MIXER

Cut the butter into $^{1}/_{4}$-inch pieces and place the butter and flour in a mixer bowl. Beat with the paddle at low speed about 1 minute, then at high speed until smooth, 30 seconds. Wrap in plastic wrap; refrigerate until cold but not hard, 15 to 20 minutes.

Enclosing the Butter Block. Remove the dough from the refrigerator and place on a lightly floured surface. Sprinkle the dough lightly with flour and roll into a 20 by 12-inch rectangle, $^{1}/_{4}$ inch thick, so that one short side is nearest you. Remove the butter block from the refrigerator and break off small ($^{1}/_{2}$-inch) pieces. Dot the butter pieces over two-thirds of the dough rectangle nearest you, leaving a $1^{1}/_{2}$-inch border around the edges. Fold as if you were folding a business letter: fold the unbuttered third over the middle and fold the remaining third over the top. Pinch the edges together so that the butter does not fall out. Tap the surface of the dough with the rolling pin to evenly distribute the butter.

First Set of Turns. Turn the dough 90 degrees so that the top flap faces your right (like a book). Sprinkle the dough and work surface lightly with flour. Roll the dough into a 20 by 12-inch rectangle, $^1/_4$ inch thick. Fold into thirds as described above, pinch the edges to seal, and tap the dough with the rolling pin to evenly distribute the butter. Rotate the dough 90 degrees and lightly sprinkle the dough and work surface with flour. Roll out as before to a 20 by 12-inch rectangle, $^1/_4$ inch thick. You may notice that rolling is slightly harder this time. Fold into thirds as described above, pinch the edges to seal, and tap the dough with the rolling pin to distribute the butter evenly. Brush off any excess flour and straighten the sides of the dough. Wrap the dough in plastic wrap and refrigerate 45 minutes to 1 hour.

Second Set of Turns. Lightly flour the work surface and the dough. Lightly tap the surface of the dough with the rolling pin. Roll into a 20 by 12-inch rectangle, $^1/_4$ inch thick, so that one short side is nearest you. Fold again as if you were folding a business letter: the top third is folded down and the bottom third is then folded up. Pinch the edges together. Turn the dough 90 degrees so that the top flap faces your right (like a book). Sprinkle the dough and work surface lightly with flour. If at any time the dough resists rolling or the

butter is noticeably soft, refrigerate it to relax the dough or harden the butter. Roll the dough into a 20 by 12-inch rectangle, $^1/_4$ inch thick. Fold the dough into thirds as described above, pinch the edges to seal, and tap the dough with the rolling pin. Wrap the dough in plastic wrap and refrigerate 4 hours or overnight. Weight the dough with a brick or 5-pound bag of sugar if it begins to rise.

Cutting. Cut the block of cold dough in two and place one half on a lightly floured surface and dust the top with flour. Tap the dough with a rolling pin to flatten it and expel some of the air. Roll into a 26 by 8-inch rectangle, frequently lifting the dough and sprinkling the work surface and dough lightly with flour to prevent sticking. Try to keep the edges of the dough as straight as possible. Trim the edges with a sharp knife, if necessary. Brush off any excess flour. To make equal size triangles for the *cornetti*, turn the dough so that one long edge is facing you. Make a parallelogram of the rectangle by first rolling on the diagonal from the middle of the dough to the upper left edge and then to the lower right edge. Trim the edges with a sharp knife and measure and mark the dough at 5-inch intervals on the top and bottom of the dough. Beginning at the bottom left-hand point, cut across at a diagonal to the first mark on the top edge. Cut diagonally back to the first mark on the bottom. Keep cutting triangles diagonally from top to bottom, connecting at the marks. Repeat with the second piece of dough.

continued

Cornetti Dolci, *continued*

Shaping. Position a triangle so that the base is nearest to you. Pull gently on the two nearest corners, stretching them slightly. Tug dough from the center of the base toward the two nearest corners so that the base of the triangle is stretched to 6 to 7 inches. Gently pull the height to 10 inches. Do not pull from the tips, because the dough will break off. With one hand, hold the tip of the triangle opposite the elongated base, stretching the dough thinner as you roll. Put pressure on the side, not the center, of the roll. Finish with the point of the triangle facing you. Repeat with the remaining triangles.

Final Rise. Place the *cornetti* on oiled or parchment-lined baking sheets. Shape each *cornetto* into a crescent by gently pulling the tips toward each other to make a half-moon shape. Cover loosely with plastic wrap and let rise until doubled, about 2 hours. To encourage the rising, you can place the sheet of *cornetti* over a bowl of warm water or place it in a turned-off oven with a pan of warm water under it. Do not let rise over direct heat, such as a pilot light or hot radiator.

GLAZE
1 large egg, beaten

Brush the risen *cornetti* lightly with the beaten egg.

Baking. Preheat the oven to 425°F. Bake 6 minutes. Reduce the heat to 375°F and bake until golden, about 15 minutes. Cool completely on racks.

Freezing. The dough may be frozen for up to 10 days after the final turn or after shaping. Wrap the dough airtight in aluminum foil or tightly cover the shaped dough on baking sheets with foil. Thaw in the refrigerator 24 hours before shaping or before the final rise and baking.

Variation. To make filled *cornetti*, use 1 teaspoon raspberry or strawberry jam, 1 teaspoon almond paste (just before baking sprinkle the tops with slivered almonds), or 1 teaspoon pastry cream (page 324) for each *cornetto*. Spoon the filling onto the stretched triangle about 1 inch from the base. Flatten the mound slightly and then roll up. Proceed as directed but allow 2 to 3 hours for the final rise. Bake the filled *cornetti* 3 to 5 minutes longer than the plain.

Girelle RAISIN-STUDDED BREAKFAST PASTRY

These raisin-studded pastries are made from *cornetti* dough. The cinnamon is definitely an American addition.

Makes 12 pastries

Cornetti dolci dough (³/₄ recipe, page 285), made through the second set of turns and refrigerated

1 large egg, beaten

3¹/₂ teaspoons (0.5 oz / 15 g) turbinado sugar

1²/₃ cups (8.8 oz / 250 g) raisins, soaked in water, drained, and patted dry

1 teaspoon (0.1 oz / 2.5 g) ground cinnamon (optional)

3 tablespoons (1.5 oz / 42 g) apricot jam

1¹/₂ teaspoons (0.3 oz / 7.5 g) water

Place the cold dough on a lightly floured surface; sprinkle the top lightly with flour. Roll the dough into a 15 by 12-inch rectangle, lifting the dough frequently with a dough scraper and sprinkling with flour to prevent the dough from sticking. Brush the entire surface of the dough with the beaten egg. Sprinkle the sugar evenly over the egg and distribute the raisins evenly over the sugar. Sprinkle with cinnamon, if using.

Shaping. Starting with the shortest side, roll up the dough tightly, without pulling or stretching, into a log. Press the seam with your fingertips to seal it. Transfer to a sheet of aluminum foil and wrap securely. Refrigerate until cold, about 20 minutes. Cut the cold dough into 1-inch slices, using a very sharp thin-bladed knife. Place the slices, cut side up, 2 inches apart on a parchment-lined or buttered baking sheet. Press down on each slice lightly with the palm of your hand to even it and then reshape into a circle. If the spirals are stuck together, gently separate with the tip of a knife.

Rising. Cover loosely with plastic wrap and let rise until doubled, 1¹/₂ to 3 hours. See rising directions for *cornetti dolci* (page 285).

Baking. Preheat the oven to 375°F. Bake until lightly browned, 25 to 30 minutes. Transfer to a rack and cool.

Glazing. Glaze *girelle* while still warm from the oven. To form a glaze, stir the apricot jam and water together over medium heat. Strain to remove any remaining chunks of fruit and lightly brush over the tops of the *girelle* with a pastry brush.

Savory Croissants

Cornetto Salato Dough SAVORY CROISSANT DOUGH

Although the Italians are famous for their collective sweet tooth, it isn't just sweet croissants or *cornetti* that they eat. Walk into any *caffè* bar in the morning to pick out a pastry to go with espresso or cappuccino, and you will always see both sweet and savory croissants. *Cornetto salato* dough is used for all kinds of appetizers and hors d'oeuvres, turnovers, and one baker's special re-creation of the famous delicate *focaccia di Recco*, the cheese-filled specialty of a tiny town near Genoa. If you've never made croissants before, start with the largest savory pastries, such as *focaccia di Recco* (page 297). The smaller turnovers and *mignon* pastries require more dexterity and familiarity with croissant dough.

Makes 3 pounds (1.4 kg) dough

3³/₄ teaspoons (0.4 oz / 10.6 g) active dry yeast

1 teaspoon (0.3 oz / 7 g) malt syrup

1¹/₃ cups (11.2 oz / 320 g) warm water

2 tablespoons (1 oz / 28 g) unsalted butter, at room temperature

2 tablespoons (1 oz / 28 g) lard or unsalted butter, at room temperature

2²/₃ cups (13.1 oz / 375 g) unbleached all-purpose flour

1 cup minus 2 tablespoons (4.4 oz / 125 g) bread flour

2¹/₂ teaspoons (0.4 oz / 12.5 g) salt

BY HAND

Stir the yeast and malt into the water in a large mixing bowl; let stand until foamy, about 10 minutes. Beat in the butter and lard. Mix the flours and salt and stir into the yeast mixture, 1 cup at a time, until the dough comes together. Knead on a lightly floured surface until smooth, firm, and velvety, 2 to 3 minutes. Do not overknead or the dough will become too elastic.

BY MIXER

Stir the yeast and malt into the water in a large mixer bowl; let stand until foamy, about 10 minutes. Beat in the butter and lard with the paddle until blended. Mix the flours and salt and mix into the yeast mixture at the lowest speed just until the flour is absorbed. Mix at medium speed for 1 minute, no longer. Knead by hand on a lightly floured surface only sixteen to eighteen times. The dough should be smooth, firm, velvety, and slightly springy.

First Rise. Place the dough in a lightly oiled bowl, cover tightly with plastic wrap and let rise until doubled, 1 to 1¹/₂ hours.

Chilling. Punch the dough down hard on a lightly floured surface; flatten to a 1-inch-thick circle without kneading it. Wrap in plastic wrap and refrigerate until the dough is absolutely cold throughout, at least 3 hours or overnight.

BUTTER BLOCK

4 sticks (1 lb / 450 g) cold unsalted butter, or 3 sticks plus 1 tablespoon (12.4 oz / 355 g) cold unsalted butter and ¹/₂ cup (4 oz / 112 g) cold lard

¹/₂ cup (2.5 oz / 70 g) unbleached all-purpose flour

BY HAND

Place the butter on a work surface. Holding a rolling pin by one handle, beat the butter until malleable and creamy. Sprinkle the flour on the work surface. Scrape the softened butter from the work surface with a dough scraper, and, using the scraper, cut the butter into the flour. Working quickly, smear the butter and flour together with the dough scraper and the heel of your hand until smooth. Scrape the mixture together into a smooth block about ¹/₂ inch thick. It should still be cold, but if it isn't, refrigerate, wrapped in plastic wrap, 15 to 20 minutes.

BY MIXER

Cut the butter into ¹/₂-inch pieces and place the butter and flour in a mixer bowl. Beat at low speed with the paddle 1 to 2 minutes; beat at medium speed until smooth, about 2 minutes. The mixture should still be stiff and cold, but if it isn't, refrigerate, wrapped in plastic wrap, 15 to 20 minutes.

BY PROCESSOR

Cut the butter into ¹/₂-inch pieces and place the butter and flour in a food processor fitted with the steel blade. Process until smooth.

Enclosing the Butter Block. Remove the dough from the refrigerator and place on a lightly floured surface. Sprinkle the dough lightly with flour and roll into a 20 by 12-inch rectangle, so that one short side is nearest you. Break off small (¹/₂-inch) pieces from the butter block and dot them over two-thirds of the dough rectangle, leaving a 1-inch border around the edges. Fold as if you were folding a business letter: fold the unbuttered third over the middle and fold the remaining third over the top. Pinch the edges together so the butter doesn't fall out. Shape the folded dough with your fingers to even the edges and keep the rectangular shape. Tap the surface of the dough lightly with the rolling pin to evenly distribute the butter.

First Set of Turns. Turn the dough 90 degrees so that the top flap faces your right (like a book). Sprinkle the dough and work surface lightly with flour. Roll the dough into a 20 by 12-inch rectangle, ¹/₄ inch thick. Fold into thirds as described above, pinch the edges to seal, and tap

continued

Cornetto Salato Dough, *continued*

the dough with the rolling pin to evenly distribute the butter. Rotate the dough 90 degrees and lightly sprinkle the dough and work surface with flour. Roll out as before to a 20 by 12-inch rectangle, ¹/₄ inch thick. You may notice that rolling is slightly harder this time. Fold into thirds as described above, pinch the edges to seal, and tap the dough with the rolling pin to distribute the butter evenly. Brush off any excess flour and straighten the sides of the dough. Wrap the dough in plastic wrap and refrigerate 45 minutes to 1 hour.

Second Set of Turns. Lightly flour the work surface and the dough. Place the dough on the surface with the top flap facing your right. Lightly tap the surface of the dough evenly with the rolling pin. Roll into a 20 by 12-inch rectangle, rolling first for length, then width. You may need to pull the dough gently with your fingers to get the right width. Adjust the corners carefully to keep the dough even. Fold the short edges to meet in the middle and then fold in half, flipping one piece over the other (as if closing a book). Brush off the excess flour and turn the dough 90 degrees so that the top flap faces your right. Lightly tap the surface of the dough evenly with the rolling pin. You may need to refrigerate the dough for 30 minutes before the next turn if

the dough is feisty and fights back. Roll again into a 20 by 12-inch rectangle and fold like a business letter (into thirds) and brush off the excess flour. Pinch the edges to seal and lightly tap the surface of the dough evenly with the rolling pin. Wrap in plastic wrap and refrigerate at least 3 hours or overnight.

Freezing. The dough may be frozen for up to 10 days after the final turn or after shaping. Wrap the dough airtight in aluminum foil or tightly cover the shaped dough on baking sheets with foil. Thaw in the refrigerator at least 24 hours.

Fazzoletti Salati SAVORY TURNOVERS

Makes 20 turnovers

1^1/$_2$ pounds (675 g) cornetto salato dough
(^{1}/$_2$ recipe, page 290)

Any savory filling on page 295

Cutting. Place the dough on a lightly floured surface and dust the top with flour. Roll the dough into an 18^1/$_2$ by 15-inch rectangle, keeping the edges as straight as possible. Trim the edges, if necessary, with a sharp knife. Cut the dough into twenty 3^1/$_2$-inch squares.

Filling and Shaping. Stretch the center of each square slightly to make a pocket for the filling. Spoon ^{3}/$_4$ to 1 teaspoon of the filling on each square. Lightly moisten a soft pastry brush with water and brush the circumference of one square; immediately fold the dough in half to make a triangle. Press the edges firmly to seal in the filling without pressing directly on the cut edges. Repeat with the remaining squares. Place 2 inches apart on buttered or parchment-lined baking sheets.

Rising. Cover with plastic wrap and let rise until doubled, 1^1/$_2$ to 2^1/$_2$ hours.

Baking. Preheat the oven to 450°F. Bake on a rack in the upper third of the oven for 6 minutes. Reduce the heat to 375°F and bake until golden brown, 12 to 14 minutes longer. Cool completely on racks.

Variation. To make smaller turnovers, which are the perfect size for hors d'oeuvres, roll 1 pound (450 g, ^{1}/$_3$ recipe) of the dough into a 20 by 10-inch rectangle and cut into 3-inch squares. Proceed as directed, spooning ^{3}/$_4$ teaspoon of the filling on each square. They will need to bake about 2 minutes less than the slightly larger turnovers.

Canoe Salate SAVORY CANOES

Makes 16 pastries

1 pound (450 g) cornetto salato dough
  (¹/₃ recipe, page 290)

Any savory filling (recipes follow)

Cutting. Place the cold dough on a lightly floured surface and dust the top with flour. Roll the dough into a rectangle slightly larger than 24¹/₂ by 8 inches, keeping the edges as straight as possible. Trim the edges, if necessary, to 24 by 7 inches with a sharp knife. Cut the dough into sixteen rectangles, each 3¹/₂ by 3 inches.

Filling and Shaping. Spoon 1 teaspoon of the filling on the center of each rectangle. Lightly moisten a soft pastry brush with water and brush the long edges of each rectangle. Fold the short edges over to meet; they will barely meet at the center because of the filling but will overlap at the sides by ³/₄ inch. Open up the center so that the filling peeks out. Press the edges firmly to seal, without pressing directly on the cut edges. Repeat with the remaining rectangles. Place 1 to 1¹/₂ inches apart on an oiled or parchment-lined baking sheet.

Rising. Cover with plastic wrap and let rise until doubled, 1¹/₂ to 2¹/₂ hours.

Baking. Preheat the oven to 425°F. Bake on a rack in the upper third of the oven for 6 minutes. Reduce the heat to 375°F and bake until golden brown, 12 to 14 minute longer. Cool completely on racks.

Savory Fillings for Cornetto Salato Dough

I was so inspired by the buttery, flaky quality of savory croissant dough that I dreamed up these fillings. Most use just a few ingredients, and you can certainly create your own variations.

Makes enough for 16 to 20 turnovers or canoes

RICOTTA, PROSCIUTTO, AND CHEESE FILLING

²/₃ cup (5.3 oz / 150 g) ricotta

1¹/₂ tablespoons (0.7 oz / 20 g) diced prosciutto

2 tablespoons (0.5 oz / 15 g) grated pecorino
    or Parmesan cheese

¹/₈ teaspoon freshly grated nutmeg

1 large egg

Press the ricotta through a wire-mesh sieve into a mixing bowl; stir in the prosciutto, pecorino or Parmesan, nutmeg, and egg with a wooden spoon or rubber spatula until well blended. Or place the ricotta in a food processor fitted with the steel blade and process with several pulses; add the prosciutto, cheese, nutmeg, and egg and process until blended.

TOMATO FILLING

4 to 6 tablespoons (1.8 to 2.6 oz / 50 to 75 g)
    chopped sun-dried tomatoes packed in oil

²/₃ cup (1 oz / 28 g) fresh bread crumbs

²/₃ cup water (5.3 oz / 160 g) or ¹/₃ cup (2.8 oz /
    80 g) water plus 5 tablespoons (2.4 oz / 70 g)
    olive oil, preferably from the jar of tomatoes

2 tablespoons (0.5 oz / 15 g) grated Parmesan
    cheese

Process all the ingredients in a blender or food processor fitted with the steel blade until blended.

OLIVE PASTE FILLING

¹/₂ cup (0.9 oz / 23 g) fresh bread crumbs

²/₃ cup (6.1 oz / 175 g) olive paste

¹/₂ teaspoon (0.07 oz / 2 g) minced garlic

2 tablespoons (0.5 oz / 15 g) grated Parmesan
    cheese

2 tablespoons (1 oz / 30 g) milk

Process all the ingredients in a blender or food processor fitted with the steel blade until blended.

ANCHOVY FILLING

2 small cans (3¹/₂ oz / 100 g each) anchovy fillets
    packed in oil, drained

1 cup (1.5 oz / 44 g) fresh bread crumbs

¹/₂ cup (4.2 oz / 120 g) milk

2 tablespoons (1 oz / 28 g) unsalted butter, at
    room temperature

Process all the ingredients in a blender or food processor fitted with the steel blade until blended.

Cornettini Mignons Salati con Cumino e Sale

TINY SAVORY CROISSANTS WITH CARAWAY SEEDS AND SALT

Serve with smoked turkey, prosciutto, or ham. These make perfect hors d'oeuvres.

Makes 26 pastries

1 pound (450 g) cornetto salato dough
 (¹/₃ recipe, page 290)

1 large egg, beaten

1 tablespoon (0.5 oz / 15 g) water

Salt

Caraway seeds

Cutting. Place the cold dough on a lightly floured surface and dust the top with flour. Roll the dough into a 28 by 11-inch rectangle. Trim to a 28 by 10-inch rectangle with a sharp knife, then cut the rectangle lengthwise in half. The croissants will be formed from triangles cut from the two pastry strips, now each 28 by 5 inches. Cover the strip of dough that you are not working with. Place one strip on the work surface so that one long edge is facing you. Measure each strip into fourteen triangles by marking off every 4 inches at the top and base. Beginning with the lower left-hand corner, cut across diagonally to the first mark on the top. Cut straight back to the first mark on the bottom. Keep cutting triangles by cutting diagonally from bottom to top and straight down from top to bottom, connecting at the marks. Repeat with the second strip of dough.

Shaping. Position a triangle so that the base is nearest you. Stretch the base to 5 inches and gently stretch the height to 9 inches. Holding the top with one hand, tightly roll up the triangle from the base with the other hand. Put firm but gentle pressure on the sides, not the center, of the roll. Mix the egg and water in a small bowl and brush the tops with the egg wash. Sprinkle with a pinch of salt and a dash of caraway seeds. Repeat with the remaining triangles. Place 1¹/₂ inches apart on buttered or parchment-lined baking sheets. Don't shape the ends into a crescent, like *cornetti,* but leave them straight.

Rising. Cover loosely with a towel and let rise until doubled, 1 to 2 hours.

Baking. Preheat the oven to 425°F. Bake on a rack in the upper third of the oven for 6 minutes. Reduce the heat to 375°F and bake until dark golden, 12 to 14 minutes longer. Cool completely on racks.

Focaccia di Recco CHEESE FOCACCIA FROM RECCO

Signs on every restaurant and bakery in the seaside town of Recco boast of *focaccia di formaggio*, which is essentially two veils of strudel-like dough enclosing delicate *straccinella* (a local cheese). This elegant fantasy with its melting cheese interior was inspired by the famous version from the restaurant Manuellina, but, as baked by Giancarlo Grignani in Milan, it uses flaky croissant dough, stracchino cheese, and a bit of salt. It is as elegant a dish as Italy offers.

Makes one 9- to 11-inch focaccia

1 pound (450 g) cornetto salato dough
  (¹/₃ recipe, page 290)

6 to 8 ounces (180 to 225 g) crescenza, stracchino,
  or Taleggio cheese, thinly sliced

1 to 1¹/₂ teaspoons (0.15 to 0.22 oz / 5 to 7.5 g)
  delicate olive oil, preferably Ligurian

Generous pinch of salt

Shaping and Filling. Place the cold dough on a lightly floured surface and dust the top with flour. Roll the dough into a 20 by 10-inch rectangle and cut crosswise in half. Pull out the sides of each square and shape each into a rough circle; trim off the square corner edges. The dough circles can be 9 to 10 inches in diameter, but they should be the same size. Place 1 dough circle on a baking sheet lined with parchment or brown paper. Arrange the cheese over the circle on the baking sheet, leaving a 1¹/₂-inch border. Brush the edge with water. Place the second dough circle over the cheese. Trim and seal the edges. Brush the surface lightly with water.

Rising. Cover with plastic wrap and let rise in a spot warm enough to aid the rising but not so warm that the butter will melt in the dough. The dough should be puffy and risen, although not truly doubled, about 2 hours for the 9-inch and 2¹/₂ to 3 hours for the 11-inch pastry.

Baking. Preheat the oven to 450°F. Just before baking, brush the top with the oil and sprinkle with a generous pinch of salt. Bake on a rack in the upper third of the oven 8 to 10 minutes. Reduce the heat to 350°F and bake the smaller focaccia 20 minutes longer and the larger focaccia 22 to 25 minutes longer. Serve warm or reheat before eating.

Puff Pastry

Pasta Sfogliata

MASTER RECIPE

Pasta sfogliata (puff pastry) is just what its name implies: sheets and sheets of fine dough, each separated by an exquisitely thin layer of butter, that rise magically from a flat rectangle about $1/2$ inch thick into a phenomenally delicate and flaky pastry dough 4 to 5 inches high. Italian bakers use puff pastry for a dazzling array of hors d'oeuvres and sweets. They sprinkle strips of dough the width of baby's fingers with cheese, anchovy paste, or sesame or poppy seeds, and then twist and bake them into straws to be nibbled upon; they make fine flaky snacks with the ironic name of *rustici*; they construct sweet puff pastry into turnovers, tarts, little horns, and fanciful boats, the vehicles for pastry cream and fruit.

Many Italian cookbooks with recipes for *pasta sfogliata* begin by suggesting that the reader go to the nearest bakery and buy the dough, or, failing that, to the supermarket for one of the frozen varieties that are now available. Unless you have a special arrangement with your baker, you probably won't be able to negotiate such a deal, but, if you have a fine gourmet grocery store in your area, you're in luck. But, since there is nothing more dramatic, delicate, and delicious than puff pastry made at home, I encourage you to make your own.

There is no question that *pasta sfogliata* takes a bit of practice and patience. The dough encloses a block of cold butter and is then rolled out and folded six times. The dough must be chilled between turns but, by the end, you'll have layered the dough into a miracle of light flakiness. You will need time—at least six hours, although you can easily refrigerate the dough overnight and work it into your schedule—and you'll need practice, because there are a few tricks to making puff pastry. But, once you've mastered it, you'll be able to make such extraordinary dishes that you'll actually be delighted that Italian bakers use puff pastry with abandon.

Because the classical method of making *pasta sfogliata* is so time-consuming, I'd recommend making a big batch and freezing what you can't use in plastic wrap or aluminum foil enclosed in an airtight plastic freezer bag. The dough keeps wonderfully in the refrigerator for two or three days and in the freezer for up to three months. Allow the dough to thaw slowly in the refrigerator over 24 hours.

A good rolling pin, 15 to 18 inches long, a good work surface—some people insist on marble, although I love my butcher-block table—and cold ingredients are essential.

The minute your dough starts to go limp or your butter block gets soft, refrigerate it until it has chilled enough to proceed, usually about 30 minutes. If the dough snaps back on itself when you are rolling it, let it rest in the refrigerator so that the gluten relaxes; after anywhere from 30 minutes to 2 hours, it will be more than happy to cooperate. Be sure to keep your work surface and your dough floured enough so that the dough can move freely on the table. You can always brush off the excess flour at the end, and you won't be caught with layers tearing because they stuck to the surface. The most important secret of puff pastry is in the chilling that is necessary after each set of turns to keep it tender and malleable as the process progresses. You'll need patience, time, and a bit of self confidence, but, once you've tackled it and succeeded, you'll be delighted with your accomplishment and can truly feel that yours is a fine Italian hand in the kitchen.

Makes 2 pounds 10¹/₂ ounces (1.2 kg) dough

DOUGH

2²/₃ cups (13.1 oz / 375 g) unbleached all-purpose flour

1 cup (4.4 oz / 125 g) pastry flour

1¹/₂ teaspoons (0.3 oz / 7.5 g) salt

1 stick (4 oz / 115 g) unsalted butter, at cool room temperature (cold if using a processor), cut into ¹/₂-inch pieces

1 cup (8.8 oz / 240 g) cold water, plus 1 to 2 tablespoons (0.5 to 1 oz / 15 to 30 g) more if needed

1 tablespoon (0.5 oz / 15 g) fresh lemon juice

BY HAND

Mix the all-purpose flour and pastry flour in a large bowl. Set aside ¹/₂ cup of the flour mixture and reserve for use in the butter block. Stir the salt into the remaining flour mixture. Add the butter and work it in with your fingertips or a pastry blender until the mixture resembles coarse meal. Mix the 1 cup of water and the lemon juice. Gradually add the liquid to the flour mixture, tossing with a fork, until the flour is evenly moistened and the dough begins to clean the sides of the bowl. If the dough is dry, add the additional water, 1 tablespoon at a time, as needed. Turn out onto a floured work surface and press (do not knead) the dough together into a round disk about 1 inch thick. Wrap in plastic wrap and refrigerate until firm and very cold, at least 1 to 2 hours or overnight.

BY MIXER

Place the unbleached flour and pastry flour in a large mixer bowl and stir to blend. Set aside ¹/₂ cup of the flour mixture and reserve for use in the butter block. Stir the salt into the remaining flour mixture. Add the butter; beat with the paddle on low speed until the mixture resembles coarse meal. Mix the 1 cup of water and the lemon juice. Pour the liquid in a thin, steady stream into the flour mixture while beating on low speed. Increase the speed slightly and beat until

continued

Pasta Sfogliata, *continued*

the dough cleans the sides of the bowl, 1 to 2 minutes. If the dough is dry, add the additional water, 1 tablespoon at a time, as needed. Beat at medium speed for 20 seconds. Turn out onto a floured work surface and press (do not knead) the dough together into a round disk about 1 inch thick. Wrap in plastic wrap and refrigerate until firm and very cold, at least 1 to 2 hours or overnight.

BY PROCESSOR

If the capacity of your food processor is 8 cups or less, process this dough in two batches. Mix the unbleached flour and pastry flour in a large bowl. Set aside $1/2$ cup of the flour mixture for use in the butter block. Stir the salt into the remaining flour mixture. Place the flour mixture in a food processor fitted with the steel blade. Place the cold butter pieces on top of the flour and process with eight to ten pulses until the mixture resembles coarse meal. With the machine running, pour the 1 cup of cold water and the lemon juice in a thin, steady stream through the feed tube. Add the additional water, 1 tablespoon at a time, as needed. Do not process until the dough gathers into a ball; it should still be ragged. Turn out onto a floured work surface and press (do not knead) the dough together into a round disk about 1 inch thick. Wrap in plastic wrap and refrigerate until firm and very cold, at least 1 to 2 hours or overnight. The dough should be completely chilled before you make the butter block.

BUTTER BLOCK

3 sticks (12 oz / 340 g) very cold unsalted butter

$1/2$ cup flour mixture reserved from the flour for the dough

Place the butter on a work surface. Holding the rolling pin by one handle, beat the butter until malleable and creamy. Sprinkle the flour on the butter. Using the dough scraper, scrape the butter from the work surface and cut the butter into the flour. Working quickly, smear the butter and flour together until the mixture is smooth. The mixture should be cool and malleable, not cold and hard or soft and runny. Flatten to a $1/2$-inch-thick block. Refrigerate or let stand at room temperature to harden or soften it if necessary. Once the butter block is the correct consistency, proceed with the remaining steps.

Enclosing the Butter Block. Lightly flour the work surface. Remove the dough from the refrigerator and lightly flour both sides. With a floured rolling pin, tap the dough gently across the surface both horizontally and vertically. Roll the dough carefully into an 18-inch circle, $1/2$ inch thick, frequently lifting the dough with a dough scraper and lightly dusting the work surface with flour to prevent sticking. Place the butter block in the center of the dough and fold the dough over the butter to completely enclose it. The edges of the dough should overlap slightly. Lift the package with the dough scraper and sprinkle flour on the work surface and the top of the dough. Tap the dough lightly with the rolling pin both horizontally and vertically. Begin to roll out the dough, pressing very lightly from the center toward you and then from the center away from you. Roll the dough carefully into an 18 by 9-inch rectangle, $1/4$ inch thick, keeping the edges as straight as possible. If the dough becomes too warm, transfer it to a baking sheet and refrigerate just long enough to chill it, usually about 30 minutes. Dust the surface of the dough and the work surface frequently with flour as you roll, lifting the edges of the dough with the dough scraper. Do not touch the dough with your hands if possible.

First Set of Turns. Fold the top third of the dough down over the middle and then fold the bottom third up over the top. Press the edges to seal. Turn the rectangle 90 degrees so that the top flap faces your right (like a book). Roll again into an 18 by 9-inch rectangle and repeat the folding. Brush off any excess flour. Wrap in plastic wrap and refrigerate 1 hour.

Second Set of Turns. Roll the dough again into an 18 by 9-inch rectangle. Fold and turn as described for the first set of turns. Reroll, dusting the work surface

and dough lightly with flour to prevent sticking. Fold and turn once again. (This is the fourth and last turn if you are making *ventaglini,* page 308). Brush off any excess flour. Wrap in plastic wrap and refrigerate 1 hour.

Third Set of Turns. Roll the dough again into an 18 by 9-inch rectangle. Fold and turn as described for the first set of turns. Reroll, dusting the work surface and dough lightly with flour to prevent sticking. Fold and turn once again. This is the sixth and final turn. Brush off any excess flour from the surface of the dough. Wrap in plastic wrap and refrigerate 4 to 6 hours before using in any of the following recipes calling for *pasta sfogliata.*

Storing. The dough can be stored in the refrigerator for up to 3 or 4 days or frozen up to 2 or 3 months. Puff pastry is best frozen after either the fourth or last turn. Wrap airtight in foil and then wrap again in plastic wrap and freeze. Thaw in the refrigerator for 24 hours. Give it the last two turns, if necessary, and refrigerate just for 2 hours before rolling out the dough for shaping.

Binario di Ricotta RICOTTA-FILLED PASTRY TART

Inside this long, thin puff pastry case is a creamy ricotta filling. Be sure to give a scalloped edge to the pastry case with the back of a butter knife.

Makes one 14 by 6 1/2-inch tart; 6 servings

2/3 cup (3.5 oz / 100 g) raisins

3 tablespoons (1.5 oz / 45 g) Marsala, rum, or maraschino liqueur

3/4 cup plus 2 tablespoons (7 oz / 200 g) ricotta

1/3 cup (2.5 oz / 70 g) sugar

2 1/2 tablespoons (0.8 oz / 23 g) unbleached all-purpose flour

2 large egg yolks, beaten

1 1/2 teaspoons (0.2 oz / 6 g) vanilla extract

1/4 cup (1.4 oz / 40 g) finely chopped candied orange peel (page 39) or mixed candied fruit, or the finely diced zest of 1/2 orange

10 1/2 ounces (300 g) pasta sfogliata (1/4 recipe, page 298)

Combine the raisins and Marsala in a small bowl; let stand until the raisins are plumped, about 30 minutes. Press the ricotta through a wire-mesh sieve or process briefly in a food processor fitted with the steel blade. Beat the ricotta and sugar with a wooden spoon in a large bowl until creamy. Stir in the flour. Add the egg yolks and beat until blended. Stir in the raisins with the Marsala, vanilla, and candied orange peel. Refrigerate, covered, while preparing the pastry.

Cutting and Shaping. Roll the cold dough on a lightly floured surface into a rectangle slightly larger than 16 by 8 1/2 inches. Pick up the edges of the dough with the dough scraper frequently while rolling to let the dough shrink back into shape before rerolling. Using a ruler and a very sharp knife, trim the dough to exactly 16 by 8 1/2 inches.

Using the straight edge of the ruler, cut a 1-inch-wide strip from each edge of the rectangle. Don't pick the strips up; just scoot them to one side. Very carefully move the remaining rectangle of dough to a parchment-lined baking sheet, placing your hands well under the dough, without pulling at the edges or stretching the rectangle. Dampen a soft pastry brush with water and brush a thin border around the rectangle. Gently move the long pastry strips to the long sides of the rectangle and the short strips to the short sides of the rectangle. Tap down gently with your fingertips in the center of the strips, without pressing on the cut edges. Dampen the strips where they overlap and trim the excess dough with a sharp knife. Prick the bottom of the tart shell evenly with a fork. Scallop the edges, using the flat side of a table knife and drawing the dough up between two fingers.

Chilling. Refrigerate the dough until cold, at least 1 hour or overnight. Cover airtight as soon as dough is cold if storing longer than 1 hour.

Baking. Preheat the oven to 425°F. Bake for 10 minutes, pricking the dough every 3 minutes to keep it from rising too much. Don't be timid; really let your fork do a vigorous dance on the bottom of the tart shell. Reduce the heat to 350°F and bake 10 minutes longer. Cool on a rack.

Filling. Spoon the filling into the baked pastry and spread evenly. Bake at 350°F until set, about 15 minutes.

Variation. To make *binario di sfoglia* (a puff pastry case), you need only line the puff pastry rectangle with strips on the long sides. Proceed as directed, but bake until golden, about 20 minutes longer at 350°F, so that the case is fully baked. Cool on a rack. Fill as desired or spread 1/4 inch of pastry cream (page 324) over the pastry and top with rows of fresh whole strawberries.

Strudel di Mele APPLE STRUDEL

The apple strudel of the northern Alto Adige region is an edible memory of the days before World War II when the whole area was the South Tirol of Austria. The German-speaking Austrians who live there have remained true to their culinary traditions as well as their language—everything is bilingual, including street signs and shop names—and apple strudel is as ubiquitous as apple pie is in America. The plains and hillsides stretching as far north as the Alps are extensively planted with orchards of the apple trees that furnish the Red and Golden Delicious and Granny Smiths of this strudel's succulent interior.

Makes 1 strudel; 8 servings (recipe can easily be doubled to make 2 strudels)

2¹/₂ cups (1 lb / 450 g) peeled and diced cooking apples (about 2 medium apples)

Grated zest of ¹/₂ lemon

³/₄ teaspoon (0.15 oz / 4 g) fresh lemon juice

³/₄ cup (5.3 oz / 150 g) turbinado sugar

³/₄ cup (2.8 oz / 80 g) crumbs from a good cake made with nuts, raisins, or dried fruit

¹/₂ cup (2.8 oz / 80 g) raisins

¹/₄ cup (1 oz / 28 g) pine nuts

2 tablespoons (1 oz / 28 g) apricot jam

³/₄ teaspoon (0.05 oz / 2 g) ground cinnamon

¹/₄ teaspoon salt

10¹/₂ ounces (300 g) pasta sfogliata (¹/₄ recipe, page 298)

1 large egg yolk

1 tablespoon (0.5 oz / 15 g) water

Toss the apples with the lemon zest and juice. Add the sugar, cake crumbs, raisins, pine nuts, apricot jam, cinnamon, and salt and stir until blended. Set aside until ready to use.

Cutting and Shaping. Roll the cold dough on a lightly floured surface into a 16 by 11-inch rectangle. Using a straight edge and a sharp knife, trim the dough to a 15 by 9¹/₂-inch rectangle. Carefully transfer, without stretching, to a parchment-lined baking sheet. Using a ruler, make light indentations in the dough 2¹/₂ inches in from each long side (see page 306). This will leave a middle strip of dough about 4¹/₂ inches wide. Spoon the apple filling evenly along this middle strip. Make 2¹/₂-inch-long cuts, 1¹/₄ inches apart, in both long sides of the rectangle. Carefully separate the dough strips with your fingers. Starting at the far end, overlap opposite strips on a modified diagonal over the filling forming a modified braid. As you work, brush the underside of each strip with a lightly dampened pastry brush. Finish the braid by using the last strips to seal the end, tucking the tips of the strips under the strudel. Refrigerate 1 hour.

Baking. Preheat the oven to 450°F. Mix the egg yolk and water and brush

continued

Strudel di Mele, *continued*

the top lightly with the egg wash. Bake on a rack in the upper third of the oven for 5 minutes. Reduce the heat to 375°F and bake 55 minutes longer. If after 30 minutes the top is too dark, reduce the heat to 325°F to finish baking. Cool on a rack.

Make light indentations in the dough 2¹/₂ inches from each long side.

Separate the dough strips with your fingertips. Brush the underside of each strip with a pastry brush.

Overlap opposite strips on a modified diagonal over the filling.

Tuck the tips of the final strips under the strudel.

Canoe di Mele APPLE CANOES

A fantasy of puff pastry: canoe-shaped pastry boats layered with rum-spiked pastry cream and topped with sugar-glazed apples.

Makes 9 pastries

1 pound 5 ounces (600 g) pasta sfogliata
(^{1}/2 recipe, page 298)

2 large eggs, beaten

9 tablespoons (5.4 oz / 144 g) pastry cream
(page 324)

2 cooking apples (about 1 lb / 450 g), peeled,
cored, and cut into ^{1}/8-inch slices

2 tablespoons (1 oz / 28 g) turbinado sugar

^{1}/3 cup plus 1 tablespoon (2.8 oz / 80 g) apricot jam

1 teaspoon (0.2 oz / 5 g) water

1 teaspoon (0.2 oz / 5 g) fresh lemon juice

Cutting. Roll the dough out on a lightly floured surface into a 16 by 10-inch rectangle, ^{1}/8 inch thick. Using a straight edge and a sharp knife, trim to a 15 by 9-inch rectangle. Cut the dough into nine 5 by 3-inch rectangles. Brush the surface with the beaten eggs. Gently stretch each rectangle very slightly from the short ends.

Shaping and Filling. Position one rectangle with a long side facing you. Place 1 tablespoon of the pastry cream on the center of the rectangle. Place 4 or 5 apple slices, slightly overlapping, diagonally across the rectangle and on top of the pastry cream. Brush the edges of the dough lightly with some of the beaten eggs. Fold one short side of the dough, from left to right, over the apples to the enter. Press the edge to seal. Don't worry if you can't see the apples inside; the center will open when it is baked. Using a dough scraper or spatula, carefully transfer to a parchment-lined baking sheet. Repeat with the remaining dough, pastry cream, and apples. Space 2 inches apart on the baking sheet.

Refrigerate, covered loosely with plastic wrap, at least 1 hour but no longer than overnight.

Baking. Preheat the oven to 400°F. Lightly brush the tops with beaten egg and sprinkle with sugar. Bake until lightly browned, about 30 minutes. Remove to a rack to cool.

Glazing. Combine the apricot jam, water, and lemon juice in a small saucepan. Place over low heat, stirring constantly, until hot. Brush over the apple canoes while they are still warm. Eat while still slightly warm or at room temperature.

Ventaglini LITTLE FANS

In France these sugar-glazed and caramelized pastries are known as *palmiers*, or palm leaves, but when you cross the border into Italy, they become *ventagli* or *ventaglini*, little fans of delicate puff pastry that are crunchy with the sugar that covers their folds and shiny surfaces.

Makes 26 pastries

1 cup (7 oz / 200 g) sugar

1 pound 5 ounces (600 g) pasta sfogliata
   (¹/₂ recipe, page 298), made through two
   sets of turns

Sprinkle ¹/₂ cup of the sugar onto your work surface, place the cold dough on top of it, and give the dough its last two turns. Roll the dough into a 15 by 12-inch rectangle. Fold it in thirds, as you would a business letter. Press the edges to seal and tap the dough lightly with the rolling pin both horizontally and vertically. Turn the rectangle 90 degrees, so that the top flap faces your right (like a book). Roll into a 15 by 12-inch rectangle about ¹/₄ inch thick, dusting the surface with the sugar on your work surface to prevent sticking and lifting the dough frequently with the dough scraper. Fold in thirds once again. Lift the dough and sprinkle the sugar that remains on the surface over and under the dough. Work in as much sugar as you can.

Shaping. Position the dough on your work surface so that the short edge is nearest you. Fold 1¹/₂ inches from the top toward the center. Fold 1¹/₂ inches from the bottom up toward the center. Con-

tinue to fold the dough from the top and bottom until they meet at the center, and then fold in half as if you were closing a book. The dough will now be ten layers thick. Tap the entire surface firmly with your rolling pin. Cut the dough crosswise into ¹/₂-inch slices, about the width of a finger. Place the *ventagli*, cut sides up, 2 to 3 inches apart on parchment-lined baking sheets. Sprinkle about ¹/₂ to ³/₄ teaspoon of the remaining sugar over each pastry and cover with plastic wrap. Reserve any more remaining sugar for the baking.

Refrigerate for about 30 minutes. The dough must be cold, but do not refrigerate too long or the sugar will ooze out during the baking and will not caramelize properly.

Baking. Preheat the oven to 400°F. Open the top of each piece of dough like a flower by separating the layers, then pinch the bottom together. *Ventagli* look like the little fans for which they are named, but they also resemble tulips or fuchsia blossoms. Sprinkle the remaining sugar over the cookies. Bake until the tops are golden brown and well caramelized, about 10 minutes. Using a spatula, check the bottoms; as each caramelizes, turn it over and bake until equally caramelized on the other side, 5 to 10 minutes. Watch them carefully, because they burn with almost no warning and they bake at surprisingly different speeds. Place the *ventagli* on a rack

to cool. Be sure they are completely cool before you stack them or they will stick to each other. They keep well for at least a week in an airtight container.

Fazzoletti Dolci LITTLE HANDKERCHIEFS OF PUFF PASTRY

These little pastries, filled with a delicate ricotta, raisin, and rum–flavored filling, are really turnovers, Italian style.

Makes 12 pastries

Scant 1 cup (7 oz / 200 g) ricotta

$^1/_3$ cup plus 1 tablespoon (2.8 oz / 80 g) granulated sugar

2 large egg yolks

3 tablespoons (1.5 oz / 45 g) rum, Marsala, or maraschino liqueur

$1^1/_2$ tablespoons (0.6 oz / 17 g) vanilla extract

2 teaspoons (0.2 oz / 6 g) unbleached all-purpose flour

$^2/_3$ cup (3.5 oz / 100 g) raisins or $^1/_3$ cup (1.8 oz / 50 g) finely chopped candied orange peel (page 39) and $^1/_3$ cup (1.8 oz / 50 g) raisins

$10^1/_2$ ounces (300 g) pasta sfogliata ($^1/_4$ recipe, page 298)

1 to 2 large eggs, beaten

Confectioners' sugar, for sprinkling (optional)

Press the ricotta through a wire-mesh sieve into a mixing bowl or process with several pulses in a food processor fitted with the steel blade and transfer to a mixing bowl. Add the sugar, egg yolks, rum, vanilla, and

flour and stir to blend. Stir in the raisins and orange peel, if using. Refrigerate, covered, until very cold, about $1^1/_2$ to 2 hours or overnight.

Cutting. Place the cold dough on a lightly floured surface and dust the top lightly with flour. Roll the dough into a rectangle $^1/_8$ inch thick and slightly larger than 20 by 15 inches. This is a very fine, thin dough that must have straight edges. Trim the edges with a sharp knife. Cut the dough into twelve 5-inch squares.

Filling and Shaping. Stretch the center of each square gently, taking care not to handle the cut edges, to make a pocket for the filling. Spoon 2 tablespoons of the filling on each square. Brush the circumference of one square with the beaten egg; fold the dough in half, enclosing the filling and making a triangle. Press the edges firmly to seal in the filling, without pressing directly on the cut edges.

continued

Fazzoletti Dolci, *continued*

Repeat with the remaining squares. Place 2 inches apart on parchment-lined baking sheets.

Chilling. Refrigerate at least 1 hour. If you don't want to bake them all, freeze the cold unbaked pastries in plastic bags. You can bake the frozen pastries without thawing them first.

Glazing. Brush the tops with the beaten egg and poke 2 or 3 little holes in each to allow steam to escape. Sprinkle the pastries with confectioners' sugar, if you want.

Baking. Preheat the oven to 400°F. Bake until golden, about 30 minutes. Transfer to racks to cool.

Cannoncini LITTLE CANNONS

These pastries look just like the little cannons they are named for, but, instead of being filled with lethal ammunition, they are rich with pastry cream, which is lethal only for the waistline. These shiny little spirals of puff pastry are found all over Italy from Piedmont and the Veneto to the tip of the boot and are favorites of children who love to bite into one side and feel the cream shoot out the other.

Makes 10 pastries

8 ounces (225 g) pasta sfogliata (about ¹/₈ recipe, page 298)

1 large egg, beaten

¹/₃ cup (2.5 oz / 70 g) sugar

1¹/₄ to 1¹/₂ cups (11 to 14 oz / 320 to 385 g) pastry cream (page 324), or ³/₄ cup (6.3 oz / 180 g) cold cream, whipped to firm peaks with 1¹/₂ tablespoons (0.7 oz / 20 g) sugar and ¹/₂ teaspoon (0.07 oz / 2 g) vanilla extract

Cutting and Shaping. Roll the cold dough on a lightly floured work surface into a 10 by 8-inch rectangle, ¹/₄ to ¹/₂ inch thick. Cut the dough crosswise into ten 1-inch-wide strips. Butter cannoli tubes. Wrap one strip of the dough around each cannoli tube, moistening it with a brush while rotating the tube; overlap the dough about ¹/₄ inch as you wrap, leaving 1 inch of the tube uncovered at one end. Lightly brush the wrapped dough with the beaten egg and then roll in the sugar. Place the tubes 2 inches apart on a parchment-lined baking sheet.

Refrigerate, covered, for 30 minutes. The dough can also be stored, wrapped airtight, in the freezer at this point and baked later.

Baking. Preheat the oven to 400°F. Bake until lightly browned and slightly caramelized, about 20 minutes. Let cool completely on a rack. Using the tip of a knife, gently remove the cannoli tubes.

Filling. Just before serving, fill a pastry bag with the pastry cream or flavored whipped cream. Pipe each *cannoncino* full of cream.

Savory Appetizers

Salatini alle Acciughe ANCHOVY-FLAVORED STRAWS

In Italy these savory appetizers are also called *stuzzichini*. This bit of slang comes from the word *stuzzicare*, which means "to prod or poke," and these lovely, buttery puff pastry straws, which surprise with the bite of anchovy at the end, are meant to excite your taste buds.

Makes about 2 dozen straws

10¹/₂ ounces (300 g) pasta sfogliata
 (¹/₄ recipe, page 298)

2 tablespoons (1 oz / 28 g) anchovy paste

Place the cold dough on a lightly floured surface and dust the top lightly with flour. Roll the dough into a 16 by 8¹/₂-inch rectangle, about ¹/₄ inch thick. Beat the anchovy paste vigorously with a fork and then spread it over half the dough. Fold the dough in half so that the short ends meet, enclosing the filling. Lightly roll into a 10 by 8¹/₂-inch rectangle, distributing the paste evenly. Straighten the edges with your hands so that the dough looks neat and trim.

Chilling. Cover the dough with plastic wrap and refrigerate until completely cold, at least 30 minutes.

Cutting and Shaping. Place the dough on a lightly floured surface. Cut lengthwise into ¹/₂-inch wide strips, using a sharp knife and a straight edge. Twist each strip three or four times so that it looks like an old-fashioned barber's pole, and place 1 inch apart on unoiled aluminum baking sheets. Press the edges down firmly to anchor them in place. If they pop up, simply retwist them and press them firmly back in place. I like to use the backs of 10-inch-wide baking pans so that the edges can be pressed into the edges of the pans; it seems to help.

Baking. Preheat the oven to 400°F. Bake until golden, 15 to 18 minutes. Transfer to racks to cool. You may reheat at 300°F for 5 minutes before serving.

Salatini al Sesamo SESAME SEED STRAWS

Makes about 2 dozen straws

10¹/₂ ounces (300 g) pasta sfogliata
  (¹/₄ recipe, page 298)

1 large egg, beaten

1 teaspoon (0.2 oz / 5 g) water

¹/₂ cup (2 oz / 60 g) sesame seeds

Place the cold dough on a lightly floured surface and dust the top lightly with flour. Roll the dough into a 16 by 8¹/₂-inch rectangle, about ¹/₄ inch thick. Beat the egg and water together in a small bowl. Using a pastry brush, brush the entire surface of the dough with the egg wash and sprinkle with half the sesame seeds. Pat the seeds gently into the dough with your hands. Turn the dough over, brush the surface with the egg wash, and sprinkle with the remaining sesame seeds. Fold the dough in half so that the short ends meet. Lightly roll the dough into a 10 by 8¹/₂-inch rectangle, distributing the seeds evenly.

Chilling. Cover the dough with plastic wrap and refrigerate until completely cold, about 30 minutes. The dough can also be refrigerated up to 24 hours or frozen, wrapped airtight, up to 3 months.

Cut, shape, and bake the straws as directed for *salatini alle acciughe* (page 312).

Variations. To make *salatini ai papaveri* (poppy seed straws), substitute ¹/₄ cup (0.5 oz / 14 g) of poppy seeds for the sesame seeds.

To make *salatini al formaggio* (cheese straws), roll out the dough in ²/₃ cup (2.3 oz / 65 g) of grated Parmesan or pecorino cheese instead of flour. You can also combine the cheese with the sesame seeds for a tender, delicate hors d'oeuvre full of toasted sesame seeds.

Rustici LITTLE PUFF PASTRY TREATS FROM LECCE

The people in Lecce eat *rustici* for quick lunches and snacks the way Neapolitans eat pizza. Every bakery and *caffè* bar has its own version, but they all start with a creamy cheese-flavored *beschiamella* sauce and a slice of tomato. Some bakers make them as tiny bite-size hors d'oeuvres and others as bigger rounds, but most make them into perfect 3^1/$_2$- or 4-inch ovals, which are as likely to turn up at birthdays and celebrations as at everyday meals. And should you go to Lecce and find people walking around eating something flaky wrapped in a napkin, you'll see *rustici* on the run.

Makes 12 pastries

BESCHIAMELLA SAUCE

6 tablespoons (3 oz / 85 g) unsalted butter

^{2}/$_3$ cup (3.3 oz / 95 g) unbleached all-purpose flour

2^1/$_3$ cups (1 lb 4 oz / 560 g) milk

1 cup plus 3 tablespoons (4.9 oz / 140 g) grated
　　Parmesan or pecorino cheese

1^1/$_2$ cups (8.75 oz / 250 g) finely sliced fresh
　　mozzarella cheese

Salt and freshly ground pepper

Melt the butter in a heavy saucepan over low heat and gradually whisk in the flour. Cook, whisking occasionally, 5 to 6 minutes. Gradually whisk in the milk; cook, stirring constantly, until thick and smooth, about 10 minutes. Stir in the cheeses, and salt and pepper to taste.

PASTRIES

1 pound 5 ounces (600 g) pasta sfogliata
　　(^{1}/$_2$ recipe, page 298)

1 large egg

2 teaspoons (0.4 oz / 10 g) water

6 sun-dried tomatoes packed in oil, cut in half,
　　or 12 slices fresh ripe plum tomatoes

12 fresh basil leaves (optional)

Place the cold dough on a lightly floured surface and dust the top lightly with flour. Roll the dough into a 21 by 15-inch rectangle. Using a 3^1/$_2$-inch round or oval cookie cutter, cut out the dough. Mix the egg and water together. Brush the circumference of half of the cutouts with egg wash and spoon about 2 to 2^1/$_2$ teaspoons of the sauce on the middle of the egg-washed circle. Cover with a slice of tomato and a fresh basil leaf (the basil is strictly my addition, but I like how it tastes). Top each filled circle with a plain circle and press the edges firmly to seal in the filling without pressing directly on the cut edges. With the edges of your palms, press gently around the filled center so that you can see the outline of the filling clearly. Place the pastries 1 inch apart on buttered or parchment-lined baking sheets. Refrigerate, covered with plastic wrap, for at least 4 hours or overnight. Brush the tops with egg wash.

Baking. Preheat the oven to 400°F. Bake 15 minutes. Reduce the heat to 350°F and bake 15 minutes longer. Serve hot, warm, or at room temperature. Do not refrigerate.

DOLCI

Crostate

Tarts

Of the two traditions of baking sweets in Italy, one is based on the simple and homey desserts that families make year after year for friends and guests. These simple desserts are much cozier than the Italian extravaganzas that look more designed than baked, architectural marvels tucked full of pastry creams and sumptuous frothy interiors. These more domestic sweets have perfumed mountain houses in the Val d'Aosta, simple farmhouses near Bologna, villas in the Tuscan countryside, and apartments in Rome. Emanating from a simple way of life, they almost invariably start with *pasta frolla*, the basic sweet dough of Italy, which dates back to the late Renaissance.

Crostate are made only with *pasta frolla*, and each dessert takes it name from the fruit or jam that fills the tart. The first *crostata* I ate in Italy was made by a woman who came to help when we had just moved into our house in a small Ligurian town. From her string bag, she pulled eggs from her chickens and a jar of homemade strawberry preserves. She went right to work, making a simple sweet dough with a bit of flour and sugar, some butter, and the two eggs that were still warm to the touch. She kneaded them together quickly with a light hand, telling me that I could pat the dough in place immediately by hand but that I would have to refrigerate it if I wanted to roll it for a thinner crust. Then she simply lined the pie plate with the dough, baked it enough to set it, filled it with her strawberry preserves, made a lattice of dough strips on the top, and baked it in the oven until it was golden. It was simple and uncomplicated, a bit of a sweet ending to a cozy country dinner. Over the time that we lived there, she repeated that *crostata*, sometimes with berries or peaches (the peaches of Italy must be the Platonic ideal, for there are none so sweet and juicy and full of flavor), and each one was always wonderful.

These *crostate* are, in fact, sold at the *forni*, bakeries where both bread and pastries are made, and the baking tends to be simple and straightforward. Nuts, fruits, and jams are the bases of most of the tarts, although bakers can transform the simplest ingredients into extravagant fare. The *torta del nonno* is essentially chocolate pudding tucked into a soft, buttery crust. Even the *torta dumont* is a simple dessert from the mountains of France that found its way over the border and into the Italian tradition. Of course, you will not be surprised that a few lemons may be transformed into a cool lemon soufflé set in a crust or that hazelnut filling may be glazed with chocolate, for Italian bakers are given to invention and can create tantalizing tastes from the simplest ingredients.

Basic Tart Doughs

Pasta Frolla SWEET SHORT PASTRY

MASTER RECIPE

Pasta frolla is the basic pastry dough of Italian baking. Although there are numerous variations on the basic theme, most recipes are based on ratios of flour to butter and sugar. The most common proportions seem to be two parts flour to one part butter and one part sugar or three parts flour to two parts butter and one part sugar. This is not to say that a baker's individuality isn't expressed in numerous personal touches. Some bakers use a lot more sugar or a lot less, while others use more butter or add a bit of lard; some use potato flour to make a finer dough, while others add baking powder when they are putting the crust together for tarts. Some use only egg yolks instead of whole eggs, and some insist that the only permissible flavoring is vanilla, while others would never use it or would add lemon or orange flavoring, orange flower water, or a liqueur, depending on the dough's destination.

Pasta frolla is often made into cookie dough and can be made with corn flour (and is then known as *pasta melgun*) or with whole wheat flour (*pasta frolla integrale*). Then there is a special *pasta frolla* used only on November 11, the saint's day of Saint Martin, when bakers in Venice sculpt a pastry portrait of Saint Martin on horseback and decorate it with a medallion of quince jam and silver and gold confetti. A chocolate-spiked *pasta frolla* from Piedmont is used mainly for cream-filled *crostate*. The great nineteenth-century cookbook writer Pietro Artusi gave only three variations for *pasta frolla* doughs: he sometimes sieved powdered sugar for his *pasta frolla*, sometimes used part lard and part butter, and in one case insisted on using only egg yolks.

There are three main *pasta frolla* recipes used in this book: a basic all-purpose one, which is the easiest to handle; a more delicate version that uses pastry flour; and a third, the finest, silkiest version, made with all-purpose flour and potato starch.

Pasta Frolla I

This recipe makes enough for three 8-inch tarts; two or three 9- or 10-inch tarts, depending on the thickness; one two-crust or two latticed 9- or 10-inch tarts; one 11 by 8-inch tart, with or without lattice; or ten to fifteen 3^1/$_2$-inch tartlets. In some cases you may have a bit of dough left over, but you can always use the extra to make a few tartlets or cookies (see Sweet Pastry Dough Cookies, pages 397–399).

Makes 1^1/$_2$ pounds (680 g) dough

2 cups plus a scant two tablespoons (10.5 oz / 300 g) all-purpose flour

^{1}/$_2$ cup (3.5 oz / 100 g) sugar

Pinch of salt

1^3/$_4$ sticks (7 oz / 200 g) unsalted butter, at cool room temperature (cold if using a processor)

1 large egg

1 large egg yolk

1 teaspoon (0.14 oz / 4 g) vanilla extract

1 teaspoon (0.2 oz / 6 g) fresh lemon juice, or ^{1}/$_2$ teaspoon (0.07 oz / 2 g) lemon extract, or grated zest of 1 lemon

BY HAND

Place the flour, sugar, and salt in a bowl and stir to mix. Cut the butter into small pieces and cut it into the flour mixture with a pastry blender or two knives until the mixture resembles coarse meal. Slowly stir in first the egg and then the egg yolk, mixing thoroughly. Then stir in the vanilla and lemon juice. Gather the dough together and knead it briefly on a lightly floured surface just until the dough comes together.

BY MIXER

Cream the butter and the sugar in a mixer bowl with the paddle until pale and creamy. Add the egg, egg yolk, vanilla, and lemon juice, one at a time, mixing thoroughly after each addition. Add the flour and salt and mix until the dough comes together and is consistent but still soft. Be careful not to overmix or the pastry will be tough.

BY PROCESSOR

Place the flour, sugar, and salt in a food processor fitted with the steel blade. Cut the cold butter into small chunks and scatter over the flour. Process with four to six pulses until the mixture resembles coarse meal. Mix the egg, egg yolk, vanilla, and lemon juice. With the machine running, pour the egg mixture through the feed tube and process just until the dough comes together on top of the blade. Do not process until it gathers into a ball or the pastry will be tough. Knead the dough very briefly on a lightly floured surface just until it is no longer sticky.

At this point you may pat the dough into place in a buttered tart pan and bake it immediately after chilling. Otherwise, divide it into thirds or halves, depending on the size of the tart you are planning, or flatten the whole amount into a 4- to 5-inch disk.

Chilling. Wrap the dough with plastic wrap or aluminum foil and refrigerate at least 30 minutes to 1 hour but no longer than 1 day.

Shaping. Let the dough stand at room temperature for 30 to 45 minutes before rolling it out. Knead the dough briefly on a lightly floured surface to loosen it and make it supple enough for shaping. Roll the dough out $1/4$ to $3/8$ inch thick with a rolling pin and ease the dough into a lightly buttered pan. Trim the edge by running the rolling pin or a dough scraper over the edge of the pan to cut the dough neatly, and then tidy the edge with your fingers.

For one 11 by 8-inch tart shell, use 1 pound (450 g) of dough and roll into a rectangle. Line a buttered 11 by 8-inch tart pan with the dough.

For one 9- or 10-inch tart shell, use 9 to 10 ounces (250 to 300 g) of dough and roll into a circle. Line a buttered 9- or 10-inch tart pan with the dough.

For one 8-inch tart shell, use 8 ounces (225 g) dough and roll into a circle. Line a buttered 8-inch tart pan with the dough.

For ten to twelve $3^{1}/_{2}$-inch tartlet shells, roll out 12 to 16 ounces (340 to 450 g) of dough $1/4$ to $3/8$ inch thick. Cut into $4^{1}/_{2}$-inch circles and line $3^{1}/_{2}$-inch buttered tartlet pans with the dough.

For one deep 8- or 9-inch tart shell, use 12 ounces (340 g) dough. Proceed as directed for other tart shells. If you find it difficult to keep the dough from sliding down the side of the pan while baking, press the dough firmly against the spring-form sides with the back of a fork after 7 minutes; bake until lightly golden, 5 to 8 minutes longer, pressing the dough against the side of the pan twice more as needed.

For latticed tarts, use two-thirds of the dough specified for each shell to line the pan. Roll a $1/2$-inch-thick rope of dough between your hands and smooth it onto the upper edge of the bottom crust, so that the edge is substantial enough for the lattice to be attached later. Partially bake the shell, if necessary, and fill. Roll out the remaining dough $3/8$ inch thick and cut into $1/2$-inch wide strips with a straight edge and a sharp knife or ravioli cutter. Arrange the strips in a diagonal lattice over the filling, trim, and press onto the edges, pinching the strips lightly onto the tart shell. Bake as directed in the tart recipe.

Storage. Store the remaining unrolled dough, including all scraps that might be used again, in the refrigerator for up to 1 to 3 days or the freezer up to 1 month. Let frozen dough thaw in the refrigerator for 24 hours before rolling it out.

Resting. Refrigerate the dough-lined pan for 20 to 30 minutes to reduce shrinking when the pastry is baked.

continued

Pasta Frolla I, *continued*

Baking. Preheat the oven to 350°F.

For partially baked shells: Line each shell with aluminum foil and fill with dried beans or pie weights. Bake until set, 12 to 15 minutes for large shells or 10 to 12 minutes for tartlet shells. Remove the foil and weights and let cool 5 to 10 minutes. Place the tart pan on top of a smaller can, such as a coffee can for large tart shells, and gently release the side of the pan from the baked tart crust. Let cool completely on a rack.

For an 11 by 8-inch partially baked shell, bake with the weights for 8 to 10 minutes; remove the foil and weights and bake 5 minutes longer, then reduce the heat to 325°F and bake until golden, 5 to 7 minutes longer.

For fully baked shells: Line each shell with aluminum foil and fill with dried beans or pie weights. Bake until the dough is no longer shiny, 12 to 15 minutes. Remove the foil and weights, prick the bottom of the dough, and bake until fully set and golden, 10 to 13 minutes longer. Let cool 5 to 10 minutes. Place the tart pan on top of a smaller can, such as a coffee can for large tart shells, and gently release the side of the pan from the baked tart crust. Let cool completely on a rack before filling.

Other Proportions. You can cut the recipe in half by dividing all the ingredients except the eggs in half. Use two egg yolks if you are making the dough by hand or by mixer, but use one whole egg if you are using a food processor.

Pasta Frolla II

2 1/2 cups (10.5 oz / 300 g) pastry flour or a combination of all-purpose flour and cake flour, sifted after measuring

1/2 cup (3.5 oz / 100 g) sugar

Pinch of salt

1 3/4 sticks (7 oz / 200 g) unsalted butter, at cool room temperature

1 large egg

1 large egg yolk

1 teaspoon (0.14 oz / 4 g) vanilla extract

1 teaspoon (0.2 oz / 6 g) fresh lemon juice, or 1/2 teaspoon (0.07 oz / 2 g) lemon extract, or grated zest of 1 lemon

Follow the instructions for *pasta frolla I* (page 320). Roll out 1/8 inch thick or slightly thicker.

Pasta Frolla III

1¹/₂ cups less one tablespoon (7 oz / 200 g) all-purpose flour, sifted after measuring

¹/₂ cup plus 1 tablespoon (3.5 oz / 100 g) potato starch

¹/₂ cup (3.5 oz / 100 g) sugar

Pinch of salt

1³/₄ sticks (7 oz / 200 g) unsalted butter, at cool room temperature

1 teaspoon (0.14 oz / 4 g) vanilla extract

Grated zest of 1 lemon

Grated zest of ¹/₂ orange

Follow the directions for *pasta frolla I* (page 320). Roll out ¹/₈ to ¹/₄ inch thick.

Pasta Frolla Integrale WHOLE WHEAT PASTRY DOUGH

Makes 14 ounces (400 g); enough for one latticed 10-inch tart or two 8-inch tarts

1¹/₂ cups (7 oz / 200 g) whole wheat pastry flour

¹/₂ cup (3.5 oz / 100 g) firmly packed brown sugar

¹/₂ teaspoon (0.08 oz / 2.5 g) salt

7 tablespoons (3.5 oz / 100 g) unsalted butter, at cool room temperature

1 large egg

1 teaspoon (0.14 oz / 4 g) vanilla extract

Follow the instructions for *pasta frolla I* (page 320). The food processor works especially well with this dough.

Basic Pastry Creams

Crema Pasticceria PASTRY CREAM

Makes 4¹/₄ cups (2 lb 6 oz /1.1 kg)

3¹/₄ cups (1 lb 12 oz / 795 g) milk

¹/₂ cup plus 2 teaspoons (3.9 oz / 110 g) sugar

3 thin strips lemon zest

7 large egg yolks

1 large egg

¹/₄ teaspoon salt

¹/₂ cup (2.5 oz / 70 g) all-purpose flour

1 to 2 tablespoons (0.4 to 0.8 oz / 12 to 23 g) vanilla extract, or 1¹/₂ teaspoons (0.2 oz / 6 g) vanilla extract plus 3 to 4 tablespoons (1.5 to 2 oz / 45 to 60 g) rum, or grated zest of 4 Meyer lemons

3 tablespoons (1.5 oz / 45 g) unsalted butter

Slowly heat the milk, 2 teaspoons of the sugar, and the lemon zest in the top of a double boiler over simmering water or in a 3-quart heavy saucepan over low heat. Meanwhile, whisk the remaining sugar, the egg yolks, egg, and salt in a small bowl until thick but still golden, 2 to 3 minutes. Sift in the flour, a little at a time, whisking briskly to mix thoroughly. Whisk ¹/₂ cup of the boiling milk mixture, 2 tablespoons at a time, into the egg mixture, then pour the egg mixture into the remaining milk mixture. Cook over medium-high heat, whisking constantly, until thickened, 2 to 3 minutes. As it begins to reach a boil and look lumpy, whisk it vigorously to smooth it. When the cream is as thick as mayonnaise, reduce the heat and whisk or stir for another minute. Remove from the heat and discard the lemon zest. Beat in the vanilla and then the butter, 1 tablespoon at a time. Cool the cream quickly by placing the pan in a bowl of cold water, by pouring through a sieve into a bowl set in an ice bath, or by spreading the cream out on two baking sheets. Smear a little butter on top and cover tightly with plastic wrap so that the cream doesn't develop a skin. Cool completely in the refrigerator. You may want to thin it with 1 to 2 tablespoons of milk before using. This pastry cream will keep 4 to 5 days in the refrigerator or in the freezer for up to 2 months.

Other Proportions. You can cut the recipe in half by dividing all the ingredients except the eggs in half and reducing the egg yolks to four and omitting the whole egg.

Crema al Limone LEMON CREAM

This lemon curd–like cream comes from Gianfranco Anelli in Rome. It makes a wonderful lemon tart in a simple *pasta frolla* shell.

Makes 2 cups

3 large eggs, lightly beaten

1¼ cups (5.3 oz / 150 g) confectioners' sugar

¾ cup (5.3 oz / 150 g) granulated sugar

Scant ½ cup (3.2 oz / 90 g) fresh lemon juice (from about 4 lemons)

Grated zest of 3 lemons

7 tablespoons (3.5 oz / 100 g) unsalted butter

Beat the eggs and sugars lightly in the top of a double boiler while off the heat until mixed. Stir in the lemon juice, zest, and butter. Heat the water in the bottom of the double boiler to a boil, then reduce the heat to maintain a steady simmer. Place the top of the double boiler over the bottom and cook the custard, whisking constantly, until as thick as cooked cereal, 10 to 12 minutes. Cool the cream quickly by placing the top of the double boiler in a bowl of cold water. Refrigerate the cream, covered tightly with plastic wrap, until set.

Glassa di Albicocca APRICOT GLAZE

Makes about ½ cup

⅔ cup (5.3 oz / 150 g) best-quality apricot jam or preserves

2 to 3 teaspoons (0.4 to 0.5 oz / 10 to 15 g) water or fresh lemon juice

Heat the preserves and water in a small, heavy saucepan over moderate heat until the mixture comes to a boil, then strain through a sieve. Use the glaze while it is still warm. Any leftover glaze will keep indefinitely in a covered jar; heat again before using. This recipe is easily halved to produce ¼ cup glaze.

Pasta di Mandorle ALMOND PASTE

Makes about 2 pounds (900 g), or 3¹/₄ cups

3¹/₃ cups (1 lb 2 oz / 500 g) blanched almonds,
  very lightly toasted

³/₄ cup plus 2 tablespoons (3.5 oz / 100 g)
  confectioners' sugar, plus more for kneading

2 cups (14 oz / 400 g) granulated sugar

¹/₂ cup (4.2 oz / 120 g) water

¹/₄ cup (3 oz / 85 g) light corn syrup

¹/₂ teaspoon (0.07 oz / 2 g) almond extract

Grind the almonds to a coarse powder in a nut grinder, blender, or food processor fitted with the steel blade. (If you use the processor, process with 2 tablespoons of the confectioners' sugar.) Add the confectioners' sugar and continue grinding to a fine powder. Transfer to a mixer bowl.

Heat the sugar, water, and corn syrup in a small, heavy saucepan over low heat and stir to dissolve the sugar. Heat to a boil over high heat and cook until the syrup registers 234°F to 236°F on a candy thermometer (a drop of the syrup should form a soft ball when dropped into a glass of cold water). Pour the sugar syrup over the almond mixture and mix by hand or with the paddle of the heavy-duty mixer at the lowest speed until blended. Cool to room temperature. Mix in the almond extract. Knead well on a surface sprinkled with confectioners' sugar until soft and elastic, about 2 to 3 minutes. Shape into a thick disk and wrap securely in plastic wrap. It will keep for months in the refrigerator.

Fruit and Jam Tarts

Crostata di Marmellata JAM TART

The famous Italian sweet tooth is indulged by the baker's art, but desserts made and served at home are usually extremely simple—a bowl of fresh fruit, a platter of cookies, or this simple jam tart, an unpretentious sweet pastry shell filled with homemade preserves. The quality of the jam is very important, because the fruit is not complicated with other flavorings. In Rome, this *crostata* is made with *visciole*, a sour dark cherry that resembles *amarena*; in Emilia-Romagna, Liguria, and Tuscany, you will most likely find the tart filled with fruit or berry preserves.

Makes one 11 by 8-inch tart; 12 servings

3 cups (scant 1½ lb / 675 g) best-quality raspberry or apricot jam

11 by 8-inch partially baked tart shell with dough reserved for lattice (pasta frolla I or II or pasta frolla integrale, pages 320–323)

½ cup (5.3 oz / 150 g) apricot glaze (page 325)

Spread the jam ½ inch thick over the tart shell. Make the lattice as directed on page 321.

Baking. Preheat the oven to 400°F. Bake until the lattice is golden brown, 15 to 20 minutes. Immediately brush the top with the glaze. Cool to room temperature on a rack.

Variations. To make *torta di marmellata* or *tartine alla marmellata*, partially bake a 9- or 10-inch tart shell or 3½-inch tartlet shells made with *pasta frolla I* or *II* (pages 320 to 322) flavored with rum instead of vanilla. You will need about 2 cups of jam for the 9- or 10-inch tart and 1½ to 2 cups of jam for ten to twelve tartlets. Make the lattice as directed on page 321. Bake as directed above; the tart will be done in 20 to 25 minutes and the tartlets in 15 to 20 minutes. Glaze and cool as directed.

Crostata di Frutta BAKED FRUIT TART

Use any of the fruits of summer to make this tart: golden-pink peaches, brilliant strawberries or raspberries, blackberries, blueberries, or cherries. I like to make alternating concentric circles of about 2¹/₂ cups (12 oz / 350 g) of sliced peaches and 1 cup (about 7 oz / 190 g) of sliced plums.

Makes one 11 by 8-inch tart; 12 servings

1¹/₄ to 1¹/₂ cups (10 to 12 oz / 285 to 340 g) apricot jam

11 by 8-inch partially baked tart shell with dough reserved for lattice (pasta frolla I or II, pages 320–322)

3¹/₂ to 4 cups fresh fruit, such as sliced peaches; halved strawberries; whole raspberries, blackberries, or blueberries; or sliced pitted cherries

1 large egg, beaten

¹/₂ cup (about 5.3 oz / 150 g) apricot glaze (page 325)

Spread the jam ¹/₄ inch thick in the bottom of the tart shell. Arrange the fruit in an attractive pattern over the jam. Make the lattice as directed on page 321. Brush the lattice with the beaten egg.

Baking. Preheat the oven to 425°F. Bake until the lattice is medium brown, 20 to 25 minutes. Immediately brush the top with the glaze. Cool to room temperature on a rack.

Variations. For a 9-inch tart, use about ³/₄ cup of jam and 3 cups of fruit. For ten to twelve tartlets, use 1 to 1¹/₄ cups of jam and 8 ounces to 1 pound of fruit.

Torta di Frutta Fresca FRESH FRUIT TART

A fresh fruit tart is a fresh fruit tart in any language you care to name, but this one comes from Italy, the land of Botticelli and Bellini, so make it as glorious to look at as it is to eat. Set curved slices of golden peaches and scarlet plums within an enclosure of pastry dough, weave pointillist fantasies of dark blueberries and red raspberries, or fan slices of strawberries in radiating circles and shine them all with apricot glaze. I like to make the smaller tart with 1¹/₂ cups (7.5 oz / 210 g) of strawberries, hulled and halved, and 1 cup (7 oz / 200 g) of sliced nectarines.

Makes one 9- or 10-inch tart; 6 to 8 servings

³/₄ to 1 cup (7 to 9 oz / 190 to 250 g) pastry cream (page 324)

9- or 10-inch fully baked tart shell (pasta frolla I, II or III or pasta frolla integrale, pages 320–323)

2 to 3 cups fresh fruit, such as sliced strawberries, peaches, or plums, or whole raspberries, blueberries, or blackberries

¹/₄ cup (about 2.3 oz / 65 g) apricot glaze (page 325)

Spread the pastry cream ¹/₄ inch thick in the bottom of the tart shell. Arrange the fruit in concentric circles over the cream. Brush the fruit with the glaze.

Variations. For an 11 by 8-inch tart, use about 1 to 1¹/₃ cups of pastry cream and 3 to 4 cups of fresh fruit. For ten to twelve tartlets, use about 2 cups of pastry cream and 1¹/₃ to 2 cups of fresh fruit. If you are using strawberries for the tartlets, arrange the slices in concentric circles to make a pyramid shape.

Crostata al Limone SOUFFLÉED LEMON TART

This delicate lemony tart is as light as a soufflé baked in crust, but it has the wonderful advantage of not having to be made at the very last minute. It could be the perfect finish to almost any meal but seems especially right at the end of a rich or complex dinner.

Makes one 9-inch tart; 6 to 8 servings

4 large eggs, separated, at room temperature

¹/₂ cup plus 2 tablespoons (4.4 oz / 125 g) sugar

3 tablespoons (0.9 oz / 26 g) all-purpose flour

¹/₃ cup (2.3 oz / 65 g) fresh lemon juice

Grated zest of 2 lemons

Deep 9-inch partially baked tart shell (pasta frolla I, II, or III, pages 320–323)

With an electric mixer, beat the egg yolks, gradually adding ¹/₄ cup of the sugar, until thick and foamy; add the flour, lemon juice, and zest and beat 2 to 3 minutes longer. Transfer to the top of a double boiler. Cook, stirring constantly, over simmering water until the mixture is thick and coats the back of a spoon. Remove the pan from the water and cool completely. Beat the egg whites until they form soft peaks; gradually beat in the remaining sugar and continue beating until stiff and glossy. Fold a quarter of the egg whites into the lemon mixture to lighten and then gently fold in the remaining egg whites with a rubber spatula. Gently pour the filling into the tart shell and smooth the top.

Baking. Preheat the oven to 350°F. Bake until the crust is deep golden, 20 to 25 minutes. Cool on a rack and then remove the sides of the pan.

Torta di Limone LEMON TART

The first time I tasted this lemon tart I loved its tart lemon flavor and smooth, buttery texture. The secret? In Italy it is made with dry pinot grigio, but I prefer to use chardonnay or Pomino Bianco to give it a rich and slightly fruitier taste. The lemon filling is best made and refrigerated for 24 hours so that the tart lemon flavor can mellow.

Makes one 9-inch tart; 6 to 8 servings

FILLING

4 large egg yolks, at room temperature

³/₄ cup plus 2 tablespoons (6.3 oz / 180 g) sugar

¹/₄ cup (1.3 oz / 35 g) all-purpose flour

³/₄ cup (6.3 oz / 180 g) pinot grigio or chardonnay

4 to 5 tablespoons (1.8 to 2.2 oz / 52 to 62 g) fresh lemon juice

Grated zest of 1 lemon

1 to 2 tablespoons (about 1 oz / 28 g) unsalted butter

Whisk the egg yolks, ³/₄ cup of the sugar, and the flour until smooth in a mixing bowl. Heat the wine and the remaining 2 tablespoons of sugar in a 2-quart nonreactive saucepan to a boil; stir in the lemon juice and zest. Whisk 3 tablespoons of the hot wine mixture, 1 tablespoon at a time, into the egg yolk mixture. Then gradually stir the egg yolk mixture into the remaining wine mixture with a wooden spoon. Heat over low heat, stirring constantly, until bubbly. If the mixture looks lumpy, whisk it vigorously to smooth it.

Cook until it is as thick as cooked cereal, about 2 minutes. Stir in the butter. Let cool to room temperature. Refrigerate, covered, for 24 hours before using, if possible.

MERINGUE

1 large egg white, at room temperature

¹/₄ cup (1.8 oz / 50 g) sugar

9-inch partially baked tart shell (pasta frolla I, II, or III, pages 320–323)

Beat the egg white in a mixer bowl until soft peaks are formed. Beat, gradually adding the ¹/₄ cup of sugar, until the peaks are stiff and shiny.

Spoon the lemon filling into the tart shell and smooth the top. Spoon the meringue into a pastry bag fitted with a large star tip and pipe a ring of rosettes around the edge.

Baking. Preheat the oven to 350°F. Bake until the meringue colors slightly, 15 to 20 minutes. Cool to room temperature on a rack.

Torta Primavera SPRINGTIME CAKE

This is a cake for all hours and occasions, from breakfast to teatime to dessert. A rich pastry crust wraps around layers of apricot jam, raisins, and a pound-cake-like filling that is topped with fanned slices of apple and crunchy sugar.

Makes one deep 8-, 9-, or 9¹/₂-inch cake; 8 to 10 servings

1¹/₄ cups (10 oz / 285 g) apricot jam

2 teaspoons (0.4 oz / 10 g) water

7 tablespoons (3.5 oz / 100 g) unsalted butter, at room temperature

¹/₂ cup (3.5 oz / 100 g) granulated sugar

2 large eggs, at room temperature

2 large egg yolks, at room temperature

Grated zest of ¹/₂ orange

¹/₂ teaspoon (0.07 oz / 2 g) vanilla extract

1 cup (4.9 oz / 140 g) all-purpose flour, or 1¹/₃ cups plus one tablespoon (6.5 oz / 185 g) pastry flour

1¹/₂ teaspoons (0.3 oz / 7.5 g) baking powder

Deep 8-, 9-, or 9¹/₂-inch unbaked tart shell with a thick rim (pasta frolla I or II, pages 320–322)

Scant 1 cup (4.9 oz / 140 g) golden raisins

2 cooking apples (14 to 16 oz / 390 to 450 g), peeled, cored, and cut into 8 to 12 slices each

1¹/₂ tablespoons (0.7 oz / 20 g) turbinado sugar

Heat the jam and water in a small, heavy saucepan until they boil, and then press through a wire-mesh sieve. Cream the butter and granulated sugar by hand with a wooden spoon or paddle, or by electric mixer (use the whisk if you have one) at high speed for 4 to 5 minutes, until fluffy and almost creamy white. Add the eggs and egg yolks, one at a time, beating thoroughly at high speed after each addition. Add the orange zest and vanilla and beat 5 minutes by hand or 1 to 2 minutes by mixer. Sift the flour and baking powder over the butter mixture and fold in gently with a rubber spatula until well blended.

Spread some of the warm sieved jam ¹/₄ inch thick on the bottom of the tart shell. Don't be tempted to add more jam, even though it seems like a good idea, because the cake will be too sweet and the jam will overwhelm the other flavors. Sprinkle the raisins over the jam; they should completely cover the jam. Pour the cake batter over the raisins and smooth the top. Arrange the apples in two concentric circles without overlapping the slices. Sprinkle with the turbinado sugar.

Baking. Preheat the oven to 350°F. Bake until a skewer inserted into the center comes out clean, 1¹/₄ to 1¹/₂ hours. Let cool on a rack. While the cake is still somewhat warm, brush with the remaining sieved jam. Serve at room temperature.

Crostata di Quattro Stagioni

FOUR SEASONS TART FROM LAKE COMO

Raspberries for summer, wild *amarena* for fall, apricot preserves for winter, and pastry cream for the spring: four seasons in four quadrants of a simple sweet-pastry tart. But don't feel confined by the ingredients listed above; you should use whatever appeals to you and arrange it with your own *fantasia*. Try poached apples or pears, fat blueberries or fresh currants, sliced peaches, or even blood oranges, if you are in the mood for something beautiful to look at as well as to eat.

Makes one 9-inch tart; 6 to 8 servings

2 ounces (60 g) pasta frolla dough (page 320)

9-inch partially baked tart shell (pasta frolla I, II, or III, pages 320–323)

¹/₂ cup (4 oz / 115 g) raspberry preserves or jam

¹/₂ cup (4 oz / 115 g) apricot preserves or jam

1 cup (9 oz / 260 g) pastry cream (page 324)

30 to 35 (3 to 4.5 oz / 110 to 130 g) preserved amarena cherries

1 large egg, beaten

¹/₃ cup (2 oz / 75 g) apricot glaze (page 325)

Cut the 2 ounces of dough in half, shape each half into a 9- or 10-inch rope with your palms, and flatten the ropes slightly. Place the ropes in the tart shell, one across the other at right angles, so that the shell is divided into four equal quadrants.

Spoon the raspberry and apricot preserves, pastry cream, and cherries each separately into one quadrant. Brush the dough with the egg.

Baking. Preheat the oven to 350°F. Bake until light golden, 20 to 25 minutes. Immediately brush the fruit with the glaze. Let cool to room temperature on a rack.

Variations. You can substitute the slices of 1 Newtown Pippin or cooking apple that have been poached briefly in sugar and white wine for the cherries. Other possible fillings are blackberry or blueberry preserves, sliced lightly blanched peaches or apricots, and pear slices that have been very lightly poached in white wine, sugar, and a few drops of lemon juice.

Torta di Pere PEAR TART

The top crust of this wonderfully rustic pear tart from Piedmont shifts and settles and even cracks over the pears beneath it like dry land after an earthquake. The slightly gritty texture of the cornmeal pastry makes a wonderful contrast to the smooth pears underneath. There is something elementally soothing and satisfying about this down-to-earth dessert.

Makes one 8¹/₂-inch tart; 8 servings

DOUGH

1 stick plus 2¹/₂ tablespoons (5.3 oz / 150 g) unsalted butter, at room temperature (cold if using a food processor)

³/₄ cup (5.3 oz / 150 g) sugar

3 large egg yolks

About 1¹/₂ cups minus one tablespoon (7 oz / 200 g) all-purpose flour

³/₄ cup plus 1 tablespoon (3.5 oz / 100 g) fine yellow cornmeal, preferably organic

1 teaspoon (0.2 oz / 5 g) salt

BY HAND

Cream the butter and sugar in a mixing bowl with a wooden spoon until well blended. Add the egg yolks, one at a time, mixing thoroughly after each addition. Sift the flour, cornmeal, and salt over the mixture and stir just until the dough comes together. Knead lightly on a floured surface until the dough is no longer sticky.

BY MIXER

Cream the butter and sugar with the paddle until well blended, 1 to 2 minutes. Add the egg yolks, one at a time, beating thoroughly after each addition. Sift in the flour, cornmeal, and salt, and mix at low speed; continue mixing until the dough comes together. Knead lightly on a floured surface until the dough is no longer sticky.

BY PROCESSOR

Place the flour, cornmeal, salt, and sugar in a food processor fitted with the steel blade. Cut the cold butter into small pieces and scatter over the flour. Process with three or four pulses until the mixture resembles coarse meal. Beat the egg yolks lightly. With the machine running, pour the egg yolks in a steady stream through the feed tube and process just until the dough comes together. You may need to add a little ice-cold water. Stop the machine as soon as the dough masses on top of the blade. Overprocessing will make a tough dough.

continued

Torta di Pere, *continued*

Chilling. Gather the dough into a ball, wrap it with plastic wrap, and refrigerate for 20 minutes to 1 hour.

FILLING

2 cups (1 lb / 450 g) full-bodied red wine; a Barolo or cabernet sauvignon would be perfect

¹/₄ cup (1.8 oz / 50 g) sugar

3 whole cloves

3 thin strips lemon zest

³/₄ to 1 teaspoon (0.06 to 0.1 oz / 2 to 2.5 g) ground cinnamon

Cornmeal or finely ground cookie or cake crumbs, for sprinkling (optional)

3 large peeled cooking pears (2 lb / 900 g, weighed after peeling), cut into fat slices and then cut crosswise in half

1 large egg, beaten, for the egg wash

Heat the wine, sugar, cloves, lemon zest, and cinnamon to a boil in a nonreactive saucepan. Gently boil until reduced to 1¹/₂ cups, about 15 minutes. Stir in the pears and cook over medium heat until tender, 15 to 20 minutes. Strain the pears; discard the cloves, lemon peel, and cooking liquid. Cool to room temperature.

Shaping. Cut the dough in half and return half to the refrigerator. This is a very delicate dough. Lightly sprinkle flour on your work surface and then lay one or two pieces of plastic wrap on it. Put the dough on the plastic wrap and cover it with a second layer of plastic wrap. This protects the dough as you roll it with your rolling pin into a circle ¹/₄ inch thick. Butter an 8¹/₂-inch tart pan very thoroughly. Remove the top layer of plastic, gently lift the dough up by the bottom piece of plastic wrap, and then carefully invert it into the prepared pan before removing the remaining plastic wrap. Trim the edge. Build up the edge of the bottom pastry with the trimmings rolled into one or two coils and flattened onto the edge, so that the edge is substantial enough for the top pastry to be attached.

Filling and Top Crust. I sometimes sprinkle a very little cornmeal or cookie or cake crumbs on the bottom of the tart shell to soak up the juices from the pears. Spoon the drained pears into the tart shell. Again using plastic wrap, roll out the remaining dough into a ¹/₄-inch-thick circle and place over the pan. Trim the overhanging dough, press the two edges together, and crimp decoratively. Lightly brush the pastry with the beaten egg.

Baking. Preheat the oven to 375°F. Bake until golden, 40 minutes. Cool on a rack. Serve warm or at room temperature.

Crostata di Zucca PUMPKIN TART

I have to admit that this particular pumpkin dessert is truly my *fantasia*. Giorgio, the baker in Venice, was busy one day and told me to take a look at his recipes, which were really just a list of ingredients and the most rudimentary instructions. After so much time spent being beguiled by the imaginations of Italian bakers and the phenomenal desserts they made with a few simple ingredients, I went to work when I got home to my kitchen on a tart I imagined would be a close cousin to Giorgio's. When I returned to Italy, I told him what I had done. He paused for a very long time, with a look of some confusion on his face, and then described his *crostata di zucca*. It was an extravaganza of two days' work, complicated processes, and fondant coverings; so, although this *crostata di zucca* is made with the ingredients listed in Giorgio's little book, it is absolutely my invention. Delicate and delicious, this tart has been the finale for our Thanksgiving dinners for many years.

Makes one 10-inch tart plus several tartlets or individual budini *(custards); tart makes 8 servings*

¹/₄ cup (2 oz / 55 g) unsalted butter, at room temperature

¹/₄ cup (1.8 oz / 50 g) sugar

3 large eggs, separated, at room temperature

2 cups (17.5 oz / 500) homemade or canned pumpkin purée

Scant ¹/₂ cup (4 oz / 115 g) milk

1 tablespoon (0.4 oz / 12 g) potato starch or all-purpose flour

Grated zest of 1 lemon

¹/₄ cup (2 oz / 60 g) rum or Cognac

10-inch partially baked tart shell (pasta frolla I, II, or III, pages 320–323)

3 partially baked tartlet shells (optional)

Cream the butter and sugar by hand with a wooden paddle or spoon or by electric mixer until light and fluffy. Add the egg yolks, one at a time, beating thoroughly after each addition. Stir in the pumpkin, milk, flour, lemon zest, and rum. Beat the egg whites until the peaks are stiff. Fold a quarter of the egg whites into the pumpkin mixture, and then gently fold in the remaining whites. Pour the filling into the tart shell to within ¹/₂ inch of the top. Pour the remaining filling either into the tartlet shells or into buttered ramekins.

Baking. Preheat the oven to 375°F. Bake until the filling is set, about 50 minutes for the tart, about 30 to 35 minutes for the tartlets, and about 35 to 45 minutes for the custards. Cool completely on a rack.

Torta di Mele e Ciliege APPLE AND WILD CHERRY TART

Set a layer of maraschino-soaked cake inside a rich pastry crust, spread it with pastry cream, and fan thinly sliced apples inside a circle of wild *amarena* cherries. I have also baked this without the cherries when I discovered that I was totally without them at the last moment. I rushed to the store while the tart was cooking and added the cherries when I got home. The unbaked cherries were fine, but they must be pressed into the pastry cream to keep them from sliding all over when you cut into the tart.

Makes one 9-inch tart; 8 servings

About $^1/_3$ baked pasta maddalena (page 365), cut into $^1/_4$-inch-thick slices, or enough slices of pound cake or genoise or cake crumbs to line the 9-inch tart shell

9-inch partially baked tart shell (pasta frolla I, II, or III, pages 320–323)

2 to 3 tablespoons (1 to 1.5 oz / 30 to 45 g) maraschino liqueur

1 to 1$^1/_4$ cups (9 to 11 oz / 260 to 320 g) pastry cream (page 324)

1 Newtown Pippin or cooking apple (6 to 7 oz / 180 to 200 g) peeled, cored and cut into about 24 slices

45 to 50 preserved amarena cherries (about 7 oz / 200 g)

2 to 3 tablespoons (1 to 1.5 oz / 28 to 45 g) turbinado or granulated sugar

$^1/_3$ cup (2.7 oz / 75 g) apricot glaze (page 325)

3 tablespoons (0.8 oz / 22 g) coarsely chopped toasted walnuts

Arrange the cake slices in a single layer in the tart shell, cutting and trimming as needed. Brush the liqueur over the cake slices and then spread with a $^1/_4$-inch layer of pastry cream. Fan the apple slices in a circle in the center of the tart. Arrange the cherries in a border around the apples and place 10 to 15 cherries in the center of the apples. Sprinkle with the sugar.

Baking. Preheat the oven to 375°F. Turn over a rimmed baking sheet and place the tart pan on it. This strange arrangement will keep the bottom from overbrowning. Bake until the apple slices are slightly browned and the cherries are plump and slightly glazed, about 25 minutes.

Brush the hot tart with the glaze and sprinkle the walnuts over the apple slices. Cool to room temperature on a rack.

Nut Tarts

Torta di Nocciole con Cioccolata
HAZELNUT CAKE WITH CHOCOLATE GLAZE

This cake is rich, densely nutty, and flavored with just a touch of orange. It is wonderful unadorned or sprinkled with a fine shower of confectioners' sugar, although it would be hard to imagine anyone objecting to the smooth dark chocolate glaze, which gives it an entirely different, elegant life.

Makes one 9-inch cake; 8 servings

1 cup (5 oz / 140 g) hazelnuts, plus more for garnish

1/2 cup plus 2 tablespoons (4.4 oz / 125 g) sugar

1/3 cup (1.8 oz / 50 g) chopped candied orange peel (page 39)

1 stick plus 2 tablespoons (4.9 oz / 140 g) unsalted butter, at room temperature

1 large egg, at room temperature

2 large egg yolks, at room temperature

9-inch partially baked tart shell (pasta frolla I, II, or III, pages 320–323)

Preheat the oven to 350°F. Toast all the hazelnuts on a baking sheet until the skins blister, 10 to 15 minutes. Rub the skins off of the nuts in a kitchen towel, or place the nuts in a food processor fitted with the plastic blade and process with one or two pulses until the skins come off. Set aside 10 to 12 perfect nuts for garnishing the cake.

Process the nuts and 2 tablespoons of the sugar to a coarse powder in a food processor fitted with the steel blade. Add the remaining sugar and the orange peel and process until finely ground. Transfer to a mixer bowl, add the butter, and cream with the paddle until very light and fluffy, about 5 minutes. Change to the whisk if your mixer has one. Add the egg and egg yolks, one at a time, beating thoroughly after each addition. Beat at medium-high speed for 3 to 4 minutes. Pour the batter into the tart shell and smooth the top.

Baking. Bake at 350°F until a skewer inserted in the center comes out clean, 35 to 45 minutes. Cool completely on a rack.

GLAZE

5 ounces (140 g) bittersweet chocolate

6 1/2 tablespoons (3.3 oz / 95 g) unsalted butter, at room temperature

1 1/2 teaspoons (0.4 oz / 10 g) corn syrup or clear glucose

Melt the chocolate in the top of a double boiler over simmering water. When the chocolate is completely melted, stir in the butter, 1 tablespoon at a time, waiting until

continued

Torta di Nocciole con Cioccolata, *continued*

each piece melts before adding the next, and then stir in the corn syrup. The glaze should be stiff and shiny. Pour the hot glaze over the cake; you may refrigerate the cake to set the glaze quickly. Garnish with the perfect whole hazelnuts.

Variations. This cake can also be baked with a top crust of pastry. Roll out 10 ounces (280 g) of pastry dough $^1/_4$ inch thick. Place over the batter before baking, trim the edges, and press onto the tart shell. Cut out small shapes from the leftover dough with a ravioli cutter or small knife and arrange on the pastry. Make a hole in the center to allow steam to escape. Brush the top with 1 egg yolk mixed with 1 tablespoon of water and, if you want, decorate the edge with skinned whole hazelnuts. Bake as directed.

Torta Piana con Mandorle ALMOND TART

There seem to be an endless number of almond tarts in Italy, all slightly different depending on the region and its traditions. This one is a delicate almond cake flavored with a bit of orange set on a fine layer of apricot jam and baked in a rich, buttery pastry shell. It is hauntingly delicious, but the *piana* in its name has nothing to do with rhapsodies, rapture, or music. Italian for "level" or "even," *piana* indicates that the top is as flat as a ribbon, although bakers always toss a couple of handfuls of sliced almonds over the top to accentuate the almond flavor and give it a lovely crunch.

Makes one 9-inch tart; 8 servings

$^1/_3$ cup (1.8 oz / 50 g) blanched almonds

$3^1/_2$ ounces (100 g) prepared almond paste

7 tablespoons (3.5 oz / 100 g) unsalted butter, at room temperature

$^1/_4$ cup (1.8 oz / 50 g) sugar

2 large eggs, at room temperature

$^1/_4$ teaspoon almond extract

Grated zest of 1 orange, or 3 tablespoons (1 oz / 28 g) chopped candied orange peel (page 39)

$^3/_4$ cup (3.5 oz / 100 g) all-purpose flour or pastry flour

$^1/_2$ teaspoon (0.08 oz / 2.5 g) baking powder

$^2/_3$ cup (5.3 oz / 150 g) apricot jam, melted and sieved

9-inch partially baked tart shell (pasta frolla I, II, or III, pages 320–323)

1 large egg, beaten

$^1/_3$ cup (1.2 oz / 33 g) sliced unpeeled almonds

You can substitute 7 ounces of almond paste (page 326) for the whole almonds, sugar, and prepared almond paste and proceed to the next step. Otherwise, grind the whole almonds to a coarse powder using a nut grinder, a mortar and pestle, or a food processor fitted with the steel blade. If you are using the processor, add 2 tablespoons of the sugar to keep the almonds from becoming oily.

Mix the almond powder, almond paste, and butter in a mixer bowl with the paddle at low speed. Add the sugar slowly but steadily and beat until smooth. If you are using the 7 ounces of almond paste from page 326, start here and beat it in the mixer bowl with the butter at low speed. Increase the speed to high and beat until light and fluffy, 2 to 3 minutes. Change to the whisk if your mixer has one and beat at high speed for 5 minutes. Add the eggs, one at a time, beating thoroughly after each addition. Add the almond extract and orange zest and beat at high speed for another 5 minutes. Sift the flour and baking powder over the batter and gently fold with a rubber spatula until blended.

Spread the jam $1/4$ inch thick on the bottom of the tart shell. Spoon heaping tablespoons of the filling evenly over the jam, sealing in the jam at the edge. It's difficult to cover the slippery jam with the filling, which is why bakers use a pastry bag to pipe the filling in a continuous spiral over the jam, but I have discovered that a little overflow of jam at the edges does no harm. Smooth the top of the filling. Very carefully brush the beaten egg over the filling and then sprinkle with the sliced almonds.

Baking. Preheat the oven to 375°F. Bake until deep golden brown, 25 to 35 minutes. Cool completely on a rack.

Variations. You can substitute raspberry jam for the apricot and hazelnuts for the almonds.

Torta di Mandorle ALMOND TART

This rich, dense, moist almond tart is made without flour. The top can be covered with handfuls of any toasted nut—hazelnut, almond, or walnut—or with a composed design of unpeeled almonds and skinned toasted hazelnuts.

Makes one 9-inch tart; 8 servings

¹/₂ cup (2.6 oz / 75 g) unpeeled almonds

¹/₂ cup plus 2 tablespoons (4.4 oz / 125 g) sugar

2 sticks plus 1 tablespoon (8.5 oz / 240 g) unsalted butter, at room temperature

1 large egg

1 large egg yolk

1 teaspoon (0.14 oz / 4 g) vanilla extract

¹/₄ teaspoon almond extract

9-inch unbaked tart shell (pasta frolla I, II, or III, pages 320–323)

1 cup (5.2 oz / 150 g) halved, skinned, and toasted hazelnuts, or halved, blanched, and toasted almonds (5.2 oz / 150 g), or toasted pine nuts (4 oz / 113 g), or a combination of hazelnuts and almonds (see page 32)

Grind the almonds and the sugar to a coarse powder in a food processor fitted with the steel blade. Transfer to a mixer bowl. If you prefer to use a nut grinder or mortar, grind the nuts, then transfer to a mixer bowl, add the sugar, and mix well. A heavy-duty mixer is best for preparing the tart filling. Beat the butter with the paddle at medium speed until light and fluffy, about 5 minutes. Change to the whisk. Add the egg and egg yolk, one at a time, as quickly as possible but whisking thoroughly at medium speed after each addition. Add the vanilla and almond extracts and whisk at medium speed 3 to 4 minutes.

Spread the nut batter in the tart shell and smooth the top. Shower the top with the toasted nuts and shake off the excess, or alternate rows of hazelnuts and almonds.

Baking. Preheat the oven to 350°F. Bake until the pastry shell is golden and the interior is set, 35 to 40 minutes. Cool completely on a rack.

Chocolate Tarts

Torta del Nonno GRANDFATHER'S TART

A homey, old-fashioned tart with a filling that definitely brings chocolate pudding to mind. Warm and reminiscent of childhood memories and pleasures, it is as comforting to eat as it is well named.

Makes one 8-inch tart; 6 to 8 servings

12 ounces (340 g) pasta frolla I, II, or III dough (½ recipe, pages 320–323), made through chilling

1 cup plus 2 teaspoons (9.5 oz / 265 g) pastry cream (page 324), at room temperature

¼ cup (0.8 oz / 25 g) unsweetened cocoa powder, preferably Dutch process

1 large egg white

1 teaspoon (0.2 oz / 5 g) water

1 teaspoon (0.2 oz / 5 g) milk

¼ cup (1 oz / 28 g) pine nuts

Cut the pastry in half and return half to the refrigerator. Roll out the remaining half to an 8½-inch circle, turning and flipping the dough frequently to keep it even. Using the bottom of an 8-inch tart pan or springform pan, trim the dough to an 8-inch circle. Place the dough circle on a buttered baking sheet and refrigerate for 1 hour.

Preheat the oven to 375°F. Prick the bottom of the pastry all over with a fork and bake until the edge is pale golden, about 12 minutes. Cool completely on a rack.

Mix the pastry cream and cocoa; set aside 2 teaspoons. Place the tart shell on a buttered baking sheet and spoon the remaining cream onto the center of the pastry. Spread the cream to within 2 inches of the edge. Beat the egg white and water together and brush over the 2-inch border. Roll out the remaining dough on a lightly floured surface to a 9-inch circle. Gently place the dough over the cream-covered pastry, centering the circle carefully. Press the edges lightly together and trim the edge of the dough even with the bottom pastry. Mold the dough to the shape of the pastry cream with the edges of your hands. The tart should look somewhat like the flat-brimmed hats worn by Italian priests.

Mix the reserved chocolate cream and the milk and carefully spread it over the dome of the tart. Lightly brush the 2-inch rim with the remaining egg white. Sprinkle the pine nuts over the painted dome.

Decorate the side of the pastry with a continuous half-moon pattern using the top half of the bowl of a teaspoon or a small cookie cutter.

Baking. Bake at 375°F until the edge is golden, about 30 minutes. Slide onto a rack and cool completely.

Torta Dumont CHOCOLATE-NUT LATTICED TART FROM VENICE

"But where did this wonderful tart get its name?" I asked the Venetian baker, for Dumont scarcely sounds Italian. As it turns out, it is French, or the Venetian fantasy of a country dessert from the mountains of France. I suspect that it acquired a little city sophistication once it came to Venice, where a bit of enchantment is to be expected.

Makes one 8-inch tart; 6 to 8 servings

2 sticks plus 1 tablespoon (8.5 oz / 240 g) unsalted butter, at room temperature

1/2 cup plus 2 tablespoons (4.4 oz / 125 g) sugar

3 large eggs

1/2 cup (2.6 oz / 75 g) blanched almonds

1/4 cup (0.8 oz / 25 g) unsweetened cocoa powder, preferably Dutch process

Grated zest of 1 lemon

Scant 2/3 cup (3.2 oz / 90 g) all-purpose or pastry flour

1 teaspoon (0.2 oz / 5 g) baking powder

8-inch unbaked tart shell with 2 ounces / 60 g dough reserved for lattice (pasta frolla I, II, or III, pages 320–323)

Using the whisk if you have one, cream the butter and sugar in a mixer bowl until light and fluffy. Add the eggs, one at a time, beating thoroughly after each addition. Grind the almonds and cocoa to a fine powder in a food processor fitted with the steel blade. Stir the almond mixture and the lemon zest into the butter mixture by hand. Sift the flour and baking powder over the batter and fold in with a rubber spatula until well blended.

Spread the filling in the tart shell. Make a lattice of six strips of dough as directed on page 321. If you want, you can roll the strips with your fingers and flatten each one slightly before setting it on top. The dough is so rich that it is easy to work by hand. Join the strips firmly to the edge of the tart shell.

Baking. Preheat the oven to 375°F. Bake until the pastry is golden, 30 to 35 minutes. Let cool 10 to 15 minutes and remove the sides of the pan. Cool completely on a rack.

Torte

Cakes

Stroll down any street in an Italian town and you'll see unmistakable evidence of the famous Italian sweet tooth. Bakeries and *pasticcerie* on almost every block boast windows and shelves full of rustic tarts and richer, creamier *dolci*, examples of satisfying simple desserts and the more ornate category of sweets that includes confections dreamed up to celebrate holidays, saint's days, festivals, and feast days. Who could be surprised? Even the Romans had a bakers' guild and loved their layer cakes, flat cheesecakes, little tarts filled with custard or cheese, and baked pastries sweetened with honey or grape must.

The craze for sweets has been with the Italians for a very long time. The entire tradition of cooking with sugar began particularly early in Italy as a result of the Crusades and voyages of Venetian traders. Sugar came to Sicily with the Arabs, who brought their elaborate pastries, as well as sugarcane and almond paste, and transformed Palermo into a city of sumptuous pastries made of lemons and sweet oranges, almonds, dates, and figs. Venice was the great center of the medieval spice trade, and its cooks were apt pupils who quickly learned the secrets of Arab pastry baking. When sugar first arrived, it was called *il sale dolce*, sweet salt, and the Italian used it as a flavoring in all food, not just desserts, which were not set aside until the end of a meal, as they are now, but interspersed with other courses. Both sugar and spices were first sold in pharmacies, because they were considered medicinal wonders with health benefits, although they were destined for luxurious preparations on the tables of the rich. By 1300 Florence allowed only one hundred special bakers to work with sugar and spices and to make marzipan, the base of almost all medieval and modern baking. Marzipan was called *frutta di martorana*, named for the convent in Palermo famous for its extraordinary trompe l'oeil fruits, vegetables, and animals.

Pastry baking became an art separate from bread baking in the late fifteenth century—the pastry cooks' guild was formed in 1492—but *torte* then were both sweet and savory, like *pasta frolla* wrapped around meats and poultry, mushrooms, and dried fruits seasoned with spices. Four and twenty blackbirds really were baked into a pie; the recipe was published in the first European cookbook, *De Honesta Voluptate et Valetudine* in 1474 (in Italy, of course). The monks of early medieval Siena may have been enjoying their *panforte*, in which spices and pepper joined forces with sweet fruits and nuts, but it wasn't until the Renaissance that most sweets came into their own. Bartolomeo Scappi, the chef of Pope Pius IV, wrote an enormous treatise that contained the first in-depth look at pastry baking; it even had a recipe for dough layered with lard and rolled and folded like the puff pastry we make today. Pastry cooks appeared in the kitchens of great houses and courts and created radical innovations in the art of desserts.

Soon the secrets of the pastry baker spread to the West. As a young bride, Maria de' Medici took her cooks to France where they taught the French cooks so well that a century later, when La Varenne wrote his first careful cookbook with its meticulous measurements and instructions, the French had become the acknowledged masters of the art. Now we tend to forget the importance of Italy's contributions. What, after all, is a genoise but the pastry of Genoa given a Gallic name? It is much easier to see the culinary stamp of other countries. *Pan di Spagna*, Spanish bread, is sponge cake brought by the Spaniards when they conquered Sicily in the fifteenth century, and plum cake came from England with the Duke of Wellington, who didn't want to leave his cake behind. These sweets mingling with the indigenous specialties and the tastes of individual regions came to life as the Genoese made sweet focaccia with raisins, the Venetians invented the cornmeal *zaletti* they still eat today, and the Sicilians made the cannoli and *cassata* that bear the culinary stamp of the earlier Normans and Arabs. The monasteries and nunneries of Sicily played such a crucial role in the making of sweets that they had a virtual monopoly on the most important recipes of the region. Until the unification of Italy in 1861, cookies, cakes, and numerous pastries were made only in these religious retreats, and it was only as the nuns began to move out of the convents that the tradition began to change.

The Italian passion for sweets has had centuries to develop, so it is no surprise that every celebration comes with dessert. Easter couldn't arrive in Naples without *pastiera* or in Palermo without *cassata*. *Panforte* is the quintessential sweet of Christmas in Siena. For birthdays, marriages, confirmations, and baptisms, the art of the pastry baker is always at the table.

Ricotta Cheesecakes and Creamy Rice Tarts

Pastiera NEAPOLITAN EASTER RICOTTA CAKE

The two ingredients that give the *pastiera* its special flavor are somewhat difficult to find, but look in Middle Eastern shops for orange flower water and try big food emporia and health-food stores for the soft white winter wheat berries. The berries must be the soft ones (the hard, red winter wheat berries will never cook to the right consistency—I know because I have tried); the white berries are often used in Naples as ornaments of the tomb of Christ in the days leading up to Easter. One Neapolitan cookbook suggests that the grain be soaked for fifteen days in a frequently refreshed water bath, but that seems excessive to me. Even three or four days require planning beyond what most of us care to undertake, but these grains need that long to soften. The berries are the lightly chewy center of the filling and are reminders of the rebirth that comes with every spring; the exotic flavors are evidence of the Phoenicians, Romans, Crusaders, and Arabs who arrived over the centuries at the port of Naples with their own spices, flavorings, and ingredients.

Makes one 9¹/₂-inch cake; 8 servings

WHEAT BERRIES

¹/₂ cup plus 1 tablespoon (3.5 oz / 100 g) soft white wheat berries

1 tablespoon (0.5 oz / 13 g) lard

2¹/₂ cups (1 lb 5 oz / 610 g) milk

1 teaspoon (0.2 oz / 5 g) sugar

¹/₄ teaspoon ground cinnamon

2 thin strips lemon zest

Three or four days before you plan to make the *pastiera*, soak the wheat berries in 2¹/₂ cups of cold water, changing the water daily, until softened. Pour the berries and the final soaking water into a saucepan and add the lard. Boil, uncovered, for 15 minutes. Drain the berries and return them to the clean saucepan. Add the milk, sugar, cinnamon, and lemon zest and cook, uncovered, over medium-low heat, stirring occasionally, until the berries are plump and split open and look creamy from having absorbed the milk, about 2 hours.

continued

Pastiera, *continued*

Drain the berries and place in a bowl; add just enough water to cover and let stand at least 3 hours or overnight.

DOUGH

2 cups plus a scant 2 tablespoons (10.5 oz / 300 g) unbleached all-purpose flour or 2¹/₂ cups (10.5 oz / 300 g) pastry flour

³/₄ cup (5.3 oz / 150 g) sugar

Pinch of salt

1 stick (4 oz / 115 g) unsalted butter, at room temperature

¹/₄ cup (1.8 oz / 50 g) lard, at room temperature

1 large egg

2 large egg yolks

BY HAND

Place the flour, sugar, and salt in a bowl and stir to mix. Cut the butter and lard into small pieces and cut it into the flour mixture with a pastry blender or two knives until the mixture resembles coarse meal. Slowly stir in first the egg and then the egg yolk, mixing thoroughly. Gather the dough together and knead it briefly on a lightly floured surface just until the dough comes together.

BY MIXER OR PROCESSOR

Refer to *pasta frolla I* instructions (page 320) for electric mixer and food processor methods.

Dough Preparation. Roll out two thirds of the dough (refrigerate the remaining third) on a lightly floured surface to ¹/₄ to ³/₈ inch thick and ease the dough into a well-buttered and lightly floured 9¹/₂-inch springform pan. Trim the edge with a sharp knife and neaten with your fingers. Build up the top edge with the dough trimmings so that the latticework will have something to grip on to. Refrigerate for 30 minutes. Remove from the refrigerator and partially bake the dough in a 350°F oven. If you find it difficult to keep the dough from sliding down the side of the pan while baking, press the dough firmly against the springform side with the back of a fork after 7 minutes. Bake until lightly golden, 8 to 10 minutes longer, pressing the dough against the side of the pan two more times or as needed.

FILLING

1¹/₂ cups (12 oz / 340 g) fresh ricotta

1¹/₂ cups (10.5 oz / 300 g) sugar

3 large eggs, separated, at room temperature

1 tablespoon (0.5 oz / 15 g) orange flower water

1 teaspoon (0.14 oz / 4 g) vanilla extract

1 cup (5.3 oz / 150 g) chopped candied orange peel (page 39)

Press the ricotta through a wire-mesh sieve into a mixing bowl, or process with several pulses in a food processor fitted with the steel blade until smooth. You may transfer the ricotta to a mixing bowl or continue in the processor. Add the sugar and beat until creamy. Add the egg yolks, orange flower water, and vanilla and stir or process with repeated pulses until thoroughly blended. If you haven't before, transfer to a mixing bowl. Drain the wheat berries and add to the ricotta mixture. Add the orange peel and stir by hand until blended. Beat the egg whites until soft peaks are formed and fold into the ricotta mixture. Pour the filling into the tart shell and smooth the top.

Roll out the remaining dough $1/4$ to $3/8$ inch thick on a lightly floured surface. Using a straight edge and a sharp knife or ravioli cutter, cut the dough into $3/4$-inch-wide strips. Arrange the strips over the filling as a lattice. Trim the strips and press onto the tart shell.

Baking. Preheat the oven to 375°F. Bake until the filling is set and the crust golden brown, 65 to 75 minutes. Cool on a rack.

Crostata di Ricotta ITALIAN CHEESECAKE OR RICOTTA TART

Although it seems unlikely that such an elegant cake could come from humble beginnings, this cheesecake, from the mountainous Garfagnana region of Tuscany, is based on the highly prized ricotta of that rustic area. Its popularity survives in various forms in Italy today, although this recipe comes from Joyce Goldstein, who lived in Italy before she became chef first at the Café at Chez Panisse and later at Square One, in San Francisco.

Makes one $9^1/2$-inch cheesecake; 8 to 10 servings

$1/2$ cup (2.8 oz / 80 g) golden raisins

3 to 4 tablespoons (1.5 to 2 oz / 45 to 55 g) Marsala

1 pound (450 g) ricotta, preferably whole milk

$1/2$ cup (3.5 oz / 100 g) sugar

1 tablespoon (0.3 oz / 9 g) unbleached all-purpose flour

4 large eggs, separated, at room temperature

$1/4$ cup (2 oz / 60 g) heavy cream

$1/4$ cup (2 oz / 60 g) sour cream

1 teaspoon (0.14 oz / 4 g) vanilla extract

$1/4$ teaspoon salt

Deep $9^1/2$-inch unbaked pastry shell (pasta frolla II or III, pages 320–323, made with 2 tablespoons Marsala and 1 teaspoon grated lemon zest instead of the vanilla)

continued

Crosata di Ricotta, *continued*

Soak the raisins in the Marsala at least 15 minutes. Drain, reserving the Marsala.

Press the ricotta through a wire-mesh sieve into a mixing bowl, or process with several pulses in a food processor fitted with the steel blade until smooth, then transfer to a mixing bowl. Add the sugar and flour and beat with a wooden spoon until creamy. Add the egg yolks, heavy and sour creams, reserved Marsala, and the vanilla; stir until thoroughly blended. Stir in the raisins. Beat the egg whites and salt until they form stiff peaks and fold into the ricotta mixture. Pour the filling into the tart shell and smooth the top.

Baking. Preheat the oven to 350°F. Bake until the filling is set and the pastry is golden brown, 50 to 60 minutes. Turn off the oven and let the cake cool with the oven door open for 30 minutes. This cake is so much better served warm that I urge you to bake it 2 to 3 hours before serving it or at least the same day you plan to eat it. If you must refrigerate it, warm it at 350°F for 20 to 30 minutes before serving.

Variation. Binario di frolla alla ricotta is essentially an Italian ricotta cheesecake in a flat strip of pastry that looks like the railroad track for which it is named. Follow the ricotta filling ingredients for the previous recipe but use 12 ounces (340 g) of *pasta frolla II* or *pasta frolla III* dough (pages 322 to 323) instead of the unbaked pastry shell.

Roll the chilled dough into a 17 by 7-inch rectangle on a lightly floured surface. Trim to about 16 by 6 inches and transfer to a buttered or parchment-lined baking sheet. Refrigerate while you prepare the filling.

Remove the rolled-out dough from the refrigerator and place on a work surface. Using a ruler and a very sharp knife, cut two long strips, each 1/2 inch wide, from one long side, and two short strips, each 1/2 inch wide, from one short side. Return the large dough rectangle to the baking sheet. Lightly brush a 1/2-inch border on the large rectangle with water and place the long strips on each side of the rectangle; then fit the short strips neatly on the short sides of the rectangle, trimming the strips as needed. Press the strips onto the rectangle lightly with your fingertips.

Spread the ricotta filling, adding 1/4 cup (1.5 oz / 40 g) of candied fruit (optional) inside the pastry strips. Sprinkle 2 to 3 tablespoons (0.5 to 0.8 oz / 15 to 22 g) of pine nuts over the filling. You may have enough filling left to make small *budini* in individual buttered baking dishes.

Preheat the oven to 350°F. Bake the *binario* until the top is set and lightly golden, 35 to 40 minutes; bake the *budini* about 20 minutes. Cool about 10 minutes on the baking sheet and transfer to a rack to cool completely.

Torta di Riso RICE TART

Rice tarts are a very ancient tradition in Italian desserts, but no one knows whether they actually date back to Marco Polo's voyage to the East, when Venetian traders, merchants, and sailors began bringing rice back from the Orient in ever-increasing amounts. By the sixteenth century there was an explosion of rice planting in the countryside around Venice, and housewives gave free rein to their imaginations and dreamed up elaborate rice dishes to satisfy their culinary fantasies. Perhaps that explains the origins of a venerable Venetian dessert exotically named *torta alla turchesca*, a Turkish tart that combined rice cooked in milk with butter, sugar, raisins, almonds, a few dates, and pine nuts bound together with eggs and egg yolks. It sounds remarkably similar to this *torta di riso*, which is but one of the many variations on the theme available in Italy today. Almonds are often included in *torta alla turchesa* and can certainly be added to this tart as well.

Makes one deep 8-inch tart; 8 servings

3 cups (25.6 oz / 730 g) milk

1¼ cups (10.5 oz / 300 g) water

½ cup plus 2 tablespoons (4.4 oz / 125 g) sugar

2 strips lemon zest

Pinch of salt

1 cup plus 1½ tablespoons (7 oz / 200 g) originario rice

1 heaping cup (5.8 oz / 165 g) raisins

¼ cup Marsala or rum (2 oz / 60 g), plus 1 to 2 tablespoons (0.5 oz to 1 oz / 15 to 30 g) for brushing

2 large eggs, separated, at room temperature

1 teaspoon (0.14 oz / 4 g) vanilla extract

5 tablespoons (2.5 oz / 70 g) unsalted butter, at room temperature

Deep 8-inch unbaked tart shell (pasta frolla I, II, or III, pages 320–323), baked 20 to 25 minutes

Heat the milk, water, sugar, lemon zest, and salt to a boil in a heavy saucepan. Stir in the rice and reduce the heat to very low. Simmer, covered, stirring occasionally, until the liquid is absorbed, 35 to 40 minutes. Spread the rice on a dinner plate to cool and discard the lemon zest.

While the rice is cooking, soak the raisins in the ¼ cup of Marsala for at least 30 minutes.

When the rice has cooled to room temperature, whisk the egg yolks and vanilla in a mixing bowl until blended. Stir in the rice. Add the butter and raisins with the Marsala and mix thoroughly. Beat the egg whites until the peaks are stiff but not dry and fold into the rice mixture. Pour the filling into the tart shell.

continued

Torta di Riso, *continued*

Baking. Preheat the oven to 400°F. Bake just until lightly creamy inside (a skewer inserted in the center should not come out completely clean), about 30 minutes. If the top is too pale, you can brown it briefly under a broiler. Cool on a rack, and brush the surface with 1 to 2 tablespoons Marsala, making a few holes with a toothpick to allow the liquid to penetrate the interior. Serve at room temperature.

Variations. To make *budini di riso*, bake the rice pudding in six fully baked tartlet shells at 400°F for 20 minutes.

Cassata EASTER CAKE OF SICILY

For centuries all the *cassate* of Sicily were made by nuns in their convents, and there are stories that those nuns worked so hard before Easter that some even forgot their regular devotions. They were busy making the quintessential Sicilian dessert that combines tastes brought by the Arabs with the *pan di Spagna* that came with the Spanish. Some think that the word *cassata* comes from the Arab *qas'at*, which means "big, deep bowl"; others convincingly argue that it comes from the old Sicilian word *caseata*, from the Latin *caseus*, meaning "cheese." Either way, it is a delicious dessert of *pan di Spagna* layered with ricotta flavored with candied fruit and bits of chocolate. In Italy the top is decorated with pale green candied strips of a squash related to the pumpkin family (I've seen it in the market as tall as a ten-year-old child), but citron makes a fine substitute. If you like, you can garnish the cake by setting a candied orange half in the center and arranging candied fruits and nuts around it.

Makes one 8- or 9-inch filled cake; 8 servings

2¼ cups (1 pound 2 oz / 500 g) ricotta

¾ cup (5.3 oz / 150 g) granulated sugar

4 to 5½ tablespoons (2 to 2.8 oz / 60 to 75 g) rum

5 ounces (4.9 oz / 140 g) chopped semisweet chocolate, or about ¾ cup (4.5 oz / 128 g) semisweet chocolate chips

Scant 1 cup (5 oz / 140 g) chopped candied orange peel (page 39) or candied fruit

8-inch pan di Spagna (page 364) or 8½-inch pasta maddelena (page 365)

7 ounces (200 g) marzipan or almond paste (page 326)

About ¼ cup (1 oz / 30 g) confectioners' sugar

Press the ricotta through a wire-mesh sieve into a mixing bowl, or process with several pulses in a food processor fitted with the steel blade until smooth and transfer to a mixing bowl. Add the granulated sugar and beat with a wooden spoon until creamy. Stir in 2 to 3 tablespoons of the rum. Add the chocolate and orange peel and stir to combine.

Cut the cake horizontally with a long thin-bladed knife into three equal layers. Place the top layer of cake, cut side up, in an unbuttered 8- or 9-inch springform pan (use an 8-inch pan for the 8-inch cake or a 9-inch pan for the 8^1/$_2$-inch cake). Brush the cake with 1 tablespoon of rum. Knead the almond paste or marzipan on a work surface sprinkled with the confectioners' sugar until stiff enough to hold its shape when rolled out and cut. Roll into a 10 by 3-inch rectangle. Line the side of the pan with parchment paper. Cut the second cake layer and the almond paste into 3-inch squares and line the side of the pan with alternating cake and almond paste squares. Trim the top edges so that the squares are even with the top of the pan.

Spoon the ricotta filling over the bottom cake layer and smooth the top. Lightly press the last cake layer, cut side down, onto the filling and fold the tops of the cake and almond paste squares over the cake. Brush the top with the remaining 1 to 1^1/$_2$ tablespoons of rum. Refrigerate, covered with waxed paper, until cold, several hours or overnight.

ROYAL ICING

2 cups plus 2 tablespoons (10.5 oz / 300 g) confectioners' sugar, sifted after measuring

3 large egg whites

2 teaspoons (0.4 oz / 11 g) fresh lemon juice

Beat the sugar, egg whites, and lemon juice in a deep mixer bowl until well blended. Beat at medium-high speed until smooth, thick, creamy, and white, about 5 minutes. Use immediately or transfer to a bowl and place plastic wrap over the surface to prevent a crust from forming. It will keep a week in the refrigerator. Invert the cake onto a serving platter and spread the top and sides with the icing. Let dry at room temperature for several hours. Refrigerate at least 3 hours before serving.

Spice Cakes and Fruitcakes

Plum Cake

Every baker in Italy has his own recipe for plum cake, an English classic that is now found all over Italy and is a favorite at teatime. It is essentially a pound cake made with the same weight of raisins as flour, sugar, and butter. It was first introduced after Waterloo when the Duke of Wellington, unmoved by French cuisine, brought his own pastry chefs with him to Paris and thus spread the recipe for plum cake. The Italians took to it with the same fervor that the English have taken to Italy, and it appears everywhere, in small towns as well as large. You might even encounter commercial versions sealed hermetically in small packages of plastic wrap. Slightly dry, this cake is permeated with the lovely fragrance of rum.

Makes one 9 by 5-inch cake

2 sticks (8 oz / 225 g) unsalted butter, at room temperature

1 cup plus 2 tablespoons (8 oz / 225 g) sugar

4 large eggs, at room temperature, lightly beaten

1 large egg yolk, at room temperature, lightly beaten

1/4 cup plus 3 tablespoons (3.5 oz / 100 g) rum

1 teaspoon (0.14 oz / 4 g) vanilla extract

1 1/3 cups (7 oz / 200 g) currants (soaked in the rum overnight, if you choose, and drained, rum reserved)

1 3/4 cups (8 oz / 225 g) pastry flour

1 teaspoon (0.2 oz / 5 g) baking powder

1/3 cup (1.2 oz / 33 g) sliced blanched almonds

Cream the butter and sugar with a wooden spoon or the paddle of an electric mixer until light and fluffy, about 5 minutes by hand or 3 to 4 minutes by mixer at high speed. Add the eggs and egg yolk, one at a time, beating thoroughly after each addition. Add the rum and vanilla and beat until light and fluffy, 5 minutes longer by hand or 2 to 3 minutes longer by mixer at high speed. Toss the currants in a bit of the flour to coat them. Sift the flour and the baking powder over the batter and fold in with a rubber spatula just until blended. Gently fold the currants into the batter.

Butter and flour an 8 1/2 by 4 1/2-inch or 9 by 5-loaf pan. Pour the batter into the pan, but don't smooth the top; instead, mound the batter a bit in the center so that it rises like a pound cake. Sprinkle the almonds over the top.

Baking. Preheat the oven to 350°F. Bake until a skewer inserted in the center comes out clean, 1 hour 10 minutes to 1 hour 15 minutes. The cake will begin to shrink away from the sides of the pan. Don't be surprised if the cake breaks open on top, as many pound cakes do. Cool for 10 minutes, then unmold by inverting onto a rack, removing the pan, and inverting onto a second rack so it can cool right side up.

Variations. To make plum cake *integrale* (whole wheat), substitute 1 cup (4 oz / 115 g) of whole wheat flour and a scant $^2/_3$ cup (2.2 oz / 65 g) of sifted unbleached cake flour for the pastry flour. Make as directed.

Torta Rustica di Noci e Caffè
A RUSTIC COUNTRY CAKE OF ESPRESSO AND WALNUTS

This simple, moist cake of walnuts and espresso was once commonly made at home on the Tuscan coast north of Viareggio. It has since become almost a memory, and today only old people still eat and remember it.

Makes one 8-inch cake or small cake ring; 6 to 8 servings

About 2 cups (7 oz / 200 g) walnut pieces

7 tablespoons (3.5 oz / 100 g) unsalted butter, at room temperature

$^1/_2$ cup plus 2 tablespoons (4.4 oz / 125 g) sugar

2 large eggs

$1^3/_4$ cups minus 2 tablespoons (7.9 oz / 225 g) all-purpose flour

$^1/_2$ teaspoon (0.08 oz / 2.5 g) baking powder

$^1/_2$ teaspoon (0.08 oz / 2.5 g) salt

$^1/_2$ cup (4.4 oz / 120 g) warm strong brewed espresso, or 3 tablespoons (1 oz / 30 g) instant espresso powder dissolved in $^1/_2$ cup (4.4 oz / 120 g) warm water

1 teaspoon (0.14 oz / 4 g) vanilla extract

Finely grind about ten of the walnut pieces and set aside for the top; coarsely chop the remaining walnuts.

Cream the butter and sugar with a wooden paddle or electric mixer until light and fluffy. Add the eggs, one at a time, beating thoroughly after each addition. Sift the flour, baking powder, and salt together. Beat in the flour mixture alternately with the coffee and vanilla in three additions, beginning and ending with the flour. Stir the chopped walnuts into the cake batter.

Butter and lightly flour an 8-inch cake pan or 6-cup ring mold. Pour the cake batter into the prepared pan and sprinkle with the ground walnuts.

Baking. Preheat the oven to 350°F. Bake the cake until a skewer inserted in the center comes out clean, 50 to 60 minutes for the 8-inch cake or 40 to 50 minutes for the ring mold. Cool completely on a rack.

Torta Speziata SPICE CAKE

Spice cake, Italian style, is very moist and tender and is delicious with rum-flavored whipped cream.

Makes one 8-inch cake

²/₃ cup (3.5 oz / 100 g) raisins

7 tablespoons (3.5 oz / 100 g) unsalted butter, at room temperature

¹/₂ cup (3.5 oz / 100 g) granulated sugar

1 large egg

1²/₃ cups (8.1 oz / 230 g) all-purpose flour

¹/₂ cup plus 2 tablespoons (2 oz / 60 g) best-quality Dutch-process cocoa

2 teaspoons (0.4 oz / 10 g) baking powder

1 heaping teaspoon (0.1 oz / 3 g) ground cinnamon

1 teaspoon (0.1 oz / 3 g) ground nutmeg

¹/₄ teaspoon ground cloves

³/₄ teaspoon (0.13 oz / 3.5 g) salt

³/₄ cup plus 1 teaspoon (6.5 oz / 185 g) warm strong brewed espresso, or 3 tablespoons instant espresso powder dissolved in ³/₄ cup plus 1 teaspoon (6.5 oz / 185 g) hot water

Confectioners' sugar

Soak the raisins in warm water to cover for 15 to 30 minutes; drain. Cream the butter and granulated sugar with a wooden paddle or electric mixer until light and fluffy. Add the egg and beat thoroughly. Sift all but 1 tablespoon of the flour, the cocoa, baking powder, cinnamon, nutmeg, cloves, and salt together. Beat in the flour mixture alternately with the espresso in three additions, beginning and ending with the flour. Toss the raisins with the remaining 1 tablespoon of flour and fold into the batter.

Butter and flour an 8-inch cake pan; pour the batter into the pan and smooth the top.

Baking. Preheat the oven to 350°F. Bake until the cake shrinks slightly from the side of the pan, 40 minutes; it should still be slightly moist inside. Cool on a rack. Invert the cake onto a serving plate and sift confectioners' sugar over the top.

Torta Contadina A COUNTRY CAKE

A rich, moist chocolate treat filled with nuts and fruits, this is neither a spice cake nor a true chocolate cake, but is, instead, the best of both worlds. When making this dish, bakeries use leftover crumbs from pound or sponge cake or ladyfingers, or whatever else they have on hand, within reason, and so can you.

Makes one 8- or 8¹/₂-inch cake

¹/₂ cup (2.7 oz / 75 g) raisins

1¹/₂ cups (7.9 oz / 225 g) candied orange peel (page 39) or half candied orange peel and half candied fruit

3 cups (13 oz / 375 g) cake crumbs

³/₄ cup plus 3 tablespoons (7.9 oz / 225 g) milk

1 large egg

1 large egg yolk

¹/₂ cup plus 1 teaspoon (1.8 oz / 50 g) unsweetened cocoa powder, preferably Dutch process

¹/₄ cup (1.8 oz / 50 g) sugar

2 teaspoons (0.4 oz / 10 g) baking powder

1 teaspoon (0.08 oz / 2.5 g) ground cinnamon

³/₄ teaspoon (0.08 oz / 2.5 g) grated nutmeg

³/₄ teaspoon (0.1 oz / 3 g) ground cloves

5 tablespoons (2.5 oz / 70 g) unsalted butter, at room temperature

About ¹/₂ cup (2 oz / 55 g) pine nuts

Coarsely chop the raisins with an oiled knife and place in a mixing bowl. Grind the orange peel and half the cake crumbs to a coarse mixture in a blender or food processor fitted with the steel blade; add to the raisins. Transfer to a mixing bowl and add half the milk and the egg and mix well. Coarsely grind the remaining cake crumbs in the food processor. Stir the cake crumbs, the remaining milk, the egg yolk, cocoa, sugar, baking powder, cinnamon, nutmeg, and cloves into the raisin mixture. Add the butter and stir until thoroughly blended.

Butter and flour an 8- or 8¹/₂-inch cake pan and pour the batter into the pan. Sprinkle enough pine nuts over the batter to cover the top.

Baking. Preheat the oven to 350°F. Bake until a skewer inserted in the center comes out clean, about 50 minutes. Cool in the pan 10 to 15 minutes, then unmold onto a rack to cool completely.

Panforte TRADITIONAL FRUITCAKE OF SIENA

Panforte means "strong bread" in Italian, and this phenomenal dessert is the best fruitcake you could ever imagine, denser than sweet bread and only slightly less rich than candy. The monks of Siena may have been among the first to find pleasure in its rich, nutty flavor, and Crusaders may have taken it as a long-lasting food to give them quick bursts of energy on their rigorous pilgrimages. No one is quite sure when *panforte* was first prepared, although there are stories that it dates back to the year 1000, when Siena was one of the first cities in Italy to use sugar and rare spices, including the white pepper that gives *panforte* its authentic medieval taste.

These days *panforte* remains the traditional Christmas treat of Siena. I once read an article by Seán Ó Faoláin in which he expressed amazement that some people went to Siena for this remarkable chewy sweet alone. It's true that Siena has numerous other enchantments—its extraordinary *campo*, which may be the most beautiful piazza in the world, its sinuous curving streets of pink and gray stone buildings, its almond-eyed madonnas, and its moment of collective madness in a horse race called the Palio—but surely there is also fascination in finding your way to Siena in a quest for *panforte*, one of the best *dolci* Italy has to offer.

Makes one 9-inch cake

1 cup (5 oz / 140 g) whole hazelnuts

³/₄ cup (4 oz / 115 g) whole blanched almonds

³/₄ cup plus 2 tablespoons (4.6 oz / 130 g) coarsely chopped candied orange peel (page 39)

³/₄ cup plus 2 tablespoons (4.6 oz / 130 g) finely chopped candied citron (page 39)

Grated zest of 2 lemons

¹/₂ cup (2.5 oz / 70 g) unbleached all-purpose flour

1 teaspoon (0.08 oz / 2.5 g) ground cinnamon

¹/₄ teaspoon ground coriander

¹/₄ teaspoon ground cloves

¹/₄ teaspoon freshly ground nutmeg

Pinch of ground white pepper

³/₄ cup (5.3 oz / 150 g) granulated sugar

³/₄ cup (8.8 oz / 252 g) honey

2 tablespoons (1 oz / 28 g) unsalted butter

Confectioners' sugar

Preheat the oven to 350°F. Toast the hazelnuts on a baking sheet until the skins pop and blister, 10 to 15 minutes. Rub the skins from the hazelnuts in a kitchen towel. Toast the almonds on a baking sheet until very pale golden, 10 to 15 minutes. Chop the almonds and hazelnuts very coarsely. Mix the nuts, orange peel, citron, lemon zest, flour, cinnamon, coriander, cloves, nutmeg, and pepper together thoroughly in a large mixing bowl.

Butter a 9-inch springform pan; line the bottom and sides with parchment paper and then butter the paper. Heat the granulated sugar, honey, and butter in a large, heavy saucepan over low heat, stirring constantly, until the syrup registers 242°F to 248°F on a candy thermometer (a little of the mixture will form a ball when dropped into cold water). Immediately pour the syrup into the nut mixture and stir quickly until thoroughly blended. Pour immediately into the prepared pan and smooth the top with the spatula. The batter will become stiff and sticky very quickly, so you must work fast.

Baking. Reduce the oven temperature to 300°F. Bake about 30 to 40 minutes. The *panforte* won't color or seem very firm even when ready, but it will harden as it cools. Cool on a rack until the cake is firm to the touch. Remove the side of the pan and invert the cake onto a sheet of waxed paper. Peel off the parchment paper. Dust heavily with confectioners' sugar.

Variation. To make *panforte scuro* (dark), add 2 ounces (60 g) of coarsely chopped dried figs and 1 to 2 tablespoons (0.2 to 0.4 oz / 6 to 12 g) of unsweetened cocoa powder.

Sponge Cakes

Amor Polenta CORNMEAL CAKE

This lightly sweetened cornmeal cake from Varese, in the upper Brianza region around Como and Bergamo, is a relative of pound cake, although it has more character, which comes from the distinctive flavor and texture of the corn and the splashes of maraschino liqueur. The delicacy of this cake belies most people's idea of cornmeal; Americans are likely to eat it at teatime, while Italians pour cream over the sliced cake for dessert.

Makes two 10 by 4-inch cakes made in Rehrücken, *or saddle of venison, pans*

3/4 cup plus 3 tablespoons (7.5 oz / 210 g) unsalted butter, at room temperature

Scant 1 cup (6.5 oz / 185 g) sugar

3 large eggs, at room temperature

6 large egg yolks, at room temperature

2 to 4 tablespoons (1 to 2 oz / 30 to 60 g) maraschino liqueur or 1/2 teaspoon (0.07 oz / 2 g) almond extract

3/4 cup minus 1 tablespoon (3.5 oz / 100 g) sifted all-purpose flour

3/4 cup (3.5 oz / 100 g) fine yellow cornmeal, plus more for the pans

2 1/2 teaspoons (0.4 oz / 12.3 g) baking powder

1/2 teaspoon (0.08 oz / 2.5 g) salt

Confectioners' sugar (optional)

This dough can be made by hand, but it requires a lot of vigorous beating and whisking to achieve its characteristic lightness. Given the choice, I'd definitely use an electric mixer.

Cream the butter and sugar with the whisk, if you have one, of an electric mixer until very light and fluffy, about 5 minutes at medium speed. Add the eggs and egg yolks, one at a time, beating thoroughly after each addition. The batter should be lemony yellow. Stir in the liqueur. Sift the flour, cornmeal, baking powder, and salt together and fold into the batter, smoothing out any lumps but taking care not to deflate the batter.

Butter two *Rehrücken* (saddle of venison) pans and coat with cornmeal. Pour the batter into the two prepared pans.

Baking. Preheat the oven to 375°F. Bake until a skewer inserted in the center comes out clean, about 30 minutes. Cool on a rack and unmold while the cake is still very slightly warm. If you like, you may follow the example of some bakeries and sift confectioners' sugar over the tops so lightly that you can still see the ridges of the cakes.

Tiramisù "PICK ME UP"

Tiramisù means "pick me up," and this version of the traditional Venetian dessert is
a dream because it is as easy to make as it is delicious to eat. *Pan di Spagna* is given
an infusion of rum and then layered with whipped cream and fresh mascarpone, the
sweet, buttery cheese from Lombardy, before it is dusted with cocoa and finished with
shavings of chocolate. If you don't find mascarpone in your market, use the freshest,
finest cream cheese instead, and, if you'd prefer to add a bit of espresso powder to the
cocoa, go right ahead.

*Makes one 2-layer rectangular cake
(14 by 8 inches); 10 to 12 servings*

1 pound 2 ounces (500 g) fresh mascarpone or
   best-quality cream cheese

3 cups (1 lb 9 oz / 720 g) heavy cream

1¹/₂ cups plus 2 tablespoons (7.9 oz / 225 g)
   confectioners' sugar

7 to 8 tablespoons (3.5 to 4.2 oz / 105 to 120 g) rum

1 teaspoon (0.14 oz / 4 g) vanilla extract

Pan di Spagna alla cioccolata (see variation for
   pan di Spagna, page 365), baked in a half-sheet
   pan and cooled completely

2 tablespoons (0.4 oz / 12 g) unsweetened cocoa
   powder, preferably Dutch process

¹/₂ ounce (15 g) semisweet chocolate (optional)

Press the mascarpone through a wire-
mesh sieve into a mixing bowl, or process
with several pulses in a food processor
fitted with the steel blade until smooth.
Add the cream, 1¹/₂ cups of the sugar, 3 to
4 tablespoons of the rum, and the vanilla
and beat with a wooden spoon or process
until smooth and creamy.

Cut the cake in half horizontally; you
will have two equal layers. Brush each
layer with 2 tablespoons of rum. Spread
half the cheese mixture on top of one
cake layer and top with the second cake
layer. Spread the remaining cheese filling
over the top layer.

Mix the cocoa and remaining 2 tablespoons of sugar and sift over the cake. If you
want, grate the chocolate over the cocoa.

Torta Savoia SAVOY CAKE

This delicious lemony chocolate cake is essentially a marble pound cake with a lovely silky texture.

Makes one 9 by 5-inch cake

2 sticks (8 oz / 225 g) unsalted butter, at room temperature

1 cup plus 2 tablespoons (8 oz / 225 g) sugar

4 large eggs, at room temperature

1 large egg yolk, at room temperature

Grated zest of 1¹/₂ lemons

2 tablespoons plus 1 teaspoon (1.2 oz / 35 g) fresh lemon juice

2 cups (7 oz / 200 g) sifted cake, or 1¹/₂ cups (7 oz / 200 g) sifted all-purpose flour

1 teaspoon (0.2 oz / 5 g) baking powder

3 ounces (85 g) best-quality bittersweet chocolate

Cream the butter and sugar with a wooden paddle or an electric mixer until light and fluffy, about 5 minutes by hand or 3 to 5 minutes by mixer at high speed. Add the eggs and egg yolk, one at a time, beating thoroughly after each addition. Beat in the lemon zest and juice and continue beating until light and fluffy again, about 5 minutes by hand or 2 to 3 minutes by mixer at high speed. Sift in the flour and baking powder, a bit at a time, over the batter and gently fold with a rubber spatula into the batter just until smooth.

Pour half the batter into another mixing bowl. Carefully melt the chocolate in a small, heavy saucepan over low heat. Quickly stir a little batter from one bowl into the melted chocolate so that the warm chocolate won't harden, and then fold into the remaining batter in that same bowl.

Butter and flour a 9 by 5-inch loaf pan. Pour half the chocolate batter into the pan and then pour half the lemon batter. Repeat with the remaining batters. The pan should be about two-thirds full. Don't smooth the top; let the batter mound in the center so that it bakes like a pound cake. To marble the cake, draw a table knife lengthwise back and forth through the cake batter several times.

Baking. Preheat the oven to 325°F. Bake until a skewer inserted in the center comes out clean, about 1 hour 20 minutes. Cool on a rack for about 10 minutes. Invert the cake onto a rack, gently remove the pan, and invert the cake onto a second rack so that it can cool right side up. Let cool to room temperature.

Pan di Spagna SPONGE CAKE

Pan di Spagna, literally "bread from Spain," actually did come to Italy with the Spanish who conquered Sicily and ruled it from 1412 to 1713. Now this delicate sponge cake is the basis for numerous sweets in Sicily, the island of extravagant desserts, including the famous *cassata*. You can certainly use it instead of genoise or *biscotti savoiardi* in any number of other desserts as well.

Makes one 17 by 14-inch or 18 by 13-inch sheet sponge cake, two 9 by 5-inch cakes, or one 8-inch round cake baked in a springform

5 large eggs, separated, at room temperature

³/₄ cup (5.3 oz / 150 g) sugar

2 tablespoons (1.5 oz / 42 g) honey

2 tablespoons (1 oz / 30 g) rum

1 teaspoon (0.14 oz / 4 g) vanilla extract

Pinch of salt

1¹/₂ cups (6 oz / 175 g) pastry flour, unsifted

¹/₂ teaspoon (0.08 oz / 2.5 g) baking powder

Beat the egg yolks, half the sugar, the honey, rum, and vanilla in a mixer bowl until light, creamy, and lemon colored, about 5 minutes using a hand-held mixer or 3 minutes using a stand mixer. Warm the egg whites in a bowl set in warm water for a few minutes, add the salt, and beat until they form soft peaks. Gradually beat in the remaining sugar and continue beating until the peaks are stiff. Sift the flour and baking powder together and return to the sifter. Fold a quarter of the egg whites into the egg yolk mixture with a rubber spatula. Sift a quarter of the flour mixture over the top and fold in. Continue folding in the egg whites and flour mixture alternately until all is incorporated.

Line the bottom and long sides of a jelly-roll or half-sheet pan (18 by 13 inches or 17 by 14 inches) with parchment paper, or flour and butter two 9 by 5-inch loaf pans, or flour and butter an 8-inch spring-form pan. Pour the batter into the prepared pan/s and smooth the top/s.

Baking. Preheat the oven to 350°F. Bake until the cake springs back when touched lightly near the center, 20 to 25 minutes for the sheet pan, 30 to 35 minutes for the loaf pans, or 40 to 45 minutes for the springform pan. Cool on a rack for 5 to 10 minutes. Use a knife to release any part of the cake that is sticking to the pan. Invert the cake/s onto a rack or baking sheet and very gently remove the pan. Peel off the parchment paper if using. Invert onto a second rack so that it can cool right side up. Let cool to room temperature.

Variations. To make *pane all'anice,* a Sardinian specialty, add 1 tablespoon (0.2 oz / 6 g) of lightly crushed aniseeds to the batter with the flour. Bake in the loaf pans as directed.

To make *anicini,* cut the baked and still hot *pane all'anice* into 1-inch-thick slices and then cut again into 4 1/2 by 1-inch strips. Bake on their sides on baking sheets at 350°F until crisp, crunchy, and a bit dry, 5 to 10 minutes. Sardinians dip these into a sweet dessert wine.

To make *pan di Spagna alla cioccolata* (chocolate), substitute 1 tablespoon (0.5 oz / 15 g) of Kahlúa for the rum, 1 tablespoon (0.5 oz / 15 g) of water for the honey, and 1/3 cup (1 oz / 30 g) of unsweetened Dutch-process cocoa and 2/3 cup (3.3 oz / 95 g) of pastry flour sifted together three times as the equivalent of the pastry flour. Omit the baking powder. Prepare as directed for *pan di Spagna,* baking in a half-sheet pan.

Pasta Maddalena GENOISE-LIKE CAKE

The virtues of *pasta maddalena* are many: it can be the base for numerous delicious desserts, such as the extravaganza known as *torta delizia* (page 367), and it can be layered with the simplest or the most elaborately flavored creams. But bakers will also tell you that if you find your tart crusts are soggy, or if you make a tart one day and expect to serve it the next, you can bake the tart with a very fine layer of *maddalena* next to the bottom crust. The cake will soak up any fruit juices and leave the crust firm and dry. You can also make several cakes and freeze what you don't need with very good results.

Makes two 8 1/2-inch cakes

1 cup (7 oz / 200 g) sugar

3 large eggs

4 large egg yolks, at room temperature

2 tablespoons (1 oz / 30 g) water

1 tablespoon (0.75 oz / 21 g) honey

1 1/3 cups (6 oz / 175 g) pastry flour, unsifted

1/8 teaspoon salt

Scant 1/2 cup (2.8 oz / 80 g) cornstarch or potato starch

1 1/2 teaspoons (0.3 oz / 7.5 g) baking powder

1 teaspoon (0.14 oz / 4 g) vanilla extract

Grated zest of 1 lemon

continued

Pasta Maddalena, *continued*

Whisk the sugar, eggs, egg yolks, water, and honey in the top of a double boiler over simmering, not boiling, water until the mixture feels lukewarm. Remove to a mixer bowl or widemouthed mixing bowl. Beat at high speed until thick, pale lemon yellow, creamy, and about tripled in volume, 3 to 4 minutes. Do not overmix or the batter will fall.

Sift the flour, salt, cornstarch, and baking powder together twice. Sift the flour mixture and fold into the egg mixture in three additions. Fold in the vanilla and lemon zest. The batter should be soft, airy, and very light and must be handled very carefully so that the air bubbles aren't inadvertently deflated.

Butter and flour two 8½-inch cake pans. Gently pour the batter into them.

Baking. Preheat the oven to 375°F. Bake until the cake springs back when lightly touched, 25 to 30 minutes. Cool the cakes in the pans 5 to 10 minutes, then invert onto cake racks and cool completely.

This cake batter is very much like that for ladyfingers (*savoiardi*) and can be used as the base for numerous filled desserts, like the *torta di mele e ciliege* (page 338), *zuppa inglese*, and other recipes calling for ladyfingers. You can brush each cake with rum and spread with pastry cream or zabaglione cream. You can also layer with whipped cream and fruits or jam or just serve it as is dusted with confectioners' sugar.

Torta Delizia LAYER CAKE WITH AN ALMOND PASTE LATTICE

This extraordinary cake is composed of layers of sponge cake or *pasta maddalena* brushed with maraschino liqueur, spread with apricot jam, and covered with a lattice of almond paste. The classic basket-weave covering is complicated. If you are trying it for the first time, practice first on waxed paper.

Makes one 2-layer cake

1 cup (8.4 oz / 240 g) water

¼ cup (1.8 oz / 50 g) sugar

⅓ cup (3 oz / 8.5 g) maraschino liqueur

1 pasta maddalena cake (½ recipe, page 365), cooled

⅔ cup (5.4 oz / 150 g) apricot glaze (page 325)

1 pound 2 ounces (500 g) almond paste, or more if needed

2 large egg yolks

3 to 4 large egg whites

Whisk the water and sugar together in a bowl until the sugar dissolves; then whisk in the liqueur. Cut the cake horizontally into two layers. Place the bottom layer on parchment paper and brush the top with half the liqueur mixture; spread a fine layer of apricot glaze over the top. Cover with the second layer, making certain to put the cut side down so that no crumbs can flake into the almond paste topping that will cover it. Brush it with the remaining liqueur mixture.

Beat the almond paste at high speed in a mixer bowl until it is well broken up and creamy. Add the egg yolks, one at a time, beating thoroughly after each addition;

then beat at high speed 2 minutes longer. The almond paste should be very thick, smooth, sticky, and able to hold its shape. Add three of the egg whites and beat thoroughly. Beat in the last egg white, a small amount at a time, until the mixture is the consistency of buttercream; it should be soft enough to be piped through a pastry bag but stiff enough to hold its shape. Have extra almond paste on hand in case you beat in too much egg.

Spoon the almond paste mixture into a pastry bag fitted with a #48 pastry tip (a flat ⅜-inch-wide tip with one serrated edge). The almond paste is traditionally piped in a basket-weave pattern. Before you start on the cake you can practice on a piece of waxed paper. When you feel confident with the pattern, you can then peel off the strips and return them to the remaining almond paste in the bag. Because fantasy is such a basic part of the Italian baker's vocabulary, you may also simplify the pattern by piping straight lines in a simple lattice pattern.

To make the basket weave, pipe one straight line very near the top of the cake. Pipe a second straight line parallel to the

continued

Torta Delizia, *continued*

first with a space the width of the piping (³/₈ inch) between the two lines. To create the illusion that the lines actually go over and under each other, you will pipe short lines that alternately go over or stop at the horizontal line. Pipe the first vertical line starting at the top center of the cake, but stop at the first line. Pipe a line next to it that goes over the first line and stops at the second. Pipe a line on the other side of your first vertical line that goes over the first line and stops at the second. Continue these short alternating lines on both sides of the top center line. Next pipe a third horizontal line ³/₈ inch below the second line. All the weaving lines that stopped at the first line can now be piped from the other side of the first line, over the second, and brought to the third line. Continue until the side is completely covered in basket weave. End your weaving lines

precisely at the edge of the horizontal lines so that the piping lines look actually woven. Be sure to clean your tip frequently and to pipe your lines completely to the edge of the cake.

Finish the cake by piping the almond paste mixture in deep swirls or waves all around the side of the cake. Let the cake dry at a cool room temperature overnight.

GLAZE

1 large egg, beaten

¹/₃ cup (2.6 oz / 75 g) apricot glaze (page 325)

Brush the top of the cake very gently and carefully with the egg, following the direction of the pattern.

Baking. Preheat the oven to 360°F. Bake on the parchment paper on a baking sheet until golden brown, about 30 minutes. Let cool completely on a rack. Brush the top and sides with the apricot glaze.

Biscotti

Cookies

The first time I was served cookies for breakfast in an Italian house, I assumed the family had run out of bread and the cookies were the best substitute they could come up with in a hurry. The second time, I realized that Italians actually ate cookies for breakfast. In fact, Italians like cookies so much that they eat them for a midmorning snack with cappuccino or *caffè latte*, as a little treat with cheese at the end of a midday meal, with abandon at teatime, and at the end of a meal dunked into wine or the local Vin Santo.

Italians have given their cookies wonderful names that sound as if they're straight out of fairy tales or nursery rhymes: *brutti ma buoni* (ugly but good), *baci di dama* (lady's kisses), *bocche di lupo* (wolves' mouths). Often the same cookie has an entirely different name in a different city or region. What are called *brutti ma buoni* in Tuscany unaccountably become *bocconcini del nonno* (little bite-size sweets for grandfather) in Rome.

Cookies have been part of the Italian way of eating for a long time. The source of the almond paste cookies that are now famous from one end of Italy to the other is probably the marzipan of Sicily that came with the Arabs, who also introduced cane sugar, almonds, and spices at about the same time that Crusaders were bringing oranges, lemons, dates, and figs to the island. Normans were refining sugar in Sicily before the twelfth century, and the Arabs brought a tradition of elaborate pastries that transformed Palermo into a city of sumptuous eating. We know that in 1308 at a banquet in honor of Clement V there were at table two trees full of all kinds of fruit—apples, figs, pears, and peaches—that seemed absolutely real but were actually made of *pasta reale*, or marzipan, made at the nearby monastery of Martorana. It was, in fact, the busy fingers and nimble hands of nuns that kept the tradition of marzipan alive as they made ever more extravagant fantasies: little lambs turned up for Easter, and perfect replicas of prickly pears, salamis, and fine slices of prosciutto proved their finesse with a paste made only of almonds, sugar, and egg whites. The nuns kept their recipes secret as they perfected them and made all kinds of elegant decorations on little cookies. Their sweets were covered with angels and fruits that resembled bas-reliefs on local churches, and some even had geometric fondant frostings and glazes inspired by local cathedral ceilings.

Today the tradition is dying out, but every region still has its own special almond paste cookies. The amaretti of Saronno are famous everywhere, but there are amaretti from Piedmont as well, *ricciarelli* from Siena, *brutti ma buoni* from Florence, *marasche* from Bologna, and *pignolate* from Sicily. Glass cases in bakeries are full of all kinds of cookies; every little *paese* and town has its own local cookie that is every bit as much a part of the regional tradition as its breads and pastas.

Nut Paste Cookies

Brutti ma Buoni alla Milanese

HAZELNUT PASTE COOKIES

Brutti ma buoni means "ugly but good," and there's no question that these cookies are aptly named. Nothing about their appearance is one bit tempting, but pop one of these chewy, crunchy little hazelnut lumps into your mouth and you'll discover that they're irresistible.

Makes 2^1/$_2$ dozen cookies

8 or 9 large egg whites, at room temperature

1 cup plus 3 tablespoons (8.4 oz / 240 g) sugar

^{3}/$_4$ teaspoon (0.1 oz / 3 g) vanilla extract

1^1/$_2$ cups (7 oz / 200 g) hazelnuts, toasted, skinned (page 32), and chopped to the size of fat rice grains

Beat 8 of the egg whites in a mixer bowl until they form soft peaks. Continue to beat, gradually adding the sugar, until the peaks are stiff and shiny. Stir in the vanilla until blended. Fold in the nuts. Transfer the mixture to a saucepan and cook over low heat for 10 minutes. Initially the mixture will soften and then, as it cooks, it should come together in a single, although not well defined, lump. It is done when it is light brown and pulls away from the sides of the pan. If the mixture is dry and crumbly, add the last egg white, a bit at a time, to moisten it. Remove the mixture from the heat. Drop the dough by the teaspoonful 1^1/$_2$ inches apart on well-buttered or parchment-lined baking sheets.

Baking. Preheat the oven to 300°F. Bake until lightly colored, 25 to 30 minutes. If the cookies seem too soft, you can turn off the oven and leave them there for 10 minutes. Cool on racks. These keep well stored in an airtight container.

Variations. Tuscans use half almonds and half hazelnuts in addition to adding about 1^1/$_2$ teaspoons of ground coriander to their dough. In Venice, the cookies are sometimes made with the addition of ^{1}/$_2$ cup (1.6 oz / 45 g) of unsweetened cocoa powder to the dough.

Brutti ma Buoni ALMOND PASTE COOKIES

Brutti ma buoni, Tuscan style.

Makes 2¹/₂ dozen cookies

1 pound 5 ounces (600 g) almond paste

2 or 3 large egg whites

¹/₃ cup (1.8 oz / 50 g) chopped candied citron (page 39)

¹/₃ cup (1.8 oz / 50 g) chopped candied orange peel (page 39)

¹/₃ cup (1.8 oz / 50 g) chopped candied lemon peel (page 39)

Confectioners' sugar

Beat the almond paste and two egg whites together with an electric mixer or in a food processor fitted with the steel blade until blended. Add the citron and orange and lemon peels and mix just until blended. The dough should be sticky but stiff enough to hold its shape. If the mix-

ture is too stiff, mix in the last egg white a bit at a time.

Shaping. Place a small bowl of cold water nearby in which to dip your fingers. Drop the dough by the rounded tea-spoonful 1¹/₂ inches apart on buttered or parchment-lined baking sheets. Pinch each cookie between your thumb and first two fingers to form an irregular pyramid. The dough should hold its shape so that the baked cookie is a one-bite experience.

Baking. Preheat the oven to 300°F. Bake until very light golden, about 25 minutes. Dust with confectioners' sugar and remove to racks to cool. Store in an airtight container.

Marasche ALMOND PASTE COOKIES ENCLOSING A WILD CHERRY

Dome-shaped cookies wrapped around a cherry and covered with sliced almonds, *marasche* are named for the wild sour cherries from Bologna that are hidden in the center of their almond paste coverings.

Makes about 40 cookies

14 ounces (400 g) almond paste

1 or 2 large egg whites

About 40 preserved amarena cherries
    (about 7 oz / 200 g)

About ³/₄ cup (2.8 oz / 80 g) sliced raw almonds

Mix the almond paste and one egg white at low speed in an electric mixer or in a food processor fitted with the steel blade until smooth. If the almond paste is too dry, mix in the second egg white, a bit at a time.

Shaping. Place a small bowl of cold water nearby in which to dip your fingers. Pinch off a piece of almond paste about the size of a walnut and roll into a ball. Flatten the ball in one hand, place a cherry in the center, and wrap the paste around the cherry. Smooth it by rolling it in your hand. The ball should be about ³/₄ to 1 inch.

Pick up a handful of sliced almonds in your other hand and roll the ball in the almonds until it is generously and thoroughly covered. Repeat with the remaining almond paste, cherries, and almonds. Place about 1¹/₂ inches apart on buttered or parchment-lined baking sheets.

Baking. Preheat the oven to 350°F. Bake 20 to 25 minutes until lightly golden. Cool on racks.

Variations. To make *bocche di lupo* (wolves' mouths), spoon the almond paste into a pastry bag fitted with a ³/₈-inch star-shaped tip. Pipe a 2-inch-long strip of the mixture on buttered or parchment-lined baking sheets, place one cherry at the beginning of each strip, and double back to meet the cherry. Repeat with the remaining almond paste and cherries. Omit the sliced almonds. Bake until lightly golden, about 18 minutes.

Amaretti I MACAROONS

Amaretti Lombard-style are crisp little almond-flavored cookies that crunch before they dissolve on the tongue.

Makes 30 cookies

3/4 cup plus 1 tablespoon (4.4 oz / 125 g)
   blanched almonds

1 cup (4.4 oz / 125 g) confectioners' sugar

1 teaspoon (0.1 oz / 3 g) all-purpose flour

2 large egg whites

1/3 cup (2.5 oz / 70 g) granulated sugar

3/4 teaspoon (0.1 oz / 3 g) almond extract (optional)

Grind the almonds to a fine powder in a nut grinder or food processor fitted with the steel blade. (If using the processor, add 1/4 cup of the confectioners' sugar, a bit at a time, to keep the almonds from becoming too oily.) Mix the nuts with the confectioners' sugar and the flour. Beat the egg whites in a bowl until they form soft peaks.

Continue beating, gradually adding the granulated sugar, until stiff and shiny. Fold in the nut mixture and the almond extract, if you are using it, until blended.

Shaping. Spoon the meringue into a pastry bag fitted with a 1/2-inch plain tip. Pipe 1 1/2-inch-wide mounds 1 1/2 inches apart on parchment-lined or buttered baking sheets. Smooth the top of each cookie with a damp finger.

Baking. Preheat the oven to 300°F. Bake 40 to 45 minutes, until very lightly brown. Turn off the oven and let the amaretti dry in the oven an additional 20 to 30 minutes. Cool on racks. Store in airtight containers.

Amaretti II MACAROONS FROM PIEDMONT

Unlike the classic amaretti from Saronno, these Piedmontese macaroons are soft and slightly chewy and taste intensely of almonds.

Makes 20 macaroons

1¹/₃ cups (7 oz / 200 g) blanched almonds

Scant 1 cup (6.5 oz / 185 g) superfine sugar

3 to 4 tablespoons (1.5 to 2 oz / 45 to 60 g) egg white

1 teaspoon (0.14 oz / 4 g) almond extract (optional)

Confectioners' sugar

Grind the almonds to a fine powder with a mortar and pestle or in a nut grinder or food processor fitted with the steel blade. (If using a food processor, add 2 table-spoons of the sugar.) Mix the ground nuts and superfine sugar in a mixing bowl. Add 3 tablespoons of the egg whites and the almond extract, if you are using it, and mix until the dough is soft enough to be piped from a pastry bag but stiff enough to hold its shape. Mix in the last 1 tablespoon of egg white, a bit at a time, if needed.

Shaping. Spoon the batter into a pastry bag fitted with a ¹/₂-inch plain tip. Pipe 2¹/₂-inch-wide rounds 1¹/₂ inches apart on buttered or parchment-lined baking sheets and flatten them a bit. Sift a little confectioners' sugar over the tops and let stand at room temperature 1 to 2 hours.

Baking. Preheat the oven to 300°F. Bake until very light tan, 25 to 30 minutes. Cool on racks. Store in airtight containers.

Pinolate CHEWY NUT COOKIES COVERED WITH PINE NUTS

Why *pinolate*? Because these fat balls of chewy hazelnut cookies are studded with *pignoli*, the famous pine nuts of Italy, which make the cookie look like a porcupine at rest.

Makes about 50 cookies

FIRST PASTE

²/₃ cup (3.5 oz / 100 g) blanched almonds

1¹/₂ cups (10.5 oz / 300 g) sugar

3 or 4 large egg whites

Grind the almonds to a fine powder in a nut grinder or food processor fitted with the steel blade. (If using the processor, add 2 tablespoons of the sugar.) Mix the nuts and the sugar in a mixing bowl. Add three of the egg whites and mix until the dough comes together in a sticky ball, adding the last egg white, a bit at a time, if needed. If using the food processor, add the remaining sugar and process to mix. Add the egg whites to the nut mixture and process to mix.

SECOND PASTE

³/₄ cup (3.5 oz / 100 g) skinned toasted hazelnuts (page 32)

²/₃ cup (3.5 oz / 100 g) raw almonds

1³/₄ cups (12.3 oz / 350 g) sugar

3 tablespoons unsalted butter (1.5 oz / 45 g), at room temperature

1 teaspoon (0.3 oz / 7 g) honey

3 or 4 large egg whites

Grind the hazelnuts and almonds to a fine powder in a mortar and pestle, a nut grinder, or a food processor fitted with the steel blade. (If using a food processor, add 2 tablespoons of the sugar.) Mix the nuts and sugar in a mixing bowl, or add the remaining sugar to the food processor and process to mix. Add the butter, honey, and three egg whites and mix until the dough comes together in a paste, adding the last egg white, a bit at a time, if needed. If using the processor, add the butter, honey, and egg whites and process until the dough comes together in a paste.

Stir both pastes together with a wooden spoon until well blended. The dough should be stiff.

COATING

1³/₄ cups (6.8 oz / 195 g) pine nuts

Confectioners' sugar

Spread the pine nuts on a large platter. Roll a bit of the dough between the palms of your hands to form a ball the size of a walnut and then roll in the pine nuts until completely covered. Repeat with the remaining dough and pine nuts. Place the balls 1¹/₂ inches apart on buttered or parchment-lined baking sheets and flatten slightly. Let stand, uncovered, overnight at room temperature.

Baking. Preheat the oven to 400°F. Sift confectioners' sugar over the dough balls. Bake until the pine nuts are light golden, 15 to 20 minutes. Cool on racks.

Bolle di Neve "SNOWBALLS" FROM THE ITALIAN ALPS

The snow that lasts all year round in some parts of the Italian Alps inspired these "snowballs" made from freshly ground almond paste and dusted with a shower of confectioners' sugar.

Makes about 4 dozen cookies

1 cup minus 2 tablespoons (4.3 oz / 125 g) blanched almonds

¹/₂ cup plus 2 tablespoons (4.4 oz / 125 g) granulated sugar

¹/₂ cup plus 2 tablespoons (3 oz / 85 g) candied orange peel (page 39)

1 cup (4.4 oz / 125 g) confectioners' sugar, plus more for the shaped dough

2 to 3 teaspoons egg white

Process the almonds and granulated sugar in a food processor fitted with the steel blade to coarse crumbs (or you can use 9 ounces / 255 grams of almond paste, page 326, and eliminate this step). Add the orange peel to the almond mixture or to the almond paste in a food processor and process to a coarse powder. Transfer to a mixing bowl and add the confectioners' sugar. Beat with an electric mixer until blended. If you are strong, you can beat the dough with a wooden spoon. Add 2 teaspoons of egg white and mix well. The dough should be firm enough to be shaped but not dry. Add the last teaspoon of egg white, a bit at a time, if needed.

Shaping. Dust a work surface with confectioners' sugar and place more sugar in a mound off to one side. Transfer the dough to the surface and roll into a log the diameter of a nickel; slice the log at 1-inch intervals. Roll each piece into a ball between the palms of your hands and then roll in confectioners' sugar so that it is completely covered. Place 1¹/₂ inches apart on buttered or parchment-lined baking sheets.

Baking. Preheat the oven to 325°F. Bake until golden brown on the outside but still soft inside, 18 to 20 minutes. Cool on racks.

Ricciarelli SOFT ALMOND PASTE COOKIES FROM SIENA

These soft and delicate cookies, shaped like the almond eyes of early Sienese painters' madonnas, are descendants of marzipan and are as ancient a Christmas sweet as *panforte*. Fragrant little cookies scented with vanilla, *ricciarelli* are best when made fresh at home, although they have become so famous that many industrial firms now package them and sell them for the holidays.

Makes 20 cookies

²/₃ cup (3.5 oz / 100 g) blanched almonds

14 ounces (400 g) almond paste

2 tablespoons (1 oz / 30 g) egg white

¹/₂ teaspoon (0.08 oz / 2.5 g) baking powder

1 teaspoon (0.14 oz / 4 g) vanilla

Confectioners' sugar

Grind the almonds to a fine powder in a nut grinder or food processor fitted with the steel blade. Transfer to a mixer bowl and mix in the almond paste with an electric mixer. Add the egg white and mix at the lowest speed until thoroughly blended. The dough should be firm. Add the baking powder and vanilla and mix until well blended.

Shaping. Transfer the dough to a floured surface and roll into a long log about ³/₄ inch in diameter. Slice the log at 2-inch intervals and shape each piece into a lozenge or diamond. Sift confectioners' sugar lightly over the shaped dough and flatten each piece slightly with a sugar-coated hand. Place the *ricciarelli* 1 inch apart on parchment-lined baking sheets and let stand, uncovered, at room temperature at least 1 hour or overnight.

Baking. Preheat the oven to 300°F. Bake until very light tan, 20 to 30 minutes. Cool on racks. Take care not to bake until brown or crisp; it is the softness that makes *ricciarelli* so delicious.

Pastine da Thé ITALIAN TEA COOKIES

The Italian sweet tooth gets its due every afternoon at teatime, when plates full of little cookies appear on tables in homes and restaurants all over the country to be consumed with a cool drink in the summer or a cup of espresso later in the year. Tea itself hasn't made much impact in Italy in the face of all those espresso beans, but these sweet morsels are perfect mid-afternoon snacks.

Makes about 3 dozen cookies

1¹/₃ cups (7 oz / 200 g) raw almonds

1 cup (7 oz / 200 g) sugar

¹/₂ cup (4.2 oz / 120 g) egg whites

¹/₃ cup (1.8 oz / 50 g) diced candied orange peel (page 39), or about 18 candied cherries, halved

Grind the almonds to a powder in a nut grinder or a mortar and pestle, or process them with 2 tablespoons of the sugar to a coarse powder in a food processor fitted with the steel blade; add the remaining sugar and process to a fine powder. Press through a wire-mesh sieve so that the powder is nearly as fine as flour. Place the almond powder and the egg whites in the food processor or in the bowl of an electric mixer and process or mix until well blended. The mixture should have enough body to be piped.

You can substitute 14 ounces (400 g) of almond paste (page 326) for the almonds and sugar. Place the almond paste in a food processor fitted with the steel blade or in the bowl of an electric mixer. Process or mix until the paste is broken up. Add the egg whites and process or mix to a smooth paste.

Shaping. Spoon the batter into a pastry bag fitted with a ³/₈ -inch star-shaped tip. Pipe 1-inch-wide stars 1¹/₂ inches apart onto buttered or parchment-lined baking sheets. Top each mound with a piece of candied orange peel or a cherry half. Let stand uncovered at room temperature overnight.

Baking. Preheat the oven to 375°F. Bake until lightly browned, 8 to 10 minutes. Cool on racks.

Butter Cookies

Baci di Dama LADY'S KISSES

These big, button-shaped, buttery cookies are fused with a spot of chocolate from Tortona in Piedmont, where sweets with somewhat frivolous, evocative names were served in the mid-nineteenth century to men seriously at work creating a unified Italy.

Makes 4 dozen cookies

1 cup minus 2 tablespoons (4.4 oz / 125 g) blanched almonds

$^1/_2$ cup plus 2 tablespoons (4.4 oz / 125 g) sugar

1 stick plus 1 tablespoon (4.5 oz / 130 g) unsalted butter, at room temperature

$1^1/_4$ teaspoon (0.2 oz / 5 g) vanilla extract

$^3/_4$ teaspoon (0.07 oz / 2 g) grated lemon zest

Pinch of salt

Scant 1 cup (4.4 oz / 125 g) all-purpose flour

4 ounces (115 g) semisweet chocolate

Grind the almonds to a very fine powder in a nut grinder or food processor fitted with the steel blade. (If using a food processor, add 2 tablespoons of the sugar so that the nuts don't become too oily.) Mix the almonds and the remaining sugar in a mixer bowl or in the food processor. Add the butter, vanilla, lemon zest, and salt and beat or process until very, very light and creamy, about 4 to 5 minutes with the mixer. If necessary, transfer the dough in the processor to a mixing bowl. Sift the flour over the top and fold in. You can refrigerate the dough overnight at this point or proceed.

Shaping. Break off pieces of the dough the size of fat cherries and roll into balls. Place $1^1/_2$ inches apart on buttered baking sheets and flatten slightly to about $^3/_8$ inch thick.

Baking. Preheat the oven to 350°F. Bake until delicate golden brown, 15 minutes. Cool on racks.

Assembling. Melt the chocolate in the top of a double boiler over simmering water. When the cookies are cool, make sandwiches by joining them in pairs with the melted chocolate, so that they do, in fact, look just a bit like the lady's lips for which they are named.

Ciambelline all'Uva RAISIN-DOTTED COOKIE WREATHS

These raisin-dotted wreaths are really just butter cookies in disguise.

Makes about 4¹/₂ dozen

1 stick plus 3 tablespoons (5.5 oz / 155 g) unsalted butter, at room temperature

1¹/₄ cups (8.8 oz / 250 g) sugar

2 large eggs, at room temperature

6¹/₂ tablespoons (3.4 oz / 98 g) milk

1 teaspoon (0.14 oz / 4 g) vanilla extract

¹/₂ teaspoon (0.07 oz / 2 g) lemon extract, or grated zest of 1 lemon

¹/₂ teaspoon (0.07 oz / 2 g) orange extract, or grated zest of 1 orange

3³/₄ cups plus four teaspoons (17.5 oz / 500 g) pastry flour or 3³/₄ cups (17.5 oz / 500 g) all-purpose flour

2 teaspoons (0.4 oz / 10 g) baking powder

Pinch of salt

²/₃ cup (3.5 oz / 100 g) golden raisins

1 large egg, beaten, for egg wash

Cream the butter and sugar in a mixer bowl until light and fluffy. Add the eggs, one at a time, beating thoroughly after each addition. Mix in the milk and vanilla, lemon, and orange extracts. Sift the flour, baking powder, and salt over the butter and mix until thoroughly blended. Stir in the raisins.

Shaping. Turn the soft, sticky dough out onto a well-floured surface. Pinch off a piece of dough the size of a walnut and roll it into a 6-inch-long log, ¹/₂ inch thick. Connect the ends to make a circle. It will resemble a little doughnut. Repeat with the remaining dough and place 1¹/₂ inches apart on buttered or parchment-lined baking sheets. Brush the tops with beaten egg.

Baking. Preheat the oven to 350°F. Bake until lightly golden, 12 to 15 minutes. Cool on racks.

Inglesine ROUND BUTTERY COOKIES WITH RUM-SOAKED RAISINS

Once they discovered Italy, the English came in drove, settling in Florence and the hills of Fiesole, bringing with them their tradition of tea and teatime. The Italians, who love a snack in mid-afternoon, were influenced by some of the English tastes and created this round buttery cookie with rum-soaked raisins in their honor.

Makes 3 dozen cookies

Scant ½ cup (2.3 oz / 65 g) raisins, soaked in rum to cover

¼ cup (2 oz / 55 g) unsalted butter, at room temperature

6 tablespoons (2.5 oz / 70 g) sugar

½ teaspoon (0.08 oz / 2.5 g) salt

1 large egg

2 tablespoons (1 oz / 30 g) milk

1 teaspoon (0.14 oz / 4 g) vanilla extract

¾ teaspoon (0.1 oz / 3 g) lemon extract

1 cup plus 1 tablespoon (5.3 oz / 150 g) all-purpose flour

¼ cup plus 1 teaspoon (1.8 oz / 50 g) potato starch

1 teaspoon (0.2 oz / 5 g) baking powder

Pinch of salt

Soak the raisins in the rum for at least 30 minutes. Drain, reserving 1 teaspoon of the rum.

Cream the butter, sugar, and salt in a mixer bowl until light and fluffy. Add the egg, milk, reserved rum, and the vanilla and lemon extracts and mix until well blended. Sift in the flour, potato starch, baking powder, and salt and mix until smooth. Fold in the raisins. Drop the dough by the teaspoonful 2 inches apart on buttered or parchment-lined baking sheets.

Baking. Preheat the oven to 375°F. Bake until lightly golden, 12 to 15 minutes. Cool on racks.

Variations. Substitute 1½ to 2 teaspoons of crushed aniseeds for the 1 teaspoon of rum.

Buranelli BUTTER COOKIES FROM BURANO

Close your eyes and picture the water stretching away from Venice, past the *palazzi* and gondolas on the Grand Canal, and think about finding your way to the little island of Burano that lies beyond Venice, where these S-shaped buttery cookies are made.

Makes about 4 dozen cookies

1 stick plus 2 teaspoons (4.3 oz / 125 g) unsalted butter, at room temperature

1 cup plus 3 tablespoons (8.4 oz / 240 g) sugar

5 large egg yolks

2 teaspoons (0.3 oz / 8 g) vanilla extract

3/4 teaspoon (0.1 oz / 3 g) lemon extract or grated zest of 2 lemons

Scant 3 cups (14 oz / 400 g) all-purpose flour

1 teaspoon (0.2 oz / 5 g) salt

Cream the butter and sugar in a mixer bowl until light and fluffy. Add the egg yolks, one at a time, beating thoroughly after each addition. Mix in the vanilla and lemon extracts. Sift the flour and salt over the mixture and mix until blended.

Shaping. Roll the dough on a floured surface into a log 2 inches in diameter. Slice the log at 3/8-inch intervals. Roll each piece into a 4-inch-long rod between the palms of your hands. Shape each rod into an inverted S and place 1 1/2 inches apart on buttered or parchment-lined baking sheets.

Baking. Preheat the oven to 375°F. Bake until pale blond and just golden at the edges, 20 to 25 minutes. Carefully remove to racks to cool.

Fregolata Veneziana FREGOLATA FROM VENICE

Fregolata means "crumbly," an apt name for this buttery, rich, slightly coarse cornmeal shortbread, which is baked as a nut-covered flat cake and cut into wedges after it has cooled.

Makes 10 to 12 cookie wedges

²/₃ cup (3.5 oz / 100 g) raw almonds

¹/₂ cup (3.5 oz / 100 g) granulated sugar

7 tablespoons (3.5 oz / 100 g) unsalted butter, melted and cooled

2 large egg yolks

2 teaspoons (0.4 oz / 11 g) lemon juice

Grated zest of 1 lemon

1 teaspoon (0.14 oz / 4 g) vanilla extract

¹/₄ teaspoon almond extract

³/₄ cup plus 1 teaspoon (3.5 oz / 100 g) fine yellow cornmeal

Scant ³/₄ cup (3.5 oz / 100 g) all-purpose flour

Pinch of salt

2 heaping tablespoons (0.9 oz / 25 g) raw almonds or skinned toasted hazelnuts (page 32), coarsely chopped

1 to 2 tablespoons (0.5 to 1 oz / 15 to 30 g) turbinado sugar

Grind the almonds to a coarse powder in a nut grinder or a mortar and pestle, or grind them and 2 to 3 tablespoons of the granulated sugar to a coarse powder in a blender or food processor fitted with the steel blade. Add the remaining sugar and process to a very fine powder. Transfer to a mixer or a large mixing bowl and beat in the butter until blended. Add the egg yolks, lemon juice, lemon zest, and vanilla and almond extracts and mix until well blended. Sift the cornmeal, flour, and salt over the almond mixture and stir just until the dough comes together. It is important not to overwork the dough.

Assembling. Butter an 8- or 9-inch pie plate. Spread the dough in the pan, using your fingers to distribute the dough to the edge. Sprinkle with the almonds or hazelnuts and the turbinado sugar.

Baking. Preheat the oven to 350°F. Bake for 20 minutes. Reduce the heat to 300°F and bake 20 minutes longer. Cool completely on a rack and cut into wedges to serve.

Ungheresi HUNGARIAN COOKIES, ITALIAN STYLE

What is the secret of this horseshoe-shaped butter cookie? Hard-cooked egg yolks give it an exceptional texture.

Makes about 80 little cookies

1 stick plus 3 tablespoons (5.5 oz / 155 g) unsalted butter, at room temperature

1 cup (4.4 oz / 125 g) confectioners' sugar

2¹/₂ large hard-cooked egg yolks, very finely sieved

1 cup plus 1 tablespoon (5.3 oz / 150 g) all-purpose flour

3¹/₂ tablespoons (1.4 oz / 40 g) potato starch

6 ounces (6 oz / 170 g) semisweet chocolate

Pinch of salt

Cream the butter and sugar in a mixer bowl until light and fluffy. Add the egg yolks, a bit at a time, beating thoroughly after each addition. Place the flour, potato starch and salt in a sifter and sift over the butter mixture while stirring by hand or mixing at the lowest speed of an electric mixer. Stir just until the dough is consistent.

Chilling. Wrap the dough tightly in plastic wrap and refrigerate 1 hour.

Shaping. Roll small pieces of the dough into logs 3¹/₂ inches long and ³/₈ inch thick; shape each log into a horseshoe. Place 1¹/₂ inches apart on buttered or parchment–lined baking sheets.

Baking. Preheat the oven to 375°F. Bake just until blond and sand colored but not golden, 10 to 15 minutes. Cool completely on racks.

Glazing. Melt the chocolate in the top of a double boiler over simmering water. Dip the ends of the cooled cookies in the melted chocolate. Place on baking sheets lined with waxed paper and refrigerate to set the chocolate.

Onde WAVES

These little ruffly cookies are dotted with a candied cherry or a single almond.

Makes 2 dozen cookies

1 stick plus 3 tablespoons (5.5 oz / 155 g) unsalted
    butter, at room temperature

1/3 cup plus 1 tablespoon (2.8 oz / 80 g) sugar

1 large egg white, plus 1 large egg white, lightly
    beaten, for brushing (optional)

1 teaspoon (0.14 oz / 4 g) vanilla extract

1/2 teaspoon (0.07 oz / 2 g) lemon extract or
    grated zest of 1 lemon

1 1/2 cups (7 oz / 200 g) all-purpose flour

Pinch of salt

24 candied cherries or raw whole almonds

Cream the butter and sugar in a mixer
bowl until light and fluffy. Beat in one egg
white and the vanilla and lemon extracts.
Sift the flour and salt over the mixture and
fold in with a rubber spatula until combined. The dough should be moist and
dense but soft enough to be piped.

Shaping. Spoon the dough into a pastry
bag fitted with a 3/8-inch star-shaped tip.
Place the pastry tip almost on a buttered or
parchment-lined baking sheet and squeeze
hard to make a 1 1/2-inch-wide mound;
release the pressure gradually and pull
forward 3 inches so that the cookies are
3 inches wide at the top but narrow to a
finer point, like a fat teardrop. The star tip

will give the cookie a lovely wavy appearance. Repeat with the remaining dough,
spacing the cookies about 1 1/2 inches apart.
Finish by setting a candied cherry or
almond at the narrow end of each cookie;
you can paint the narrow tip of the dough
with a little of the beaten egg white to hold
the cherry or almond in place, if you wish.

Baking. Preheat the oven to 350°F.
Bake until lightly golden, 15 to 20 minutes. Cool on racks.

Tegole d'Aosta TILE-SHAPED COOKIES FROM THE VAL D'AOSTA

These thin, round hazelnut cookies are named for the fine slate tiles that line the roofs of houses in the Val d'Aosta. You can either shape the warm cookies on a rolling pin or wine bottle or let them cool flat. This dough also makes wonderful *lingue di gatto* (page 388). These are wonderful tea and after-dinner cookies, but they don't keep well—especially the lighter and more delicate variety—because the humidity in the air causes them to lose their slight crunch.

Makes 4 dozen cookies

1 stick plus 3 tablespoons (5.5 oz / 155 g) unsalted butter, at room temperature

³/₄ cup plus 3 tablespoons (6.8 oz / 195 g) sugar

¹/₂ teaspoon (0.07 oz / 2 g) vanilla extract

²/₃ cup (3.3 oz / 95 g) hazelnuts, toasted and skinned (page 32)

3¹/₂ ounces (100 g) leftover cookies, preferably butter or sugar

¹/₄ cup (1.2 oz / 35 g) all-purpose flour

Pinch of salt

Scant ¹/₂ cup (3.7 oz / 105 g) egg whites

Cream the butter and sugar in a mixer bowl until light and fluffy. Add the vanilla and mix well. Grind the hazelnuts to a coarse powder in a nut grinder or food processor fitted with the steel blade; remove and set aside. Grind the leftover cookies to crumbs. Add the hazelnuts to the crumbs and process to a fine powder. Add to the butter mixture and mix until thoroughly blended. Stir in the flour and salt and fold until blended. Beat in the egg whites. The batter should be light and almost runny.

Shaping. You can shape these cookies either with a pastry bag or by hand. Spoon the batter into a pastry bag fitted with a ¹/₂-inch plain tip and pipe 2¹/₂-inch circles onto buttered and floured or parchment-lined baking sheets. Smooth the tops with the back of a spoon without flattening them. The cookies will spread during baking, so leave at least 3 inches between the circles. To shape by hand, drop 2 teaspoonfuls of the dough onto prepared baking sheets without flattening them, and smooth into 2¹/₂-inch circles using the back of a spoon dipped in cold water.

Baking. Preheat the oven to 375°F. Bake until the edges of the cookies are evenly browned, 7 to 10 minutes. Let cool on the baking sheets 3 to 4 minutes and then gently dislodge and transfer to racks to cool. You may shape the warm cookies over a rolling pin or wine bottle if you wish.

Variations. For a slightly less delicate cookie, use ¹/₃ cup plus 1 tablespoon (2.8 oz / 80 g) of egg white in the dough.

Lingue di Gatto CAT'S TONGUES

A *langue de chat* becomes a *lingue di gatto* in Italy, a delicate, crispy little cookie that is long and narrow and curled like a cat's tongue.

Makes 5 dozen cookies

1 stick (4 oz / 115 g) butter, at room temperature

$1/2$ cup plus 2 teaspoons (3.8 oz / 110 g) sugar

Grated zest of 1 lemon

1 teaspoon (0.14 oz / 4 g) vanilla extract

$1/4$ cup plus 2 tablespoons (3.5 oz / 100 g) egg whites

$3/4$ cup plus 2 teaspoons (3.9 oz / 110 g) all-purpose flour

$1/8$ teaspoon salt

Cream the butter and sugar in a mixer bowl until light and fluffy. Mix in the lemon zest and vanilla. Add the egg whites gradually, beating thoroughly after each addition. Sift the flour and salt together three times. Sift the flour mixture, a third at a time, over the batter, beating thoroughly after each addition.

Shaping. Butter and flour or line a baking sheet with parchment paper. Spoon the batter into a pastry bag fitted with a $1/4$-inch flat tip. Pipe $1^1/2$- to 2-inch-long strips about 1 inch apart onto the prepared baking sheet.

Baking. Preheat the oven to 350°F. Bake until the edges are crispy brown but the centers are still pale, about 10 minutes. Let cool for a moment or two, and then place each cookie over a rolling pin or wine bottle, immediately pressing the cookie to the rolling pin or bottle so that the cookie conforms to its shape. Remove when the shape is set. If the last cookies on the baking sheet are hard before you can mold them, return to the warm oven for a minute to soften.

Variations. To make *lingue di suocera* (mother-in-law's tongues), melt 5 ounces (140 g) of semisweet chocolate in the top of a double boiler over simmering water while the cookies are baking. Remove a just-baked cookie from the baking sheet with a spatula. Spread a little melted chocolate on the bottom with a knife. Remove another cookie and sandwich the chocolate between them. Immediately place over a rolling pin or wine bottle to mold as directed for *lingue di gatto.* Repeat with the remaining cookies and chocolate.

Biscotti

Biscotti al Latte VANILLA-SCENTED TEA BISCUITS

Another of those familiar vanilla-scented, slightly dry cookies so redolent of Italy, this delicate and buttery tea biscuit resembles a wreath-shaped sugar cookie.

Makes 6 dozen cookies

1 stick plus 3 tablespoons (5.5 oz / 155 g) unsalted butter, at room temperature

1 cup (7 oz / 200 g) sugar

1 tablespoon (0.7 oz / 21 g) honey

3 or 4 large eggs, at room temperature

1/2 cup plus 3 tablespoons (5.8 oz / 165 g) milk

1 teaspoon (0.14 oz / 4 g) vanilla extract

1/2 teaspoon orange extract (0.07 oz / 2 g), or grated zest of 1/2 orange

1/2 teaspoon lemon extract (0.07 oz / 2 g), or grated zest of 1 lemon

3 3/4 cups (17.5 oz / 500 g) all-purpose flour

2 teaspoons (0.4 oz / 10 g) baking powder

Pinch of salt

1 1/2 tablespoons (0.6 oz / 16.5 g) coarsely ground raw almonds

Cream the butter, sugar, and honey in a mixer bowl until light and fluffy. Add two of the eggs, one at a time, beating thoroughly after each addition. Mix in the milk and vanilla, orange, and lemon extracts. The batter may look curdled at this point, but don't worry; it will smooth out later. Sift the flour, baking powder, and salt over the batter; mix well.

Shaping. Transfer the dough to a floured surface. Break off pieces of dough the size of fat cherries; roll each piece into a thin 6-inch rod, and connect the ends to form a 3-inch ring. Place 1 inch apart on buttered or parchment-lined baking sheets. Beat one egg in a small bowl and brush the tops of the rings with the beaten egg. Sprinkle lightly with the ground almonds. Use the remaining egg if you run out of egg wash.

Baking. Preheat the oven to 325°F. Bake until lightly browned, 20 minutes. Cool on racks.

Biscotti d'Anice ANISE COOKIES

These anise-flavored cookies puff up like little sponge cakes in the oven and have the delicate, airy texture of ladyfingers when first cooked. Cut them in diagonal slices and bake them a second time to make the traditional crunchy anise-scented cakes of Sardinia.

Makes 2 dozen cookies

4 large eggs, at room temperature

¾ cup plus 2 tablespoons (6.3 oz / 180 g) sugar

1 teaspoon (0.17 oz / 4 g) vanilla extract

Grated zest of ½ lemon

1½ cups minus 1 tablespoon (7 oz / 200 g) all-purpose flour

Pinch of salt

¼ teaspoon baking powder

2 teaspoons (0.2 oz / 5 g) aniseeds, crushed

Beat the eggs and sugar in a mixing bowl until the mixture forms a slowly dissolving ribbon when the beaters are lifted, 5 to 10 minutes. Mix in the vanilla and lemon zest. Sift the flour and salt and sift again with the baking powder over the egg mixture; fold in gently. Stir in the aniseeds.

Shaping. Spoon the batter into a pastry bag with a plain tip. Pipe the batter in strips, 4 inches long and 1 inch wide, onto buttered or parchment-lined baking sheets. The piped batter should look like large ladyfingers.

Baking. Preheat the oven to 375°F. Bake until slightly crisp and brown on the edges, 20 minutes. Remove from the pan. If you want drier, crunchier biscotti, reduce the heat to 325°F. Cut each strip in half on the diagonal and bake on the baking sheet 5 to 10 minutes longer. Cool on racks.

Biscotti di Prato DIAGONALLY CUT ALMOND BARS FROM PRATO

These nut-studded bars are dry and crunchy because they are baked not once, but twice. Tuscans serve them after dinner with Vin Santo, the sweet dessert wine reserved for special occasions. Keep the biscotti in a cookie tin and they will last for a long time, but, if you let them dry out at room temperature, the flavor gets even better, and they will soften up immediately when dipped in a late harvest wine or port, if you can't find the special Vin Santo of Tuscany.

Makes about 4 dozen cookies

3³/₄ cups (17.5 oz / 500 g) all-purpose flour

2 cups (14 oz / 400 g) sugar

4 large eggs, at room temperature

2 large egg yolks, at room temperature

1 teaspoon (0.2 oz / 5 g) baking powder

Pinch of salt

1 teaspoon (0.14 oz / 4 g) vanilla extract

1¹/₃ cups (7 oz / 200 g) raw almonds, toasted (page 32) and coarsely chopped

Pour the flour in a mound on a work surface or in a big bowl. Make a well in the center and place the sugar, three of the eggs, the egg yolks, baking powder, salt, and vanilla in the well. Gradually work the flour into the ingredients in the well and mix with your hands until smooth. Knead the almonds in thoroughly and keep kneading, sprinkling with additional flour if needed, 4 to 5 minutes in all.

Shaping. Line two baking sheets that are at least 15 inches long with parchment paper, or butter and flour them. Divide the dough into quarters. Roll each piece of the dough on a floured surface into a log 2 by 2¹/₂ inches in diameter and place the logs at least 2 inches apart on the prepared baking sheets. Beat the remaining egg and brush it over the tops of the dough logs.

Baking. Preheat the oven to 350°F. Bake for 30 to 35 minutes until they are golden. Remove from the oven and reduce the temperature to 325°F. When they are cool enough to handle, use a serrated knife to cut the logs diagonally into ³/₄- to 1-inch slices and lay them cut side up on the sheets. Return to the oven for another 10 to 15 minutes. Cool on racks.

Variations. In Pistoia, these biscotti are made with a mixture of almonds and hazelnuts.

Tozzetti HAZELNUT AND ORANGE COOKIES FROM VENICE

These glossy little blond bars from Venice look as squat and chunky as the name implies (*tozzo* means "stocky"). But bite into one and you'll find a pale, soft interior with big chunks of hazelnut and hints of orange—a delicious, elegant surprise.

Makes twenty 4½ by 1½-inch bars, twenty-four 2¼-inch squares, or sixty 1½-inch squares

1 stick plus 1 tablespoon (4.5 oz / 130 g) unsalted butter, at room temperature

½ cup plus 2 tablespoons (4.4 oz / 125 g) sugar

2 large eggs, at room temperature

1 large egg yolk, at room temperature

¾ teaspoon (0.1 oz / 3 g) vanilla extract

½ teaspoon (0.07 oz / 2 g) lemon extract, or 1 tablespoon (0.5 oz / 15 g) lemon juice

½ teaspoon (0.07 oz / 2 g) orange extract, or 2 tablespoons (1 oz / 30 g) orange juice

Scant 2 cups (8.8 oz / 250 g) all-purpose flour

¼ teaspoon salt

1⅔ cups (8.2 oz / 235 g) toasted and skinned hazelnuts, each coarsely chopped into 2 or 3 pieces

⅓ cup (1.8 oz / 50 g) finely chopped candied orange peel (page 39)

Cream the butter and sugar in a mixer bowl until light and fluffy. Beat in one of the eggs and then the egg yolk. Mix in the vanilla, lemon, and orange extracts. Sift the flour and salt over the butter mixture, sprinkle with the nuts and orange peel, and gently fold in. If the dough seems too soft to be rolled out, refrigerate, covered, 1 to 1½ hours.

Shaping. Transfer the dough to a lightly floured surface and roll into a 15 by 9-inch rectangle. Roll up the dough on the rolling pin and unroll on a buttered and floured or parchment-lined baking sheet. Beat the remaining egg and brush over the dough.

Baking. Preheat the oven to 375°F. Bake until shiny and blond but not golden, 15 to 20 minutes. It should still be slightly soft inside. Remove from the oven and let stand 10 to 15 minutes. While still warm, cut into 4½ by ½-inch bars or 2¼-inch or 1½-inch squares. Transfer to racks to cool.

Cookies of Various Grains

Crumiri BUTTERY HORSESHOE-SHAPED COOKIES FROM PIEDMONT

These delicate, crumbly horseshoe-shaped cookies come from Piedmont, where the oldest families of the region traditionally made them every Saturday. Rich and surprisingly tender, they get their special taste from the slight crunch of cornmeal. This recipe can easily be doubled.

Makes 2 dozen cookies

1³/₄ sticks (7 oz / 200 g) unsalted butter, at room temperature

³/₄ cup (5.3 oz / 150 g) sugar

2 large eggs, at room temperature

1³/₄ cup (8.4 oz / 240 g) all-purpose flour

Pinch of salt

Scant 1 cup (4.5 oz / 120 g) fine yellow cornmeal

Cream the butter and sugar in a mixer bowl until very light and fluffy. Add the eggs one at a time, beating thoroughly after each addition. Sift the flour, salt, and cornmeal together and sift again over the batter; mix well.

Shaping. You can shape these cookies either with a pastry bag or by hand (I think the latter is easier). If using the pastry bag, spoon the dough into a bag fitted with a ³/₈-inch star-shaped tip (the traditional cookies are ribbed). Pipe 4-inch-long logs, ¹/₂ inch thick, about 2 inches apart on buttered and floured or parchment-lined baking sheets. Or, roll pieces of the dough, each about the size of a walnut, into long, thin logs of the same dimensions. Place 2 inches apart on the prepared baking sheets. Bend each piped or rolled log into a horseshoe.

Baking. Preheat the oven to 325°F. Bake until slightly golden, about 12 minutes. Cool on racks.

Variations. To make *lunette siciliane*, another polenta cookie of the same dough and shape, brush the tops of the unbaked cookies with beaten egg and coat with sesame seeds. Place seed side up on the baking sheets and bake as directed for *crumiri*.

Zaletti RAISIN CORNMEAL COOKIES FROM VENICE

There are probably as many recipes for this diamond-shaped cornmeal cookie as there are Venetian bakeries and families, but they all feature raisins, the same shape, and the same golden color (*gialetti*), from which the cookie gets its name.

Makes about 5 dozen cookies

³/₄ cup (4 oz / 115 g) dark seedless raisins or currants, soaked in rum to cover

1 stick plus 3 tablespoons (5.5 oz / 155 g) unsalted butter, at room temperature

¹/₂ cup plus 1¹/₂ tablespoons (4.2 oz / 120 g) sugar

2 large eggs, at room temperature

1 teaspoon (0.14 oz / 4 g) vanilla extract

1¹/₂ cups (7.7 oz / 220 g) all-purpose flour, plus 1 to 2 tablespoons (0.3 to 0.6 oz / 9 to 18 g) for the raisins

1¹/₂ cups (7 oz / 200 g) fine yellow cornmeal

2 teaspoons (0.4 oz / 10 g) baking powder

³/₄ teaspoon (0.13 oz / 3.5 g) salt

Soak the rasins in the rum at least 30 minutes and drain. Beat the butter and sugar together in a mixer bowl until light and fluffy. Add the eggs one at a time, beating thoroughly after each addition. Sift in the 1¹/₂ cups of flour, the cornmeal, baking powder, and salt and mix well. Toss the raisins with 1 to 2 tablespoons of flour and stir into the dough.

Shaping. Transfer the dough to a lightly floured surface. Roll into an 18-inch log, about 1³/₄ inches thick, and slice the log at ³/₈-inch intervals. Using your fingers, pat and shape each piece into a diamond or oval about 3 inches long. Place about 2 inches apart on buttered baking sheets (they puff and spread as they bake).

Baking. Preheat the oven to 375°F. Bake until lightly browned, about 20 minutes. Cool on baking sheets for a few minutes and then transfer to racks.

Biscotti di Crusca BRAN COOKIES SPIKED WITH RUM

The Italian concern with health is apparent in this cookie, which bakes to a granola-like crunchiness.

Makes about 3 1/2 dozen cookies

1 stick plus 1 tablespoon (4.5 oz / 130 g)
   unsalted butter, at room temperature

1/4 cup (1.8 oz / 50 g) sugar

1/2 cup plus 2 tablespoons (4.3 oz / 125 g)
   firmly packed light brown sugar

1 large egg, at room temperature

2 tablespoons (1 oz / 30 g) rum

1/2 teaspoon (0.07 oz / 2 g) vanilla extract

1 1/3 cups (6.1 oz / 175 g) pastry flour

1 cup (1.8 oz / 50 g) wheat bran

1 teaspoon (0.2 oz / 5 g) baking powder

Pinch of salt

Cream the butter and sugars in a mixer bowl until light and fluffy. Add the egg, rum, and vanilla and mix at medium speed for 1 minute. Sift the flour, bran, baking powder, and salt over the batter and mix until thoroughly blended, 30 seconds to 1 minute. The dough should be fairly stiff and easy to roll; the trick is to use as little flour as possible to roll out the dough so that it doesn't dry out. Transfer the dough to a very lightly floured surface and dust the top with a minimal amount of flour. Roll out 1/4 inch thick and prick all over with a fork. Cut out 2 1/2-inch scalloped circles with a cookie cutter. Place 1 inch apart on buttered or parchment-lined baking sheets. Gather and reroll the scraps; cut out as many circles as possible.

Baking. Preheat the oven to 350°F. Bake just until firm, 8 to 10 minutes. If overbaked, the cookies will be dry and lose their appealing moistness. Cool on racks.

Biscotti Integrali WHOLE WHEAT COOKIES SPIKED WITH RUM

These little cookies have a wonderful nutty, crunchy taste that is enhanced by a lacing of rum. The Mediterranean diet, which has been so heartily promoted as a healthy way of living, depends in part on whole grains, so you might even feel virtuous consuming these.

Makes about 3 1/2 dozen cookies

1 stick plus 2 tablespoons plus 1 teaspoon
     (5 oz / 145 g) unsalted butter, at room
     temperature

1/2 cup plus 2 tablespoons (4.4 oz / 125 g) sugar

1 large egg, at room temperature

2 tablespoons (1 oz / 30 g) rum

1/2 teaspoon (0.07 oz / 2 g) vanilla extract

Scant 2 cups (8.8 oz / 250 g) whole wheat flour

1 teaspoon (0.2 oz / 5 g) baking powder

Pinch of salt

Cream the butter and sugar in a mixer bowl until light and fluffy. Add the egg, rum, and vanilla and beat 2 minutes. Sift the flour and baking powder over the batter and mix until thoroughly blended. The dough should be fairly stiff and very easy to roll. Transfer the dough to a lightly floured surface and dust the top of the dough with a minimal amount of flour. Roll out 1/4 inch thick and prick all over with a fork. Cut out 2 1/2-inch scalloped circles with a cookie cutter. Place 1 1/2 inches apart on buttered or parchment-lined baking sheets. Gather and reroll the scraps for more circles.

Baking. Preheat the oven to 350°F. Bake for 8 to 12 minutes, until firm. Cool on racks.

Sweet Pastry Dough Cookies

Savoiardi LADYFINGERS, ITALIAN STYLE

We call them "ladyfingers," but these, one of the most basic Italian cookies, are traditionally known as *savoiardi* after the house of Savoy, the most powerful dynasty in Italy in the seventeenth century, when they became popular. They are often used for desserts with and without fillings. *Pasticcio della nonna* from Piacenza, for example, alternates layers of *savoiardi* bathed in rum with amaretti dipped in maraschino.

Makes 30 cookies

5 large eggs, separated, at room temperature

³/₄ cup (5.3 oz / 150 g) granulated sugar

2 drops white vinegar

1 teaspoon (0.14 oz / 4 g) vanilla extract

³/₄ cup plus 2 tablespoons (4.4 oz / 125 g) all-purpose flour

Scant ¹/₄ cup (1.4 oz / 40 g) potato starch

Pinch of salt

Confectioners' sugar

Beat the egg yolks and 3 tablespoons of the granulated sugar in a large mixer bowl until the mixture is light, thick, and forms a slowly dissolving ribbon when the beater is lifted, 7 to 10 minutes. Beat the egg whites in a warmed bowl at high speed with clean beaters until foamy. Gradually beat in the remaining granulated sugar and continue beating at high speed until the peaks are stiff and shiny. Beat in the vinegar and vanilla. Sift the flour, potato starch, and salt together. Fold a quarter of the egg yolks into the whites, then alternately fold the flour mixture and the egg whites into the egg yolks.

Shaping. Spoon the batter into a pastry bag fitted with a ¹/₂-inch plain tip. Pipe 5-inch-long strips of the batter about 1 inch apart on greased and floured or parchment-lined baking sheets. Sift confectioners' sugar generously over the tops.

Baking. Preheat the oven to 425°F. Bake until lightly golden, 10 to 15 minutes. Cool on racks. Ladyfingers keep 2 to 3 weeks in an airtight container.

Fagottini LITTLE JAM-FILLED POCKETS

The perfect snack, these buttery pockets of pastry dough are filled with apricot or raspberry jam.

Makes about 2¹/₂ dozen cookies

Pasta frolla I (page 320), made through chilling

1 or 2 large eggs, beaten

6 or 8 tablespoons (3 to 4 oz / 85 to 115 g) apricot or raspberry jam

Roll out the cold dough ¹/₄ inch thick on a floured surface. Cut out 3-inch plain or scalloped ovals with a cookie cutter. Gather and reroll the scraps and cut out as many ovals as possible. Brush the top of each one with the beaten egg and spoon a little less than 1 teaspoon of the jam in the center of each. Fold the ovals in half and seal the edges securely using the tines of a fork or the tips of your fingers. Place 1¹/₂ inches apart on buttered or parchment-lined baking sheets. Brush the tops with beaten egg.

Baking. Preheat the oven to 350°F. Bake until golden, 20 minutes. Cool on racks.

Buccellati FIG- AND ALMOND-FILLED COOKIES FROM SICILY

Imagine, if you can, a Fig Newton Sicilian-style, with figs and nuts rolled inside sweet pastry dough and topped with a dusting of powdered sugar. These fat little nougats look more like *pfeffernüsse* than Fig Newtons, but wait until you bite into them.

Makes 3 dozen cookies

²/₃ cup (3.5 oz / 100 g) finely chopped Calimyrna or light figs

Scant 1 cup (3.5 oz / 100 g) walnuts, toasted (page 32) and chopped

²/₃ cup (3.5 oz / 100 g) blanched almonds, chopped

Grated zest of 1 orange

¹/₂ to ³/₄ teaspoon (0.04 to 0.05 oz / 1 to 1.5 g) unsweetened cocoa powder, preferably Dutch process

³/₄ cup plus 4 teaspoons (7 oz / 200 g) red wine

2¹/₂ teaspoons (0.6 oz / 18 g) honey

1 tablespoon (0.4 oz / 13 g) granulated sugar

Pasta frolla I (page 320), made through chilling

Confectioners' sugar

Combine the figs, walnuts, and almonds in a saucepan. Add the orange zest, cocoa, wine, honey, and granulated sugar and stir to combine. Cook, stirring occasionally, over medium heat until it forms a rather dry paste. Remove from the heat. Pinch off one piece of the cold pastry dough about the size of a walnut, roll between your palms into a ball, and then flatten to a circle. Place 1 teaspoon of nut paste in the center and wrap the pastry over the paste, enclosing it completely. Roll into a ball. Repeat with the remaining pastry and paste and place 1¹/₂ inches apart on buttered or parchment-lined baking sheets.

Baking. Preheat the oven to 350°F. Bake until lightly browned, 25 minutes. Transfer to racks and immediately sift confectioners' sugar over the tops. Let cool completely.

Variations. For an unorthodox but delicious cookie, substitute *pasta frolla integrale* (page 323) for the *pasta frolla I.*

Chocolate Nut Cookies

Ossi da Morto BONE-SHAPED COOKIES FOR THE DAY OF THE DEAD

These crunchy, chocolatey cookies, with unexpected air pockets in their centers, are traditionally shaped like a human bone. This recipe is only one variation of the cookie, which can be found from Venice to Piedmont in the north all the way south to Sicily, where they are sometimes shaped to resemble skeletons, the infant Jesus, and even grape clusters. These cookies keep very well and, in fact, are actually better the second day.

Makes 2 dozen cookies

²/₃ cup (3.5 oz / 100 g) blanched almonds

Scant 1³/₄ cups (7 oz / 200 g) confectioners' sugar

3 tablespoons plus 1 teaspoon (0.7 oz / 20 g) unsweetened cocoa powder, preferably Dutch process

3 to 3¹/₂ tablespoons (1.5 to 2 oz / 45 to 60 g) egg whites

1 tablespoon (0.5 oz / 15 g) milk

Grind the almonds to a coarse powder in a food processor fitted with the steel blade. Add the sugar and cocoa and process to a fine powder. Add 3 tablespoons of the egg whites and process to a stiff, solid paste.

Add another ¹/₂ tablespoon of egg white if necessary.

Shaping. Pinch off pieces of dough the size of a fat cherry and roll between your hands into balls. Place 2 inches apart on buttered or parchment-lined baking sheets. Lightly brush the tops with milk.

Baking. Preheat the oven to 325°F. Bake for 20 to 22 minutes. At first the cookies will flatten out and look like nothing at all, but, given a few more minutes, each of these little cookies will puff up and their tops will become cracked and shiny. Cool on racks.

Baci d'Alassio CHOCOLATE KISSES FROM ALASSIO

These chewy, nutty, pebble-shaped cookies look as if they might have come right off the beach of a Ligurian seaside town. The secret to making them is getting the dough the right consistency and allowing them to dry overnight before baking.

Makes 15 cookies

1 heaping cup (5.3 oz / 150 g) hazelnuts, toasted and skinned (page 32)

³/₄ cups (5.3 oz / 150 g) superfine sugar

11 ounces (300 g) almond paste

1 teaspoon (0.2 oz / 7 g) honey

4 large egg whites, at room temperature

3 to 4 tablespoons (0.8 to 1 oz / 22 to 30 g) unsweetened cocoa powder, preferably Dutch process

Leftover cookies, such as butter, sugar, or chocolate, if needed

2 ounces (60 g) semisweet chocolate

Grind the hazelnuts with 2 tablespoons of the sugar to a coarse powder in a food processor fitted with the steel blade. Add the remaining sugar and process to a fine powder. Add the almond paste and process to a smooth paste, or mix the nut mixture and the almond paste with an electric mixer until smooth. Transfer the mixture from the food processor to a mixer bowl if necessary. Mix in the honey. Stir in the egg whites with a wooden spoon and then stir in the cocoa. The dough should be gooey and sticky but definitely not runny. When you pull a piece between your hands, it should stretch to a ribbon. If the dough is runny, grind leftover cookies to fine crumbs and stir a bit at a time into the dough to correct the consistency.

Shaping. Spoon the dough into a pastry bag fitted with a ³/₈-inch star tip. Pipe small button stars 1¹/₂ inches apart on buttered or parchment-lined baking sheets. Let stand uncovered overnight at room temperature to dry.

Baking. Preheat the oven to 375°F. Bake 8 to 10 minutes. The cookies should be chewy inside and look almost a bit undercooked. Cool completely on racks. While the cookies are cooling, melt the chocolate in the top of a double boiler over simmering water. Join two cookies together with melted chocolate. They should rest on their sides and be refrigerated 15 to 30 minutes to set the chocolate.

APPENDIX:
Source Guide to Ingredients and Equipment

VARIED PRODUCTS

A.G. FERRARI FOODS

(877) 878-2783 • www.agferrari.com
Flours, sea salts, herbs and seasonings, olive and anchovy pastes, oils, vinegars, meats, and salumi.

AMAZON.COM

www.amazon.com
Numerous flours, yeasts, salts, herbs, amarena cherries, Pernigotti cocoa, and even diastatic barley malt syrup and powder. A great collection of equipment includes the Sassafras La Cloche brick oven, baking stones, pizza stones, pizza peels, and a retractable razor blade scraper for slashing bread.

CHEF SHOP

(800) 596-0885 • www.chefshop.com
An amazing Italian pantry that includes anchovies, capers, Pernigotti cocoa, San Marzano tomatoes, and amarena cherries, as well as June Taylor products and lard from the Mangalitsa pig.

ITALIAN GOURMET SHOP

(305) 788-3093
www.italiangourmetshop.com
Olive oil, dried porcini mushrooms, dried cannellini beans, Taggiasca olives, San Marzano tomatoes, and Tuscan wild pine nuts from Radici of Tuscany, basil pesto from Genoa, and salted capers from Sicily. Most products are sold in large quantity.

KING ARTHUR FLOUR

58 Billings Farm Road,
White River Junction, VT 05001
(800) 827-6836 • www.kingarthurflour.com
Excellent one-stop shopping for flours, including "00" Italian-style flour, plus cocoa, Nielsen-Massey vanilla, lemon, and orange extracts, natural citrus oils, espresso powder, chocolate, and panettone flavoring, as well as all kinds of baking equipment.

KITCHEN KRAFTS

(800) 298-5389 • www.kitchenkrafts.com
Vanilla, lemon, orange, and clear vanilla extracts and rosewater flavoring. Also bowls, a layer cake slicing kit, Microplane zesters, KitchenAid mixer attachments, rolling pins, scales, piecrust shields, sifters, whisks, and many other useful tools.

MARKET HALL FOODS

The Pasta Shop at Market Hall,
5655 College Avenue, Oakland, CA 94618
(510) 250-6005
The Pasta Shop, 1786 4th Street,
Berkeley, CA 94070
(510) 250-6004
National phone number: (888) 952-4005
www.markethallfoods.com
A wonderful source for baking supplies such
as Agrimontana candied citrus peels (lemon,
orange, and citron), almond paste, nuts, flours,
flavorings and essences, and amarena cherries,
as well as tomato paste from Maria Grammatico and Gia, olive paste, Italian cheeses,
olive oils, and cured meats.

WILLIAMS-SONOMA

(877) 812-6235 • www.williams-sonoma.com
Honeys, jams, and vanilla extracts, among
many other ingredients. Excellent inventory of
equipment in its stores and catalogue, including nut grinders, spice grinders, Pullman loaf
pans, Microplane cheese mills, pizza stones and
peels, and pastry blenders.

ZINGERMAN'S

610 Phoenix Drive, Ann Arbor, MI 48108
(888) 636-8162 • www.zingermans.com
Many Italian cheeses (e.g., Fontina from the
Val d'Aosta, taleggio, piave, Parmigiano Reggiano), olive oils, various salts, dried figs, coarse
salt from Trapani, some herbs from Sicily.

FLOURS

ANSON MILLS

(803) 467-4112 • www.ansonmills.com
Flours ground fresh weekly include coarse and
fine cornmeal, coarse and fine polenta, graham
wheat flour, pastry flour, bread flour, bread
flour, and rye flour.

ARROWHEAD MILLS

(800) 434-4246 • www.arrowheadmills.com
Organic and stone-ground flours, including
organic pastry and rye flours, organic stone-
ground whole wheat flour, a particularly nice
organic fine corn meal, and oat and buckwheat flours.

BOB'S RED MILL

(800) 349-2173 • www.bobsredmill.com
Many flours called for in this book, including organic unbleached all-purpose flour,
organic whole wheat flour, organic buckwheat
flour, various cornmeals and corn flours, and
organic brown rice flour.

COMMUNITY GRAINS

www.communitygrains.com
A new company from Oliveto restaurant
offering a variety of whole-grain flours grown
and milled in Northern California. The flours
offer the whole grain in its entirety, which
means that doughs made with them need
a greater percentage of water. Their flours
include bread flour, unbleached all-purpose
flour, and hard-to-find durum flour, as well
as whole wheat pastry flour, brown rice flour,
and Italian polenta.

GIUSTO'S

(888) 884-1940 • www.giustosf.com
An enormous variety of natural (pesticide-
free) and organic flours for the home and
professional baker. They include unbleached
all-purpose, bread, pastry and cake, pizza, and
pasta flours, plus their version of the Italian
"00" and durum flour. They also make flours
with malt included in them.

HODGSON MILL

(800) 525-0177 • www.hodgsonmill.com
Many organic flours, including organic
natural unbleached white, rye, whole wheat

and whole wheat pastry, stone-ground rye, and unbleached all-purpose, as well as several cornmeals.

FRESH YEAST

ALL IN KOSHER
27 Orchard Street, Monsey, NY 10952
(845) 774-8753 or (877) AIK-4-USA
www.allinkosher.com
Cakes of Red Star and Fleischmann's fresh yeast.

CHEESES

ARTISANAL CHEESE
(877) 797-1200 • www.artisanalcheese.com
Includes several pecorino cheeses, Parmigiano-Reggiano, piave, taleggio, and two types of Gorgonzola.

COWGIRL CREAMERY
Ferry Building Marketplace,
San Francisco, CA 94111
(866) 433-7834 • www.cowgirlcreamery.com
Fifteen to twenty types of Italian cheeses, plus Italian-style fresh mozzarellas, fior di latte in fresh filtered water, and sheep's milk ricotta made in America.

FORMAGGIO KITCHEN
(888) 212-3244 • www.formaggiokitchen.com
Italian cheeses, olive oils, and flours, including "00," as well as baking supplies and extracts.

GIOIA CHEESE COMPANY
1605 Potrero Avenue,
South El Monte, CA 91733
(626) 444-6015 • www.gioiacheeseinc.com
Fresh mozzarella and burrata, the creamy cousin of mozzarella.

IDEAL CHEESE
(800) 382-0109 • www.idealcheese.com
A particularly good variety of Italian cheeses, including Parmesan, piave, several pecorini, mascarpone, provolone, and mozzarella di bufala from Campania as well as fresh, lightly salted American mozzarella.

PASTA CHEESE
(800) 386-9198 • www.pastacheese.com
An excellent selection of Italian cheeses, including sheep's milk ricotta; mascarpone; fresh buffalo mozzarella from Campania; and fiore di latte, cow's milk mozzarella in brine.

CURED MEATS

BOCCALONE SALUMERIA
Ferry Building Marketplace,
San Francisco, CA 94111
(415) 433-3500 • www.boccalone.com
Excellent cured Italian-style meats, including salumi, lardo, and mortadella.

LA QUERCIA
(515) 981-1625 • www.laquercia.us
Outstanding prosciutto made in the United States.

SALUMERIA ITALIANA
(800) 400-5916 • www.salumeriaitaliana.com
Imported cured meats, including pancetta, plus cheeses, olives and olive paste, anchovies, caperberries, and Antico Molino "00" flour.

SALUMI CURED MEATS
(207) 223-0816 • www.salumicuredmeats.com
Many types of Italian salumi cured by master artisan salumist Armandino Batali, father of Mario.

OLIVE OIL

OLIO2GO

(866) 654-6246 • www.olio2go.com
A very large selection of Tuscan olive oils from Avignonesi, Badia a Coltibuono, Castello di Volpaia, and Laudemio, among many others.

FRUITS, NUTS, JAMS

JUNE TAYLOR COMPANY

(510) 548-3266 • www.junetaylorjams.com
Impeccable candied orange peel, lemon peel, bergamot, and jams.

TRUFFLEBERT FARMS

(541) 686-6186 • www.trufflebertfarms.com
Organic hazelnuts from Oregon.

SPICES

PENZEY'S

(800) 741-7787 • www.penzeys.com
A multitude of spices; almond, orange, and lemon extracts; cinnamon, clove, and white pepper for *panforte*.

SPICE BARN

(866) 670-9040 • www.spicebarn.com
Offering almost every conceivable spice, herb, and extract.

EQUIPMENT

AWEIGH SCALES

www.aweighscales.com
Excellent source of scales, including the KD 7000 and 8000.

BRAM

493 First Street West, Sonoma, CA 95476
(866) 970-2726 • www.bramcookware.com
The moist cooking environment of Bram's handmade glazed ceramic bakers creates an ideal crisp crust and full-flavored interior crumb for the bread baker.

BREADTOPIA

www.breadtopia.com
Equipment for bread and pizza bakers, including pizza peels, La Cloche brick ovens, dough scrapers, and a variety of scales.

CHEF'S CATALOG

(800) 338-3232 • www.chefscatalog.com
Pastry tools, whisks, baking mats, springform pans, and measuring tools, among other items.

COOKWARE.COM

(888) 478-4606 • www.cookware.com
Kitchen scales, Taylor thermometers, molds for panettone and *pandoro*, all types of baking pans, Microplane graters, pizza stones, cake pans, pie pans, and more.

FORNO BRAVO

(800) 407-5119 • www.fornobravo.com
Complete range of home pizza-baking equipment, including professional pizza stones.

SCALES GALORE

(800) 832-0055 • www.scalesgalore.com
A source of many scales.

SUR LA TABLE

(800) 243-0852 • www.surlatable.com
All manner of baking equipment, including thermometers, scales, and pans.

INDEX

This book is for John, who has eaten it all.

All rights reserved. Published in the United States by Ten Speed Press, an imprint
of the Crown Publishing Group, a division of Random House, Inc., New York.
www.crownpublishing.com
www.tenspeed.com

Ten Speed Press and the Ten Speed Press colophon are registered trademarks of
Random House, Inc.

Originally published in somewhat different form by Harper & Row Publishers, Inc.,
New York, in 1985.

Library of Congress Cataloging in Publication
Field, Carol.
  The Italian baker : the classic tastes of the Italian countryside—its breads, pizza, focaccia,
cakes, pastries, and cookies / Carol Field ; photography by Ed Anderson. — 1st rev. ed.
      p. cm.
  Includes index.
  1. Baking—Italy. 2. Bread—Italy. 3. Pastry—Italy. 4. Cooking, Italian. 5. Cookbooks. I. Title.
TX763.F53 2011
641.5945—dc23

                        2011017004

ISBN: 978-1-60774-106-0

Printed in China

Design by Chloe Rawlins

10 9 8 7 6 5 4 3 2 1

First Revised Edition